St Antony's Series

General Editor: **Jan Zielonka** (2004–), Fellow of St Antony's College, Oxford

Recent titles include:

Simone Bunse
SMALL STATES AND EU GOVERNANCE
Leadership through the Council Presidency

Judith Marquand
DEVELOPMENT AID IN RUSSIA
Lessons from Siberia

Li-Chen Sim
THE RISE AND FALL OF PRIVATIZATION IN THE RUSSIAN OIL INDUSTRY

Stefania Bernini
FAMILY LIFE AND INDIVIDUAL WELFARE IN POSTWAR EUROPE
Britain and Italy Compared

Tomila V. Lankina, Anneke Hudalla and Helmut Wollman
LOCAL GOVERNANCE IN CENTRAL AND EASTERN EUROPE
Comparing Performance in the Czech Republic, Hungary, Poland and Russia

Cathy Gormley-Heenan
POLITICAL LEADERSHIP AND THE NORTHERN IRELAND PEACE PROCESS
Role, Capacity and Effect

Lori Plotkin Boghardt
KUWAIT AMID WAR, PEACE AND REVOLUTION

Paul Chaisty
LEGISLATIVE POLITICS AND ECONOMIC POWER IN RUSSIA

Valpy FitzGerald, Frances Stewart and Rajesh Venugopal (*editors*)
GLOBALIZATION, VIOLENT CONFLICT AND SELF-DETERMINATION

Miwao Matsumoto
TECHNOLOGY GATEKEEPERS FOR WAR AND PEACE
The British Ship Revolution and Japanese Industrialization

Håkan Thörn
ANTI-APARTHEID AND THE EMERGENCE OF A GLOBAL CIVIL SOCIETY

Lotte Hughes
MOVING THE MAASAI
A Colonial Misadventure

Fiona Macaulay
GENDER POLITICS IN BRAZIL AND CHILE
The Role of Parties in National and Local Policymaking

Stephen Whitefield (*editor*)
POLITICAL CULTURE AND POST-COMMUNISM

José Esteban Castro
WATER, POWER AND CITIZENSHIP
Social Struggle in the Basin of Mexico

Valpy FitzGerald and Rosemary Thorp (*editors*)
ECONOMIC DOCTRINES IN LATIN AMERICA
Origins, Embedding and Evolution

Victoria D. Alexander and Marilyn Rueschemeyer
ART AND THE STATE
The Visual Arts in Comparative Perspective

Ailish Johnson
EUROPEAN WELFARE STATES AND SUPRANATIONAL GOVERNANCE OF SOCIAL POLICY

Archie Brown (*editor*)
THE DEMISE OF MARXISM-LENINISM IN RUSSIA

Thomas Boghardt
SPIES OF THE KAISER
German Covert Operations in Great Britain during the First World War Era

Ulf Schmidt
JUSTICE AT NUREMBERG
Leo Alexander and the Nazi Doctors' Trial

Steve Tsang (*editor*)
PEACE AND SECURITY ACROSS THE TAIWAN STRAIT

C. W. Braddick
JAPAN AND THE SINO-SOVIET ALLIANCE, 1950–1964
In the Shadow of the Monolith

Isao Miyaoka
LEGITIMACY IN INTERNATIONAL SOCIETY
Japan's Reaction to Global Wildlife Preservation

Neil J. Melvin
SOVIET POWER AND THE COUNTRYSIDE
Policy Innovation and Institutional Decay

Julie M. Newton
RUSSIA, FRANCE AND THE IDEA OF EUROPE

Juhana Aunesluoma
BRITAIN, SWEDEN AND THE COLD WAR, 1945–54
Understanding Neutrality

Helen Belopolsky
RUSSIA AND THE CHALLENGERS
Russian Alignment with China, Iran and Iraq in the Unipolar Era

St Antony's Series
Series Standing Order ISBN 978–0–333–71109–5 (hardback)
978–0–333–80341–7 (paperback)
(*outside North America only*)

You can receive future titles in this series as they are published by placing a standing order. Please contact your bookseller or, in case of difficulty, write to us at the address below with your name and address, the title of the series and the ISBNs quoted above.

Customer Services Department, Macmillan Distribution Ltd, Houndmills, Basingstoke, Hampshire RG21 6XS, England

Small States and EU Governance

Leadership through the Council Presidency

Simone Bunse

Assistant Professor,
INCAE Business School, Costa Rica

In Association with
St Antony's College, Oxford

First published 2009 by
PALGRAVE MACMILLAN

Palgrave Macmillan in the UK is an imprint of Macmillan Publishers Limited, registered in England, company number 785998, of Houndmills, Basingstoke, Hampshire RG21 6XS.

Palgrave Macmillan in the US is a division of St Martin's Press LLC, 175 Fifth Avenue, New York, NY 10010.

Palgrave Macmillan is the global academic imprint of the above companies and has companies and representatives throughout the world.

Palgrave® and Macmillan® are registered trademarks in the United States, the United Kingdom, Europe and other countries.

ISBN-13: 978–0–230–53731–6 hardback

A catalogue record for this book is available from the British Library.

Library of Congress Cataloging-in-Publication Data
Bunse, Simone, 1973–
   Small states and EU governance : leadership through the Council presidency / Simone Bunse.
      p.   cm. — (St Antony's series)
   Includes bibliographical references and index.
   ISBN 978–0–230–53731–6
   1. Council of the European Union—Presidents.   2. European Union countries—Politics and government.   I. Title.   II. Title: Small states and European Union governance.
   JN34.B86 2009
   341.242'2—dc22   2008052847

10   9   8   7   6   5   4   3   2   1
18   17   16   15   14   13   12   11   10   09

Transferred to Digital Printing in 2010.

To my parents

Contents

List of Tables and Figures   x

Foreword   xi

Acknowledgements   xiv

Abbreviations   xv

1 Introduction   1
  I.   The Council presidency and small states   1
  II. The gaps in our understanding of the presidency   2
  III. Hypotheses, methodology, and theoretical
       underpinnings   4
  IV. The cases   10
  V.   Limits and caveats   14
  VI. Structure and propositions   16

**2 The Presidency within the EU's Institutional Balance
    and its Evolution**   18
  Introduction   18
  I.   The presidency as the guardian of equality: the EU'S
       institutional balance   19
  II. The evolution of the presidency   31
  Conclusion   37

**3 The Council Presidency as a Policy Entrepreneur:
    Nature, Agenda-setting Power, and Conditions for
    Success**   39
  Introduction   39
  I.   Policy entrepreneurship and agenda-setting in the EU   40
  II. Conceptualising the presidency: neutral broker versus
       policy entrepreneur   43
  III. Conditions for Success   55
  Conclusion   70

4   **The 1999 Finnish Presidency: Internal Market and**
    Foreign Policy Priorities and Achievements   **74**
    Introduction   74
    I.   Finnish internal market and foreign policy
         presidency objectives   75
    II. Obstacles: the leadership environment, institutional
         hurdles, and preference divergence   79
    III. Overcoming the obstacles: the strategic process   83
    IV. Conditions for success   94
    V.   Revision of achievements: assessing the counterfactuals   103
    Conclusion   111

5   **The 2001 Belgian Presidency: Internal Market and**
    Foreign Policy Priorities and Achievements   **114**
    Introduction   114
    I.   Belgian internal market and foreign policy
         presidency objectives   115
    II. Obstacles: the leadership environment, institutional
         hurdles, and preference divergence   120
    III. Overcoming the obstacles: the strategic process   126
    IV. Conditions for success   139
    V.   Revision of achievements: assessing the counterfactuals   150
    Conclusion   156

6   **The 2003 Greek Presidency: Internal Market and**
    Foreign Policy Priorities and Achievements   **159**
    Introduction   159
    I.   Greek internal market and foreign policy presidency
         objectives   160
    II. Obstacles: the leadership environment, institutional
         hurdles, and preference divergence   164
    III. Overcoming the obstacles: the strategic process   169
    IV. Conditions for success   184
    V.   Revision of achievements: assessing the
         counterfactuals   192
    Conclusion   199

7   **Conclusion**   **202**
    I.   The presidency, national interests, and levels of
         influence   202
    II. A question of size? On the presidency's resources and
         constraints   206

III. The presidency as a policy entrepreneur 210
IV. The value of the rotating Council presidency 212
V. Are the alternatives better? 215

Appendix 218

Notes 222

Bibliography 244

Index 282

List of Tables and Figures

Tables

1   Four Categories of Presidency Influence   9
2   Similarities and Differences & Internal Market and CFSP
    Presidency Priorities   13
3   Evolution of QMV in the Council of Ministers   22
4   The Evolution of the Commission Composition   25
5   The Evolution of the EP's Composition   27
6   The Council Presidency Rota (1958–2008)   29
7   The Council Presidency's Formal Tasks   36
8   The Council Presidency's Informal Powers   56
9   Expectations of High/Low Levels of Council Presidency
    Influence   69
10   The Level of Presidency Influence in Selected IM and
    Foreign Policy Dossiers   205

Figures

1   The Policy Entrepreneur's Impact on Bargaining Outcomes   41
2   The Presidency as a Policy Entrepreneur: Nature, Agenda-
    Setting Power, and Conditions for Success   72
3   Finnish System of Inter-ministerial Co-ordination During
    the 1999 Presidency   98
4   Inter-ministerial Co-ordination During the Belgian 2001
    Council Presidency   145
5   The Council Presidency's Resource/Constraint Structure   207

Foreword

Kalypso Nicolaïdis

There is no doubt that Simone Bunse has given us both a highly topical book, the stuff of headlines and an impressive scholarly achievement. Her book provides the most systematic assessment to date of the EU's rotating Council presidency, the political objectives such an institution has served over time, and the influence it has had on European affairs in general.

Such a study is clearly timely. As even the average European citizen may have realised, the rotating presidency has been at the center of the EU's institutional reform debates since constitutional fever took over the European project for the best of the last decade. Indeed, the Draft Constitution and its reincarnation under the guise of the Lisbon Treaty contains the most far-reaching reform of the EU presidency to date. The rotating presidency has been at the core of the EU institutional design since the foundation, the result of a sensitive bargain between small and big states. And while rotation may not be entirely abolished as the headlines would have us believe, it would and most probably be decapitated, and replaced by a permanent (if a two and a half year renewable term can be called so) chair of the European Council. Did the rotating presidency deserve such fate? What impact has it had on European developments and political bargains? Are some countries better at presiding over EU affairs than others? Are some issues better served by some countries which may use the presidency to provide renewed momentum? Is the presidency a mediating or activist role?

These questions discussed by Simone Bunse in the book are of interest not only for EU scholars but for anyone interested in broader issues of regional and global governance, the role of political leadership as well as comparative federalism. The book should also appeal to practitioners, particularly those in the new Member States preparing for their first presidency!

Although the literature on the presidency has been rapidly expanding over the past few years, Simone takes us one step further. While most EU research has focused on the big states, she explores the presidencies of three small states, Finland, Belgium, and Greece. She takes variance seriously by asking under what condition the influence of

the presiding country may be maximised and presenting novel empirical insights into the pros and cons of alternative presidency strategies
and behaviour. She takes domestic politics seriously by showing how
they influence presidency priorities and strategies in specific circumstances. She takes theory seriously and enriches the institutionalist
framework with her notion of the presidency as an intergovernmental
policy entrepreneur.

Her argument will provide grist to the mill of Europe's small and
medium Member States who have staunchly defended the rotating
Council presidency demonstrating as it does small states' capacity to
make creative use of it and shape dossiers in line with domestic preferences. In short, size does dictate influence. Instead, Simone shows how
other factors matter: the leadership environment, the heterogeneity,
intensity and distribution of governmental preferences in the Council,
inter-institutional relations with the Commission and the Parliament,
and the presidency's skill and effective use of the Council Secretariat.

This does not mean that the presidency can become a blunt instrument for savvy Member States. The Council's culture of consensus and
the logic of reciprocity across presidencies as well as the short time span
of the office tend to prevent the presidency holder from abusing the
power of the chair. In such repeated games, it pays off in the long run
to be accommodating of other states' interests – Member States cannot escape the fact that for one presidency, they will have 26 rounds as
ordinary Council member!

I share Simone's assessment of the broader value of the EU's rotating presidency. Indeed, it has served as an important symbol of the
commitment to shared leadership and formal equality between states
in the EU, reinforcing the idea that the EU was created to prevent
the (re-)emergence of hegemons on the European continent; it helps
national administrations as well as societal actors learn about the EU
and get socialised into its formal and informal networks; and it periodically channels new dynamism and creativity into Europe's decisions
processes, as every presidency attempts to leave its own positive imprint
to the EU's agenda.

It would be hard to close this book without being convinced that some
of the main arguments against rotation, namely that the EU needs a
powerful figurehead and that small states are overburdened with the
task, rest on shaky empirical ground. The rotating presidency it seems
has served the Member States well and made the EU as a whole more
effective, legitimate, and interesting.

The book ends with an overview of the potential risks and opportunities of the most recent presidency reform proposals as included in the 2007 Lisbon Treaty provisions and asks whether the key values of the Council presidency, including the Council's consensus culture, the spirit of shared leadership in the EU, and the incentives for policy innovation, would be upheld under the new provisions. Clearly, and whatever the answer, the presidency is likely to remain on the agenda, both scholarly and policy, for the years to come. Simone Bunse' work will undoubtedly stand as a core reference.

Oxford, September 2008

Acknowledgements

I would like to thank Kalypso Nicolaïdis and Anand Menon for their academic and personal support throughout my academic journey. Paul Magnette, Jan Zielonka, Derek Beach, Ben Crum, and Hartmut Lenz gave useful comments on earlier drafts of my work. The feedback by an anonymous reviewer helped me sharpen the analytical edge of my arguments. Roberto Ramirez assisted with the appendix. Most of the research was carried out between 2002 and 2005, while a doctoral student at the University of Oxford, visiting researcher at the European Studies Institute at the Free University of Brussels, and a junior fellow at the Finnish Business and Policy Forum EVA. It would not have been possible without the support of the numerous national and EU civil servants who provided me with their insights into EU decision-making and the role of the Council Presidency. Thanks go also to all the governments and Keppens Design for the permission to use their country's presidency logo for the book cover which is to illustrate the principle of the EU's rotating leadership. Finally, I want to thank my husband Kevin Casas who learned a lot about European politics during the past years. I am grateful for his academic advice, patience, and his confidence in me. His passion for politics and political science is utterly contagious!

Abbreviations

ACP	African, Caribbean, and Pacific
A	Austria
AE	*Agence Europe*
Agalev	*Anders Gaan Leven* (Belgium's Flemish Green Party)
ANA	Athens News Agency
APPG	All Party Parliamentary Group on the Great Lakes and Genocide Prevention
ATMs	Autonomous Trade Measures
AU	African Union
B	Belgium
BCM	Baltic Council of Ministers
BEAC	Barents Euro-Arctic Council
BIP	Balkan Integration Process
BM	Blocking Minority
Bu	Bulgaria
CAP	Common Agricultural Policy
CARDS	Community Assistance for Reconstruction, Development and Stabilisation Programme
CBSS	Council of the Baltic Sea States
CEECs	Central and Eastern European Countries
CEPS	Centre for European Policy Studies
CFSP	Common Foreign and Security Policy
CONV	Convention
COREPER	Committee of Permanent Representatives
CPC	Community Patent Court
CR	Czech Republic
CRoP	Council's Rules of Procedure
Cy	Cyprus
D	Germany
DDRR	Disarmament, Demobilisation, Reintegration and Repatriation
DK	Denmark
DRC	Democratic Republic of Congo
E	Spain
EBRD	European Bank for Reconstruction and Development

EC	European Community
ECB	European Central Bank
ECJ	European Court of Justice
Ecolo	*Parti Politique Francophone Belgique, Écologie* (Belgian Francophone Green Party)
EcoSoc	European Economic and Social Committee
ECOWAS	Economic Community of West African States
ECSC	European Coal and Steel Community
EDF	European Development Fund
EEA	European Economic Area
EEC	European Economic Community
EIB	European Investment Bank
EIS	European Information Service
ELIAMEP	Hellenic Foundation for European and Foreign Policy
EMS	European Monetary System
EMU	European Monetary Union
EP	European Parliament
EPC	European Political Co-operation
EPO	European Patents Office
Es	Estonia
ESI	European Stability Initiative
EU	European Union
Euratom	European Atomic Energy Community
Europol	European Police Office
EV	European Voice
F	France
FAZ	*Frankfurter Allgemeine Zeitung*
FDF	*Front Democratique des Francophones* (Belgium's Francophone Democratic Front)
Fin	Finland
FT	Financial Times
FYROM	Former Yugoslav Republic of Macedonia
FRY	Federal Republic of Yugoslavia
g	Gram
GAC	General Affairs Council
GAERC	General Affairs and External Relations Council
GB	Great Britain
GDP	Gross Domestic Product
Gr	Greece
H	Hungary
I	Italy

ICD	Inter-Congolese Dialogue
ICG	International Crisis Group
ICT	International Criminal Tribunal
ICTs	Information and Communication Technologies
ICTY	International Criminal Tribunal for Former Yugoslavia
IGC	Intergovernmental Conference
IM	Internal Market
IMF	International Monetary Fund
INTERREG	Interregional Co-operation
Ire	Ireland
IT	Information Technology
JHA	Justice and Home Affairs
L	Luxembourg
La	Latvia
LDCs	Least Developed Countries
Li	Lithuania
M	Malta
MCC	*Mouvement des Citoyens pour le Changement* (Belgian Citizens' Movement for Change)
MEP	Member of European Parliament
MFA	Ministry of Foreign Affairs
MONUC	United Nations Mission in the Democratic Republic of Congo
MP	Member of Parliament
MRU	Mano River Union
NATO	North Atlantic Treaty Organisation
NCM	Nordic Council of Ministers
ND	Northern Dimension
NEPAD	New Partnership for Africa's Development
NGO	Non-Governmental Organisation
NI	New Institutionalism
NIB	Nordic Investment Bank
NIP	National Indicative Programme
NL	Netherlands
NPOs	National Patent Offices
NYT	New York Times
OAU	Organisation of African Unity
OCTs	Overseas Countries and Territories
P	Portugal
PASOK	Panhellenic Socialist Movement
PCA	Partnership and Co-operation Agreement

PHARE	Poland and Hungary: Aid for Restructuring Economies
Pl	Poland
PM	Prime Minister
PRL	*Parti Reformateur Liberal* (Belgian Francophone Liberal Party)
PS	*Parti Socialiste* (Belgian Francophone Socialist Party)
PSC	Political and Security Committee
QM	Qualified Majority
QMV	Qualified Majority Voting
R	Romania
RCI	Rational Choice Institutionalism
S	Sweden
SAAs	Stabilisation and Association Agreements
SAP	Stabilisation and Association Process
SEA	Single European Act
SEE	South Eastern Europe
SEECP	South East Europe Co-operation Process
SGP	Stability and Growth Pact
Slo	Slovenia
SMEs	Small and Medium-Sized Enterprises
SP	Stability Pact
SU	Soviet Union
SZ	*Süddeutsche Zeitung*
TACIS	Technical Assistance to the Commonwealth of Independent States
TEU	Treaty on European Union
UACES	University Association for Contemporary European Studies
UK	United Kingdom
UPU	Universal Postal Union
US	United States
VF	Virtual Finland
VLD	*Vlaammse Liberalen en Demokraten* (Belgium's Flemish Liberal Party)
WB	World Bank
WTO	World Trade Organisation
ZEI	*Zentrum für Europäische Intergrationsforschung*

1
Introduction

I. The Council presidency and small states

Over the past years the issue of the rotating Council presidency has been at the centre of the European Union's (EU's) institutional reform discussions disclosing a deep divide between the small and the big Member States. The former, including the Benelux, Austria, Finland, Ireland, Portugal, and most of the EU's newest members, have fiercely defended the rotating office. The latter, especially France, the UK, and Spain, have strongly advocated the creation of a new more permanent arrangement. The critics claimed that small states are overburdened with the presidency's administrative, organisational, and mediation tasks and that the resources and political clout of big states are needed to broker compromises and manage the EU's growing external role. The supporters of the current arrangement responded by highlighting the inefficiencies of big administrations and contending that small states are better mediators in the EU's internal and external affairs. In May 2003, the rift over the presidency nearly caused the breakdown of the Convention on the Future of Europe. The issue moved back into the spotlight in June 2008 with the Irish rejection of the Lisbon Treaty. The treaty contains the most far-reaching Council presidency reforms to date and the outcome of the referendum can partly be explained by voters' concerns over the impending institutional changes and new balance between big and small Member States. The perception that the large EU countries decide matters was cited by 4% of the voters as their reason to reject the treaty. Another 3% saw their No vote as a means to protect the influence of the EU's small members.[1]

Neither the intensity of the conflict between 'small against big' nor the prominence of the Council presidency reform over other institutional arrangements was the most anticipated. While quarrels between large and small Member States are not new, they have never been as stark or explicit in the EU's history of grand bargains.[2] In addition, when the presidency was established in the 1950s it had been a complete afterthought – its creators having little more in mind than to share out the responsibility for chairing Council meetings in some orderly fashion.[3] Finally, the academic literature has described the rotating presidency as a 'responsibility without power'[4] – a 'neutral broker'[5] with burdensome administrative and organisational tasks that put particularly small states under great strain. If this were indeed the case, two inter-linked questions arise: (a) Why has the reform of the Council presidency been so contentious? and (b) Why are especially small states such adamant supporters of the status quo? This book investigates this puzzle. It is an attempt to analyse the political objectives the Council presidency serves and present a systematic and comparative assessment of its influence in the European integration process by looking at three small states – Finland, Belgium, and Greece.

To date, the presidency literature is relatively sparse. Given that the presidency lacks formal institutional status, its importance and influence have often been overlooked. Thus, few books are dedicated to the Council presidency.[6] Instead, most work on the presidency is found in studies on the European Council and the Council of Ministers and focuses on its legal status and formal functions.[7] A second body of research consists of single country cases reviewing the office holder's performance.[8] They are generally descriptive accounts of a presidency's main achievements. Hardly any studies analyse the presidency's peculiar hybrid nature of an intergovernmental policy actor (with its own preferences, areas of expertise, and political and administrative culture) in charge of a supranational institution, its importance within the EU's institutional balance, or subtle power and leadership capacity – this book's starting points of analysis. This has led to a number of gaps in our understanding of the Council presidency.

II. The gaps in our understanding of the presidency

The presidency's influence in the integration process remains under-researched and under-theorised. Kirchner's (1992) study of the institution's centrality in EU decision-making is one of the few research endeavours with theoretical aspirations.[9] Favouring co-operative federalism, whereby national governments and supranational institutions engage with each other to impact the integration process, he analyses the dynamics of the Single European Act (SEA) and the work of the Intergovernmental Conference (IGC) on European Monetary Union (EMU) and Political Union. However, Kirchner does not develop the theoretical concepts in his empirical chapters. Moreover, he seems to assume only two possible outcomes: a presidency either fostered co-operation enhancing integration or promoted national interests – two simplified scenarios that may not be mutually exclusive.

The empirical literature also typically lacks a broader comparative framework. O'Nuallain (1985) and Wurzel (1996a, 1996b, 2001) are amongst the few exceptions.[10] O'Nuallain reviews ten different country experiences between 1973 and 1983 to detect the presidency's effect on national administrations. It is argued that the key ingredient to a successful presidency (however success may be defined) is the combination of 'a co-ordinated strategy with tolerant flexibility'.[11] While this account is a significant contribution to comparative public administration, it does not tackle the leadership capacity of the presidency.

Wurzel's work examines how the Council presidency works within the environmental field by comparing past British and German presidencies. Finding little difference in the way both governments run their presidencies (despite considerable divergence in their national styles), he concludes that the presidency's importance lies in fostering the Europeanisation of national policies.

The leadership aspect and the presidency's potential causal influence have been disregarded in the bulk of the presidency literature. Bulmer and Wessels (1987), for example, attribute a crucial role to the presidency in the preparation and organisation of European Summits which – through their package deals – shape Community business. However, they ignore the role of the presidency in brokering such deals. As most studies limit their analysis to investigating the presidency's formal operating rules, they tend to find that it is charged with a multitude of different tasks but 'falls well short of being a tool for collective leadership'.[12] The importance of its informal powers and resources to help it in its political tasks is dismissed.[13]

The literature is particularly sceptical with regard to the presidency's agenda influence. Agenda-setting in the EU is a collaborative process between the presidency and the main EU institutions. It involves collecting pending items and initiatives by the presidency, other member governments, and the Commission.[14] Additional constraints are the heavy administrative burden and short term of the office. Most analysts therefore conclude that the presidency's influence in terms of policy development should not be exaggerated:[15]

A presidency's responsibility is to ensure that the Union functions. The political responsibility of a presidency comes down to the task of piloting dossiers through the given procedures in order to arrive at balanced solutions within a reasonable period.[16]

Interestingly, the leadership capacity of the chair is neglected not only in the Council literature, but also in international bargaining more generally. As Tallberg finds, in much of the international bargaining literature the negotiating parties – while varying in their preferences and strategies – are seen as 'functionally equivalent' and fail to recognise the powers of the chair.[17] Thus, within the Council, asymmetrical relationships of influence (between the presidency and the other Council members) are overlooked.[18]

Recently, a more encouraging body of research is emerging which examines the presidency at IGC negotiations. Svensson (2000) talks about an 'engineering presidency' at the Amsterdam IGC.[19] Gray and Stubb (2001) characterise it as the provider of 'political guidance'. The first to examine the presidency in the context of day-to-day Council negotiations is Metcalfe (1998). He identifies six categories of presidency leadership resources including rewards, coercion, socialisation, legitimacy, expertise, and information.

As to the presidency's agenda-shaping capacity, Bunse (2000, 2004) and Tallberg (2003, 2004, 2006) have argued that it has been underestimated and that there is scope for manipulating the agenda and for active initiation.[20] In addition, Thomson (2008) and Kollman (2003) argue that the presidency influences decision outcomes and Elgström (2003) questions its neutrality. Overall, however, the presidency has largely remained isolated from the comparative politics and international relations literature. To date there are few systematic, comparative accounts of the Council presidency that analyse its importance and influence in the course of European integration or the nature of the outcomes brokered.

III. Hypotheses, methodology, and theoretical underpinnings

This book attempts to address these gaps and adds to the growing latter category of research. It challenges the assumption that the presidency has responsibility without power and looks for theoretical concepts that are sensitive to the presidency's hybrid nature and combination of formal and informal powers.

From the intensity of the presidency reform debate and the arguments raised, three inter-linked conclusions can be drawn. First, contrary to the overriding picture that emerges from the literature, the institution must fulfil a political objective within the EU's institutional set-up that is particularly valued by the small EU members. Second, rather than placing a disproportionate burden upon smaller states, the office must entail privileges or powers which seemed worth defending by seven out of the EU's then 15 members plus most of the accession states. Third, other factors than size must determine the extent to which the office holder, including small states, can exploit these privileges. Institutionalists point to variables, such as the leadership environment, decision takers' preferences, inter-institutional relations, as well as their skill and use of information advantages. The central hypotheses which emerge and that this book aims to investigate both theoretically and empirically can subsequently be formulated as follows:

- The rotating Council presidency is a mechanism to equalise power differences between the EU's small and big Member States.
- The presidency evolved into an influential institution providing the office holder with a comparative advantage to shape the EU's agenda and policy outcomes in line with its national interests.
- Factors such as the leadership environment, the heterogeneity, intensity and distribution of preferences in the Council, inter-institutional relations, and the office holder's skill and use of the Council Secretariat are more important than size to explain a presidency's ability successfully to pursue its national interests.

To probe these hypotheses, the book first explores the Council presidency's importance and agenda influence within the institutional balance and multi-leadership constellation of the EU. Second, in-depth case studies of the recent Finnish, Belgian, and Greek Presidencies and their effects in two policy areas (internal market (IM) and foreign policy) construct a detailed empirical account of presidential leadership and influence of three small countries. Leadership is defined as 'an asymmetrical relationship of influence in which one actor guides or directs the behaviour of others towards a certain goal over a certain period of time'.[21] Influence, in turn, is understood pragmatically as the capacity 'to change an outcome from what it otherwise would have been in the absence of an action'.[22] In the context of the agenda-setting power of the presidency, this includes the ability not only to initiate new policies, but also to structure or limit policy choices.[23] Both the theoretical chapters as well as the case studies have the broader goals of reflecting on the nature of the EU and the outcomes brokered by three presidencies. The results, in turn, allow us to contribute to the discussion whether the rotating presidency benefits the EU and its Member States or not, and hence offer some normative conclusions for the ongoing reform debate.

The methodological approach of this book falls into the category of 'Process and Institution Studies'.[24] The latter select a small number of institutions or a process that appear similar in important ways to then use them to illuminate the nature of either the institution or the process.[25] In line with much public policy analysis that traces the process through which causality operates,[26] the core of this book examines how the agenda-setting process unfolds under the selected presidencies, how the office holders exert their influence, and with what effects.

Theoretical tools: an institutionalist approach

In placing the presidency within a broader framework of incentives, resources, and constraints, this book expresses a preference for new institutionalism (NI). NI attributes a crucial role to institutions in explaining political behaviour and outcomes – the central assumption being that institutions make a difference:

> by shaping not just actors' strategies, but their goals as well and by mediating their relations of co-operation and conflict, institutions structure political situations and leave their own imprint on political outcomes.[27]

While older forms of institutionalism consist mostly of descriptions of formal institutions and detailed structures, NI seeks to explain phenomena with institutions as the independent variable. In this case, the presidency is seen as a separate institution (a set of established rules, expectations, and incentives) and the independent variable that shapes policy outcomes. Its degree of influence, in turn, is the dependent variable, which may vary not only from presidency to presidency, but also from one policy or issue to another. The challenge consists in explaining the channels through which, and the conditions under which, the presidency can or cannot pursue its political objectives and thereby exercise leadership in the institutional constellation of the EU.[28] To determine the extent to which the presidency acts as an independent or intervening variable allowing national governments to further their own interest, the analysis attempts to distinguish between the Council presidency as an institution and the individual national presidencies as policy actors.

New institutionalists' definition of institutions is useful here because it is not only based on formal rules, but also on informal procedures[29] – so far hardly touched upon in the presidency literature. Thus, in addition to the formal, structural aspects of institutions, it focuses on *actual* behaviour, in this case how the presidency country tries to influence Council decision-making and outcomes in line with the office holder's preferences.[30] The institutionalist concept of a 'policy entrepreneur' who seeks informal ways to shape the EU agenda and mobilise support for his or her preferred solution is introduced in this context. As stressed above, the book tries to separate the question to what extent institutions have independent effects (can be treated as causes in their own right) from the degree to which national governments are able to use the opportunities and institutional mechanisms the presidency offers. In other words, it attempts to distinguish the generic features of the Council presidency which shape policy outcomes from the contingent Member State idiosyncrasies at play.

Rational Choice Institutionalism (RCI) seems particularly useful when looking at the presidency given its emphasis on utility maximising and strategic interaction.[31] Actors with well-defined preferences are assumed to act strategically to achieve policy outcomes that are closest to their individual preferences. Contrary to other versions of rational choice theory, rational choice institutionalists accept that the sources of preferences and definitions of personal interests may not all be exogenous. Individuals and institutions also interact to create preferences and to be successful they have to accommodate certain norms and institutional values.[32]

The presidency is seen as a utility 'maximiser' which operates within a well-defined set of boundaries constraining individual maximising behaviour. The book shows how the presidency affects the interaction among strategic players and the choices available to them.[33] By looking at the sequence of this interaction and depicting the relationship between the presidency and policy outcomes, it attempts to draw a precise picture of the mechanisms underlying a policy choice.

NI is being applied with increasing sophistication to the EU.[34] Crucially, it combines elements of both major integration schools: Neofunctionalism[35] and Intergovernmentalism.[36] From Neofunctionalism it accepts that institutions 'take a life on their own' influencing policy choices in ways that cannot be predicted from the preference and power of the Member States alone.[37] Thus, it draws upon principal-agent analysis whereby – once established – agents cannot be fully con-trolled by their principals, but become entrepreneurs that pursue their own interest.[38] Under this scenario the presidency is expected to have a degree of autonomy of the Member States and other institutions. From the intergovernmental approach, NI borrows insights about the centrality of national governments and their preferences in the EU's development.[39] Most crucially, however, it seeks to determine how and under what conditions Community institutions are successful in pur-suing their goals. In our case, this task involves examination of the resource/constraint structure within which the presidency operates as well as the skill of the office holder to exploit the opportunities which present themselves with the chair position to pursue national objectives.

Methodological and conceptual tools

The analysis relies more heavily on descriptive than causal inference. It attempts to link the detailed description of a process to a causal rela-tionship and identify (with the help of institutionalist theory) potential causal mechanisms. This involves analysing the presidency as an insti-tution, as well as individual presidencies' agenda priorities, preferences, strategies, and achievements. Crucially, we have to investigate how the different variables interact and relate to policy outcomes. The key question is to what extent and how was a presidency initiative or compromise accepted unaltered, modified, or rejected.

The presidency's influence will vary from case to case. This book puts forward four categories of influence as the key conceptual tool to asses an individual presidency: high, medium, low, and no influence. A high correlation between the preferences of the presidency country and the final outcomes despite significant opposition would imply that the gov-ernment in the chair had a high level of influence. Medium levels of influence imply progress or agreements that reflect the office holder's point of view in some parts and do not go against its interests in others. When some issues are solved in line with the presidency country's view, but no overall agreement is reached, we can classify the outcome as a low level of influence. Finally, if an agreement brokered goes against the presidency's view, the office holder has clearly had no influence. Table 1 outlines these four categories of influence. The strength of this type of categorisation is that it is sensitive not only to the presidency country's preferences, but also to the intensity of these preferences and opposi-tion forces. It focuses on the provisions that were most important to the office holder.

Table 1 Four Categories of Presidency Influence

Level of Influence	Definition
High ⟶	High correlation between presidency country's preferences and outcomes brokered despite significant obstacles/opposition.
Medium ⟶	Medium correlation between office holder's preferences and outcomes brokered, but no provisions agreed are against national interests.
Low ⟶	Some issues are solved in line with the presidency holder's preferences, but no overall agreement is reached.
No influence ⟶	The agreement reached is against the presidency country's national interests.

Wozniak Boyle (2006) measures influence by counting the number of provisions an institution put forward that were accepted, modified (with or without intent), and rejected. She argues that an institution (in her case the Commission) has had a strong influence in a given reform, if it 'attained an acceptance rate greater than or equal to 60 per cent and if the total percentage of accepted provisions plus those modified within intent is greater than or equal to 80 per cent'.[40] This method seems to disregard: (a) the weight of these individual provisions; and (b) the opposition forces at work. Were the provisions agreed (or rejected) the most important ones for the institution under consideration? How do we isolate the actor's influence, if many provisions were agreed but there was little opposition? The approach used in this book refrains from any precise numerical analysis, but relies on qualitative analysis that takes the intensity of preferences and opposition into account.

Potential variance in presidency influence can arise from two separate factors: those that are outside the presidency's control (circumstantial) and those that are influenced by the office holder.[41] The former include unpredictable internal or external political or economic developments (the presidency's leadership environment) and institutional obstacles the presidency country faces in pursuit of its priorities. These vary from presidency to presidency, but no matter which government assumes the office, its preferences and strategic choices will be influenced by them. Factors that depend on the presidency country include the skill, reputation, inter-institutional relations, and strategies of the office holder, as well as the efficiency of its system of inter-ministerial co-ordination and its use of the Council Secretariat to exploit information advantages. The latter are more predictable and have consistent consequences. The goal of inference is to detect whether the circumstantial elements overwhelm the second set of factors which are contingent Member State characteristics. The case studies thus begin with an overview of the presidency's leadership environment and the obstacles it faced. This is followed by an empirical analysis whether particular policy outcomes are the result of the presidency country's entrepreneurial activity and skill.

As all methods the approach has its flaws: the problem of anticipated reactions.[42] If the chair anticipates other actors' interests and only puts forward what it believes will be acceptable, this would clearly not be an example of agenda influence. To mitigate this weakness I analyse the individual presidencies' preferences, the obstacles they faced in the pursuit of these preferences, and the actions they undertook to change the outcome from what it would have been in the absence of this action. Through counterfactual analysis I try to dismiss other causes (than the chair) to explain a policy outcome. The counterfactuals include considerations such as: How does the influence of a Member State vary when it holds/does not hold the presidency or what is the comparative advantage of the presidency? And what role/influence did other decision-makers, such as the other Member States, the Commission, and the European Parliament (EP), have in the outcome?

IV. The cases

The book relies upon a small number of in-depth case studies – a growing trend in comparative Political Science. The merit of this approach is that it is capable of saying a good deal more about the institution and countries chosen and shows greater contextual detail than quantitative methods can exhibit.[43] The bulk of the research thus comprises a comparative study of the Finnish, Belgian, and Greek Presidencies (1999, 2001, and 2003 respectively) and their influence in IM and foreign policy issues.

This selection is motivated by a number of methodological considerations. First, for our explanatory purposes the appropriate 'universe of cases' is not unlimited by time. The presidency has evolved with successive treaty revisions and the EU's growing external role. To avoid difficulties of comparability connected with institutional change, all three cases are presidencies, which took office after the Amsterdam

Treaty entered into force and before the Nice Treaty's institutional changes were applied.

Second, only small country presidencies have been selected. Small size is frequently equated to a lack of power to influence policy outcomes.[44] Hence, this is the hardest possible test our central hypothesis about the institution's agenda influence can be exposed to. The underlying assumption is that if even *small* states acquire additional agenda influence when holding the presidency, then there is little reason to doubt that big states could too. Small states here are defined in absolute terms, as those with significantly less than 40 million inhabitants. Within the EU these are the Netherlands, Greece, Belgium, the Czech Republic, Portugal, Hungary, Sweden, Austria, Slovakia, Denmark, Finland, Ireland, Lithuania, Latvia, Slovenia, Estonia, Cyprus, Luxembourg, Malta, Romania, and Bulgaria. In other words, all Member States except for six: the founders France, Germany, and Italy, and, after successive enlargements, the UK, Spain, and Poland.[45]

Third, selecting only small states allows us to investigate the empirical claim whether small states do indeed struggle with the demanding presidency role. By holding the size-variable constant, we can test whether the (small) size of the office holder conditions its success or rather there are other variables which may be more powerful than size in explaining the level of presidency influence.

However, even though Finland, Belgium, and Greece are all small, they differ along a number of variables that analysts have identified as crucial in explaining variations in presidency performance. These are resources, interests and identity (North/South), the degree of commitment to European integration, and level of experience.[46] Finland can be characterised as a wealthy, inexperienced, northern pragmatic pro-European country. The 1999 Finnish Presidency was its first. Belgium is one of the EU's well-off founding members with federalist aspirations. It has held the presidency 11 times. Greece, in contrast, is a comparatively poor, southern, relatively experienced EU country. It has a history of being a reluctant Member State, but is recently becoming more mainstream. The 2003 Presidency was Greece's fourth.

This combination of similarities (size) and differences (resources, interests and identity, the degree of commitment to European integration, and level of experience) makes the selection problematic from the standpoint of a 'most-similar' or 'most-different systems' comparative inquiry. Clearly, the comparison does not fall neatly in either category. However, the countries are sufficiently different as to allow the logic of the 'most-different system' approach of comparative study to work.[47] The idea is to begin with contrasting starting points, but detect similarities of strategy and process. Instead of focusing on different characteristics across countries, the focus becomes individual national behaviour and the relationship of variables within countries. The challenge lies in explaining a presidency's influence by its strategic, goal-oriented actions, including intra- and inter-institutional relations rather than specific country characteristics.[48]

The final methodological consideration that underlies the case selection is that the presidency's influence may vary according to policy area. To gain a more comprehensive picture of the institution, its influence in two policies is analysed. The IM is the EU's oldest Pillar I policy and issues related to it form the bulk of each presidency's day-to-day work.[49] In IM matters the Community method of decision-making grants the Commission an important role in proposing legislation and the EP in co-legislating. Areas connected with the IM usually fall under qualified majority voting (QMV). In contrast, the EU's common foreign and security policy (CFSP), or Pillar II, is essentially intergovernmental. Governed by the unanimity rule, it is driven by the Council rather than the Commission or EP. The underlying assumption is that both the influence of the other actors in the EU's different pillars and the decision-making rules matter when trying to determine the power of the presidency as an institution. In addition, in both areas small states' leadership has been regarded as highly limited due to their lesser votes in the Council or their lack of political weight.

The selected dossiers are the information society (e-commerce and copyright directives) and the Northern Dimension (ND) under the Finnish Presidency; postal liberalisation and the EU's policy towards Africa (the Great Lakes region) under the Belgian Presidency; and the Community Patent regulation and EU relations with the Western Balkans under the Greek Presidency.[50] They have in common that they were, according to the countries' respective presidency agendas and public officials, amongst the most important national priorities in the policy areas under consideration. Hence it is likely that the chairs tried to exploit all resources at their disposal to shape the legislative outcomes in these dossiers and that we can trace this process from the preparation phase of each presidency. Indeed it would make little sense to select dossiers of little interest to the office holder, as here it may be willing to leave the leadership to others, for example the Commission or other Member States. Nonetheless, even in priority dossiers presidential influence varies depending on the presidency country's leadership capacity and the strength of the constraints at work. Table 2 summarises each country's characteristics and IM and foreign policy priority dossiers.

Table 2 Similarities and Differences & Internal Market and CFSP Presidency Priorities

Small State Presidency	Resources	Interests/ Identity	EU policy	Experience	Internal Market Priority	CFSP Priority
Finland 1999	wealthy	Northern	pragmatic mainstream	inexperienced	Information Society (e-commerce & copyright directives)	Northern Dimension
Belgium 2001	wealthy	Northern	federalist	experienced	Postal Liberalisation	Africa (Great Lakes)
Greece 2003	poor	Southern	mainstream, historically reluctant	relatively experienced	Community Patent	Western Balkans

For a good comparison between countries with very different features, not only the similarities, differences, and research hypotheses must be clearly identified. The case studies must also be structured around well-specified, initial research questions.[51] Organised to illustrate the hypotheses posed and according to the observable implications of the hypotheses, each case study is structured around the following questions:

- What were the presidential priorities/preferences in the selected policy areas and how far did they reflect national priorities, values, and ideas?
- What were the obstacles the presidencies were facing in pursuit of their aims?
- How were objectives pursued and obstacles overcome? How did the presidency countries rally consensus behind their preferred policy solutions and initiatives, which strategies were applied, how were deals being struck?
- To what extent did the presidencies reach their goals and what shape did agreements take?
- What variables explain presidency success or failure? How important was the size of the office holder?
- To what extent can the outcomes be attributed solely to the presidency? Are there plausible counterfactual scenarios?

Overall, the book pursues two main aims: (a) reveal whether/to what extent the presidency country's national stance is reflected in the outcome of the negotiation; and (b) detect whether the small size of a country conditions the presidency's ability to manage the office effectively and broker agreements. In addition, the research design allows us to reflect on the nature of the outcomes reached and hence establish whether presidency compromises are positive-sum or not. Positive-sum (or *Pareto* efficient) outcomes are deals which make some Member States much better off, others a little better off, nobody worse off and are preferable to the status quo by all. This point has important implications for the presidency reform debate.

V.   Limits and caveats

The analysis has a number of limits and caveats. As all theoretical approaches, NI has its problems. The most important are: (a) refutation may be difficult (the hypotheses posed may not be falsifiable);

(b) isolating the impact of institutions as independent variables is difficult; and (c) institutional theories have difficulties in grasping the role of cultural factors in explaining outcomes.[52] As much social science literature, NI may be better in describing process than determining the ultimate cause. These problems, while significant, should, however, not lead to the rejection of institutionalist approaches. They can, at least in part, be mitigated by a careful assessment of the counterfactuals – as this book attempts. In addition, by analysing the factors that condition the successful pursuit of an actor's preferences, institutionalist approaches can identify important building bricks in the search to break the impasse between Intergovernmentalism and Neofunctionalism.

The case studies try to strike a balance between process and substance with the latter relying heavily on interviews with officials from national administrations and EU institutions, news sources, parliamentary debates, official EU documents, and Council press conferences. Nonetheless, some information is difficult to obtain. Council meetings are held behind closed doors and the details of presidency confessionals are not recorded.[53] Thus, the analysis tends to tilt towards describing the process.

Cases that follow the 'most different, similar outcome' logic are generally not particularly interested in countries, but more in identifying variables that explain outcomes and in generating new hypotheses. However, they do not provide any means to test them. Thus, while this book identifies potential explanatory variables, it is unable to rank them, or check their robustness – a general disadvantage of small N studies. Furthermore, by concentrating on the negotiation outcome, this analysis pays little attention to subsequent implementation.

Finally, selecting only small state presidencies has clear limitations. While it may allow us to present an empirical critique of affirmations that small states are unable to deal with the office and provide answers to questions why the rotating Council Presidency been so important for small states, it does not offer conclusive validation or refutation of other empirical claims made by critics and defenders of the presidency which are well worth analysing. These include, for example, that there are considerable differences between the small and the big states in terms of their strategies and approach to the office. If this is true, are these differences between small and big states systematic and what does this mean for the presidency country's ability to exert agenda influence? These questions can only be answered by systematic comparisons between small and big presidencies, which is beyond the scope of this book.

Despite these limitations, the findings of this investigation are very useful additions to the debate surrounding the Council presidency and EU decision-making more generally: they help illuminate key aspects of the institutional dynamics in the EU and contribute novel empirical insights into individual presidency behaviour and are therefore of heuristic value.

VI. Structure and propositions

This book is divided into seven chapters. The following chapter examines the presidency's importance within the EU's institutional balance and traces the evolution of its tasks. It introduces the institution as the most far-reaching equalising mechanism that – by sharing out leadership – tames power politics in the EU and prevents the emergence of a hegemon. Given the proposals for a permanent presidency would tilt the EU's traditional institutional balance more clearly in favour of the big states, the small countries have strongly defended the current arrangement. In addition, the chapter shows how the presidency unexpectedly emerged into a key institutional player with crucial leadership functions. Unsurprisingly, small states in particular have come to see it as an additional arena to exert influence and means to compensate for their limited power.

Chapter 3 explores the presidency's agenda-setting power and the conditions under which its influence is maximised. It challenges the view that the presidency is a neutral chair with limited capacity to shape the EU agenda. The concept of policy entrepreneurship is introduced as a way to conceptualise the strategic behaviour of the presidency and capture its formal procedural and informal agenda-setting powers. The chapter argues that the presidency can – under certain conditions – shape EU policy in line with the office holder's national interests despite the formal neutrality rule. Although its formal powers are constrained, it enjoys subtle informal powers to direct the other decision-making players towards its goals. The concept of political entrepreneurship captures this form of leadership and inherent bias of the presidency. Particularly the presidency's agenda control and information advantages grant the chair a significant comparative advantage over other decision-makers.[54] Factors that condition a presidency's success to shape policy outcomes in line with its own preferences include a combination of context-specific, institutional, and country factors: the leadership environment; the heterogeneity, intensity, and distribution of preferences in the Council; inter-institutional relations; and the holder's skill and use of the Council Secretariat.

Chapters 4, 5, and 6 present the case studies of the three selected presidencies and evaluate their impact on IM and foreign policies. They analyse the means by which the presidency exercises political entrepreneurship and establish the level of individual presidency influence in each case according to the above categories. Their objective is twofold: (a) to illustrate the *ways* in which, the *extent* to which, and the *conditions* under which, the presidency has been a causal or intervening factor; and (b) analyse the outcomes the three presidencies generated. The case studies illustrate the complex interaction among the presidency, the member governments, the Commission, as well as other actors which establish the context for presidency autonomy and influence. They build upon, and empirically substantiate, the theoretical discussions of Chapters 2 and 3. To ensure that causal influence can be isolated, in each case two questions were posed: (a) whether the presidency was the driving force behind the initiative or agreement reached; and (b) what was the role of the other decision-makers. Within the case studies potential explanatory factors that appear to enable small states to overcome the constraint of size and to produce changes in the dependent variable are highlighted.

The concluding chapter summarises the key results and theoretical implications of the study and highlights directions of further research. It also places the findings within the pending reforms, focusing in particular on their normative ramifications. It argues that the presidency's political objective of guarding equality in the EU, its potential to introduce new priorities and innovative solutions, as well as the positive-sum nature of its outcomes ensure that the institution is not only in the interest of small states, but also beneficial to the EU as a whole.

2
The Presidency within the EU's Institutional Balance and its Evolution

Introduction

The EU is a unique or, as some prefer, 'experimental'[55] political and economic construct. Lacking a sovereign centre and homogeneous constitutional demos, it is less than a nation state. However, given that its common supranational institutions perform executive, legislative and judicial functions in areas traditionally the privilege of nation-state power, it is more than an international organisation.[56] The tension between state versus non-state defines its compromise design, which is based on a deliberate diffusion of political authority between three pillars of co-operation, the Community institutions, and the Member States.

Analysts struggle to describe the EU's 'in-between' nature. Amongst its many different labels are 'dynamic international regime based on intense multilateralism',[57] 'novel confederation',[58] 'regulatory state',[59] 'political system',[60] or 'quasi-federal union'.[61] Whatever label we may feel most comfortable with, the EU exhibits federal characteristics. It is based on the ideals of community and shared leadership and relies on a delicate institutional balance guarding equality between its members and managing potential tensions between 'big and small'. This chapter reviews the EU's institutional balance and the importance of the Council presidency within it. Subsequently, it traces the evolution of the presidency's functions. The aim is to investigate whether the rotating Council presidency is indeed a tool to equalise power differences between the Member States – as our starting hypothesis states – and shed light on the question why the Lisbon Treaty reform of the Council presidency has been so contentious.

The chapter argues that the rotating Council presidency is the most far-reaching mechanism in guarding equality between the EU's 'big and small'. Neither the balance between supranational and intergovernmental institutional arrangements nor the careful design of weighted votes in the Council of Ministers or the composition of the Commission and the EP have exemplified the equality principle to the extent the presidency does.[62] Unsurprisingly, small Member States have fiercely defended the office. In any federal construct, institutional equality is vital to small states to avoid the emergence of a hegemon and safeguard legitimacy. The analysis of the presidency's evolution shows that – contrary to the expectations of its creators – it evolved from a mainly administrative task into a leadership function providing all states equally with the opportunity to guide the EU's Council business and external affairs. Hence, a disequilibrium emerged that particularly the big states – concerned about loosing power to a growing group of smalls – wanted to address.

I. The presidency as the guardian of equality: the EU'S institutional balance

To achieve co-operation and consensus, any pattern of relations with federal traits has to ensure that none of its constitutive units is permanently disadvantaged. Differing territorial interests and unequal size have to be combined in a complex web of checks and balances. How to devise and maintain such a system has been the key concern throughout the European integration process. From its early beginnings as the European Coal and Steel Community (ECSC), European Economic Community (EEC), European Community (EC), and – since 1992 – the EU, a number of institutional mechanisms have sought to tame pure power politics in the Union and introduce a degree of equality between its members.[63] They include a delicate balance of supranational and intergovernmental elements, a complicated system of weighted votes in the Council of Ministers, and sensitive appointment procedures to the Commission, the EP, and the Council presidency. To assess the importance of the rotating presidency within this institutional balance, these mechanisms are analysed in turn.

The EU's supranational and intergovernmental balance
The EU's combination of intergovernmental and supranational elements has been its key characteristic ever since its creation. It comprises: (a) a supranational, independent Commission – formerly High

Authority – with the monopoly on the right to initiate Community legislation and put proposals to the intergovernmental Council of Ministers which has to accept them before becoming law; (b) a supranational EP – initially Assembly and largely consultative body – which gradually developed into a co-legislator alongside the Council; and (c) an independent, supranational European Court of Justice (ECJ) to interpret the treaties.

Particular stress was laid on the supranational institutions. Their independence was to ensure that size would no longer equal might. The Commissioners, for example, were explicitly prohibited to '[either seek or take] instructions from any government'.[64] Similar provisions were made for the judges and advocates general of the ECJ, which – since establishing the primacy of Community law – is probably the most independent EU institution.[65] Nonetheless, small states initially feared potential *dirigisme* and Franco-German dominance of the supranational institutions, particularly the Commission.[66] They insisted on the establishment of an intergovernmental counterweight to the Commission leading to the creation of the Council, which represents the Member States. However, over time, the Commission developed a reputation as the 'guardian of the treaties'[67] and 'catalyst of a European interest'.[68] Thus, small states have come to see it as their strongest ally and defender of minority interests.[69] Big states, in turn, tend to assert their power in the Council's various layers and substructures, which emerged as intergovernmentalism strengthened in the EU.

The sensitive mix between supranational and intergovernmental elements also manifests itself across its pillars. While decision-making in Pillar I (EC, ECSC, and Euratom) is dominated by the Commission–Council–EP triangle, the *modus operandi* in Pillars II and III (CFSP and Justice and Home Affairs (JHA)) is essentially intergovernmental. Deprived of its right of initiative the Commission's powers in these areas is limited. So are the ECJ's and the EP's who do not have jurisdiction or the right to co-legislate in Pillars II and III. To balance the lack of power of small states in Pillars II and III – often at the expense of efficiency – the prevailing decision-making rule has been unanimity.

The Community method kept a balance between small and big states that has been crucial for the EU's overall functioning. However, while the mix of intergovernmental and supranational institutions and operating modes moderate pure power politics and guarantee that no state is systematically disadvantaged, it does not make the Member States equal. Indeed, *de-facto* inequality has always been a central feature of the institutional design through the weighting of votes in the Council of Ministers and the composition of the Commission and EP.[70]

Weighted votes

By definition, a weighted system allocates a different number of votes to its constitutive units granting them unequal power in the decision-making process. The EU's system of weighted votes in the Council of Ministers arose as a consequence of the enormous size differences of the six founding members. Luxembourg was much the smallest country, with barely over 300,000 inhabitants, while at the other end of the scale France, Italy, and West Germany had populations of over 50 million. Giving each Member State one vote was clearly not an option. However, the smaller states needed safeguards against the larger. Hence, the weightings were framed to over-represent the small (and under-represent the big) with respect to their population size. While the allocation of votes was adjusted periodically to accommodate new members, this principle remained unchanged. In fact, bigger countries' under-representation has grown over time, particularly since German reunification in 1990 and as the number of acceding smaller states increased. As Table 3 shows, initially the three large states could, theoretically, force through a Commission proposal opposed by the Benelux states.[71] Since 1973, they no longer have enough votes to do so. Indeed, their electoral weight fell from 70% of the vote in 1958 to below 50% in 2007 despite representing 70% of the EU population.

Until recently Germany, the UK, France, and Italy had ten votes; Spain eight; the Netherlands, Belgium, Portugal, and Greece five; Sweden and Austria four; Denmark, Finland, and Ireland three; and Luxembourg two votes. With over 82 million inhabitants, Germany wielded only one vote per eight million citizens, while Luxembourg with 460,000 inhabitants got one vote per 230,000 citizens. A qualified majority (QM) required 62 out of the total 87 votes resulting in a blocking minority of 26 votes. Thus, the four big states needed at least two other Member States to get proposals adopted. Or, put differently, six small states representing 25% of the EU's population could block a proposal.[72] The blocking minority (BM) remained more or less constant throughout the Community's successive enlargements at approximately 30% of available votes.

In May 2004, Poland, the Czech Republic, Hungary, Slovakia, Lithuania, Latvia, Slovenia, Estonia, Cyprus, and Malta were accommodated into this system. Poland received eight votes; the Czech Republic and Hungary five; Slovakia, Lithuania, Latvia, Slovenia, and Estonia three;

Table 3 Evolution of QMV in the Council of Ministers

Bigs	1958	1973	1981	1986	1995	May 2004	Nov. 2004 (1)	2007	2014 (3) %	2014 (3) Gain(+)/Loss(–)	Pop. mil.
D									16.7%	+8.3	82.438
F	4 (23.5%)	10 (17.2%)	10 (15.9%)	10 (13.2%)	10 (11.5%)	10 (8.1%)	29 (9%)	29 (8.4%)	12.8%	+4.4	62.886
I									11.9%	+3.5	58.752
GB	–								12.3%	+3.9	60.422
E	–	–	–	8 (10.5%)	8 (9.2%)	8 (6.5%)	27 (8.4%)	27 (7.8%)	8.9%	+1.1	43.758
Pl	–	–	–						7.7%	+0.1	38.157
Total	12 (70.6%)	40 (69%)	40 (63.5%)	48 (63.2%)	48 (55.2%)	56 (45.2%)	170 (53%)	170 (49.3%)	~70%	~+20	346.413
Smalls											
R	–	–	–	–	–	–	–	14 (4.1%)	4.4%	+0.3	21.61
NL	2 (11.8%)	5 (8.6%)			5 (5.7%)		13 (4%)	13 (3.8%)	3.3%	–0.5	16.334
B			5 (7.9%)	5 (6.6%)					2.1%	–1.4	10.511
Gr						5 (4%)	12 (3.7%)	12 (3.5%)	2.3%	–1.2	11.125
P	–	–	–						2.1%	–1.4	10.57
CR									2.1%	–1.4	10.251
H									2.0%	–1.5	10.077
S									1.8%	–1.1	9.048
A	–	–	–	–	4 (4.6%)	4 (3.2%)	10 (3.1%)	10 (2.9%)	1.7%	–1.2	8.266
Bu									1.6%	–1.3	7.719
DK	–	3 (5.2%)	3 (4.8%)	3 (3.9%)	3 (3.4%)				1.1%	–0.9	5.428
Ire									0.9%	–1.1	4.209
Fin									1.1%	–0.9	5.256
SR						3 (2.4%)	7 (2.2%)	7 (2%)	1.1%	–0.9	5.389
Li									0.7%	–1.3	3.403
La									0.5%	–0.7	2.295
Slo							4 (1.2%)	4 (1.2%)	0.4%	–0.8	2.003
Es									0.3%	–0.9	1.344
Cy									0.2%	–1.0	0.766
L	1 (5.9%)	2 (3.4%)	2 (3.2%)	2 (2.6%)	2 (2.3%)	2 (1.6%)	3 (0.9%)	3 (0.9%)	0.1%	–1.1	0.46
M	–								0.1%	–0.8	0.404
Total	5 (29.4%)	18 (31%)	23 (36.5%)	28 (36.8%)	39 (44.8%)	68 (54.8%)	151 (47%)	175 (50.7%)	~30%	~–20	146.468
QM	12 (70.6%)	41 (70.7%)	45 (71.4%)	54 (71.1%)	62 (71.3%)	88 (71%) (2)	232 (72.3%) (2)	258 (74.8%) (2)	65% of pop./55% of MS (4)		
BM	6 (35.3%)	18 (31%)	19 (30.2%)	23 (30.3%)	26 (29.9%)	37 (29.8%)	90 (28%)	88 (25.5%)	4 MS		
Total	17	58	63	76	87	124	321	345	100		492.881

Notes: Due to rounding totals may not add up to 100%. (1) Nice Treaty (2) Cast by a majority of MS on a Commission proposal (in other cases, cast by at least two-thirds of MS) and 62% of the EU's total population. (3) Double Majority System as per Lisbon Treaty. Full Implementation by 2017. (4) Where the Council is not acting on a proposal of the Commission or initiative of the Union Minister for Foreign Affairs, the QM is obtained with 72% of the MS representing 65% of the EU population. Council members representing at least three-quarters of a BM (either at the level of MS or population) can demand that the Council should further discuss the issue. The Council may decide to withdraw the latter measure in 2014. Population estimates, Eurostat, 7.11.2006. Commission Doc 15124/06. QM = Qualified Majority, BM = Blocking Minority, MS = Member State, Pop. = Population.

and Cyprus and Malta two. The QM and BM thresholds were raised to 88 and 37 votes respectively. The ten new states' accession implied that the six biggest states with a total of 56 votes representing more than 70% of the EU's population needed to generate another 32 votes (support by at least six smalls) to get a proposal adopted. Blocking a proposal, in turn, required at least eight small states representing less than 20% of the EU population.

This allocation of votes, however, was short-lived. As the 2004 and 2007 enlargements consisted overwhelmingly of small states, favouring them to 'equal out' size differences became contentious. The bigger states feared future scenarios of being 'held hostage' by smaller ones. Hence, the Nice Treaty, whose institutional provisions entered into force in November 2004, redesigned the EU's traditional voting arrangement. First, it increased the number of votes of the bigger states from five times to almost ten times of that of the smallest member. Second, it raised the QM threshold from roughly 70% to almost 75% of the votes. Third, when acting upon a Commission proposal, the votes must be cast by a majority of the Member States. In other cases, the Council requires votes to be cast by at least two-thirds of the members. Finally, the requirement was added that a QM must represent at least 62% of the total EU population.[73] Overall, the new arrangements changed the weightings in favour of the bigger states.[74]

The Lisbon Treaty proposes to replace the EU's system of weighted votes with a double majority system. When the Council acts on Commission proposals, votes must be cast by 55% of the Member States, rather than a simple majority. In addition, the population minimum increased to 65%. In highly sensitive matters, when the Council acts on its own initiative, a Member State, the European Central Bank, or the High Representative, the required QM is to consist of 72% of the Member States representing 65% of the EU's population. A blocking minority, in turn, must comprise at least four states. Further safeguards introduced include the provision that states can appeal to the European Council when vital national interests have been violated.[75] Population thresholds generally benefit the bigger states, while Member State thresholds benefit the more numerous smalls. This double majority system is to be phased in 2014 and fully implemented by 2017. If ratified, the Lisbon Treaty will further boost the power of the EU's largest members (see Table 3).[76]

The above discussion shows that the EU's system of weighted votes offers a degree of security for the interests of smaller states overrepresenting them in proportional terms. In absolute terms, however, larger states retain much greater weight in the decision-making game. As Irish Prime Minister (PM) Bertie Ahern stated, 'If I had to depend on Ireland's weighted vote to promote our interests in the Council, I would not bother to turn up.'[77]

The Commission composition

Differentiated weightings have also been characteristic of the Commission. While all states have had the right to appoint one Commissioner to the college, the EU's big states have traditionally been granted two Commission posts (Table 4).

The equality principle is theoretically guarded by the fact that Commissioners should be independent (see above).[78] However, given that they are nominated by the national governments, they cannot be expected to be fully impartial. Should they disregard key national interests of their Member State, they are simply not re-appointed. Examples of partiality on behalf of the Commissioners include the debate whether to take Germany and France to the ECJ over their effective suspension of the Stability and Growth Pact (SGP) in November 2003. The Commissioners from the bigger countries were in favour of dropping the case, while those from the smaller states supported legal action.[79] Similarly, echoing the Greek Cypriot government, the Greek and Cypriot Commissioners expressed concerns over Commission proposals to establish trade links with the Turkish Cypriot north of the Island.[80]

> While [...] not supposed to represent his or her government formally, "their" Commissioners often become the ears and voice of a country in the EU executive.[81]

Surely, two additional ears and voices have been advantageous for the bigger states, especially as the Commission takes its decisions by simple majority. A Commission official argued,

> One could not honestly pretend that national or other pressures are never exercised to influence Commissioners or officials in shaping Commission's decisions and initiatives. Of course, interests of large member states are likely to be voiced more loudly.[82]

The Commission composition has also altered with the last enlargement. On accession of the ten new members, a transition started. Each accession state was granted one Commissioner while the EU's five biggest states retained their two posts until their end of term. This raised

Table 4 The Evolution of the Commission Composition

	Number of Commissioners									
	1958 EEC6	1973 EEC9	1981 EEC10	1986 EC12	1995 EU15	May 2004 EU25	Nov 2004[1] EU25	2007 EU27	2009[1] EU27	By 2014[2] EU27+
Bigs	2	2	2	2	2	2	1	1		
Smalls	1	1	1	1	1	1	1	1		
Total	9	13	14	17	20	30	25	27	<27	2/3 of MS

[1]Nice Treaty. From 2009 the number of Commissioners will be less than the number of MS and the Commissioners will be chosen according to a rotation system based on the principle of equality. [2]Lisbon Treaty.

the college from 20 to 30 Commissioners. Since November 2004 the Nice provision of one Commissioner per state applies. Although this theoretically equals out the differences between small and big, Nice further stipulated that once the EU grows to 27 states, the number of Commissioners should be less than the Member States and chosen according to a rotation system based on the principle of equality and reflecting the demographic and geographical range of all.[83] This system should come into force in 2009.

Alternatively, the Lisbon Treaty sets the number of Commissioners at two-thirds of the number of Member States by 2014. While this provision implies that the Commission will grow with further enlargements, at any point in time one-third of Member States will not have a Commissioner. Either development is not good news for the smalls. While bigger states can compensate for the lack of a Commissioner through their weight in the other institutions or their Commission staff, smaller countries will find themselves at a greater disadvantage. This explains their fierce defence of the principle of one Commissioner per state at the 2003/2004 IGC and the inclusion of a provision in the new Treaty that enables EU members to appeal the envisaged reduction of the size of the Commission by 2014 if circumstances justify. It also features amongst the reasons why the Irish rejected the Lisbon Treaty. Six per cent of the Irish voters stated their opposition to loosing their right to have an Irish Commissioner in every Commission. One official argued, 'As a small state, if you do not have a Commissioner you are in a sense out of the game.'[84]

Representation in the European Parliament

De-facto inequality is also visible in the EP. The attribution of seats in the EP is degressively proportional, half way between equal representation and population proportionality.[85] Albeit overrepresented in terms of population size, most small states are either three or four times less represented in the EP than the big ones (Table 5). Currently, the EP has 785 members. The smallest Member State, Malta, has five seats and the largest, Germany, 99. While subsequent enlargements increased the overall representation of the smalls from 24% in 1958 to 44% in 2007, the big state share is still 56%.

The Lisbon Treaty continues this trend. It states that representation of citizens should be degressively proportional and raises the minimum number of seats for the small states to six, lowers the highest number of MEPs per country to 96, and fixes a maximum of 750 MEPs. The EP

Table 5 The Evolution of the EP's Composition

	Number of MEPs											Degree of Under (–)/Over (+) Representation				
Bigs	1958	1973	1976	1981	1986	1991	1995	2004	2007	2009–2014[1]	2009–2014[2]	% of EU pop.	2007–2009 % of seats	2007–2009 (–)	2009–2014[2] % of seats	2009–2014[2] (–)
D	36	36	81	81	81	99	99	99	99	99	96	16.7	12.6	-4.1	12.8	-3.9
F	36	36	81	81	81	81	87	78	78	72	74	12.8	9.9	-2.9	9.9	-2.9
I	36	36	81	81	81	81	87	78	78	72	72[3]	11.9	9.9	-2.0	9.6	-2.3
GB	—	36	81	81	81	81	87	78	78	72	73	12.3	9.9	-2.4	9.7	-2.6
E	—	—	—	—	60	60	64	54	54	50	54	8.9	6.9	-2.0	7.2	-1.7
Pl	—	—	—	—	—	—	—	54	54	50	51	7.7	6.9	-1.8	6.8	-0.9
Seats (%)	76	73	79	75	74	75	68	60	56	56	56	~70	56		56	
Smalls														(+)		(+)
R	—	—	—	—	—	—	—	—	35	33	33	4.4	4.5	0.1	4.4	0.0
NL	14	14	25	25	25	25	31	27	27	25	26	3.3	3.4	0.1	3.5	0.2
B	14	14	24	24	24	24	25	24	24	22	22	2.1	3.1	1.0	2.9	0.8
Gr	—	—	—	24	24	24	25	24	24	22	22	2.3	3.1	0.8	2.9	0.6
P	—	—	—	—	24	24	25	24	24	22	22	2.1	3.1	1.0	2.9	0.8
CR	—	—	—	—	—	—	—	24	24	22	22	2.1	3.1	1.0	2.9	0.8
H	—	—	—	—	—	—	—	24	24	22	22	2.0	3.1	1.1	2.9	0.9
S	—	—	—	—	—	—	22	19	19	18	20	1.8	2.4	0.6	2.7	0.9
A	—	—	—	—	—	—	21	18	18	17	19	1.7	2.3	0.6	2.5	0.8
Bu	—	—	—	—	—	—	—	—	18	17	18	1.6	2.3	0.7	2.4	0.8
DK	—	10	16	16	16	16	16	14	14	13	13	1.1	1.8	0.7	1.7	0.6
Fin	—	—	—	—	—	—	16	14	14	13	13	0.9	1.8	0.9	1.7	0.8
SR	—	—	—	—	—	—	—	14	14	13	13	1.1	1.8	0.7	1.7	0.6
Ire	—	10	15	15	15	15	15	13	13	12	12	1.1	1.7	0.6	1.6	0.5
Li	—	—	—	—	—	—	—	13	13	12	12	0.7	1.7	1.0	1.6	0.9
La	—	—	—	—	—	—	—	9	9	8	9	0.5	1.1	0.6	1.2	0.7
Slo	—	—	—	—	—	—	—	7	7	7	8	0.4	1.0	0.6	1.1	0.7
L	6	6	6	6	6	6	6	6	6	6	6	0.3	0.8	0.5	0.8	0.5
Es	—	—	—	—	—	—	—	6	6	6	6	0.2	0.8	0.6	0.8	0.6
Cy	—	—	—	—	—	—	—	6	6	6	6	0.1	0.8	0.7	0.8	0.7
M	—	—	—	—	—	—	—	5	5	5	6	0.1	0.6	0.5	0.8	0.7
Seats (%)	24	27	21	25	26	25	32	40	44	44	44	~30	44		44	
Total	142	198	410	434	518	536	626	732	785	736	750[3]	100	100		100	

[1] Nice: Distribution of Seats according to Art. 189 TEC as modified by Art. 9 of the BG/RO – Act of Accession. [2] As proposed by EP report of 12.10.2007. Population estimates from Table 3. [3] To be increased by 1.

presented a proposal on the precise allocation of seats in October 2007 which the IGC accepted. However, it decided that the number of MEPs would be 750 plus its president. The additional seat is to be attributed to Italy.

The rotating Council presidency and its importance for the EU

The Council presidency is the EU's only institution where 'equality between states [has throughout been] applied in its pure form'.[86] A pre-established six-monthly rota is followed regardless of size, economic power, or merit.[87] Originally the Member States rotated in alphabetical order and any newcomers were accommodated into this system (Table 6). The order of rotation was changed twice. After Spain and Portugal joined, the Council reversed the alphabetical sequence each calendar year from 1993 onwards. This ensured that countries would hold both first and second semester presidencies given the different workloads each semester involves. The rota was revised a second time in the Accession Act for Finland, Sweden, and Austria. It is currently decided unanimously by the Council. Initially countries held the presidency every three years. This time frame increased over time.

Regardless of the precise order and number of years in between a country's presidency turn, the rotation principle allows equal access of the institution to the EU's members enabling them 'to make diplomatic contributions independent of their political and economic weight'.[88] This has been particularly important for smaller states:

> The presidency affords an opportunity to show the world how well a small country can tackle politically sensitive issues.[89]

The presidency can thus be seen as the 'guardian of equality' in the EU. While equality may not be a merit in and itself – to be effective and credible decision-making procedures should reflect power realities – replacing the rotating with a permanent presidency would upset the EU's founding principle and tilt its traditional institutional balance more clearly in favour of the big states. This partly explains the hostility by the small states towards the creation of a permanent European Council president. As a Finnish Convention member said,

> If we were to reject the rotation system, we would lose a symbol of equality between the Member States. There is no place for [...a permanent] president of the Union.[90]

Table 6 The Council Presidency Rota (1958–2008)

Year	First Semester	Second Semester
1958 (EU6)	Belgium	Germany
1959	France	Italy
1960	Luxembourg	Netherlands
1961	Belgium	Germany
1962	France	Italy
1963	Luxembourg	Netherlands
1964	Belgium	Germany
1965	France	Italy
1966	Luxembourg	Netherlands
1967	Belgium	Germany
1968	France	Italy
1969	Luxembourg	Netherlands
1970	Belgium	Germany
1971	France	Italy
1972	Luxembourg	Netherlands
1973 (EU9)	Belgium	Denmark
1974	Germany	France
1975	Ireland	Italy
1976	Luxembourg	Netherlands
1977	United Kingdom	Belgium
1978	Denmark	Germany
1979	France	Ireland
1980	Italy	Luxembourg
1981 (EU10)	Netherlands	United Kingdom
1982	Belgium	Denmark
1983	Germany	Greece
1984	France	Ireland
1985	Italy	Luxembourg
1986 (EU12)	Netherlands	United Kingdom
1987	Belgium	Denmark
1988	Germany	Greece
1989	Spain	France
1990	Ireland	Italy
1991	Luxembourg	Netherlands
1992	Portugal	United Kingdom
1993 (reversed order)	Denmark	Belgium
1994	Greece	Germany
1995 (EU15)	France	Spain
1996	Italy	Ireland
1997	Netherlands	Luxembourg

Table 6   (Continued)

Year	First Semester	Second Semester
1998 (balanced order)	United Kingdom	Austria
1999	Germany	Finland
2000	Portugal	France
2001	Sweden	Belgium
2002	Spain	Denmark
2003	Greece	Italy
2004 (EU 25)	Ireland	Netherlands
2005	Luxembourg	United Kingdom
2006	Austria	Finland
2007 (EU 27)	Germany	Portugal
2008	Slovenia	France
2009	Czech Republic	Sweden

Others called the replacement of the rotating presidency by a permanent president an 'institutional *coup d'etat*'[91] fearing such a president would '[nibble] away at the Commission's powers'[92] and create a state of 'permanent cohabitation with the Commission president'.[93]

Rotation prevents the development of a strong permanent centre that 'may come to dominate the autonomy of the constituting members' and 'undermine the EU's legitimacy'.[94] It offers assurance that 'no single Member State can exert a long-term determining influence on the Council'[95] and is a mechanism that guarantees non-centralisation avoiding precisely the kind of hegemonic power structures that have troubled Europe in the past. As the then Austrian Foreign Minister Benita Ferrero-Walder commented,

> I see no additional value in [...] a European Council president [...]. It is not so good to concentrate so much on one person and to establish such strong centralisation. After all, we are a Europe consisting of many individual states and I think this should be taken into account. One must ask which states might produce the European Council president. I am afraid it would be primarily the major states that would fill this post.[96]

Similarly, Portuguese Secretary of State for European Affairs Carlos Costa Neves feared that the abolition of the Council presidency would 'in the long term lead to the creation of a leading EU core group of larger countries'.[97] The rotating principle is perceived as an important safeguard against such a big state directorate and for the interests of the

EU's small states. Even former Spanish PM Jose Maria Aznar, who joined French President Jacques Chirac and British PM Tony Blair in advocating the abolition of the rotating presidency, saw it as a tool to avoid an 'imbalance of interests'.[98] This notion of shared leadership has been the 'historical underpinning of the Union'[99] contributing to an ongoing process of successful co-operation among the EU's ever more diverse group of Member States.

The issue of institutional equality between big and small states is at the heart of any federal construct. In the debates of the 1787 Federal Convention in Philadelphia, for example, a proportional composition of the US Senate was ruled out on the grounds that it 'strikes at the existence of smaller states'.[100] The 13 sovereign American states would only be equal if the Senate was composed of an equal number of delegates from each state. Interestingly, both the Senate and the Council presidency – albeit completely different institutions with different purposes – were defended on the same grounds as both systems were wrestling with the same issues: designing political systems with enduring legitimacy.[101]

But if the Council presidency was accepted without any controversy by the big states in 1958, why did they start pursuing its abolition? Or, in institutionalist jargon, how to explain this disequilibrium that has arisen and hence the incentive to alter an institution that has previously been in equilibrium? Looking at the evolution of the presidency offers a partial answer.

II. The evolution of the presidency

The conflict over the future of the Council presidency could not have been in starker contrast to the debates leading to its creation. When the presidency was established in the 1950s, it had been a complete afterthought. The Schuman Plan of 9 May 1950 had not even foreseen a Council, nor did Jean Monnet's blueprint for the ECSC envisage a leadership role for national governments and their ministers. Thus, the initial conception of the presidency was very modest. The 1951 Paris Treaty merely stated that each government would hold the Council chair for three months in rotation and that it would be responsible for convening meetings.[102] The presidency term was extended to a six-month period in 1957 by the Rome Treaties.[103] The precise functions of the presidency were never specified in the original Community Treaties. Instead, its main duties were set out in the 1958 provisional standing orders of the Council and included chairing all Council formations; agenda and minute drafting; signing documents and notifying decisions; and representing the Council before the Assembly. These tasks were generally viewed as 'irksome' rather than offering scope for influencing policy-making.[104] The presidency was accepted without controversy and remained essentially unreformed over successive treaty revisions.

Over time, however, the presidency unexpectedly evolved into an institution with important leadership functions and opportunities for shaping public policies. According to New Institutionalist Theory, two main reasons explain this transformation: changes in the relative power of the actors since the time of the design of the EU institutions and developments in the policy environment posing new challenges to existing institutional forms. Both are examined in turn.

Changes in the relative power of the Commission, the Council, and the EP

Community decision-making was designed as a tandem relationship between the Commission and the Council, with the Commission as the sole drafter of legislation and defender of the collective interest and the Council representing national priorities. It was assumed that the Commission would take the lead and evolve into the stronger partner.[105] This assumption proved wrong. It was the Council rather than the Commission that emerged as the main decision-making institution. The importance and leadership potential of the presidency increased correspondingly. The Commission weakened considerably after the 'empty chair crisis' in the mid-1960s which resulted in the institutionalisation of Member States' veto rights of Commission proposals when vital national interests were at stake. As Wallace put it: '1965–6 marked a turning point which altered the institutional balance and specifically activated the previously dormant potential of the presidency'.[106] French President De Gaulle and disagreements between the Member States on the institutional balance contributed significantly to the curtailing of the Commission's powers and to the strengthening of intergovernmental elements in the 1960s. The subsequent leadership gap was filled by the Council presidency.

The Council's role and with it the importance of the presidency grew further after the institutionalisation of the European Council and thus regular Summits by the EU's heads of state or government. The heads of state or government had met sporadically since 1961. In 1974, on the suggestion of the then French President Valéry Giscard d'Estaing, it was agreed that the new body would meet at least three times a year and be chaired by the presidency. The European Council's task became to 'provide the Union with the necessary impetus for its development and

[...] define the general political guidelines thereof'.[107] Indeed, it turned into the EU's 'principal agenda-setter' and 'core of the EU's executive',[108] its summits being the most important presidency events. A Commission official said,

> [Initially] the Council presidency was a pure management task and only consisted of the chairing of meetings. However, its task has become a lot heavier and now involves providing direction and agenda-setting.[109]

In addition, the creation of the European Council strengthened the intergovernmental element in EU co-operation. As Kirchner argued,

> Whilst the intergovernmental method could effectively sideline the Commission in EC decision-making, it required a replacement for the Commission's role [...] – the Council presidency.[110]

Successive rounds of enlargement contributed to the greater importance of the European Council and mediator role of the presidency. As the number and diversity of the EU's members increased, agreement was harder to reach. Especially after the first enlargement in 1973 and throughout the 1970s, Member State solidarity reached a low point. The EU entered a period of Euro-sclerosis marked by political and economic flux. In addition, the UK demanded a re-negotiation of entry terms, there were disagreements over the Common Agricultural Policy (CAP), and transatlantic relations deteriorated. The Commission was still ineffectual and the large Member States failed to play a leadership role. Decisions became the outcome of difficult intergovernmental negotiation and the presidency turned into an important arbiter and decision-making mechanism in the Council. This development increased the office holder's opportunities to settle major conflicts and launch policy initiatives.[111] As more and more issues started being pushed up to European Council level, a more active role of the presidency was required.[112]

The presidency's mediator tasks further expanded with the growing importance of the EP and its transformation into a co-legislator. Initially the EP only had a supervisory role. Its competences, however, were extended to include legislative and budgetary powers. Since the Amsterdam Treaty, the EP's task to co-legislate together with the Council has become the standard procedure. The co-decision procedure put the two institutions on an equal footing by abolishing the third reading which used to allow the Council to go back to positions formulated at an earlier stage (unless an absolute majority of MEPs pronounced its opposition). By eliminating the possibility of recurring to texts rejected earlier, Amsterdam granted equal weighting to the opinion of either institution.[113] Thus, within the co-decision procedure the Council can no longer impose its position on the EP. In short, it underlined the need of effective liaison with the EP for agreements to be reached – a task the Council presidency took on.[114]

However, the presidency assumed important leadership roles not only because of the changes in the relative power of the Community institutions, but also as the EU deepened and broadened its policy scope.

Changes in the policy environment

The SEA and subsequent treaty changes increased the Community's volume of work, the Community went into many new policy areas, and more active management by the presidency, for example to facilitate the implementation of the IM programme by 1992, was required. In addition, many of the general aims raised in the SEA enabled the presidency to employ an innovative role. This is particularly visible in the sphere of foreign policy. Title III of the SEA on European Political Co-operation (EPC) established that the Council presidency would be responsible not only for the management of political co-operation activities, convening and organising meetings, but charged with initiating action, coordinating, and representing the position of the Member States in relations with third countries in respect of EPC activities.[115] The Council Secretariat was to assist the presidency in preparing and implementing the activities of EPC and in administrative matters.[116] With each treaty revision the scope of the presidency's role in foreign policy matters grew. Inevitably, the role of the presidency changed with this development. It began to emerge as a 'collective face' for the EC as a whole.[117]

De Bassompiere (1988) finds that the Council presidency became the sole forum through which Council of Ministers' activities were initiated, co-ordinated, and represented. Given the lighter institutional structure in foreign policy, foreign policy management became highly dependent upon the presidency. The consolidation of the position of the Council and its presidency is also visible in JHA. Both are driven by the Council rather than the Commission.

With the growth in the Council's legislative activity, the number of sectoral Councils and preparatory working groups, the presidency's organisational tasks also increased substantially. Since the SEA and Maastricht Treaty, not only the number of decisions to be taken by the EU but also the complexity of the issues leading to a greater reliance on working groups increased dramatically.[118] Council configurations grew to the point that for reasons of efficiency, steps to gradually cut the number of Councils were initiated at the Helsinki Summit in December 1999 and reduced to nine Councils at the 2002 Seville Council.[119]

Finally, the presidency acquired representative roles with regard to not only other EU institutions, but also the press, media, and wider world. This function also grew more by 'default rather than by design'.[120] Besides the presidency, the Council had no other means of representing itself *vis-à-vis* other players.[121] As the Community's external role expanded and it began to conduct negotiations on trade and development with third states (for example, with the African, Caribbean, and Pacific (ACP) states) and seek special relations with its neighbours (for example, with Turkey), the presidency assumed further external representative roles.

The Council's Rules of Procedure (CRoP) which replaced its provisional standing orders setting out the presidency's basic operating rules were revised sporadically to reflect these developments. The CRoP of 1979, for example, stated that the presidency would convene Council meetings, lay out the timetable seven months before beginning its term, draw up provisional agendas, chair meetings (including the Committee of Permanent Representatives (COREPER) and working groups), sign the minutes of meetings and all official decisions, ensure that decisions are notified, and represent the Council before the EP. In the 1987 CRoP the presidency's role in the decision-making process increased by adding that the Council shall vote on the initiative of its president. The 1993 CRoP further added that the presidency should submit a six-month working programme, that it can propose issues for policy debate, a written vote procedure for urgent issues including CFSP issues, may chair preparatory meetings ahead of its official term and shall ensure that Committee and working group reports are available before the relevant COREPER meetings.

Since 2000 the presidency has had various strategic tools available to facilitate agreement: it can restrict the numbers per delegation present in the meeting room for discussion of particular items, set the order in which items are to be taken, and allot the time for discussion of a particular item. These were extended in 2002 by granting the presidency the right to ask delegations to present in writing their proposals for amendment of a text under discussion before a given date and ask delegations which have similar positions on a particular item or text to choose one of them.[122]

Table 7   The Council Presidency's Formal Tasks

Function	Formal Tasks	Reasons for Development
Leadership/ Initiative	• Submit 6-monthly, annual, and multi-annual work programmes • Set Council agendas • Initiate policies/debates • Mediate diverse viewpoints • Initiate votes	• Emergence of Council as main decision-maker/decline of Commission • Creation of European Council • Search for new targets/broadening policy scope
Management/ Co-ordination	• Chair all Council meetings and ensure discussions are conducted in a businesslike manner • Co-ordinate agendas with other EU institutions	• Increased volume of work with subsequent treaty changes • Successive rounds of enlargement
Organisation/ Administration	• Convene all Council meetings • Draft documents, minutes, conclusions	• Increased number of Council meetings/growth in Council's legislative activity • Increased complexity of issues
Representation	• Represent Council *vis-à-vis* other EU institutions, third countries	• Need for representation *vis-à-vis* other decision-making institutions • Growing external role

Sources: Council Rules of Procedures 1996, Consolidated TEU, Presidency Handbook.

In sum, the presidency over time developed from a mere organiser into an important initiator and promoter of political initiatives; chair of all Council meetings; manager of the Council; the co-ordinator, mediator and broker of different viewpoints between the Member States and the other Community institutions; and the representative of the Council *vis-à-vis* the Commission, the EP, as well as third states communicating common positions and negotiating on behalf of the EU.[123] Each Member State preparing for the presidency office faces a complex set of tasks having to:

> ...plan, direct and inspire a programme of work in a multitude of fields in the smoothest and best-co-ordinated manner, to search for the compromise that makes decision possible, to represent the Community and negotiate on its behalf *vis-à-vis* the EP in situations becoming more and more frequent, where real skilful negotiation is called for as well as vis-à-vis public opinion and the press.[124]

Table 7 groups this multitude of tasks into four broad and overlapping categories and summarises the reasons for their development.[125]

Conclusion

This chapter investigated the presidency's potential equalising effects by examining the EU's institutional set-up and the presidency within it. It showed that since its inception in the 1950s, the EC has been based on a delicate institutional framework, which – as any federal construct – tried to balance the vast size differences of its members. This institutional framework has relied upon combining supranational with intergovernmental arrangements, a complicated system of weighted votes in the Council, and sensitive appointment procedures to the Commission, the EP, and the Council presidency.

Of all these mechanisms, the Council presidency is the most far-reaching in terms of putting big and small states on an equal footing. While the other institutional arrangements favour small states in proportional terms, in absolute terms the differentiated weightings ensure that the Member States are not equally represented across the EU's institutions. Bigger states carry more weight given their number of votes, MEPs, and – until recently – the number of Commissioners. *De-facto* inequality between big and small Member States will increase, should the Commission be reduced to two-thirds of the Member States and rotation be abandoned at European Council level.

This chapter further argued that the rotating presidency has ensured non-hierarchical and decentralised leadership of the Council thereby avoiding the emergence of a single power centre. Preventing the rise of a hegemon is particularly important in the EU – a system that, for its effective functioning, relies heavily on consensus and that derives its democratic legitimacy indirectly.

As to the presidency's evolution, this chapter showed that as long as the presidency remained a low key administrative actor with little political influence, it hardly offered possibilities to shape the EU's integration path. Thus, pure equality between big and small states in terms of access to the office did not cause controversy or rejection by the larger countries. However, given that the presidency gradually evolved from an organisational function into an important leader of EU affairs guiding the work of the Council across the EU's policy pillars, managing inter-institutional relations and external affairs, its potential agenda influence has grown. This is one of the factors that led to a disequilibrium with the bigger states seeking to abolish it and smaller states fiercely defending it. The latter see the presidency as an additional arena to exert their influence *vis-à-vis* the bigger Member States. Most recently, this has become visible in the Irish referendum on the Lisbon Treaty.

NI puts forward two main reasons for the emergence of such disequilibria: changes in the relative power of the institutions or in the policy environment. Both reasons seem to hold. The relative power of the actors since the creation of the EU changed with the decline of the Commission and the increasingly important role of the Council and the EP. The EU's policy environment, in turn, changed with successive treaty changes and its growing external role.

NI further suggests that once created, institutions cannot be fully controlled by their masters. In this case, NI would predict that the presidency enjoys discretion from the collective preferences of the Member States and its role and actions can only be controlled imperfectly. This would imply that individual presidencies have both the incentive and means to use the office to shape the EU's agenda and policies in line with its national priorities – the subject of the next chapters.

3

The Council Presidency as a Policy Entrepreneur: Nature, Agenda-setting Power, and Conditions for Success

Introduction

Chapter 2 examined the presidency within the EU's institutional balance and its evolution. This chapter analyses the nature and agenda-setting power of the office. In doing so it sets out the theoretical framework for the following case studies.

The Council presidency is a peculiar hybrid: it is neither intergovernmental nor supranational. On the one hand, the presidency illustrates the importance of national actors and interstate bargains in EU decision-making. Council meetings are chaired by Member State officials whose *raison d'être* normally is to negotiate deals that best reflect national preferences. Individual national presidencies can therefore be seen as policy actors. On the other hand, the presidency is supranational in its operation and an institution in its own right. It is expected to put the general interest first and broker compromises acceptable to all the other decision-makers within a culture of consensus. Unsurprisingly, it has been called 'schizophrenic'.[126] It faces the contradictory task to combine sector-specific national concerns with impartiality.[127]

Hybrids are difficult to conceptualise. The dominant presidency conceptualisation in the literature has been that of a 'neutral arbitrator'[128] who facilitates agreement by the impartial fulfilment of its tasks. This chapter challenges this view on theoretical and empirical grounds. It first introduces the framework of policy entrepreneurship in the EU and evaluates the neutral broker versus policy entrepreneur concept. Second, it seeks to explain variance of presidential influence by outlining four categories of factors that we should expect to condition the extent to which the office holder can pursue its political objectives. Some of these factors are generic to the Council presidency;

others are specific to individual Member States. Particular attention is paid to potential limitations related to the small size of the presidency country.

The chapter argues that although the presidency's formal powers are constrained, the office holder can direct the other decision-making players towards its goals. This is achieved by exploiting its informal powers and information advantages – underestimated in much of the literature. Regardless of size, the presidency's privileged position in the EU's decision-making system allows it to shape agenda items, advance or delay legislation, and initiate new policy debates. The concept of political entrepreneurship captures this form of leadership, the biased nature of the presidency office, and its subtle informal powers. Nonetheless, presidencies' entrepreneurial success varies. It depends not only on the institutional position of the chair – the same for each office holder – but also on the particular circumstances at the time, the institutional environment, and specific country characteristics. But rather than on size, we can expect the presidency's level of influence to depend on: the leadership context; the heterogeneity, intensity, and distribution of governmental preferences in the Council; inter-institutional relations; and the office holder's skill and effective use of the Council Secretariat.

I. Policy entrepreneurship and agenda-setting in the EU

Policy entrepreneurship is a form of leadership. It focuses on actors' autonomy within the given institutional set up. Policy entrepreneurs initiate policies, mediate, and broker deals. They favour congeniality and consensus, but defend a distinctive ideal point. Their agenda-setting power stems from the control over specific resources, including their material resources, reputation, information, expertise, and ability to mediate.[129] They are biased brokers who 'invest their resources to promote a position in return for anticipated future gain'.[130] Rather than enjoying considerable formal powers they seek informal ways to launch discussions by highlighting certain problems, proposing possible solutions, and mobilising support for their preferred solution.[131] In brokering deals they 'help to dissolve or circumvent the collective-action problems associated with institutional bargaining'.[132] With their superior knowledge policy entrepreneurs can both get the parties *to* the Pareto frontier and hence reach Pareto efficient (or positive-sum) outcomes and shift them *along* the Pareto frontier into their preferred

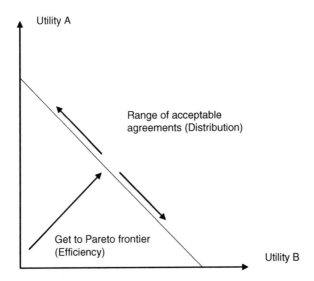

Figure 1 The Policy Entrepreneur's Impact on Bargaining Outcomes
Source: Adapted from Beach (2005).

direction.[133] Hence, they affect both efficiency of an agreement and the distribution of gains among actors (see Figure 1).

Policy entrepreneurs play an important role in Kingdon's agenda-setting theory.[134] Agenda-setting is the first crucial stage in the policy process.[135] Agendas are 'lists of subjects or problems to which government officials and people [...] closely associated with those officials are paying serious attention at any given time'.[136] Kingdon distinguishes between 'systemic' and 'decision' (or active) agendas. Systemic agendas comprise all legitimate issues for concern while decision agendas are smaller items under active discussion in the decision process. In the EU, elements of the systemic agenda include the Council's multi-annual and annual programmes which outline broad priority areas; the individual six-monthly presidency working programmes in which governments set out their goals for their term; and European Council conclusions. The agendas for individual Summits, sectoral Councils, COREPER, and working group meetings can be seen as active agendas.

According to Kingdon, policy entrepreneurs act within three simultaneous 'streams' in the agenda-setting process: the identification of problems; the proposing of specific policies or policy alternatives; and politics (political changes or actors direct attention to certain agenda items). At certain times a 'coupling' of these streams takes place. A problem comes to the fore, policy proposals exist, and the political climate for decision emerges opening a 'policy window' for successful adoption or policy change. Policy entrepreneurs wait for such windows 'like surfers wait for a big wave' to propose or sell carefully pre-prepared proposals to the decision body.[137] Predictable policy windows include scheduled renewals of certain programmes. Unpredictable windows open frequently, if briefly, after changes in political conditions or leadership environments.

The EU's agenda-setting process is much friendlier to policy entrepreneurs than individual national systems.[138] This is mainly due to: the high number of national and transnational participants in policy-making and multitude of alternative solutions; the numerous access points; and the general fragmentation of policy-making with no exclusive leadership.

Particularly the multiple access points and fragmented nature of policy-making open opportunities for agenda-setters. However, this openness can also lead to indeterminacy, stalemate, or political instability. More precisely, while the likelihood to put issues on the agenda might be higher than at national level, there is no guarantee that such issues will move to the decision-making stage.[139] The EU's loosely articulated policy-making system and blurred functions between the Commission, Council, and EP lead to competing conceptualisations of the same issue and make it difficult to push an issue on the active agenda. The resulting combination of multiple opportunities and powerful constraints triggers a need for strong political entrepreneurship.

Policy entrepreneurship by the Commission has so far been the focus of most studies.[140] This is due to its important agenda-setting powers in terms of drafting legislation but its lack of decision-making power. Potential entrepreneurship by the Council presidency has been ignored by most analysts,[141] particularly by the two main integration schools neofunctionalism and intergovernmentalism. While the former has argued that supranational entrepreneurship is one of the major factors shaping decision-making in the EU, the latter finds that its role is 'greatly exaggerated and sometimes even counterproductive'.[142] Instead, governments with the greatest interest in reaching agreement are believed to initiate, mediate, and mobilise negotiations and agendas.[143] How does the presidency fit into this debate? Is it a 'fairly passive [manager]'[144] and neutral broker that changes its 'national hat' for a supranational one while at the EU's helm? Or is it a 'double-hatted' active policy entrepreneur that tries to shape policy outcomes in line with its domestic preferences?

II. Conceptualising the presidency: neutral broker versus policy entrepreneur

Formal rules: The presidency as a neutral broker

The explanatory strength of the neutral broker conceptualisation of the presidency relies on formal rules and procedures. Implicit in this approach is that the presidency does not seek to widen its influence and is heavily constrained because: it is formally required to be neutral; it has a weak legal base and lacks formal powers of legislative initiative; it is a heavily organisational/administrative task; and it represents the EU externally.

The neutrality constraint

According to the Presidency Handbook 'the presidency must, by definition, be neutral' and 'cannot favour either its own preferences or those of a particular Member State'.[145] The country in the chair is asked explicitly to distance itself from speaking for its government. It occupies two seats in the Council, one as president and one as the national delegation whose position may not be the same.[146] The neutral broker approach further contends that the EU's challenging negotiating set-up leaves little room for presidency interests. Effective co-operation is achieved by impartial brokerage by the presidency – a trusted player from amongst the Council members. Agreements contribute to a shared political project, which distinguishes the EU from other multilateral negotiations.[147] The Member State in the chair is thought either to have been socialised to behave impartially or to fear 'sanctions' by its principals[148] should it break the 'neutrality norm':

> States which appear to engage in the 'aberrant' behaviour of nakedly pursuing national [...] objectives ahead of those of the EU face heavy criticism and a difficult presidency. Thus, paradoxically, the presidency may not provide a good opportunity for advancing national [...] policy objectives.[149]

Small states, it is argued, are particularly constrained by the neutrality norm given that they 'cannot afford to affront the more powerful members of the system'.[150] The fact that the presidency has remained unreformed for so long is seen as evidence that sanctions for pursuing national interests have not been necessary.

Limited formal powers

The second constraint stressed by the neutral broker approach is the presidency's restricted formal powers and weak legal foundations. To date the Council presidency does not have formal institutional status.[151] Brief references to it are spread throughout the treaties. In addition, the presidency lacks formal powers of legislative initiative (in Pillar I) or shares it with the Commission (in Pillars II and III). The Commission's agenda-setting power is particularly significant under conditions of QMV when the Council can only alter it by unanimity.[152] Agenda-setting in the EU is a collaborative process between the EU institutions and the Member States. The customary presidency tour of the European capitals ahead of each term and the major Summits, for example, serve to collect Council members' opinions:

> The *tour des capitals* allow you to get other Member States' input. You cannot ignore other Member States – the agenda is a compromise agenda and also follows the Commission work programme.[153]

Furthermore, the EU's agenda is a rolling agenda. Unfinished initiatives have to be continued and the general Community timetable (including annual budgetary and agricultural price reviews or the renewal of external trade and co-operation agreements) has to be followed. Enlargement or economic and monetary union (EMU), for example, had been on every presidency agenda for a decade. Thus, many analysts see the presidency as 'phases of an ongoing process'[154] or 'cheerleader for a well-established programme, rather than a powerful executive position'.[155] Voss and Bailleul argue,

> The daily running of Europe cannot be split up in six-month parts. It has its own dynamics and these are to a large extent determined by the rolling programme. Especially in the [...] first pillar, a legislative proposal can be 'pending' for months, even years.[156]

In terms of policy outcomes, the neutral broker concept argues that six months are too short to leave a mark, particularly as each presidency acts in a climate of constant flux. Unexpected events can rapidly change presidency priorities and goals.

In sum, the presidency's agenda-setting capacity and ability to steer integration is downgraded. Agenda-setting is interpreted as an impartial collection of sufficient points to continue EU business and conclude broad package deals on issues that impose themselves on the agenda. The presidency is thought to identify the 'ingredients' of the package and set the bargaining process in motion[157] with the aim of serving the EU rather than steering it. The scope for pursuing national priorities is minimal. As Voss and Bailleul conclude,

> The European agenda is governed mainly by its own dynamics, which are dissociated from the president's wishes, demands, or priorities.[158]

The presidency's administrative burden

The neutral broker approach regards the presidency's administrative role as a burden rather than a comparative advantage:

> At the heart of the Union business is the daily running of a great number of meetings. Chairing these meetings skilfully and efficiently is perhaps what the duties of the presidency, in the final analysis, come down to.[159]

Each incoming presidency faces the organisation and chairing of 1500–2000 meetings at all levels. At present, there are about 240 working groups and individual committees. COREPER I (the deputy Permanent Representatives) and COREPER II (the Permanent Representatives) meet at least once a week. On average there are between 35 and 40 ministerial Councils and two Summits per presidency. In addition to these formal meetings, the presidency organises around nine to ten informal sectoral Council meetings in its home country. Sometimes presidencies convene emergency ministerial meetings, as the case after the outbreak of the Russia–Georgia war in 2008, the disagreements over the Iraq war under the 2003 Greek Presidency, or the September 11 terrorist attacks in 2001. All require logistical arrangements, chairmanship, and the preparation of agendas, minutes, decisions, statements, and press conferences. The meetings held outside of Brussels, where the presidency cannot rely on the organisational apparatus of the Council Secretariat, are a particular strain on resources.

The financial burden is also considerable, particularly for the small Member States. Finland spent in the region of 50–60 million euros on its 1999 presidency.[160] After the May 2004 enlargement presidency costs increased even further. Ireland's 2004 presidency bill, for example, approximated 90 million euros.[161]

Furthermore, the neutral broker approach downgrades the powers of initiative of the presidency and stresses the importance of smooth management instead:

> The smooth management of business in the Council is the least glamorous but most important function of the presidency.[162]

Representing the Union

The final constraint highlighted by the neutral broker approach concerns the presidency's representational task. The presidency speaks for the EU in bilateral and multilateral meetings and regularly issues presidency declarations on behalf of it. It represents the EU within the established frameworks of political consultation with the US, Canada, and Japan and co-operation with the Ukraine and Russia. Presidency declarations are usually elaborated with the General Secretariat and demonstrate the EU's concerns about external events, human rights issues, or natural disasters. The neutral broker approach stresses that in its relations with third states, the presidency serves the Union as a whole guarding its character of an economic and political union defending peace and democratic values. Thus, it sees limited opportunity for a presidency to use its representational task to pursue domestic interests.

Overall, by relying heavily on formal roles and constraints, the neutral broker conceptualisation disregards differing cultural norms/styles and national preferences and the informal powers that a presidency can exploit, especially in the agenda-setting process. This contrasts sharply with new institutionalist analysis and the policy entrepreneur framework.

Informal practices: the presidency as a policy entrepreneur

New institutionalists take informal practices into consideration and examine how the presidency country with its differing styles and preferences operates within formal institutional constraints. The policy entrepreneur concept argues that the presidency actively seeks to enhance its influence and circumvent formal constraints. It stresses: the biased nature of the presidency; its informal agenda-setting powers and the strategic dimension of its formal administrative/organisational task; and the presidency's information advantages.

Presidency bias

In line with principal agent theory, the policy entrepreneur approach assumes that the presidency seeks a degree of autonomy from the other Member States. Rather than being 'self denying in the chair'[163] it 'adapt[s] to other sources of power as [it tries] to find [its] place in the larger order'.[164] Instead of being neutral, it develops its own initiatives, participates in shaping ideas, and engineers consensus behind them by adjusting to, and working with, other actors in the system. Member States' general attitude to the EU, certain policies, and other players will influence their behaviour and strategies.[165] The result is a certain bias in favour of one's own government's position no matter which Member State holds the presidency.[166]

Illustrative cases challenging the neutral broker position are found across the EU's policy areas. In the area of JHA, for example, the Greek 2003 Presidency drafted a compromise on visas for sailors that reversed the 2002 Spanish Presidency approach. Concerned about combating illegal immigration more effectively, Greece wanted to free border authorities from the responsibility to issue visas to sailors by handing this task to embassies. Spain, in contrast, had tried to cut red tape by authorising border guards instead of embassies to supply visas.[167]

In the foreign policy arena, the 1998 UK Presidency aligned itself with the American position threatening military action in Iraq without any previous consultation. Rather than representing the EU, Blair was accused of 'seeking to impose the views of Mr Clinton on Europe'.[168] This example is no exception. A strong ally of Israel, Italian PM Silvio Berlusconi made little effort to play an even hand in the Middle East conflict under his 2003 presidency.[169] Contrary to EU policy he also praised Russian President Vladimir Putin's actions in Chechnya – widely criticised for human rights abuses. Similarly, past Greek Presidencies have not shied away from defending national foreign policy interests during their terms in office.

Other examples of presidency bias include presidencies' attempts to shape IGC agendas. During the 1991 IGC on Political Union the Dutch Presidency introduced a draft Treaty on European Union that reflected the federalist convictions of politicians within the Dutch coalition government rather than built upon that of its Luxembourg predecessor.[170] Similarly, during the 2000 IGC Council President Jacques Chirac 'unashamedly championed his country's own interests' rather than continuing the discussions from the Portuguese Presidency.[171] All but impartial, Chirac advocated 'a shift in the balance of power in Community decision-making decisively towards the larger Member States'.[172]

Thus, the formal expectation of neutrality is no credible constraint on a presidency's actual behaviour. Neutrality may instead be highly issue specific. For example, the 1998 Austrian Presidency was judged by the Member States' ambassadors as a passive, honest broker waiting for initiatives by others in many areas, while in its key priority areas (employment, tax, and security affairs) it was seen as a defender of national interests.[173] The 2000 French Presidency was perceived as a genuine broker in the negotiations on the flexibility dossier; however, it was strongly biased in case of extending QMV. Hence the government holding the presidency may only be a genuine neutral broker in dossiers where it has few key interests at stake or when its concerns are close to the centre ground.[174]

Finally, to avoid the neutrality constraint the presidency can mobilise other Member States to speak for its interests. A practitioner confirmed,

> If there is an issue we do not really like, but we know other Member States will do the opposing for us, why should we openly form part of the group being accused of hindering the progress? Therefore we can use them as assets. If subsequently there are issues that we really want, they know that we have been a good presidency and are not the ones always hindering everything.[175]

The above suggests that the presidency's leadership is subtle. It aims at pursuing its priorities without alienating other negotiating parties and guarding the EU's decision culture of consensus. Institutionalised collaboration with supranational actors and other Member States may not necessarily lead to rivalry, but the pooling of resources. The presence of formal constraints stressed by the neutral broker advocates does not prevent seeking informal ways to exercise power.

The presidency's informal agenda-setting powers and the strategic dimension of its organisational task

Despite dismissed by the neutral broker conceptualisation, closer examination of the presidency's informal powers reveals considerable agenda influence. Such informal powers include the fine-tuning of agendas, moving items onto active agendas, and structuring debates around certain proposals. The combination of these informal with formal procedural powers allows the presidency to exclude items from the discussion or hinder its progress, emphasise/understate issues, and introduce new issues.[176] The exclusion of issues is probably the most obvious presidency power. As various analysts put it:

> Agenda-setting is an initial crucial veto point in the policy making process at which political and administrative leaders can exercise their power, whether to make policies happen, or to prevent anything from happening [...].[177]

> Some issues are organised into politics – others are organised out.[178]

'If a government holding the presidency does not like a Commission proposal, the presidency can simply refuse to put it on the agenda.'[179] One of the most prominent examples is the 1965 French Presidency which ignored the Commission proposals on agriculture.[180] More recently, the Barroso Commission 'begged' the 2005 UK Presidency to continue the EU's 2007–2013 budget negotiations – a request the UK ignored until its final presidency month.[181]

In case of Member State proposals it may be more difficult to exercise the power of exclusion. A British official said,

> It is the presidency's prerogative to set the agenda. However, if we feel something has been omitted, we ask for it to be put on the agenda. It would be very unwise for a presidency not to accept this. This ensures that issues are not simply dropped off the agenda.[182]

Nonetheless, presidencies do sometimes ignore issues raised by other Member States. Tallberg (2003) cites the case of the Swedish 2001 Presidency in this context. Despite British and Dutch demands to dedicate part of the March 2001 Stockholm Summit to the growing crisis over the spread of foot-and-mouth disease, the presidency did not change its focus on employment – one of Sweden's key priorities. Similarly, despite the importance some Member States attached to the proposal to scrap the right to opt out of the maximum 48-hour week contained in the EU's working time directive, the 2005 UK Presidency stalled discussions on it by excluding it from Council agendas.

A more subtle power than outright exclusion is the facilitation of 'non-decisions'[183] and hence the use of the chair position to hinder progress in areas it dislikes. This can be done in at least two ways. First, the presidency will have a decisive impact on whether a proposal falls or is adopted by deciding if and when an issue is put to the vote.[184] Second, the presidency can present or push forward proposals that lack the ingredients of a real compromise.[185] Consequently, progress is put on halt for six months not to compromise national interests. The failure of the 1999 German Presidency to reach agreement on the liberalisation of the railway sector and freight traffic and on the end-of-life car directive, for example, were attributed to some details being against German interest.[186] The Italian 2003 Presidency was accused of preventing any progress on the introduction of a Europe-wide arrest warrant out of national interest.[187] The initial lack of progress under the 2003 Greek Presidency with regard to relations between the EU and NATO (Berlin Plus) was ascribed to 'Greece hiding behind the presidency to stir things in the way it would like'.[188] Another prominent example is the 1983 Greek Presidency, which – partly because of its stance on enlargement – delayed Spain's accession to the EU by facilitating a 'non-decision' on the accession date.

While excluding dossiers or hindering progress may be the presidency's most obvious power, the possibility to emphasise some issues while understating others is its most important comparative advantage. Once a government decides which areas to emphasise/understate, resources are allocated accordingly.[189] This will affect which, when, and if certain issues move onto decision agendas during the six months. Sometimes this has longer-term effects. An illustrative example is the 1988 German Presidency – the first to use its time in office to drive forward the road to EMU, calling for a strengthening of the European Monetary System (EMS) and a European Central Bank (ECB). The June Hanover Summit subsequently established a committee charged with exploring how and when EMU could be phased in which kept it firmly on the EU agenda. The French 2000 Presidency, in turn, diverted attention away from the liberalisation of energy sectors, which had been on previous presidency agendas. Momentum towards liberalisation of energy sectors thereafter slowed considerably not only in 2000, but also in 2001.[190] Contrary to the neutral broker proposition, the rolling nature of the EU agenda does not hinder this subtle, informal presidency power.

While formally given the task to rank the items on the agenda of each meeting and allocate time of discussion to it, informally, the presidency can do so according to its own perception of priorities. National interests at stake, the 1997 Luxembourg Presidency, for example, ranked the dossier dealing with banking secrecy highly on the Council agenda and the 2004 Dutch Presidency focused the Council's attention on flood prevention measures. Contrarily, the 2000 Portuguese and French Presidencies did not show much enthusiasm for harmonising energy taxes and the Dutch 2004 Presidency was not prepared to pay much attention to the Community Patent or the harmonisation of alcohol taxation. Thus, while issues close to a presidency's national interest are likely to 'top the agenda' in Council meetings[191] and given more time for debate, issues that a presidency is not particularly interested in move to the bottom.

In addition, while formally asked to organise all meetings, the presidency can exploit this task informally by selecting its preferred themes for individual events. This leverage is particularly visible in informal Council meetings – often dedicated to a particular topic. The Austrian 1998 Presidency, eager to give impetus to the discussion on a European security policy, organised an informal Defence Council. To commit the EU to an Action Programme for flood protection, the 2004 Dutch Presidency scheduled an informal Environmental Council on this issue. During informal Councils the presidency holder is most likely to be in a position to push national priorities and generate allies,[192] as they are used to pool ideas and facilitate the free exchange of views without being accompanied by too many officials.[193] Thus, informal Councils are also frequently used to brainstorm new initiatives. Although no decisions are taken at informal Councils, broad agreements reached are usually followed up at COREPER level.[194]

In the past, presidencies have also formed new sectoral Councils to draw attention to certain policy areas.[195] For example, the consumer protection Council was initiated by the 1983 German Presidency. Following the informal meeting on cultural affairs under the Greek Presidency in November 1983, a cultural affairs Council was formally set up under the 1984 French Presidency. Other Councils, that have a history of meeting infrequently, depending on the priorities of the presidency, include youth and tourism. The latter is usually convened by economies with a large tourist sector.[196] Instead of being a burden, as the neutral broker approach suggests, convening meetings and deciding their themes turns into an opportunity to advance Council members' thinking on issues close to the presidency country.

Presidencies pay particular attention to European Council agendas attempting to plan them to their own advantage in terms of content and publicity.[197] European Council meetings are the most important events, as their logic is to define the main policy orientations, new areas of activities, and guidelines for integration. For example, the 2000 Lisbon Summit initiated a decade-long economic reform process aimed at increasing Europe's competitiveness and the 1993 Copenhagen Council decided to enlarge to Central and Eastern Europe. Enjoying procedural control over the EU's most authoritative institution and holding a privileged position to manipulate its agenda should clearly not be underestimated.

Tallberg detects 'agenda structuring' along three lines.[198] First, presidency initiatives reflect the culture, tradition, or values of the office holder. Mirroring the distinct levels of transparency of their national administrative cultures, Council transparency, for example, progressed significantly under the Nordic Presidencies, but received little concrete impetus under the recent Portuguese or French Presidencies. Belgium, a strong advocator of the federalist principle, made the 'Future of Europe' the theme of its 2001 presidency, while Denmark, a euro-sceptic state concerned about its sovereignty, did virtually not pay any attention to the work of the Convention on the Future of Europe under its 2002 presidency.[199] Second, governments differ in the levels of importance and approach to broad policy areas, such as economic, social, or environmental policy.[200] Environmental policy, for example, figured prominently under the recent Scandinavian and German Presidency, but received little attention under the 2002 Spanish Presidency. UK Presidencies have had IM and further liberalisation high on their agenda while Greece has taken a more sceptical approach on IM issues stressing the creation of a 'proper European Social Area' instead.[201] One official emphasised,

> It does make a difference if the chair takes a more liberal market approach or is more protectionist. This can clearly affect the outcome of the negotiations and the final decision taken.[202]

Third, presidencies vary according to their regional priorities. They tend to focus on their immediate neighbourhood or countries with former colonial links. Amongst the priorities of Spain's past Presidencies (1989, 1995, and 2002) was strengthening EU ties with Latin America.[203] The relaunch of the Barcelona Process featured highly on the 2003 Italian and 2008 French Presidency programmes.[204] The 1998 Austrian Presidency, concerned about a possible flow of refugees, concentrated on the situation in Yugoslavia.

Finally, the presidency may attempt to introduce new initiatives by organising open Council debates or special conferences on them. To float its ideas, it can submit 'papers' or 'non-papers'. A paper is an informal document to provoke discussion and a presidency or Commission initiative. A non-paper is intended to propose solutions, which may ultimately lead to either a modified Commission proposal or a

Council decision.[205] The 2001 Belgian Presidency, for example, issued a non-paper in preparation for the Laeken declaration on the future of the Union. To tackle disagreements concerning the CAP, the 2000 French Presidency circulated a non-paper on the sustainable development of agriculture. While Member States and the Commission also enjoy the right to submit such papers, this measure is mostly used by the presidency.[206]

Awareness raising campaigns about new issues usually commence well before a presidency takes office given that 'recognised community problems are closer to being agenda items than unrecognised ones; discussed problems closer than un-discussed ones'.[207] Indeed, putting a new issue on the agenda without previous discussion can be counterproductive:

> A bad agenda-setter is somebody who suddenly puts a new issue on the agenda. At working group level this is a great source of irritation, because frequently we have no instructions from our capitals on these points. Ad-hoc initiatives are usually not a good idea.[208]

Examples of presidencies promoting new initiatives include past Spanish Presidencies and the EU's Mediterranean policy, the Northern Dimension under the Finnish Presidency, or the 2003 Greek Presidency's initiative to introduce the southern Mediterranean countries into the EU's so-called 'New Neighbourhood Initiative'. A preliminary conclusion is that new initiatives are pursued particularly in the area of foreign policy where countries enjoy greater expertise on regional problems than other Member States. This increases their power to persuade them that EU action is necessary. Despite the potential institutional constraint of the unanimity rule that prevails in Pillar II, the presidency country has more leverage in this area because of the lighter institutional structures. Thus, contrary to the neutral broker line of argument, presidencies may well attempt to leave their imprint on the EU's agenda by focusing on foreign-policy initiatives:

> The rotation principle ensures that each country can add a special touch and personal flair, particularly in the area of foreign policy. Each country has an angle from which to approach the themes on the agenda. Thus the Nordic countries promoted Nordic dimensions, Greece focuses on the Balkans and this will continue during the Italian Presidency.[209]

Information advantages

The last aspect stressed by the policy entrepreneur concept is its information advantage:

> The presidency clearly has a big information advantage. We did not quite realise how drastic this is. The presidency started and it was a radical change. The phones were ringing all the time. The information traffic was crazy. [...] We knew exactly what would happen tomorrow and how Member States would react – which was not the case before. We could then take this into consideration. This is a good possibility of influencing things, which is a liberty given to the presidency. It gives it a lot of influence.[210]

> The presidency means the privilege of knowing more than others. You know more than others through the bilateral contact and Community structures. Then you have to think, elaborate, and really work on how to achieve a common position.[211]

The chair's information advantages can help it to develop focal points of discussion and compromise solutions that are closest to its national interests and around which bargaining can converge.

Besides the sheer running of the office, the tools which the presidency can employ to establish information advantages include the *tours des capitals*, 'confessionals', and questionnaires. Rather than being a neutral exercise to collect agenda points and priorities of all Member States, touring the capitals helps a presidency to detect potential negotiating positions of other Member States and subsequently to identify its negotiation strategy:

> The *tour des capitals* are very useful. People explain what they think to you. They are more relaxed and you have the opportunity to establish what to expect in the future. It is a tool to determine the negotiation margin.[212]

'Confessionals' are private sessions between the presidency and the representatives of selected Member States. They consist of confidential talks to establish where a compromise may be found and what the margins of manoeuvre are. The president is under oath not to reveal a Member State's position to any other player.[213] During the Nice IGC negotiations the French Presidency made extensive use of confessionals which significantly altered negotiation texts.[214] Sometimes, presidencies issue questionnaires to determine Member States' positions. The 2003

Greek Presidency, for example, issued a questionnaire facilitating the exchange of views on education, youth, and cultural policy. The 2002 Danish Presidency prepared a questionnaire on actions taken by Member States to eliminate barriers to the cross-border provision of services. Thus, the very task of chairing is not necessarily constraining, but can be seen as providing information advantages over the other players at the negotiating table.

To conclude, in contrast to the neutral broker conceptualisation, the policy entrepreneur approach captures the inherent conflict between self-interest and neutrality. It accepts the limitation of formal powers and is based on a more subtle idea: the leadership capacity to exploit informal powers. Rather than a neutral operation, each agenda is carefully constructed and contains important nuances or ideas. These reflect the presidency's emphasis of certain issues despite the formal neutrality requirement, the predetermination of much of the EU's systemic agenda, and the possibility of externally imposed crises that may alter pre-established agendas. The lack of formal powers, the requirement of impartial chairmanship or the rolling nature of the EU's agenda do therefore not constrain presidencies from being a strategic actor and 'national interests can find a legitimate and acceptable position on the presidency agenda and may lead to new initiatives or debates within the EU'.[215] Hayes-Renshaw and Wallace (1997) argue,

> The presidency is the one clear and only occasional opportunity for a member government to imprint a particular style on the Council, to impose a particular topic on the colleagues, or to ride an individual minister's hobby horse.[216]

Only in cases when the presidency's national position is very close to the Council's centre of gravity and when it has no vital interests at stake, it is likely to be a genuine neutral broker. The overall mixture of formal agenda-setting powers, managerial and administrative duties gives the country in the chair clear scope informally to select priorities in line with national interest, expedite or delay negotiations on particular issues, or introduce new ideas. Table 8 illustrates these informal presidency powers.

III. Conditions for Success

Although the presidency's informal powers are considerable, not all presidencies will be equally successful in their agenda-shaping efforts.

Table 8   The Council Presidency's Informal Powers

Functions	Informal Power/Manipulation
Leadership/ Initiative	• Emphasise/understate issues depending on national perceptions • Introduce new issues/debates of interest to the office holder • Lead debates towards preferred focal point (exploit information advantage and heterogeneity of viewpoints) • Initiate votes when outcome is clear
Management/Co-ordination	• Advance/hinder policies by proposing biased compromises or strategic timing • Rank/allocate time to items according to national priorities
Organisation/ Administration	• Decide themes and number of meetings in line with national priorities
Representation	• Forge inter-institutional and international alliances to pursue national priorities

Their level of influence depends on the resources and constraints the office holder faces which vary according to time, issue, and country. These can be grouped into four sets of factors: (a) the leadership environment; (b) the heterogeneity, intensity and distribution of governmental preferences in the Council; (c) inter-institutional relations with the Commission and the EP; and (d) the office holder's skill and use of the Council Secretariat.

The leadership environment

Any country assuming the Council presidency has to fine-tune its ambitions with the leadership context at the time.[217] If political and economic developments in the presidency country and other Member States, the state of the EU's internal affairs, or external events are hostile to the exercise of leadership, the extent of presidential agenda influence is likely to be modest. A favourable environment, in turn, allows for the incoming presidency country to exploit the presidency institution – and hence the window of opportunity that opens with the office – to shape the EU agenda and legislation.

During the 1989 French Presidency, for example, its stable economy enabled France to take the risk of abolishing exchange rate controls and achieve agreement on EMU (despite revolutionary external events). Conversely, domestic turmoil and presidential elections during the 1995 French Presidency prevented it from being wholeheartedly present in Community matters. Similarly, the UK Presidency in 1992 found it difficult to pursue a consistent policy line on the European level because of severe domestic pressure. PM John Major faced a large parliamentary opposition, a split government over the new Maastricht Treaty, a severe economic recession, and speculative attacks against the British Sterling leading to the withdrawal of the pound from the exchange-rate mechanism of the EMS.

Political and economic developments in other Member States have also had an impact on the presidency's agenda-shaping capacity. Referenda on EU issues or elections, for example, can greatly upset Council business. The Danish 'No' to the TEU interfered with the work programme of the 1992 British Presidency which had already made plans for its implementation. The rejection of the Constitutional Treaty in France and the Netherlands put the 2005 Luxembourg Presidency into a difficult situation and the Irish rejection of the Lisbon Treaty derailed a key issue on the French 2008 presidency agenda. France had been keen to chair the negotiations on who would occupy the new post of European Council President during its term. Similarly, elections have had a paralysing effect on presidency objectives.[218] The 1996 Irish Presidency, for example, had to scale back its ambitions for the IGC due to forthcoming elections in the UK. As the *Irish Times* argued, a high-profile draft Treaty and 'stark choices would [have been] a gift to British Euro-sceptics' election campaign' which no one with high aspirations for the IGC wished for.[219] The Finnish and Portuguese Presidencies in 1999 and 2000 had to deal with tensions in the Council following the 1999 Austrian election result which led to a new coalition government including the far Right. The struggle for Germany's chancellorship after the failure of the 2005 German election to produce a clear majority complicated Council business under the UK Presidency. Similarly, after its 2007 election Belgium was plagued by difficulties to form a coalition and remained without a government for six months. This complicated the work of numerous presidencies.

Regarding the economic situation of other Member States, in periods of prosperity the Member States may be more inclined to make costly compromises than in periods of economic hardship. During the severe recession of the 1970s and early 1980s, for example, the

Council members became more inward looking and searched for national rather than European solutions. Consequently, presidencies had to scale back their ambitions. More recently, divisions over how to respond to the global financial crisis and grim economic outlook for 2009 have become visible. A number of Member States rejected proposals by the 2008 French Presidency to create a eurozone 'economic government'.[220]

The aspirations of the presidency are further circumscribed by internal EU affairs. European integration has not been a smooth process. The 'empty chair crisis', during which French ministers did not participate in any Council meetings and the French permanent representative was withdrawn from Brussels, paralysed the presidency. More recently the resignation of the Commission over allegations of fraud and mismanagement threw the EU into a deep crisis affecting the German and Finnish 1999 Presidencies. Similarly, the rejection by the EP of a number of Commissioners for the 2004–2009 Commission and the subsequent reshuffle meant that the Dutch 2004 Presidency was without a fully functioning Commission for some weeks. Other recent examples of internal crises affecting the presidency's agenda-setting capacity include the breakdown of the IGC negotiations in December 2003 or the 2005 budget dispute.

Finally, external events can act as powerful constraints hindering any advancement of predetermined national priorities.[221] The French 2008 Presidency unexpectedly had to deal with the Russia–Georgia war. The Iraq war heavily overshadowed the 2003 Greek Presidency. The Belgian Presidency in 2001 was not the same after the September terrorist attacks in the US. The Kosovo war and NATO intervention in 1999 dominated the German Presidency, and the Bosnian crisis hampered the aims of several presidencies. The presidency's agenda-setting capacity will depend on its skill to take advantage of favourable developments and deal with unexpected events. The latter are powerful constraints as they cannot be prepared for or manipulated by the presidency and require flexibility and additional resources by the office holder.

Governmental preferences

The second category of factors influencing presidential success concerns the heterogeneity, intensity, and distribution of governmental preferences. Progress on EU dossiers will depend on the ability of the presidency country to reconcile the views of 27 Member States with diverse interests stemming from their different geographic, political, and economic situation. Especially when unanimity-voting applies, initiative to find out delegations' negotiation leverage as well as active persuasion and brokerage is required.[222] But even with QMV, there is a need to accommodate many interests and the evolution of the EU's voting system and increased diversity has made coalition-building more complicated.[223] Hence, while the voting arrangements, especially unanimity, are formal constraints specific to the presidency as an institution, the skill to facilitate agreement largely depends on the individual office holder.

A presidency's capacity to shape policy outcomes in line with its own preferences is highest the greater the heterogeneity of views in the Council – given that it can effectively pick out of several coalitions the one closest to its own preferences and use its informal powers to push it into the dominant position. Conversely, should the presidency find itself isolated in the Council with a majority of Member States converging on an alternative compromise, it is unlikely to be successful in shifting the balance in favour of its own viewpoint.

The intensity and distribution of preferences also matters. The greater the intensity of Member State preferences, the less the likelihood that the presidency can persuade them to change their views. States will be particularly unlikely to compromise if they have vital national interests at stake. Indeed, the presidency country does well to accommodate Member States with 'real national interests' to guard a consensual climate and set informal norms for future presidencies.[224]

As to the distribution of preferences, a presidency must avoid big state opposition against its initiatives given their political clout and weight in the Council. Instead it should generate big state support and exploit existing coalitions to get initiatives and proposals adopted. Of particular relevance has been, in many cases, in how far the Franco-German axis could be won as an ally for presidency initiatives and compromises.[225] Since the creation of the Community the Franco-German axis has often set the broad direction of European integration, despite occasional tensions and changing leadership.[226] If France and Germany are against an initiative, the presidency can be thrown into the shadow by the Franco-German couple who may try to rule the Council through their bilateral relations. Werts found this to be the case on a number of occasions between 1974 and 1981 when President Giscard d'Estaing and Chancellor Schmidt had the habit of presenting their own agreed agenda.[227] More recent examples of Franco-German 'mastery' include their suspension of the euro rules in November 2003 or their alliance in the Convention and subsequent IGC.[228]

Since the 2004 enlargement the UK has shown eagerness to join the Franco-German axis and institutionalise regular trilateral meetings.[229] It aligned itself with France and Germany in the Convention's institutional reform debates and joined them in their diplomatic mission to halt Iran's suspected nuclear weapon's programme. In addition, despite a recent fall out over the EU's budget and future economic model, the three countries have attempted to co-ordinate their approach in European defence affairs.[230] Particularly small state presidencies will need to be vigilant of potential coalitions formed by the EU's big Member States.

Inter-institutional relations

Active collaboration with the Commission and the EP are also crucial for a presidency country to maximise its entrepreneurial success. Both institutions compete with the presidency for agenda influence and can either act as a resource or as a constraint.

The presidency shares policy initiation, implementation, and representational functions with the Commission. Presidency initiatives in Pillar I have no legal powers unless they go through the official stage of Commission proposals. While the presidency can invite the Commission to prepare a text, it cannot dictate it and – at least legally – the Commission need not respond. If a presidency wants to have any influence on the precise content and timing of a Commission proposal, a close relationship with the institution is therefore indispensable. A number of practitioners described the interdependent nature of Commission–presidency relations:

> The presidency cannot do it alone, but the Commission cannot do it alone either.[231]

> Sometimes you are in the hands of the Commission, for example when they are late to present their proposal and you were really counting on it. Of course, the presidency can push the Commission for proposals. Being pushed by the presidency is actually in their interest as well, as they realise you are eager to take a certain proposal forward.[232]

Thus, there are in-built incentives to co-operate and both the Commission and the presidency share the striving for agreements. In addition, the Commission participates in Council negotiations as the 28th member and with its additional expertise and knowledge of Member States' negotiating positions may help a presidency to identify the ingredients of a compromise.[233] In this sense both institutions potentially have a mobilising effect on decision-making:

> [The presidency and the Commission] always have very strong political agendas. What unites them is that both want to drive the agenda forward, thus there is usually a high degree of areas of communality.[234]

While the Commission's influence is greatest at the outset of the legislative process, its proposals change – often significantly – in subsequent Council negotiations and the co-decision procedure.[235] The Commission's power to shape final policy outcomes will partly depend on the voting and amendment rules in the Council of Ministers – highest in cases of QMV with unanimity amendment.[236] Should the Council try to change a proposal without unanimous agreement, the Commission has the possibility to disagree or withdraw it. Hence, despite incentives to collaborate, the Commission–presidency interdependence can also lead to antagonistic relations.[237]

Particularly small states generally consider the Commission as an important ally. As the Council presidency, the Commission is perceived as an important counter-weight to the predominance of the large EU members. Ireland during its 1996 presidency, for example, co-ordinated its priorities closely with the Commission contributing to the presidency's success to put the issue of organised crime firmly on the Community agenda.[238] Similarly, after the Maastricht ratification crisis the Belgian 1993 Presidency worked closely with the Commission resulting in the 1993 White Paper. The British 1992 Presidency, on the other hand, proved rather conflictual. The UK's and the Commission's viewpoints converged on few issues, relations between Commission President Jacques Delors and British PM John Major were tense on a personal level, and the British even proposed a reform to downgrade the role of the Commission.[239] The 2003 Italian Presidency also openly clashed with the Commission.[240]

In Pillars I and II the presidency's leadership is less constrained given the dominance of the Member States. Indeed 'due to its intergovernmental and relatively unbureaucratic nature, foreign policy may be an area in which the presidency feels able to leave its mark'.[241] However, here leadership is also shared. The High Representative assists the presidency in the co-ordination and representation of the CFSP. The External Relations Commissioner – although denied the monopoly right of initiative – is 'fully associated' to all aspects of CFSP, including implementation and representation. Hence, in CFSP matters, potential Commission–presidency antagonism concerns not so much in the policy formulation phase, but in the implementation process:

> Although the Commission and Member State governments may make policy proposals, policy initiation [of CFSP matters] tends to fall to the presidency. However, policy implementation almost invariably involves major input from the Commission. Since the Commission does not regard itself as the servant of the Council, this arrangement is a source of considerable cross-pillar tension.[242]

Depending on the issue concerned, the presidency represents the EU in five different configurations: by itself (communicating presidency declarations and common positions); with the Commission (in trade or Pillar I issues); with the High Representative (inaugurating and implementing CFSP projects); with both the Commission and the High Representative (to discuss the political, security, and economic situation of a third state or to meet with acceding or candidate countries); or with the Commission, the High Representative, and the succeeding presidency (when horizontal issues are likely to require follow-up under the next presidency).[243] To succeed, presidential foreign policy initiatives therefore need the backing of multiple actors, including the other Member States, the Commission, and the High Representative.

In case of the EP, its co-legislator status also grants it agenda-setting powers – albeit restricted ones. By placing before the Council provisions that it can more easily adopt than amend, the EP is in a position to structure the choices of the Council members.[244] A presidency does therefore well to generate support within the EP while at the same time striking a deal in the Council.[245] In addition, as the EP is the only directly elected EU institution, one can argue that a presidency initiative gains significantly in legitimacy and weight if it has its support.

Overall, inter-institutional relations and the level of collaboration with the Commission and the EP will depend on the presidency in office.[246] The successful policy entrepreneur will adapt to the institutional environment and ensure that the Commission and EP do not turn into powerful constraints, but into allies instead.

Skill and use of the Council Secretariat

Finally, a presidency's ability to act as a successful policy entrepreneur is, in part, influenced by its level of preparation and skills, including co-ordination, political finesse, and credibility. Thus, country-specific factors impact the entrepreneurial potential of the presidency.

However, the office holder's size is not necessarily one of them. Different advantages and disadvantages may arise in connection with size. In terms of material resources small states are generally far more constrained than bigger Member States. A Finnish official explained,

> One problem we have is that we are a bit thin on the ground. Where larger countries have a unit of three or four people we have only one single desk.[247]

An additional small state handicap is the lack of political clout and bargaining power, particularly needed in foreign affairs or to solve major deadlocks.[248] Small state Council presidencies may have difficulties to access US officials and be taken seriously in foreign affairs.[249] On occasion, even other EU members have chosen to bypass small state presidencies. The recent Greek Presidency was not consulted before Tony Blair and seven other leaders published a statement calling for Europe to support the US over the 2003 Iraq crisis. Similarly, at the outset of the 2001 war in Afghanistan, the large Member States made direct arrangements with the US without involving the Belgian Presidency.

However, presidency influence (or the lack thereof) is not systematically related to size. The 1997 Luxembourg Presidency, for example, was judged as 'the best of the last few years'.[250] Similarly, Belgium and Ireland have the reputation of effective Council presidents. The efficiency of the recent Nordic presidencies has also been praised. The 2000 French Presidency in turn was judged as chaotic and 'probably one of the worst in the history of the EU'.[251] As a practitioner argued, '[much depends upon] how you play the cards you have been given'.[252]

A more systematic comparison of the Council's legislative activity under small and big presidencies since 1999 shows no evidence that small states systematically adopt less/or more directives, regulations, decision, or other types of legislation than big states (see Appendix). While the 2002 Spanish Presidency adopted 36 directives, for example, the Irish 2004 and Finnish 2006 Presidencies adopted 47 and 43 directives respectively. However, to manage the immensely demanding presidency tasks small states are often prepared to put domestic politics 'on hold' during their term. One commentator wrote in case of Luxembourg's 1997 Presidency: 'Almost every day of Jean-Claude Juncker's days was dedicated to Europe – no head of government of a large country could dedicate all their days to Europe, nor chair personally two Council sessions a month, in addition to the Summits.'[253]

More important factors than size to conclude dossiers and shape them in line with domestic interests, seem to be effective inter-ministerial co-ordination; efficient organisation/administration and management; the contacts, political judgement and power to persuade of the president-in-office; and the strategic use of the Council Secretariat. Effective inter-ministerial co-ordination is necessary to ensure consistency in a presidency's agenda-shaping effort. Arguably a presidency will be more influential the more effective its national inter-ministerial co-ordination.[254] Co-ordination weaknesses in the management of EU affairs were clearly visible during the German presidency in the first half of 1999 or the 2000 French Presidency. In small administrations, in turn, information flows are often easier and quicker resulting in better communication and a more effective handling of the presidency tasks.

Each system of inter-ministerial co-ordination has its own merits and faults. Amongst the key differences is the extent to which and how the presidency country involves its Permanent Representation. Some countries run their presidency almost entirely from their Permanent Representation. They tend to select chair persons from the Permanent Representation due to their expertise and negotiation skills gained in the pre-negotiating phase of policy proposals and their familiarity with the other decision-makers. The latter reduces the potential conflictual nature of the negotiations.

On the other extreme are countries that keep tight control in the capital. They tend to select people from the ministries as chairpersons and tightly circumscribe the decision power of working group chairs. The concern here is that officials based at the Permanent Representations might sacrifice national positions more easily ('go native') due to their personalised relations with their counterparts at the other Permanent Representations. In addition, although they theoretically receive instructions exclusively from the organs responsible for inter-ministerial co-ordination, they are in close contact with individual ministries which sometimes try to circumvent inter-ministerial co-ordination, thus reducing the efficiency of negotiation outcomes. In pursuing their objectives, presidencies are best served by systems that rely heavily on their Permanent Representations without undermining or debilitating the overall control by the capital.

To increase the likelihood of success, efficient organisation and management ensuring that dossiers move up the Council hierarchy is also key. This includes tasks such as delivering documents on time. Under the 1999 German Presidency, for example, many envoys felt in no position to negotiate given the late distribution of documents.[255] Similarly, the 2005 UK Presidency was criticised for the lack of providing information ahead of the Hampton Court Summit.[256]

Efficient organisation and management furthermore implies the effective use of the Mertens and Antici groups. Chaired by the presidency, the latter are composed of members of the Permanent Representations and the Commission. They prepare the timetables and agendas for COREPER I and II respectively as well as Council meetings. At the same time they are highly confidential forums in which the presidency will inform the Member States how it intends to handle particular problems. They ensure that permanent representatives are fully briefed, new issues are commented upon, and problems are identified. They also enjoy close contacts with the Commission and hence allow the Member States and the Commission to co-ordinate their negotiating positions before the formal Council meetings.[257] Thus, the Antici and Mertens can be seen as the 'transmission belt' between the political, negotiating sphere and the administrative, advisory sphere.[258]

Co-ordination and organisation in the context of the presidency are, however, disputed. Some find that the contacts, skills, and personality of the chairpersons are more important in shaping policy outcomes than national co-ordination mechanisms:

> Much depends on the role the heads of government plays and what kind of contacts he has and uses.[259]

Bilateral informal contacts have frequently served to solve major impasses in the past. During the 1984 French Presidency, for example, Mitterrand engaged heavily in bilateralism. He organised at least 30 meetings with other government heads resulting in a highly successful Summit resolving major stalemates at the time.[260] Member States differ in the time they devote to such informal consultations.

Individual skills include not only contacts but also political judgement and the power to persuade. Political judgement is vital to decide when an issue is ripe for decision. A skilful chairperson will use his or her temporary authority to keep the attention of his or her colleagues on the presidency priorities and will know when to intervene, call for a vote, and accelerate or delay negotiations. Some of the formal tools the presidency has to do this have already been examined (restricted sessions and confessionals). The presidency can also 'stop the clock' and keep all negotiating parties in the room until agreement has been found. Any policy initiative – however necessary it might appear to its initiator – is doomed if the presidency misreads the constraints of the day. Equally, if an office holder fails to act in a favourable situation, the opportunity could be missed.[261]

The power to persuade, in turn, is the ability 'to induce [others] to believe what the president wants of them is what their own appraisal of their own responsibilities requires them to do in their own interest, not his'.[262] Therefore, it is more than mere reasoned argument. Additional expertise, the presidency's information advantages, and skilful marketing increase its power to persuade. General diplomatic, mediation, and communicative skills are crucial. These were completely lacking during Italy's 2003 presidency. The Foreign Press Association named Berlusconi 'miscommunicator of the year',[263] his mismanagement of the constitutional talks contributed to the break down of the IGC, and his presidency was judged a 'personal failure'.[264]

The power to persuade can also increase with a country's reputation and style. Small states generally have a good record of reconciling competing interests and more unassuming style gearing all their efforts towards effective consensus building. As the scope of their interests tends to be narrower, they are often perceived as better placed to facilitate compromise and can afford to be neutral on issues that either do not concern them or are of lesser importance for them:

> You have to be flexible and adaptable [under the presidency]. This is often more difficult for the bigger countries than for smaller countries which have less political luggage to carry and often not so many strong national positions to defend.[265]

The 1977 and 1981 UK Presidencies, for example, found it hard to mediate in Community negotiations. Wallace (1986) argues that the British political style was ill-suited to the role of coalition-building.[266] This may have to do with the UK's lack of experience of coalition government. Even though the efficacy of the British Civil Service, inter-ministerial co-ordination, and implementation records are admired, their style of running the presidency after years of experience still causes awkward situations. At the launch of the British 1998 Presidency Blair caused an outcry by stating:

> I see this presidency as a test for Britain to show that we can and do offer strong leadership in Europe. I want our presidency to lead the

process of change and reform. [...] Our presidency is an opportunity to demonstrate that Britain now has a strong voice in Europe.[267]

Empirically, presidencies that manage to guard a consensual style have been most influential. Due to the EU's logic of repeated games to broker compromises a presidency does well to 'gain the confidence of [its] peers'.[268] To generate such confidence, the seniority of the head of government can play a role, a country's reputation, political colour or personal factors. However, a presidency can also pursue several strategies. It may try to portray the *image* of an impartial broker, for example 'by convincing the Member States that it is also pushing on their priorities' or creating a 'positive-sum' atmosphere so that all feel they get something out of the negotiations.[269] It may look for unanimous agreement even in matters governed by QMV and refrain from isolating any group of Member States. Several interviewees indicated that the principle of diffused reciprocity and hence knowing that one day they may be in a similar position (or, indeed, if they enjoyed similar support at some time in the past, that they are repaying an old debt) is at work in the Council especially under small state presidencies. One official described his government's strategy:

When there was a real national interest at stake for a country, then we tried to accommodate it even if we already had a QMV.[270]

In sum, the particular combination of skills and strategies of the presidency-in-office will influence the abilities to use the power resources and institutional setting to find opportunities to influence the EU agenda.

Puchala concludes that the effectiveness of a policy entrepreneur stems *inter alia* from its command of information, technical expertise, and ability efficiently to orchestrate and mediate collective international problem-solving.[271] Rather than on size, this will partly depend on training, preparation, and strategic planning, which differ from country to country:

Very much depends on the level of preparation. Preparation [...] is key to success. Member States must be confident that the presidency knows what it wants.[272]

Sometimes Member States are against, sometimes in favour [of an initiative], but with extensive planning you can get things your way.[273]

Even issues that may not be relevant to the country holding the chair need thorough examination to identify cross-sectoral trade-offs and establish the reputation of a competent chair. An awareness of different negotiating strategies and styles of the national delegations is an additional advantage.[274]

Finally, presidential influence will depend on its effective use of the Council Secretariat. The Council Secretariat assists the presidency in the preparation of its term and ensures that Council activities correspond closely to the presidency's work programme.[275] Initially it had a low-key servicing role, but as the presidency functions grew, it developed into an important presidential resource with over 2000 staff.[276] The Council Secretariat's prime motivation is to enable the presidency to broker consensus. In addition to supplying technical and secretarial back-up for meetings (including providing conference rooms, interpreting services, and drafting documents), it briefs the president before each meeting, offers policy advice, formulates compromise proposals and generally performs a wide range of activities that are necessary to ensure that decisions are taken in the Council.[277] Most important for the presidency are the Council Secretariat's reports and notes on progress made in working parties, its assessment of the discussions between Member States and knowledge about Member State attitudes, its procedural advice and proposals of alternatives. Thus, it also has an active political dimension, which distinguishes it from an ordinary Secretariat.

Crucially, the General Secretariat assists the presidency in building up extensive information advantages. Having followed many dossiers over several years, it is the Council's 'institutional memory' and can offer the presidency in-depth knowledge and expertise on these dossiers. Moreover, as its members are in constant contact with the permanent representatives and national experts, their insider knowledge is extensive. A practitioner summarised,

> The Council Secretariat is a reliable and professional resource for the presidency. [...] They usually have a good feeling of 'what will fly'.[278]

In addition, it provides the presidency with legal advice. Having a legal service at its disposition enhances the acceptability of presidency conduct and initiatives. Small states in particular rely heavily on technical and legal assistance from the Council Secretariat and have developed the custom of working closely with it. Luxembourg and Ireland, for example, have among the best records of using the Council Secretariat and its legal service. Some of the larger states such as the UK, in turn, often rather rely on their national administrations instead. However, it is doubtful that even the largest administrations can match the Council Secretariat's knowledge of procedures, overview of the machinery, and assessment of other States' attitudes.[279] The extensive use of the Council's resources can compensate small states' relative lack of resources to some extent and allows them to run consensual presidencies. As seen above, a consensual climate in turn enhances the likelihood that a presidency is successful in pursuing its aims and priorities.

However, in three ways the Council Secretariat may also act as a potential constraint on the presidency. First, it is *communautaire* and does not take any instructions from the governments.[280] Its master is the Council not the presidency. Thus, it will remind the presidency of its formal role if an initiative takes on excessive national colouring.[281] Second, it ensures that a presidency does not drop agenda issues on which policy decisions have been taken previously. It thereby provides an important degree of continuity in the Council's legislative activity. Third, contrary to early assessments of the Council Secretariat as a provider of totally impartial advice[282] or a neutral assessor of other State's attitudes,[283] the

Table 9 Expectations of High/Low Levels of Council Presidency Influence

	High level of presidency influence	Low level of/no presidency influence
Leadership environment	• the leadership environment is favourable (domestic and external political and economic developments are positive)	• the leadership environment is unfavourable (the office holder faces internal and external crises)
Heterogeneity, intensity, and distribution of governmental preferences	• the heterogeneity of views in the Council is high and the intensity of preferences low, allowing the presidency country to construct winning coalitions around its favoured viewpoint • the presidency mobilises big state support	• the presidency country is isolated with its viewpoint and the other Member States converge around a different compromise • the presidency faces big state opposition

Table 9   (Continued)

	High level of presidency influence	Low level of/no presidency influence
Inter- institutional relations	• presidency–Commission relations are collaborative • the presidency mobilises support in the EP	• presidency–Commission relations are antagonistic • the EP opposes a presidency compromise or initiative
Skill and use of the Council Secretariat	• the presidency country prepares its priorities well, legitimises them at EU level, ensures efficient domestic co-ordination and skilfully exploits its information advantages through extensive use of the Council Secretariat	• the presidency country is unprepared, openly pursues its national interests, lacks effective inter-ministerial co-ordination, and fails to exploit its information advantages by under-using the Council Secretariat

Council Secretariat is not always unbiased itself. Its political powers have grown over the years hand in hand with the complexity and diversity of the issues the Council had to deal with. Several interviewees compared it to an evolving 'second Commission'.[284] Thus, each presidency must 'use the Secretariat without letting it dominate [its] agenda'.[285]

Overall, relying extensively on the Council apparatus offers the presidency – no matter whether small or big – positional advantages over the other Council members. The extensive use of the Council Secretariat is particularly important for small states to overcome their lack of resources, to find compromise solutions, co-ordinate work, and arrive at an overall view before each Council meeting. Table 9 summarises when to expect high and low presidency influence.

Conclusion

This chapter has conceptualised the Council presidency as a hybrid or 'double hatted' policy entrepreneur that attempts to influence the

EU's agenda and shape policy outcomes according to domestic preferences while at the same time preferring consensus. The institutionalist policy entrepreneur framework captures the presidency's biased nature and key roles of proposing initiatives and rallying consensus behind them. The Council presidency presents a window of opportunity for national governments to shape the EU agenda through the institution's combination of formal and informal powers. However, once in office, a presidency does not – as Kingdon's theory assumes – patiently wait for further opportunities to shape the agenda. This chapter has argued that individual presidencies actively seek to create such opportunities or policy windows to shape legislation. These stem from the presidency's procedural powers and the information advantages of the chair position which grant the office holder a comparative advantage over other potential entrepreneurs in the EU, such as fellow Member States, the Commission, or the EP.[286] Thus, it is not 'merely one amongst equals',[287] but *primus inter pares* or the 'spindle in the web'.[288]

However, the level of presidency influence will vary. The second part of the analysis has focused on the conditions that either smooth or impede the way for successful policy entrepreneurship. Some of them have to do with the political and economic context, others with the EU's institutional environment, and a third category of factors are country specific. The chapter argued that the influence of the country in the presidency chair is likely to be highest when the leadership environment is favourable; the heterogeneity of views in the Council is high, the intensity of preferences low, and the presidency country can mobilise big state support; inter-institutional relations are collaborative; and the office holder is highly skilled. Key skills include thorough preparation, efficient domestic co-ordination, a consensual style, and the effective use of the Council Secretariat. While the presidency cannot control the leadership environment or the intensity of preferences in the Council, the other conditions can be manipulated by the chair, for example, through ally building and collaboration with the Commission and the EP. 'The initiative with the greatest chance of success is one that can mobilise combined national and [supranational] leadership.'[289] Figure 2 illustrates the theoretical framework and arguments that emerge from this analysis.

Contrary to the arguments raised by opponents of the rotating presidency, the size of the presidency country does not seem to condition its success to pursue national interests. Instead it directly affects the behaviour and strategies chosen by the office holder. Smaller states have strong incentives to overcome their lack of resources through

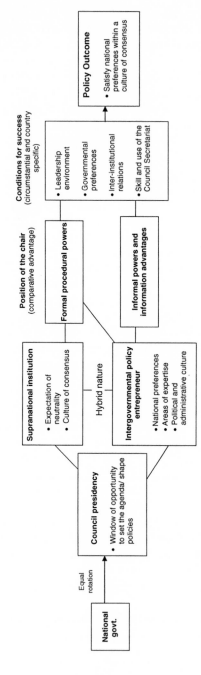

Figure 2   The Presidency as a Policy Entrepreneur: Nature, Agenda-Setting Power, and Conditions for Success

extensive use of Council assets, close collaboration with the Commission, intensive preparations, and efficient inter-ministerial and vertical Council co-ordination – precisely the factors that promise a successful presidency.

Overall, the above analysis shows that the presidency does not act in an institutional vacuum. Its operating modes are highly structured by the overall decision-making system and culture, as well as the presidency's operating environment. Hence, the presidency does not shape the agenda by imposing its will, but by using its combination of procedural powers and coalition-building skills. Given that these are particularly important for small states, they tend to invest heavily into their presidency. How influential they are in their priority areas compared to other agenda setters in the EU, in particular the Member States, the Commission, and the EP, and what kind of policy outcomes are generated is the subject of investigation in the following case studies.

4

The 1999 Finnish Presidency: Internal Market and Foreign Policy Priorities and Achievements

The EU Council presidency will be Finland's chance to stamp its brand of Nordic entrepreneurship and diplomacy on the region.[290]

Introduction

The Finnish Presidency from 1 July to 31 December 1999 was Finland's first time in the Council chair. Since joining the EU in 1995, Finland has developed into the only 'mainstream'[291] Nordic member firmly committed to Community projects despite its lack of federalist political culture and often critical public. It views the EU as an 'ever developing union of independent states' granting it – a small country long caught between two power blocs – security, market access, and increased influence in international affairs.[292] The presidency was regarded as the 'greatest international challenge since Finnish independence'[293] and a means to complete the country's integration into the West, cease being a newcomer, and promote distinct Nordic interests.

This chapter examines the Finnish Presidency's objectives and leadership in the areas of the IM and foreign policy. Within the IM, Finland prioritised the information society (InfoSoc), in particular the e-commerce and copyright directives. In the area of foreign affairs the ND was Finland's main emphasis. The chapter investigates the extent to which Finland managed to use the presidency to push domestic concerns onto the EU agenda and shape policy outcomes in line with its national preferences. In addition, it analyses the nature of the decisions taken. The chapter starts by identifying the link between Finland's presidency priorities and its domestic interests. Second, the obstacles the presidency faced in pursuing its aims are outlined, including its leadership environment, diverging preferences in the Council, and inter-institutional relations. An analysis of Finnish strategies and resources to overcome these obstacles and the conditions for success follows. The chapter closes with an assessment of the presidency's achievements, which critically considers the role of other decision-makers.

The chapter shows how Finland, despite its small size and a challenging context, exploited the presidency office to pursue initiatives of national interest and succeeded to adopt the e-commerce directive. No agreement was reached on copyright, although negotiations progressed significantly. In case of the ND, Finnish entrepreneurship is even clearer. Finland anchored the ND on the EU agenda after legitimising it in anticipation of its presidency. In both policy areas, Finland attempted to shape the EU according to its own ideals by generating positive-sum outcomes. Besides relying upon its expertise, mediation, and marketing skills, it minimised constraints by careful preparation including enhanced inter-ministerial co-ordination, effective use of Council resources, and a solid alliance with the Commission. The biggest constraints to success in case of the copyright directive were the intensity of preferences in the Council and external events in case of the ND.

I. Finnish internal market and foreign policy presidency objectives

Developing the InfoSoc

Developing the InfoSoc and a 'smooth-running digital market place' had been an EU goal since the 1994 Corfu Summit.[294] To do so, the Finnish Presidency prioritised the adoption of the draft directives on certain legal aspects of e-commerce and on the harmonisation of certain aspects of copyright.[295] Neither of them was new. The Commission had first published the e-commerce directive in November 1998.[296] It was to 'contribute to the proper functioning of the IM by ensuring the free movement of InfoSoc services' through the approximation of national legal provisions.[297] These related to the establishment of service providers, information requirements, commercial communications, electronic contracts, the liability of online service intermediaries (telecommunication operators and access providers), codes of conduct, out-of-court dispute settlements, court actions, and co-operation between Member States. The cornerstone of the directive was the country of origin principle which requires providers to comply only with the laws of their country of origin as opposed to all the countries where they offer their products.

The copyright directive had been on the EU agenda since 1997. Its rationale was to adapt existing legislation to the growing impact of digital technology on the dissemination of information and ease of reproducing copyright-protected material.[298] Adequate protection of copyright materials and harmonisation of diverse national laws were needed to facilitate cross-border trade, guarantee undistorted competition, and address costs associated with rising piracy levels. The directive covered reproduction rights, communication to the public, distribution, exceptions (copying for private use), and technological measures (coding and encryption) to control unauthorised copying.

Prioritising the development of a single market in online services reflected both Finnish economic preferences and sectoral expertise.[299] Finland keenly supports the IM and is amongst the leading nations in producing and using information and communications technologies (ICTs). In the 1990s the Finnish electronics industry was the country's largest export earner and generated more than 30% of economic growth.[300] Within the EU, Finland headed the statistics of online users in 1999 with more than 30% of its population[301] (compared to the EU average of 8.3%).[302] Unsurprisingly, the country felt well suited to drive this area forward:

> There are a couple of things that we will stress strongly [during our presidency]. One is [...] the information society [...] and there we feel that Finland is well placed to set the tone.[303]

In the light of the above, it was crucial to Finland that the final shape of the directives would benefit its electronics market. In the case of e-commerce this meant that Finland wanted to limit the legal liabilities of intermediaries. As to copyright, Finland favoured – in addition to limited liability for intermediaries – international rather than Community exhaustion of the distribution right. Community exhaustion implied that authors, who accept the sale of their works in one Member State, agree that they may be sold throughout the EU. With international exhaustion the distribution right is exhausted wherever work was marketed for the first time with the author's consent. Furthermore, Finland preferred an open list of exemptions of copyright-protected material and flexibility for individual national decisions.

Constructing the Northern Dimension

The ND was a new Finnish initiative. It sought to strengthen EU foreign policy in the North, especially towards Russia. Other partner countries included Estonia, Latvia, Lithuania, Poland, Norway, and Iceland. The aim was to create an umbrella to coordinate existing regional activities more efficiently.[304] As the Commission put it:

> Within the framework of [the] existing contractual relationships, financial instruments, and regional organisations, the Northern Dimension is a concept than can [...] contribute to the strengthening of the Union's external policies and reinforcement of the positive interdependence between Russia and the Baltic Sea region and the European Union, notably by achieving further synergies and coherence in these policies and actions.[305]

Being rather vague at the outset, Finland's objective was to fill the ND with content during its presidency. It envisaged enhanced co-operation in the areas of: infrastructure; environment and nuclear safety; education, research, and human resources; public health; cross-border co-operation; trade and investment; the fight against cross-border crime; and Kaliningrad. Hence the ND cut across policies and overlapped with the Common Strategy on Russia which concentrated on integrating Russia into a wider economic area and addressing common interests and challenges.[306] The ND was a tool to give additional impetus to the common strategy's specific initiatives and to integrate its objectives into a broader regional framework.

At least four reasons account for Finland's interest in developing an ND for the EU. First, the disintegration of the USSR had brought new soft security threats with it.[307] The ND was regarded as an instrument to stabilise the region, integrate Russia and the Baltic States into European security structures, and continue Finland's traditional pragmatic Russia approach on the EU level.

Second, Finland was interested in closing the large gap between Finnish and Russian living standards – a further source of potential instability – through increased trade and economic co-operation, efficient exploitation of Russia's vast natural resources, the development of infrastructure, and social programmes. Indeed, Finnish PM Paavo Lipponen saw economic possibilities for it in return for a more stable and prosperous Russia:

> Finnish national interests are very much involved. [...] Finland
> will be involved as business centre for the region, with global
> opportunities.[308]

In addition, facilitating greater economic stability in Russia and its former satellites meant a more secure market for Finnish exports. In other
words, Finland saw it as a means to reduce its economic vulnerability
caused by its export dependence on the region.

Finland's third motivation was the environmental threat in the Baltic
Sea and Russia. Finland was especially concerned about the pollution by Russian energy production and two ageing power plants with
poorly maintained Chernobyl-type reactors near the Finnish border.
The Kola region also contained enormous deposits of nuclear waste
while lacking reprocessing facilities and safe storage capacities. Given
Russia's limited financial resources to address these problems, Finland
saw the ND as a means to direct political attention to the need to
co-operate with Russia in the area of nuclear safety and environmental
protection.

Finally, sharing a 1300-km border with Russia, Finland wanted to
strengthen border management and prevent illegal immigration and
drug trafficking.

In sum, developing closer relations with Russia and the Baltic region
was more important for Finland than for any other Member State. The
EU seemed the most adequate forum for the pursuit of an ND, as it
offered supranational institutions, which were seen as best equipped
to monitor and co-ordinate the activities and objectives by the diverse
actors in the region. In addition, the funds the EU had at its disposal
were much larger than the small budget the Nordic Council of Ministers
or the Nordic Investment Bank offered for joint Northern initiatives.[309]
Unsurprisingly, the presidency programme declared the promotion of
this new initiative an important goal:

> Promoting the new Union policy of a ND will be an important objec-
> tive for the Finnish Presidency. The aim is to get the ND concept
> firmly incorporated into the external relations of an enlarging Union
> especially with regard to Russia and the Baltic region.[310]

Given that both the InfoSoc and the ND had 'a strong national background',[311] Finland invested heavily in them. Nonetheless, neither the

adoption of the InfoSoc directives nor the construction of the ND were foregone conclusions.

II. Obstacles: the leadership environment, institutional hurdles, and preference divergence

The InfoSoc directives

As Chapter 3 showed, each presidency faces a unique leadership environment arising from the internal and external economic and political situation of the office holder and the EU. Domestically, Finland assumed the office with considerable assets. Finnish GDP growth almost doubled the EU average and the re-election of the 'Rainbow Coalition' in March 1999 under social democrat Lipponen provided for continuity.[312] The EU's internal state, however, provided for a challenging leadership context for a newcomer. At the start of the Finnish Presidency, the EU was in an unprecedented state of uncertainty caused by the Commission resignation over fraud and mismanagement and complicated further by the low voter turn-out in the EP elections, the new Amsterdam Treaty, and a weak euro.

Given the joint Commission resignation, there was uncertainty whether the InfoSoc directives could be amended before the new college had taken office. The shape of the new Commission remained unclear during the whole first month of the Finnish term and the traditional July presidency–Commission meeting to co-ordinate their agendas had to be postponed. Finland was reportedly so worried about the likely inability to advance with the EU's IM agenda that Permanent Representative Antti Satuli suggested that the EP should convene the hearings to approve the new Commissioners in August (the EU's traditional holiday month) rather than September – causing an outcry amongst MEPs.[313]

The EU's legitimacy crisis deepened after the June EP elections registered the lowest voter turnout since 1979. The new influx of inexperienced MEPs and the post election vacuum made a slow start inevitable. The Treaty of Amsterdam, which came into force on 1 May 1999, added to the challenges as it turned the EP into a genuine co-legislator. Finally, at the start of Finland's presidency there was a scare about the weak euro and Italy dropping out.

Apart from this directional uncertainty, Finland picked up the InfoSoc directives from a crowded IM agenda and at a difficult point in the decision-making process. Both directives were complicated and highly political trying to strike a balance between the divergent interests of software companies, service providers, publishers and recording companies, authors/artists, and consumers. Disagreements between the Finnish Presidency, the EP, the Commission, and the Council members developed on a number of aspects of both directives.

Contrary to Finnish interests, the EP sought to modify the legal liability of intermediaries in the e-commerce directive. It rejected the Commission's series of exemptions to intermediary liability. Its approach was more consumer- than business-oriented and it sought clarification on a number of issues to protect consumers.

The issue of the responsibility of intermediaries was also a major point of conflict in the Council. Austria, Denmark, Italy, the Netherlands, and Sweden rejected the argument that providers do not have the resources to control information on the networks. In addition, they argued that future technological developments might allow any intermediary to monitor the transmitted information, so that limiting intermediaries' liability may become inappropriate.[314] Sweden, in particular, expressed fears that the directive could limit the scope of combating computer crime and child pornography[315] and requested to review criminal law aspects of the e-commerce directive by the Justice Ministers.[316]

Furthermore, the compatibility of the draft directive with the framework for distance selling of financial services presented a major problem. Italy, Belgium, and Spain argued that the two directives were incompatible and wanted to exclude financial services. Some delegations also questioned the coherence of the text in relation to international law[317] and Finland still had to settle 162 technical notes.[318] Finally, the e-commerce directive was dependent upon agreement on a directive on electronic signatures.

The copyright directive was not less conflictive. The EP had voted significant amendments placing greater emphasis on the interests of right holders. They related to 'fair compensation' of right holders in case of private copying, the prohibition of circumventing technical protection measures, and the need to obtain permission from the right holders for temporary copies. The Commission rejected the provision that authorisation would be necessary for temporary copies and any additional exceptions and provisions that called into question its general approach and balance of interests.[319] Contrary to Finnish preferences, the Commission also pursued a closed list of exemptions to the exclusive rights of authors to authorise or prohibit reproduction and distribution of their works leaving little flexibility for national decisions.

The article on exemptions also emerged as a serious point of divergence in the Council. Germany supported the Commission and defended an exhaustive list of exemptions, whereas the UK, Ireland, and the Nordics preferred an open list. Just ahead of the Finnish Presidency term, the UK asked for a substantial re-discussion of all exemptions.

As in the case of e-commerce there was discussion to what extent intermediaries were to be held liable in the event of infringements. In addition, the relationship between the legal protection of technical measures and the exception (Article 6) was difficult. The German Presidency had not yet opened discussions on Article 6, so that there was still confusion about its meaning. In essence, Article 6 made it illegal to de-activate technological measures and to produce, sell, and distribute equipment for neutralising them. In case of digital copying, legal protection for technical measures would prevail over the exception and right holders could apply protection measures to stop private digital copying. However, in the case of analogue copying, Article 6 proposed that de-activating a technological measure would be allowed. Sweden, France, Italy, Spain, Greece, and the Commission were in favour of this proposal. Other delegations had their reservations.[320]

Further points of conflict included the exhaustion of the distribution right and the EP's introduction into the copyright directive of the concept of fair compensation. The UK, Austria, France, Spain, Italy, Germany, Greece, and Belgium supported Community exhaustion, whereas Finland, Sweden, Denmark, Portugal, the Netherlands, and Luxembourg recommended international exhaustion. As to fair compensation, only Finland, Belgium, Spain, Austria, and Greece accepted the directive's wording and concept of fair compensation. Denmark, the UK, Ireland, Sweden, and the Netherlands objected it given the concept's unclear scope as to Member States' obligations. The Council's draft merely stated that to determine the form, arrangements, and level of such compensation, the circumstances of each case would have to be taken into account.[321] The wording 'fair compensation' was also questioned by France and Germany who preferred 'fair remuneration'.

Another handicap to achieve agreement on the InfoSoc directives was the generally tense climate in the Council caused by a dispute between the UK and Spain over Gibraltar and the UK's red-line negotiation style. The Finnish Presidency had to spent valuable time on reconciling tensions between the UK and the other Council members.

The German Presidency's progress reports presented at the June IM Council indicated that neither directive was anywhere close to agreement. Finland had set itself ambitious presidency goals prioritising issues of national interest which promised to be complicated and troublesome.

The Northern Dimension

The hurdles the ND encountered were even greater including external events in Kosovo and Chechnya, as well as enlargement issues. Even though Finnish President Martti Ahtisaari had secured a peace deal for Kosovo, its situation remained precarious. The reconstruction process imposed itself on top of the agenda inflicted spending cuts in existing EU programmes and risking that there would be 'little spare cash for the Northern Dimension'.[322]

In addition, the ND became 'hostage' to Russia's decisions. EU–Russia relations were already strained after NATO's air campaign over Kosovo, but worsened after Russian military action in Chechnya. Both the Council and the EP distanced themselves from Russia making it difficult, if not impossible, for Finland to pursue efforts to 'enhance positive interdependency' in the North.

Other pressing issues on the EU's external agenda included preparations for the next round of WTO negotiations, the renewal of the Lomé agreement, and enlargement which had been neglected under the German term due to Kosovo. Against this difficult external climate and heavy agenda, it seemed inadequate to prioritise a new, national initiative.

A further obstacle was the Commission's scepticism towards the ND.[323] Given its horizontal nature, the ND relied upon effective co-ordination between different Directorates General (DGs) with conflicting views on the EU's approach to regional co-operation. The ND exposed this weakness in the Commission, which – much to its reluctance – had to establish an Interservice group composed of officials belonging to all relevant DGs under the supervision of the DG for external relations. In short, the ND triggered the need to increase co-ordination – the 'very thing that [did] not go down well in the Commission'.[324]

The Commission was also reluctant to set up a new fund for the ND's implementation. It did not regard the ND as a new regional initiative, but as a 'concept within the framework of existing contractual relationships, financial instruments, and regional organisations'.[325]

Moreover, Finland faced Member State and partner country scepticism. Spain, fearing a distraction away from the Barcelona Process, was particularly hostile. France questioned the role the US would play in the ND and the UK thought the ND would not concern all Member States. Italy and Belgium – while not opposed – were very uninterested at most. Even the Nordics' initial reaction to the initiative was unenthusiastic. Both Denmark and Sweden felt that they had not been consulted properly about the ND and preferred intergovernmental forums, such as the

Council of the Baltic Sea States (CBSS).[326] As to the partner countries, Russia complained that the ND saw the country solely as a source of raw materials[327] and national parliamentarians portrayed the ND as neo-colonialist. Overall, the ND's reliance on close dialogue with applicant and non-applicant states, regional organisations and sub-regional bodies were new elements that caused suspicion amongst the Member States and the Commission.[328]

How then did Finland try to overcome this long list of obstacles in case of both the InfoSoc and the ND and to what extent did it reach its goals?

III. Overcoming the obstacles: the strategic process

Ex-ante presidency preparations

To overcome the numerous obstacles, meticulous strategic planning began well before the Finnish Presidency term. In case of the InfoSoc this meant a careful assessment of the state of play. As to the ND the most important step was to 'denationalise' it ahead of the presidency.

The InfoSoc directives: Assessing the state of affairs

The decision to dedicate considerable resources to the InfoSoc directives was the result of careful inter-ministerial consultation before the presidency. As early as in 1997 the ministries, together with the Finnish Permanent Representation, were invited by the PM's office to submit 'ground memorandums' on all potential presidency projects. The aim of these consultations was to establish 'what were the things on the table, what [Finland] would really like to push, and what [it] did not like that much'.[329] The memorandums highlighted the elements Finland would have to take into consideration to achieve its aims, including the opinions of other Member States and EU institutions. They were generally done, and regularly updated, in close collaboration with the future working group chairs – selected one and a half years before the presidency to accumulate expertise. Once the PM's EU co-ordination unit (see below) had determined that 'all ministries wanted something on the information society', an expert group was convened which singled out e-commerce and copyright as the two areas of action for the Finnish Presidency.[330]

As soon as it was clear that the InfoSoc would be a priority, Finland contacted the Council Secretariat and the Commission to agree upon a joint approach and investigate countries' negotiation positions.[331] Given that the InfoSoc directives fell under the co-decision procedure, presidency preparations also included early informal contact with the relevant EP rapporteurs.[332]

Another ally that Finland could use in its goal to advance the InfoSoc was the business lobby whose interest in e-commerce had increased steadily. A number of business initiatives, such as the Memorandum of Understanding on Open Access to E-Commerce and the Global Business Dialogue (GBD) on e-commerce, served as platforms to build consensus on the directives.

Denationalising the Northern Dimension

The ND originated at the PM's office. Contrary to the InfoSoc, the ND was a new concept which Finland first had to legitimise at EU level given the neutrality expectation of the presidency. The strategy became to get 'its pet proposal ready'[333] by anchoring the ND on the EU's systemic agenda *before* the Finnish Presidency to then push it onto active decision agendas and forward it legitimately *during* its term of office:

> We realised that the only legitimate way to push forward [the ND] was to make it an integral part of the EU agenda beforehand. Therefore we thought we should start with the concept of the ND early. Right now [during the Finnish Presidency] we can be active on the ND without people thinking that we are pushing forward our national agenda.[334]

The two most important means to anchor the ND on the EU agenda and ensure its content would reflect Finnish ideas were to overcome Commission scepticism and get the blessing of the European Council. This was achieved through close bilateral contacts with the Commission and other PMs and Heads of State, which commenced two years ahead of Finland's presidency.

In April 1997 Lipponen proposed the ND in a letter to Commission President Jacques Santer. However, 'the political will had to come from the Member States'.[335] Thus, a month before the Luxembourg Summit, in November 1997, Lipponen toured EU capitals to discuss the concept with his counterparts and the Council presidency. When Finland put the ND forward as part of the EU's external relations, the European Council reacted favourably. Luxembourg supported the inclusion of the ND in the Summit Conclusions and requested the Commission to submit an interim report which was presented a year later at the December 1998 Vienna Summit. The Vienna Summit was the political breakthrough to get the ND concept acknowledged. It stressed the importance of the ND for the EU's internal and external policies, especially towards Russia and the Baltics. The Council of Ministers was invited to identify, on basis of the Commission report, guidelines for action in the relevant fields.

The Commission's interim report resembled the initial concept of the Finns closely. It recalled the EU's activities and instruments with regard to the ND and set out the region's challenges and where the EU could provide added value. In addition, it established the guidelines and operational recommendations for future activity in this area.[336] Most importantly, it recommended that 'contacts are taken within the appropriate forums with Estonia, Latvia, Lithuania, Poland, Iceland, Norway, and the Russian Federation to further exchange views and develop the ND concept'[337] – even though these countries were not called 'partner' countries yet.[338] However, contrary to early Finnish hopes, it became clear that the Commission was unwilling to set up a special fund for the ND's implementation and the interim report was still vague.

Throughout this period the Finns increased their diplomatic activity. The post of Ambassador for the ND was specifically created in view of the presidency[339] and the ND was introduced in many seminars and conferences by regional organisations.[340] The ND was also on the agenda of all key bilateral meetings.[341] Germany was won as an ally early on. Chancellor Helmut Kohl strongly supported co-operation with the Baltic Sea Region and the reconstruction of the countries East of the Baltic Sea.[342] Since reunification, Germany had assisted Russia as a consequence of the agreements about the former GDR. The UK turned out to be especially supportive of the ND's nuclear dimension. At the end of the 1998 UK Presidency, it organised a meeting for Finland, inviting the Commission, Austria, and Germany to analyse how to take the ND forward. This was significant as the Austrian and German Presidencies preceded Finland's term.

To overcome the scepticism of the Mediterranean countries of the ND, Finland pursued a strategy of 'reciprocal solidarity' by showing an active interest in the Barcelona Process. Finland hosted, for example, the first ministerial Euro-Mediterranean meeting on the environment in the winter of 1997 and advanced various projects related to the Barcelona Process (the association agreements, negotiations on the MEDA II Regulation and the preparations for a common strategy on the Mediterranean) during its presidency. Bilateral meetings also served to dismiss Spanish and Portuguese fears about adverse effects of the ND on Mediterranean co-operation.[343] Portuguese PM Guterres announced his support of the ND at the Luxembourg Summit arguing that the Barcelona Process should be complemented by 'something in the North'.[344]

Similarly, high-level meetings took place with Russia[345] and the other partner countries. The latter were offered an opportunity to influence EU policy-making without being members. They were urged to produce papers to feed into the ND. Finland thereby gave them the feeling of being 'pre-EU not post-Soviet [republics]'.[346] Never before had third states been offered 'to influence EU policy in such a direct and institutionalised manner'.[347]

The Finnish 'marketing strategy' rested on three pillars: emphasising the positive-sum nature of the ND; using Community language and existing structures; and highlighting its cost-effectiveness.[348] Finland devised an initiative that would make better off not only the Northern region, but also the EU in general through additional soft security including increased stability, the exploitation of resources of the area, enhanced nuclear safety, and a strengthened external presence. In addition, Finland stressed that the ND would contribute to clarifying Russia's understanding of the EU.[349] It launched the ND when accession negotiations with the CEECs were soon to start – the idea being to link it with enlargement which was to dominate the EU agenda for some time to come. The Finnish administration argued that relations with Russia would increase in importance with the accession of the Central and Eastern European Countries (CEECs) when the Russian border would become the EU's permanent external border. A senior official summarised,

> You have to present your initiative as a European one in order to be influential.[350]

The second and third pillars of Finland's marketing strategy served to demonstrate the ND's compatibility with existing EU policies and, after the Commission had established that the ND would be promoted through existing budget frameworks, the Finnish strategy became to highlight the initiative's cost-effectiveness. Combined this made for a 'politically correct' strategy that proved effective.

Once Finland had the backing of the European Council, the next crucial task became 'to work [its] way down the Council hierarchy'[351]:

> The European Council sets the agenda, but to establish an official position we needed a decision to be taken in the General Affairs Council which was much more complicated because the Member

States now started to study the substance of the ND, not having seen the details yet. Only during the German Presidency did we start to look at all the details, and the problems are always in the small details, priorities, and financing programmes.[352]

Finland's aim was not only to get the General Affairs Council (GAC) to examine the ND, but also obtain its backing for a ministerial conference and an action plan. This was partly achieved by the GAC on 31 May 1999 which agreed the main guidelines for ND policies and sectors that were of particular importance. These reflected those that Finland had lobbied for. The May GAC further decided that the implementation and development of the ND should be done in close consultation with the partners – now formally accepted as such – through the existing agreements (Europe Agreements, PCA, EEA) and within regional bodies such as the CBSS and the Barents Euro-Arctic Council (BEAC).[353] At the Cologne Council a few days later, EU leaders reconfirmed the political backing for the ND initiative and welcomed Finland's intention of holding a ministerial conference on the ND and drawing up an action plan. The significance of the May GAC and the Cologne Summit was that Finland could now carry the ND further without being accused of introducing a new national initiative under its presidency. In sum, the Finland successfully 'denationalised'[354] the ND before its presidency:

The ND is an example of something that two years ago was a Finnish initiative, but which has now, in due time before the presidency, become joint EU policy.[355]

However, at the start of the Finnish Presidency the ND was still lacking policy content.[356] To fill the ND with concrete measures, Finland used the Council presidency's formal procedural and informal agenda-setting powers.

The presidency's agenda-setting powers

E-commerce and copyright: Towards political agreement?

The agendas of Council, COREPER, and working group meetings as well as special presidency events closely reflected Finnish priorities. By putting the InfoSoc on the agendas of all IM and industry-related events, as well as meetings concerning education and courts of law, Finland developed it into a key horizontal theme. The Finnish Presidency first explored the significance of the InfoSoc at informal ministerial level. The discussions were accompanied by a series of conferences and expert meetings. Their results were subsequently fed into working group discussions before pushing the dossiers up the Council hierarchy again.

In the case of e-commerce, Finland scheduled an informal Industry Council at the outset of its presidency (2–3 July), in the high-tech city Oulu, where it presented a paper on how to increase EU competitiveness through ICTs. The ministers agreed that 'in Europe the legislative framework for [...] the InfoSoc is still rather undeveloped' and urged the adoption of the InfoSoc directives.[357] A forum and conference on different aspect of growth and competitiveness through technology complemented the Council discussions on e-commerce. Both events were organised with the Commission and put forward recommendations on how to promote entrepreneurship through technology. The conclusions of the forum were subsequently discussed by COREPER[358] before being forwarded to the Industry Council, which agreed to integrate the issue into the EU's annual competitiveness debate.

The most important meeting to give the copyright directive renewed impetus was the Informal Council on Cultural and Audio-visual affairs which Finland focused specifically on copyright. The ministers decided to investigate the obstacles to the free mobility of production within the IM and agreed that measures at both EU and national level were needed to address illegal copying. The debate continued in monthly events: a forum for authorities responsible for audio-visual policy and enterprises in September, an expert meeting on copyrights in the digital environment in October and at the November Culture/Audio-visual Council. To bridge the different interests the presidency brought together governments, copyright authorities, and the providers of telecommunication services at these meetings.

As the development of the InfoSoc (e-commerce in particular) was linked to legislation negotiated in the Telecommunications Council, Finland also had the Telecommunications Council deal intensively with the issue. The presidency scheduled a debate titled 'The information society of the future: responding to the challenges of global electronic commerce' in the November Council and presented a paper highlighting the fundamental changes e-commerce is creating for citizens, business, and government. The discussions built upon recommendations that were made at the GBD's annual Conference concerning problem areas in e-commerce (such as consumer confidence, intellectual property rights, jurisdiction, and liability).

Crucially, the November Telecommunications Council formally adopted the directive on electronic signatures. While most of the work on this had been done by the German Presidency, Finland ensured that co-decision worked smoothly. The EP's amendments in the second reading were minor and acceptable to both the Council and the Commission.

Finally, part of Finland's strategy was to set a positive example in the area of the InfoSoc by relying heavily upon communications technology itself. The Foreign Ministry's Press and Culture Department ran the most extensive presidency internet and extranet service to that date providing access to Council agendas and submitting live press conferences. Overall, the informal ministerial meetings, conferences, as well as the presidency website developed the InfoSoc into a *leitmotiv* for the Finnish Presidency. The long list of e-commerce and copyright-related events generated momentum towards the adoption of the directives.

However, to solve the outstanding technical issues, Finland had to broker a compromise in the Council. Hence it increased its efforts at working group level. In case of the e-commerce directive, Finland raised the working group meetings from monthly discussions under the German Presidency to almost weekly sessions.[359] At COREPER level it dealt three times with e-commerce[360] and set a strategic target for each meeting.[361] Each COREPER meeting was staged beforehand with the chairperson imagining which country would come in when and deciding at what point the Commission would comment. Having meetings between COREPER and the Commission was unusual – COREPER normally just meets with the Council Secretariat.[362]

Tensions over intermediary liability dominated much of the Council discussions. As seen above, Finland favoured the exclusion of service providers' liability for the information they transmit or store. Enjoying procedural control over the agendas, the Finnish Presidency did not give in to Swedish requests of discussing liability at the JHA Council. It asked Sweden to improve its inter-ministerial co-ordination instead.[363] To overcome Sweden's fear about the directive's potentially adverse implications for combating computer crime and Member States' general concerns about exempting intermediaries from liability, the presidency compromise strengthened the Member States' role of supervision and their ability to establish certain obligations for intermediaries.

To address reservations that in the future technological development would enable all service providers to effectively monitor the information they transmit and thus make exemptions of liability inadequate, the presidency compromise expanded the directive's 're-examination' clause. This clause asked the Commission to adapt the directive to developments in InfoSoc services as necessary. To accommodate Sweden, Finland integrated into this provision a particular focus on crime prevention and the protection of minors. In addition, it added that Commission reports should analyse 'the need for additional conditions for the exemption from liability provided for in Articles 12 and 13 in the light of technical developments'.[364] These changes removed Member States' reservations regarding the liability issue and ensured that Finland's objective of exempting intermediaries was not compromised.

To dismiss Italian, Spanish, and Belgian concerns about the compatibility of the draft directive with the framework for distance selling of financial services, the presidency convincingly argued that the e-commerce directive would contribute to the creation of a legal framework for the online provision of financial services rather than contradict the directive on distance marketing of financial services. Finland's compromise clarified that the e-commerce directive did not pre-empt future initiatives in the area of financial service. Crucially, it made explicit that Member States can – under certain circumstances – restrict the freedom to provide InfoSoc services to protect consumers and that this would cover measures aimed at protecting investors. This allowed financial services to be included despite initial reservations.[365]

To disregard doubts regarding the directive's relation to international law, it was changed in line with recommendations by the Council's legal service. Trying to accommodate all Member States by offering important safeguards, the Finnish Presidency pushed for a positive-sum compromise that would be a considerable advancement to the status quo. This strategy worked. At the December IM Council Finland reached unanimous agreement on the e-commerce directive with Belgium abstaining[366]:

> We identified the most critical points at each stage and if they went right we would move to the next stage. And, stage after stage went right and in the end we had the deal we wanted. Everybody was on board.[367]

COREPER was invited to finalise the text for its adoption without further discussion at the next Council meeting.[368]

Finland pursued a similar strategy with regard to copyright. From September onwards it increased working group meetings to almost weekly sessions[369] and issued a non-paper on the issue as the basis for debate. As in the case of e-commerce it was pushing for a common position by December. Contrary to the German strategy, Finland postponed the discussion on exemptions (Article 5) and opened the debate on other politically sensitive issues, such as obligations as to technological measures (Article 6). The July and September discussions centred almost exclusively on Article 6.

However, progress on the copyright dossier was slow.[370] Differences continued on the issue of exceptions, fair compensation, the exhaustion of the distribution right, and legal protection for systems designed to outlaw illegal copying. Agreement could, however, be achieved on other technical details and the liability issue. Once the liability of intermediaries was limited in the area of e-commerce, this also applied to copyright. But as some of the issues Finland had planned to solve at working group level could not be agreed, only one COREPER meeting dealt with the copyright directive, mainly to elaborate a progress report on it for the December IM Council. Despite Finland's considerable effort and the high number of meetings it organised to advance the directive, it failed to agree the dossier.

The Northern Dimension: from systemic to active agenda?

In case of the ND, Finland managed to engage the relevant institutions, Member States, and partner countries in a constant dialogue despite the crowded agenda.[371] The ND's horizontal nature and links with the Common Strategy on Russia gave it ample opportunities to do so. The ND featured on the agendas of seminars, EU meetings with third states, relevant Council of Ministers meetings, the Helsinki Summit, and a special foreign ministerial conference.

The seminars were important stepping stones for concretising the ND. They included an unprecedented EU–Russia seminar on migration right at the start of the Finnish term.[372] In other sectors (forestry and energy) Finland seized upon expert seminars by the BEAC and the CBSS and invited them to present their results at the ministerial meeting on the ND.[373] The Finnish Presidency also organised an ND Business Forum in November which brought together key players from commerce, investment, transport, and energy to discuss the problems and prospects for developing business opportunities in Europe's North. The Forum examined the specific needs of commercial growth, financial bases for this growth, and the development of business relations with Russia.

The EU's bilateral meetings which discussed the ND included summits with Russia, the US, and Canada. Within the framework of the Common Strategy on Russia, the ND was examined when the EU Troika met with Russia's Foreign Minister Igor Ivanov and Deputy PM Viktor Kristenko and at the EU–Russia Summit in October 1999. To consolidate transatlantic co-operation on Northern Europe, the Finnish Presidency discussed the ND at the EU–Canada and EU–US Summits. Both issued joint statements reaffirming their shared objectives in the region. Interestingly, in 1998 the Clinton administration had developed a parallel framework, the Northern European Initiative (NEI), to help the Baltic states integrate into European and Euro-Arctic institutions, enhance co-operation between the US, Europe and north-western Russia as part of an American strategy to engage Russia and reinforce US–Nordic relations.[374] The NEI and US support for more effective institutions in the North aided Finnish attempts to concretise the ND.[375]

Further results on the ND were achieved at sectoral Councils. Most notably, the Finnish Presidency put the ND on the agendas of the November Health and December Energy Council. At the Health Council, the Member States took note of the latest developments on health questions in relation to the ND and the common strategy on Russia. The Council also agreed on a negotiating position in view of the Euro-Mediterranean Conference of Health Ministers as part of the Barcelona Process. The December Euro-Mediterranean Conference was important as it touched upon the same health issues that concerned the ND. A meeting of high-level health experts from the EU and applicant countries about possibilities of intensifying co-operation in the health area had been organised a month before.

More significant was the outcome in the energy field. A ministerial conference on Energy and Co-operation in the Baltic Sea paved the way for the adoption of the priorities of energy co-operation at the December Energy Council. It brought the EU delegations together with the energy ministers of the Baltic Sea states and representatives from the candidate states, the US, international organisations, and financial institutions to discuss further integration of the northern energy market. The Commission subsequently adopted a communication on the 'ND of EU Energy Policy'.[376] It examined what action to promote and existing EU initiatives. The conclusions adopted at the Energy Council were based on this communication. The Commission highlighted the energy role of the Baltic Sea and insisted that the EU enhance energy co-operation with the region. It was agreed to entrust the practical measures to implement these recommendations to a group of senior officials in which all the Member States of the CBSS would be represented for the following two years. The Commission, too, was participating in the group's work.

Most important to advance the ND, however, was Finland's initiative to hold – in partnership with the Commission – the first ministerial conference on the ND in Helsinki. By means of this high-level meeting Finland hoped to consolidate the dialogue on Northern issues, establish clear commitment of the Member States, the Commission, and the partner countries towards the ND and lay the groundwork for future implementation. It served 'to take the ND beyond general discussion to concrete action'.[377]

The conference participants were the EU Member States, the ND partner countries, and the Commission. The Committee of the Regions, the Economic and Social Committee (EcoSoc), the CBSS, the BEAC, the Nordic Council of Ministers (NCM), and the Baltic Council of Ministers (BCM) had observer status. Financial institutions (the EBRD, the EIB, the NIB, and the World Bank) also participated as observers. Bringing together these different actors was a new format under which to draw up the ND action plan. The participants focused on the promotion of stability through economic integration, trans-border challenges, and perspectives for regional co-operation.

The conference clarified the ND's institutional framework, priority areas, and future steps. The presidency conclusions highlighted energy networks and market development, natural resources, industrial development, and trade as priorities. Transport and communication, nuclear waste management, public health, and social issues were also underlined. As to future steps, participants emphasised the need for deeper multilateral co-operation between socio-economic organisations, the growing interest in the ND at the sub-national level, the necessity to establish closer contacts between regions at sub-national level and corresponding North American initiatives. The central role of international financial institutions in the EU was highlighted with regards to the implementation of the policy.

The most significant outcomes of the ND ministerial conference were the support it generated for an action plan to 'be taken into account by relevant actors wherever appropriate'[378] and the future commitment it secured towards the ND by the Commission, the Member States, and the partner countries. Commissioner Patten congratulated the Finns 'for pushing the ND up the EU agenda' and stressed the Commission's determination 'to play an active part both in the preparation and implementation of the action plan [...] to take forward this important initiative'.[379] Illustrating its close co-operation with Finland, the Portuguese delegation presented the concluding statement of the conference and made the adoption of the ND action plan one of its presidency aims for the 2000 Feira Summit. Denmark indicated that it would organise a special conference on Kaliningrad to be fed into the action plan in May 2000 and Sweden announced its intention to hold a follow-up ND conference and Business Forum during its 2001 presidency.

As to the partner countries, they expressed eagerness to contribute to the ND's development. Russian Foreign Minister Ivanov stressed its reciprocal nature:

> Apart from huge resources of raw materials, wood, oil and gas, we have many other things to offer ranging from industrial and scientific potential to skilled labour force and advanced technologies. Here we hope for reciprocity. We would like to get down to modernisation of our industry, agriculture and social and cultural spheres, to the conversion of our defence industries and facilities.[380]

Overall, the preconditions for ensuring the consolidation of the initiative were set. The results were forwarded to the Helsinki Summit which acknowledged the conclusions of the conference and repeated the intention to draw up an action plan.[381]

However, Chechnya clearly overshadowed the ND conference. Amongst the major disappointments was that although the partner countries were represented by their foreign ministers, the EU countries – apart from the presidency – were not. The EU ministers were reportedly busy at other events. The more obvious reason for their absence, however, was the strain Chechnya had put on EU–Russia relations.[382]

While the war in Chechnya did not derail the agenda of the ND conference – primarily because of Finnish persistence and because it did not invalidate the importance of the initiative's long-term goals – the absence of the ministers diminished the conference's political and symbolic significance and the war reduced the feasibility of successful implementation. Unsurprisingly, the international press dismissed its results.[383] After diplomatic relations between the EU and Russia worsened ahead of the European Council, it became clear that the prospects for the initiative' future success would depend upon Russia. One official concluded,

> While nice words were said at the Helsinki summit and in its communiqués […] the ND initiative still [had] a long way to go.[384]

IV. Conditions for success

The leadership environment, skill, and use of the Council Secretariat

Although the challenging leadership environment was beyond the presidency's control, Finland handled the EU's internal crisis and adverse external developments skilfully. The political void caused by the Commission resignation meant that the Council members had to rely more than usually on the presidency.[385] Finland used its position to pressure both the EP and the Commission. As a result the EP hearings started on August 30 and the EP approved the new college by mid-September. Upon Finnish insistence that even the 'care-taker' Commission was legally bound to revise the InfoSoc directives after the EP vote, the proposals were amended in time to forge the compromise on e-commerce.

In case of its foreign policy objectives, Finland tried to divorce Chechnya, as far as possible from the ND. It discussed the issue in private with Russia's foreign minister and the Commission and held a separate GAC on Chechnya. Finland insisted that the dialogue with Russia needed to be maintained[386] and a month later even agreed a joint action establishing a cooperation programme on disarmament with Russia.[387] The Commission was an important ally to fend off Member State reservations and EP calls to cut off funding to Russia.[388] Patten stressed repeatedly that interrupting relations with Russia could undermine the democratisation process and the ND's long-term goals. Hence, Finland managed to reduce the potentially detrimental impact of internal and external crises on a presidency's agenda influence. Finland's newcomer status and reputation as a constructive Member State was an important asset.

Moreover, Finland's expertise in the InfoSoc was well respected in the Council and its past experience as bridge-builder in the Cold War era lent it high credibility in the area of external relations. As Greek MEP Katiforis said,

> Finland is a country with great experience of surviving peacefully under difficult conditions and with difficult neighbouring countries.[389]

In addition, through exceptionally early preparations Finland skilfully overcame its size constraint:

> If you prepare well, it brings results. As a small country, if you want to have results, that's what you have to do.[390]

To exert agenda influence the three most important factors singled out by Finnish officials as part of these presidency preparations were: (a) well-trained staff; (b) efficient organisation and administration; and (c) effective inter-ministerial co-ordination. All three were taken very seriously. Seminars on the presidency with scholars, MEPs, Commission staff, and former presidency representatives commenced in 1996. Chairpersons attended negotiation simulations and hundreds of officials received language courses. Closer to the presidency term, officials were encouraged to attend Council meetings. Training was especially intense at working group level. In addition, a group of special presidency aids was recruited and staff from all ministries was sent to the Finnish Permanent Representation to get to know their Brussels counterparts and their daily routine. To overcome potential personnel shortages during the presidency, Finnish civil servants were asked to either put their summer holidays on hold or stagger them.[391]

Furthermore, efficient administration and a consistent policy line – two requisites to facilitate agreement – were key objectives. This included ensuring that documents were delivered on time to enable the respective governments to formulate a co-ordinated approach before the next meeting:

> Organisation is key. It serves political aims and is necessary to achieve political victories, to get results.[392]

Finnish administrative skill and professionalism was acknowledged throughout[393] and undoubtedly contributed to advancing the negotiations on both the InfoSoc dossiers and the ND.

To enhance consistency and ensure that Finland spoke with a single voice in Brussels, Finnish inter-ministerial co-ordination was improved for the presidency term. The importance of inter-ministerial co-ordination for small states was stressed by various practitioners:

> A country's institutional arrangements of policy co-ordination are likely to have an impact on the capacity to reach its policy objectives and on the relative capabilities of various political actors.[394]

> Big countries can afford doing a little this here and a little that there. Small countries cannot. If we give a splintered image or the idea that we do not know what we are talking about, we can much more easily be ignored as the presidency.[395]

Three major changes were undertaken to aid presidency co-ordination, preparation, and running. First, a new EU co-ordination unit was set up at the PM's Office in 1997. It consisted of the State Secretary and Under-secretary for European Affairs, two counsellors, an advisor, and two administrative assistants. It supported the PM by overseeing the presidency preparations and political co-ordination. The State Secretary for EU Affairs, Alec Aalto, was the PM's former advisor. The State Under-Secretary, Antti Peltomäki, was a former MP from the second largest party of the government coalition (KOK), which ensured close contact with the Finnish Parliament.

To avoid potential friction or overlap with the EU Secretariat at the Foreign Ministry, the unit's function was narrowed down to the co-ordination of the presidency agenda. The EU Secretariat, in turn, oversaw the overall co-ordination of EU affairs. It also prepared the European Councils and – together with the relevant ministries – the instructions to the Finnish Permanent Representation. It served as the secretariat for the main decision-making bodies in the Finnish co-ordination system: the Cabinet EU Committee directed by the PM and the so-called Committee for EU Affairs. The former defines the ministers' room of manoeuvre in Council meetings and consists of the ministers, the State Secretary for EU affairs, the Permanent Representative to the EU and other permanent experts. The latter – situated directly below (see Figure 3) – is an advisory body headed by the State Secretary for EU affairs and includes high-level officials employed by the ministries (their Permanent Secretaries or deputies), the PM's Office, the Office of the Presidency of the Republic, the Bank of Finland, the Office of Attorney General, and Åland.

The key strengths of the new EU unit were that it created with little bureaucracy: (a) a direct informal network between the people responsible for the substance of EU matters in the ministries; and (b) a link between the PM and the individual ministries. This was particularly important for the ND which was 'so horizontal that it [would] not really [have been] possible to co-ordinate it through the EU Secretariat'.[396] It also mattered in the case of the InfoSoc, where not only the Ministry of Trade, but also the Ministries of Labour and Social affairs, of Justice and Education had a stake. In addition, the new EU unit was perceived as a more neutral mediator than the Foreign Ministry:

> The EU unit was key to solve disputes between ministries. The Prime Minister's office is more neutral – it is not even called Prime Minister's office, but Council of State.[397]

The second change was the creation, in July 1996, of a Secretariat for the EU Presidency charged with organising all events taking place in Finland. For political and practical reasons Finland opted for an unprecedented fully centralised system. This set up avoided competition

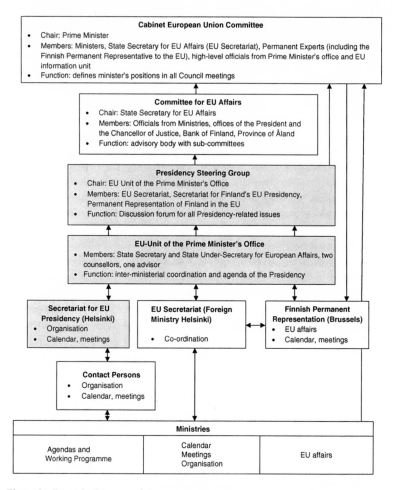

Figure 3 Finnish System of Inter-ministerial Co-ordination During the 1999 Presidency

Source: Adapted from EU Unit, Prime Minister's Office, State Under-Secretary Antii Peltomäki.

between the ministries for resources and ensured efficient co-ordination between them regarding meetings and their practical arrangements. It further allowed Finland to create one visual image and was also more economical in terms of personnel and more practical to overcome interpretation bottlenecks.[398]

The final change undertaken to enhance co-ordination was the formation, in 1997, of a presidency steering group bringing all key units (the directors from the Secretariat of the EU Presidency, the EU Secretariat, and the Finnish Permanent Representative) together. The group was chaired by the PM's EU unit and although it had no right of decision, uniting people from the PM's office with those responsible for organisation, permitted identifying problems early and in-depth discussion of any agenda item and the events held on it. Figure 3 describes the national co-ordination of EU affairs during the Finnish Presidency.

The set-up encouraged the formation of non-hierarchical teams consisting of the COREPER chairs, their counterparts in Helsinki and the relevant minister and resulted in a direct line of communication between the different levels.[399] This system worked well, so that the Foreign Ministry's EU Secretariat was moved permanently to the Council of State in 2000 and the set-up was repeated for the 2006 Finnish Presidency.[400]

In addition, co-operation between the key co-ordinators was judged as a key asset. As the EU Secretariat and the Permanent Representation were under the political backing of the PM's Cabinet EU Committee, a clear chain of political command was ensured. Since Ambassador Satuli participated in the Cabinet EU Committee, he was more integrated in domestic EU policy co-ordination than the norm in other Member States.[401] Although the overall steering of policy was done from Helsinki, the day-to-day management of the presidency could therefore be entrusted to the Permanent Representation:

> We trusted our Permanent Representation and their expertise and had very good co-operation with them. What facilitated this good co-operation was of course that we knew our people – there are not so many of them.[402]

Nonetheless, the link between administrative efficiency and policy effectiveness is not as straightforward as the foregoing analysis may suggest. A presidency's success is also conditioned by a number of other country specific factors, including its style, relations with the Council members, and the use of the Council Secretariat.[403]

Finland's presidency style was consensual and pragmatic[404] showing itself in both the area of foreign policy where the unanimity rule dominates and the negotiations of the e-commerce and copyright dossiers where QMV sufficed. Despite the QMV rule, Finland attempted to accommodate all Member States and sought positive-sum outcomes:

> We tried to have everybody on board for as long as possible, particularly where we felt a Member State had a key interest at stake. Only

in the final stages, if not everybody was on board, the presidency searched for a qualified majority.[405]

In addition, rather than merely concentrating on generating support by the countries with most votes, the Finnish Presidency also consulted the small states.

However, despite Finland's attempt to generate a consensual climate in the Council, some 'beginner mistakes' could not be avoided.[406] An unforeseen political conflict broke out over the languages used at informal Councils. For practical reasons and following custom, the Finns had limited the working languages at informal ministerial sessions to English, French, and Finnish. This offended Germany and Austria who decided to boycott some of the informal meetings. After their successive presidencies both countries had assumed that German would continue to be used. In the end, the language problem only concerned four meetings[407] and Finland increased the languages 'where necessary'.[408] However, it refused to raise German to the level of English or French particularly given Spanish and Italian concerns about favoured German treatment. The language row overshadowed the start of the Finnish Presidency, particularly the informal Industry Council.

Finally, the Finnish Presidency's use of the Council Secretariat was extensive. This was in many ways a natural strategic step by a small, inexperienced presidency. As a practitioner said,

> It was our first presidency and we needed a lot of help. So we wanted to use all the resources we had as much as we could.[409]

This was particularly true for the InfoSoc directives. In case of the ND, Finland relied less on the expertise of the Council Secretariat. It was after all its own initiative.

However, while relying heavily on the Secretariat's traditional services, such as organising meetings and taking notes, Finland did not allow it to dominate the course of the negotiations[410]:

> The Commission and the Council Secretariat really tried to take more space and powers, [because we were] a small, new chair.[411]

> The Council Secretariat can help to strike a deal, but it is not instrumental in striking the deal. It is very much the presidency which does this.[412]

A senior official from the Council Secretariat confirmed,

> The presidency brokers the deals, but with input from the Commission and the Council Secretariat.[413]

Various interviewees suggested that the power of the Council Secretariat depends on the way a presidency is run: the greater the control of the presidency's capital, the smaller the Council Secretariat's influence. Since Finland seemed to have developed a healthy balance between direction from Helsinki and input from Brussels and as the InfoSoc was one of its areas of expertise, it is unlikely that it let the Council Secretariat dominate its priority dossiers. Crucially, a number of officials argued that the Council Secretariat was sceptic about rushing the InfoSoc dossiers given their complicated legal side:

> During the 6 months you really try to speed things up and get things done in the little time you have. Some people complain that this results in bad quality legislation. The Council Secretariat, for example, is often unhappy about this.[414]

This was confirmed by an official at the Council Secretariat responsible for the IM who complained about the 'great tendency to rush things'.[415]

Heterogeneity, intensity, and distribution of governmental preferences

The heterogeneity, intensity, and distribution of preferences in the Council were favourable in the e-commerce directive, unfavourable in the copyright directive, and could be manipulated in case of the ND. As seen above, the views on the e-commerce directive in the Council were sufficiently heterogeneous to rally consensus behind Finland's preferred viewpoints. On the issue of intermediary liability, Finland had the additional advantage, that it did not face major big state opposition (except Italy) and had the Commission on its side. This made it easier to convince the Member States that limiting intermediaries' liability – with some addition safeguards – was the approach that best reflected the 'common interest'. Where Finland faced greater big state opposition with regard to the compatibility of the e-commerce directive with the framework for distance selling of financial services, it made sure that their concerns could be dismissed through further clarification within the directive. Even though Belgium abstained, the compromise did not make the country worse off and it did not veto it.

With regard to copyright, preferences were less heterogeneous and opposing camps were forming on the issues of the exhaustion of the distribution right and the concept of fair compensation. On both points Finland was in the minority facing Franco-German opposition. In the first case France and Germany were joined by the UK, Spain, and Italy. Hence, Finland was unable to broker a compromise in line with its own preferences.

As to the ND, once Spain's scepticism could be overcome through reciprocal strategies, there was no intense Member State opposition to it. Precisely the success of the Finnish Presidency was to design a positive-sum initiative that was hard for anybody to oppose and contained some initiatives for everybody in priority areas as diverse as nuclear safety and the environment, immigration, and energy.

Inter-institutional relations

Close relations with the EP and the Commission was undoubtedly another factor that contributed to Finland's success. The Finnish Presidency agenda was well-received in the EP and was judged as 'balanced', pragmatic, and forward looking.[416] Finnish ministers regularly attended parliamentary plenaries and committee meetings[417] and the presidency's many informal discussions with the EP led to the adoption of a number of directives. As seen above, ever since the first reading of the InfoSoc directives close contact with the EP was sought and – partly thanks to extensive lobbying by Finnish MEPs – the EP was also supportive of the ND.[418] In the July discussions of the Finnish priorities, MEP Harbour attributed Finland a leading role in the area of e-commerce[419] and Finnish MEPs stressed the importance of furthering the ND.[420] In addition, even though the EP's role in the EU's foreign policy is limited, Finland encouraged it to present its opinions and involved it in the policy preparations.[421] Nonetheless, after Russia's military action in Chechnya the EP heavily criticised Finland for not taking immediate action to suspend TACIS and increase humanitarian aid.[422] This put into questions the ND's future implementation.

Close co-operation with the Commission had been key to Finland ever since it became a member of the EU. Halonen said repeatedly that a strong Commission is the best support for a small Member State wishing to keep an eye on the 'bigs'.[423] According to Rehn, Finland regards the Commission 'as the defender of small states' equal rights in the EU decision-making'.[424] However, the Commission does not systematically defend small state or a presidency's interest. Much depends on the specific proposal or initiative under consideration.

In the case of the InfoSoc, using the Commission as a resource was not difficult. Finland's preferences coincided with the aims of the Commission to establish a legal framework that provided 'sufficient legal security, encourage on-line innovation and trust in order to accelerate the growth of e-commerce in Europe'.[425] Both the emergence of a clear legal framework for e-commerce and the adequate protection of intellectual property rights featured within the institution's new IM Strategy. In addition, the Commission was an obvious ally because it had already done the preparatory work to eliminate legal obstacles to e-commerce in other difficult dossiers (on regulatory transparency mechanisms, protection of personal data and conditional access services, electronic signatures). This had involved extensive lobbying of Member States and other institutions in favour of developing the InfoSoc. While the Commission's approach in the e-commerce directive broadly reflected Finnish preferences, in the case of copyright, the Commission, joined by the big states, formed a powerful alliance against the Finnish Presidency.

Despite the limited Commission powers in foreign policy, presidency–Commission relations over the ND were tense at the beginning and subsequently developed into a collaborative relationship. Finland had to convince the institution of its ambitious initiative and liaise closely with the people who drew up the interim report. The institution's eventual backing of the ND at the ministerial conference suggests that Finland managed to bring the Commission on its side.[426]

V.   Revision of achievements: assessing the counterfactuals

To check the robustness of the causal process developed above, the counterfactuals are analysed next. How does Finnish Presidency entrepreneurship in the InfoSoc and the ND compare with the leadership by other Member States, the Commission, and the EP?

The InfoSoc directives

Presidency achievements and the role of other Member States

The Finnish Presidency clearly elevated the adoption of InfoSoc legislation into a key priority. By exploiting the procedural powers of the chair and scheduling numerous meetings related to the directives, Finland contributed to the recognition that e-commerce urgently required a clearer legal framework. Its approach, including long-term preparation and the strategic use of the Council Secretariat and the Commission, was successful in generating agreement on the e-commerce directive. In line with Finnish interest, the presidency compromise limited the legal liability of intermediaries and ensured a high level of consumer protection. Given Finland's expertise in e-commerce, the other Council members did not challenge Finnish leadership in the dossier. None of them put forward their own compromise solution or input papers around which the final compromise on the e-commerce directive was constructed.

Despite the strength of its strategic approach, Finland did not reach agreement on the copyright directive. The distribution of preferences in the Council was the biggest constraint to presidential success. Nonetheless the dossier 'got a considerable push' by Finland.[427] In particular, the presidency solved the sensitive article on liability, so that the Portuguese Presidency could relatively swiftly move the directive to COREPER level and adopt it by June. However, Portugal's common position on the copyright directive differed on two key aspects. First, Portugal brokered agreement on an exclusive list of exemptions rather than an open list, as Finland had preferred. Second, contrary to Finland, Portugal bowed to the big-state coalition that favoured Community exhaustion over international exhaustion. None of the following presidencies turned the InfoSoc into a major priority theme on their presidency agendas.

The role of the Commission

The Commission was an important actor to generate momentum towards advancing the InfoSoc. Finland co-hosted a number of events with the Commission and the Commission took some initiatives itself. For example, it held a public hearing on 'Electronic Commerce: jurisdiction and applicable law' to address questions such as which court has jurisdiction to hear a dispute and which law that court applies to determine the rules applicable to that dispute. In addition, it launched its so-called 'eEurope – An Information Society for All' initiative proposing ambitious targets to maximise citizens' benefits of the InfoSoc. But was it the Commission who set the priorities, pursued them vigorously, and brokered the final compromise on e-commerce?

A Commission official admitted that they are unable to elevate certain issues over others. Instead, the Commission adjusts its agenda to the presidency priorities:

> The Commission sets the agenda in the sense that it proposes the initial agenda. However, it is the presidency who has the possibility to set the priorities on the agenda. The presidency gives direction to the

process. It tells us what their views are and what they would like to focus on. Our response then is, for example, to advance putting forward certain proposals or the date for adoption. This speeds proposals up that may have otherwise been adopted or emerged 6 months or more later.[428]

Hence, it is unsurprising that the Commission launched its 'eEurope' initiative under the Finnish Presidency. A strategic actor itself, it knew it would receive adequate attention under the Finnish term.

On the detailed content of the e-commerce directive the Commission proposal broadly reflected the Finnish Presidency approach. Especially on the liability issue, the Commission defended – as Finland – the exemption from liability for intermediaries where they play a passive role as a 'mere conduit' of information from third parties and limit service providers' liability for other intermediary activities such as the storage of information. Hence it is difficult to isolate Commission or indeed Finnish Presidency influence. •

However, two aspects suggest that Finland was key in both the drafting and negotiation phase of the directive. First, particularly on the liability issue Finland had actively lobbied the Commission during the drafting stage of the proposal doing the 'pre-influencing'.[429] Generally, small states are most likely to be heard by the Commission: (a) when they form coalitions with at least one or two big states; (b) when they have well-developed networks within the Commission; and (c) when they can offer special technical expertise on an issue.[430] Finland fulfilled all three conditions. On the liability issue it enjoyed the support by the UK, France, and Germany. Within the Commission Finland found reliable allies in both IM Commissioner Bolkestein and Finnish Commissioner for enterprise and information society Erkki Liikanen. The Commission also respected Finland's expertise on the issue. Furthermore, Finland was backed by the business lobby and the Cologne Council conclusions which had specifically demanded 'an [e-commerce] directive which has the support of the industry'.[431] In sum, the shape of the proposal already reflected the Finnish Presidency's key interests, so that the Commission–Presidency tandem worked smoothly.

Second, the Commission proposal did undergo some important changes in the Council negotiations suggesting that the presidency was more influential than the Commission. The Finnish Presidency compromise did not only strengthen Member States' role of supervision and ability to establish certain obligations for intermediaries, but more importantly, it deleted a number of articles granting the Commission

additional powers. These included provisions 6 of Article 19 and
Article 20. The former stated that the Commission would lay down
the rules governing cooperation between national authorities. The latter
gave the Commission the power to take measures to ensure the proper
functioning of electronic media between the Member States.

In case of copyright, Commission influence was also limited. While
it got its way on the list of exemptions, the Portuguese compromise entailed Community rather than international exhaustion of the
distribution right as the Commission had defended.

In sum, the evidence regarding the power of the Commission in shaping final policy outcomes is mixed. A practitioner argued that the success
of a Commission proposal depends on 'the quality of the initial proposal
and how well it reflects the overall balance of interests' in the Council.[432]
This means in essence that neither the presidency nor a major delegation is against it. In contrast, whether a presidency is successful or not
will depend to a large extent on its leadership capacity including:

> how well the presidency structures the debate, how good it antici-
> pates problems, how good it is in bilateral contacts, and how well it
> formulates a compromise.[433]

In the case of the InfoSoc Finland was well placed to lead and anticipate
problems, formulate compromises, and tend bilateral contacts. Overall then, it seems to have been the Finnish Presidency rather than the
Commission who brokered the final compromise on e-commerce:

> The presidency often asks/consults the Commission, but it is the pres-
> idency who is in the lead. I have to stress that we had an extremely
> able Minister who was on top of the issues because of his personal
> commitment. He knew every nuance of every word in the compro-
> mise and their implications. I have seen opposite examples where the
> presidency does not play a role at all. Then other Member States or
> the Commission try to jump in to fill the leadership gap.[434]

The role of the EP

The EP's influence in shaping the e-commerce directive was even more
limited. Only those amendments that were acceptable to the Commission and the Finnish Presidency made it into the final compromise.

The vast majority of EP amendments was minor and did not question the Commission approach. They included, for example, reference
to the fact that the development of e-commerce can enhance Europe's

competitiveness and benefit European citizens. Other amendments suggested inserting that e-commerce is an opportunity to provide public services in the cultural, education and linguistic fields and that the free movement of InfoSoc services is 'a reflection of the freedom of expression enshrined in the European Convention for the Protection of Human Rights and Fundamental Freedoms'.[435] As the Finnish Presidency, the EP was also trying to increase transparency. Hence Finland supported the EP amendments regarding information requirements about prices and unsolicited commercial communications. They ensured a higher level of transparency and could generate greater consumer confidence in e-commerce. Indeed the majority of EP amendments were minor and could be accepted in whole or in part.

However, the EP's more substantial amendments regarding the legal liability of online service providers acting as intermediaries were rejected. As seen above, the EP argued that intermediaries should be held liable for the content they transmit or store. This was rejected by both the Commission and the Finnish Presidency. Once the Finnish Presidency reached a unanimous common position on limiting intermediaries' legal liability, the EP did not propose any further changes to it – perhaps because the new centre-right EP was more business oriented than the previous Socialist-dominated one.

The Northern Dimension

Presidency achievements and the role of other Member States

By mid-2006 a second ND Action Plan had been implemented and a Northern e-Dimension, an ND Environment Partnership, and an ND Partnership on health and social welfare agreed. In addition, an ND Information System was launched in 2004. Most important for Finland, the nuclear waste disposals of Kaliningrad and North-West Russia became recipients of significant amounts of ND funding, and a project was launched to finalise the construction of St Petersburg's south-west waste water treatment plant to clean up the Gulf of Finland. On Finland's border with Russia the ND's most significant project has been the new border crossing station in Salla.

Although analysts disagree on the ND's overall effectiveness given its mixed implementation record, the overriding fact remains that Finland – in the presidency chair – succeeded in translating the Cologne Summit's general approval of the ND into a concrete initiative for deeper co-operation in the North. Particularly the adoption of the Commission's inventory of ND activities at the ministerial conference and the decision to prepare an action plan were key Finnish achievements in the efforts to concretise the initiative.

By placing the ND on active Council agendas and closely co-operating with the Commission, Finland advanced the initiative particularly in the energy sector.[436] Long-term projects such as plans to build the Northern Gas pipeline combining Russia, the countries in the Northern Region, and central Europe progressed. Both can be seen as stepping stones towards the EU–Russia energy dialogue launched a year later. Moreover, the ND developed in the health and environmental sectors.

While some of the ND projects may have come about within existing bilateral frameworks, bilateral contacts are unlikely to have achieved at least three of the ND's key aims: to encourage greater synergies between the programmes in the region; to generate better inter-operability between the different Commission DGs and their financial tools; and to alert the Commission to Kaliningrad. Working towards better co-ordination between INTERREG, PHARE, and TACIS has been a distinct feature of the ND. A guide for project applicants on how to link the three together was presented in April 2001 and follow-up initiatives have since taken place. As seen above, an Interservice group was created within the Commission to bridge co-ordination difficulties between the institution's DGs. It was within the ND context that the Commission first started thinking about Kaliningrad's problematic position after enlargement. Neither Russia nor the Commission, or other Member States had brought up the issue before Finland put it – through the ND – on the agenda.

Three further achievements are noteworthy. First, Finland created a new format under its presidency consisting of ministerial conferences that bring together the candidate states, regional and financial institutions. Second, Finland 'normalised' the ND under its presidency, laying the groundwork for subsequent chairs. Portugal endorsed the first ND action plan at its Feira Summit in June 2000 – a remarkable achievement considering that the initiative was initially seen as a 'rival initiative' to the South. The Gothenburg European Council, in turn, adopted a 'Full Report on ND Policies' that took stock of the activities to implement the Feira Action Plan and outlined proposals for the ND's continuation. It also asked the Commission to produce annual progress reports on the implementation of the ND, which it has done since 2002. Finally, Denmark produced the draft of the ND's second action plan to pursue the initiative beyond 2003. The ND's second Action Plan underlined the initiative's importance in the context of EU enlargement and its contribution in carrying forward the Union's new neighbourhood policy in the region. It was endorsed by the European Council under the 2003 Greek Presidency and came into effect on 1 January 2004.

Finally, the ND encouraged contacts at administrative level, especially with Russia. Never before had Russian authorities been as involved with a presidency. Regional bodies became more closely engaged and their expertise was used to establish priorities and continues to be vital in the implementation process.

However, Finland did not achieve everything during its term. While it secured the continuation of the ND, the Finnish Presidency did not secure the joint financing of the initiative between the Community, EU Member States, partner countries, regional bodies, and international finance institutions. When asked if Finland would have done anything differently in retrospect two senior officials stated,

> I think we have been a little too modest with the ND in the sense that we were very careful not to propose anything that would need more money and make things more complicated. If you look at the Spanish Presidency and their way of handling what is known as the 'Mediterranean facility,' but what they are developing very determinedly into a Euro-Mediterranean Development Bank – I think there has been a lot of activism in and from the South which outnumbers ours.[437]

> This is a complicated issue. The implementation process suffers from the lack of a single budgetary instrument. We are now discussing the possibility of a new financing instrument, building on TACIS, PHARE, and INTERREG. We think we need a new start in this sector. However, the reality in 1999 was that the budget package was just in place, Agenda 2000 had just been agreed, there was little chance for us to get a separate budget for the ND.[438]

In addition, despite Finland's heavy dialogue with the Russian administration, co-operative initiatives by Russian parliamentary bodies at federal and regional level were still lacking. By the end of the Finnish term, many reforms necessary to facilitate further co-operation in line with the ND concept had been either rejected or postponed by such parliamentary bodies.

The ND was a Finnish initiative, developed with little input from the other Member States who were lacking the level of expertise Finland had on the region's problems. It took a lot of marketing by the Finns to interest the Member States and partner countries, overcome their scepticism or opposition, and convince them of the long-term benefits of the ND.

Before the Finnish Presidency, the initiative was still lacking a concise focus. Up to this point it was a 'notion used in many different ways and a variety of different contexts'[439] rather than a routine item that any Member State or other EU institution would have readily invested in. Unsurprisingly, despite Finland's progress at the Luxembourg and Vienna Councils, the German Presidency in the first half of 1999 did not even refer to the ND in its presidency programme. In addition, following the Chechnya war, Russia's human rights abuses and doubts about Russia's ability to implement the ND, Member States' attitude towards the initiative cooled markedly. Only after great efforts during the Finnish Presidency term, Sweden and Denmark decided to hold follow-up ND conferences. The only enthusiastic Nordic supporter was Norway as the ND offered it influence in the formulation of EU policies without being a member.

The role of the Commission

The Commission's contribution to the development of the ND included its interim report, inventory of EU policies affecting the ND, a position paper on the environment in the ND, a document on gas supplies and energy policy, and the subsequent action plan. However, the initiative behind these contributions did not come from the Commission who was initially resistant to the ND because it challenged its traditional working modes. While the ND enjoyed the 'intergovernmental push' by the Finnish Presidency, it was left without the 'supranational pull' that could come from the Commission had it fully embraced the initiative.[440]

Most of the work was done by Finnish civil servants, so that the interim report and action plan reflected closely Finnish intentions and emphasis.[441] Patten recognised the Commission's limited role in the development of the EU's foreign policy and regional co-operation organisations and the leadership of the Council presidency:

> There are legal limits to our competence in regional co-operation organisations. We must therefore rely on strong leadership from the EU Presidency to keep up the momentum and to ensure the involvement of non-EU partner countries. The Finnish government has set an excellent example.[442]

The role of the EP

The EP issued a resolution and report on the ND in the spring of 1999 in response to the Commission's interim report.[443] Its contributions agreed with the ND objectives and sought to concretise the Commission report, for example, by proposing greater inter-regional and cross-border cooperation. They focused on the Baltic Sea region and stressed the role of national organisations in cooperation projects. Contrary to Finland, however, the EP wanted the ND to develop into a regional policy rather than anchoring it firmly into the EU's foreign policy and security dimension. In addition, it sought to flesh out a greater role for itself:

> The Northern Dimension should not remain a matter of high foreign policy. It is about real issues affecting the daily lives of our citizens. It therefore cries out for treatment and involvement of elected representatives at a more immediate level. It is more regional policy than foreign policy.[444]

Other substantial suggestions included the creation of a 'Northern Summit' as a follow up to the Finnish Presidency's ministerial conference. The 'Northern Summit' was to be attended by all countries encompassed within the ND, Canada, and the US. To date no such Northern Summit has been convened. In addition, the ND is still within the EU's foreign rather than regional policy realm. While Finland acknowledged the EP's opinions, its influence in shaping the initiative was highly limited. Indeed, as seen above, towards the end of the Finnish Presidency, the EP questioned the ND's heavy focus on Russia and demanded a freezing of funds.

Interestingly also, the EP did not present any input papers for the ND's first action plan. To develop 'a clear voice in the ND process' it only became active during the preparations for the second action plan.[445] During the initial years of the ND, the EP did neither challenge Finnish leadership in introducing nor developing the initiative.

Conclusion

Both in the area of the IM and foreign policy, Finland used the presidency as a window of opportunity to orient the EU to Finnish economic and political concerns. Although the IM agenda mirrored the EU's ongoing legislative process, the Finnish Presidency set its own distinct priorities. The Council chair served as a tool to develop the InfoSoc into the presidency's *leitmotiv* and focus the Member States on the e-commerce and copyright directives.

According to our categories of presidential influence set out in Chapter 1, in the e-commerce dossier Finland had a high level of influence. Despite considerable obstacles including a challenging leadership environment and Member State differences, the directive was agreed and its key controversies – such as the legal liability of intermediaries – were solved in line with the presidency's preferences and the interests of the Finnish telecommunications and electronics market. Finland's influence over the copyright dossier, in turn, was low. The directive progressed considerably and – as in the e-commerce case – limited the legal liability of intermediaries. However, no overall agreement was reached. Indeed, the succeeding Portuguese Presidency compromise differed from Finland's preferred solutions on the issues of exemptions and exhaustion of copyrights.

The presidency's power to set the active agendas for six months and its extensive dialogue with other decision-makers was crucial to facilitate results on the directives. Its combination of formal and informal powers granted it a comparative advantage to move the dossiers from working group level up the Council hierarchy. The triangular relationship between Council, Commission, and Parliament shaped the strategies employed by the presidency. Given Finland's proactive IM approach, it could pool resources with the Commission to raise awareness about the significance of the InfoSoc. To detect individual Member States' positions and find a compromise on the dossiers, Finland relied heavily on its Permanent Representation and the Council Secretariat. Influencing other Member States and the EU institutions was considered easier while holding and preparing for the presidency:

> When you have to prepare for the presidency it is much easier to approach the Commission and other Member States. You have a system for doing that and a programme.[446]

Nonetheless, the failure to adopt the copyright directive illustrates that the presidency cannot impose its will. The intensity and distribution of Member State preferences were the biggest constraints to presidential influence in the copyright dossier.

Finnish Presidency leadership was even more evident in the case of the ND. Despite initial opposition to the ND, Finland developed it from a catchword and peripheral Finnish interest to a central theme in the EU's external relations.[447] Apart from some initial concession to the Commission with regards to the financing of the initiative in the period before the presidency, Finland's influence in concretising and shaping the ND during its presidency was high. The Commission interim report reflected Finland's original approach, drew upon Finnish expertise on Northern issues and the idea of an action plan was endorsed. As in the case of the InfoSoc this success was achieved through exploiting the presidency's formal procedural power and the informal power to emphasise its regional interests after effective and 'politically correct' marketing of the ND, much of which preceded the presidency.[448]

The content of the ND and the intergovernmental institutional framework meant that Finland first had to legitimise the initiative at the highest level. Once it generated European Council approval, it needed to concretise it lower down the Council hierarchy. Linking the ND to enlargement, the Common Strategy on Russia, and the Mediterranean Dimension gave it ample opportunities to develop it during its term. Influencing the Commission was crucial to shape the precise content of future EU action in this area and secure the implementation of the initiative. Member State scepticism was overcome by choosing a reciprocal and pragmatic approach avoiding the neglect of other foreign policy issues and continuity of the ND was achieved by winning future presidencies as allies.

Despite the challenging leadership environment, this chapter has shown that a small, inexperienced presidency could handle the presidency office well and achieve results by careful preparation, efficient co-ordination, and seeking positive-sum outcomes. Cherishing a special legislative dossier or idea did not automatically lead to results. In both pillars Finland's own entrepreneurial activity was central to adopt the e-commerce directive, advance copyright, and concretise the ND.

In sum, even within the constraints of the EU institutions and the preferences of other Member States, the Finnish Presidency acted as an important agenda setter:

> My biggest criticism of Finland has always been that we were too reactive and not proactive enough. We did not really have an EU policy; we reacted to other countries' EU policy. During our presidency we had for the first time an agenda. We had fixed positions. It forced us to think before hand and be pro-active.[449]

5

The 2001 Belgian Presidency: Internal Market and Foreign Policy Priorities and Achievements

The presidency of the Council of the European Union [...] is for us an exceptional opportunity to put our brand on the European integration project.[450]

Introduction

Belgium is one of the EU's founding members with a positive presidency track record in terms of policy breakthroughs and managerial capacity. It is also the most outspokenly federalist Member State that has placed European integration at the centre of its economic and foreign policies. Initially Belgium saw it as key to contain potential future Franco-German hegemony. Later Europe grew into a means 'to adapt [Belgium's] increasingly open economy to globalisation while preserving some features of the European socio-economic model' and 'to enhance its influence in foreign affairs'.[451] The 2001 Belgian Presidency from 1 July to 31 December was the country's eleventh Council presidency.

This chapter analyses the 2001 Belgian Presidency's achievements in its most important IM and foreign policy priorities: the postal services directive and the development of the EU Africa policy, in particular the peace process in the Great Lakes. As the previous chapter, this chapter investigates the extent to which Belgium could use its presidency to shape policy outcomes in line with its national preferences and reflects on the nature of the decisions taken.

The analysis shows that in the chair Belgium facilitated agreement on further opening the postal sector without compromising its own positions and despite an ideological split in the Council. The Council Secretariat was its key ally in building bridges between the two camps and constructing a near unanimous compromise. As to the EU's Africa policy Belgium focused attention on the Great Lakes and pushed for a more holistic policy with a diplomatic, development, and conflict prevention dimension. Its presidency initiatives, including the first EU troika to the region, the first ministerial meeting at continental level, and increased diplomatic activity with regional organisations led to the adoption of a series of Council conclusions and more pro-active EU Africa policy than ever before.

I. Belgian internal market and foreign policy presidency objectives

Liberalising postal services

The adoption of the postal services directive of May 2000 formed part of a gradual liberalisation effort that the EU had started in 1997. The 1997 directive on common rules for the development of Community postal services[452] had liberalised 3% of the market and set up a common regulatory framework by defining:

- the minimum characteristics of a mandatory universal postal service; quality standards for cross-border services; tariff principles; and principles governing the transparency of accounts;[453]
- the maximum limits for those services where competition was deliberately restricted (reserved areas) to fund unprofitable universal service activities (effectively 350 g); and
- the principles to govern the licensing of the provision of non-reserved postal services.

The 2000 postal services directive proposed liberalising an additional 20% of the sector by 2003 through decreasing the weight/price limits of letters and direct mail from 350 g to 50 g and fully opening express and outgoing cross-border mail to competition. Universal services would continue and a compensation fund would pay for the less commercially viable sectors. Moreover, special services (for example, express mail or delivery on appointment) were to be fully liberalised and the directive set a timetable for further market liberalisation. A follow-up directive was to be presented before 2005, adopted by the EP and the Council before 2006, and enter into force before 2007.

In its presidency programme Belgium emphasised postal liberalisation as a key area of concern[454] and PM Verhofstadt said in his July EP speech:

> [. . .] to exploit the advantages of the single market to the full, we must also integrate the financial markets, liberalise gas, electricity, telecommunications, post, and transport [. . .].[455]

This was a U-turn. Belgium had opposed the 1997 directive and formed part of a veto alliance led by France against postal liberalisation. Even though the Belgian economy is highly integrated into the IM, the country has been hesitant to liberalise. As a Belgian official said,

> We have got some problems [. . .] when it comes to liberalisation. We have a background of monopolies. 51% of our basic services remain under state control. We do not want them to be too expensive, but we want basic guarantees for a minimum service and protect consumer rights.[456]

The change of government in 1999 which broke 40 years of conservative rule had much to do with this turnaround. Verhofstadt had – for most of his political life – been a fervent free-market supporter and 'the nearest Belgium [had] to a Thatcherite'.[457] His party's key themes were deregulation, privatisation, and slimming down social security. To be elected, he had to moderate his discourse, but driving forward liberalisation remained his priority. In the area of postal services Verhofstadt wanted to go much further than some of his coalition partners. The Council presidency offered him a tool to do so. Ludlow argued,

> Verhofstadt was in a difficult coalition together with Socialist parties who did not favour postal liberalisation. There was no consensus in Belgium on this issue. Thus Verhofstadt's strategy was to push it on the EU agenda. Once agreement on the EU level would be reached he could use this as a political tool to forge internal consensus.[458]

This became increasingly important, as investigations of the Belgian *La Poste* for abuse of its dominant position were underway. These led to formal antitrust proceedings in June 2001 and in December the Commission fined the Belgian Post Office 2.5 million euros. Paradoxically, *La Poste* was also asking for additional financial support from the Belgian government to guarantee the universal service – the reason for having a monopoly in the first place.

The Belgian Presidency goal was to reach a common position on the new postal directive by the October Telecommunications Council. Verhofstadt favoured a gradual lowering of the weight threshold below which Member States would be allowed to hold a monopoly and setting 2009 as the deadline to reach full liberalisation.

Peace and conflict prevention in the Great Lakes

In the foreign policy realm, the Belgian Presidency's main goal was a more pro-active and coherent EU Africa policy. A Belgian official stated,

> We saw the need to europeanise Africa policy. [...] The most important for us was to generate a body of Council conclusions on the issue. We wanted to bring together the very divergent views. I call it policy building or developing a shared vision.[459]

In particular, Belgium wanted to commit the EU more deeply to the peace process in the Great Lakes (Burundi, the Democratic Republic of Congo (DRC), Rwanda, and Uganda). It pursued two objectives: sketching out a European policy towards the Great Lakes focussing on peace and conflict prevention; and enhancing the EU–Africa dialogue.[460]

Economic relations between the EU and Central Africa date back to the 1950s. The Rome Treaty provided for the association of the overseas countries and territories (OCTs) with the Community and a European Development Fund (EDF). After most OCTs gained their independence, EU–Africa relations gradually changed. The Yaoundé Conventions of 1964 and 1971 (Yaoundé I and II) established preferential trade agreements with the associated African States and Madagascar. They also promoted regional co-operation and created joint institutions to oversee the Conventions' work. However, the limited concessions failed to provide the developing countries with a greater share of world trade and enhanced the dependency relationship.[461]

In the mid-1970s and early 1980s – mainly due to UK accession – the EU restructured its relations with the developing world through the Lomé Conventions of 1976 and 1981 (Lomé I and II) which now also included the Caribbean and Pacific states. The new group of ACP states were to be put on a more equal partnership and their economies integrated into to the global market. This implied dropping the principle of political conditionality – characteristic of the previous arrangements. The main policy objectives became the promotion of trade, agricultural and industrial development, special aid for the least developed countries (LDCs), and support for regional co-operation.

The two follow-up Conventions of 1986 and 1990 (Lomé III and IV) shifted EU attention from the promotion of industrial development to self-sufficiency and food security and emphasised new political issues including human rights and democratic governance. Lomé IV re-introduced the conditionality principle allowing the retrieval of allocated funds should a country disrespect democracy and the rule of law. Nonetheless, Africa's economies steadily declined and Lomé's poor results combined with the end of the Cold War, globalisation, and progressive trade liberalisation eventually led to a more fundamental revision of EU–Africa relations: the Cotonou Partnership Agreement of June 2000.

Cotonou placed even greater emphasis on the political aspects of development.[462] While retaining Lomé's institutional structure, it included institutional capacity building, the support of civil society, the role of non-state actors in promoting development, gender equality, and sustainable resource management. Second, the principle of trade liberalisation effectively replaced that of non-reciprocal privileged access. The agreement covers the period until 2020. However, a genuine political dialogue with the Great Lakes and the whole African continent, as Belgium advocated, was slow to develop. As one interviewee stated, 'We have had no real Africa policy – for decades we just had economic relations.'[463]

The first steps towards a political dialogue with the Great Lakes and the whole continent were taken in 1996 and 2000. In 1996 the EU sent a Special Envoy to the region and, on initiative of the Portuguese Presidency, the first EU–Africa Summit was held in Cairo in April 2000. It brought together the African countries of the ACP group with those of the Mediterranean littoral and sought to 'develop an effective framework for promoting a constructive dialogue on political, economic, social, and development issues'.[464] The Summit agreed common priorities in the Cairo Action Plan. To monitor their implementation it decided to hold a follow-up summit in 2003 and have ministerial and bi-regional group meetings at senior official level in between summits. In sum, while a continental dialogue had barely started, the Belgian Presidency could build on four decades of economic relations with Central Africa and the mechanisms laid down at Cairo.

At least two interlinked reasons account for Belgium's emphasis on the Great Lakes. First, Belgium has had colonial ties with the Congo since 1885 when King Leopold created the Congo Free State as his own private empire. Under the Verhofstadt government new evidence of the cruelties of Belgian colonialism and Belgium's involvement in the assassination of the Congo's first democratically elected PM, Patrice Lumumba, was revealed. It caused an outcry and forced the country to re-evaluate its colonial past. The response of the new government, particularly Foreign Minister Louis Michel, was to launch a new 'ethical foreign policy' and embark on fresh relations with Belgium's former colonial territories. He repeatedly stressed Belgium's 'moral responsibility to demonstrate solidarity with the region in Africa it knows best and where it still has numerous ties'.[465] Verhofstadt's and Michel's recommendation of an official parliamentary inquiry into Belgium's role in Lumumba's death and their visit to Rwanda in April 2000 to publicly apologise for the lack of action to prevent the 1994 genocide were to mark the beginning of Belgium's new ethical foreign policy. The Council Presidency was seen as a platform to pursue Belgium's new approach internationally.

The second motivation for prioritising Africa was to restore Belgium's international reputation by taking the lead in peace initiatives, conflict prevention, and humanitarian aid. Michel wanted to reorient Belgian and the EU's Africa policy on the defence of human rights and encourage the international community to get involved in the Great Lakes peace process. He was particularly interested in intensifying the EU's diplomatic relations with the DRC and had personal ambitions to carve out Africa as an area for Belgium and for himself:

> From the beginning Michel decided that Africa should be his remit. He wanted to put both himself and Belgium into the picture. Mr Africa in the GAC. It is no coincidence that he is now Commissioner for Development.[466]

The Belgian presidency programme dedicated various paragraphs to Africa:

> The Presidency will work to ensure that the EU becomes more closely involved in accompanying the peace processes in Central Africa and in the Great Lakes region. [...] it plans to draw up an inventory of all humanitarian needs and the requirements for rebuilding the health sectors, national infrastructures, judicial systems, and the democratisation process. The Presidency will submit proposals to its partners with a view to developing a plan of action for peace and development in Central Africa.[467]

Other sections highlighted Belgium's intention to launch discussion on conflict prevention in Africa, hold a ministerial meeting on issues concerning the future of Africa, to intensify dialogue between the EU and African regional organisations, and to '[make] the Cotonou Agreement operational via thematic cooperation plans with countries involved in conflicts and the involvement of civil society in helping identify, plan, and implement cooperation actions'.[468] In addition, Belgium hoped to send the first ever EU troika to Africa and generate support for increasing EU aid to the region.

Central Africa also featured in all key speeches upon assuming the presidency. During his first EP plenary Verhofstadt argued,

> The Balkans and the Middle East may be more important politically. I am not going to dispute that. From a humanitarian point of view, however, the tragedy that is unfolding in the Great Lakes region is a thousand times greater. [...] I say to you that the Union can no longer stand idly by. Political, diplomatic and economic action is urgently required and the presidency will present an action plan to that effect.[469]

Belgium was particularly keen to abandon the conditionality approach to aid, increase political and financial commitment to the region, and search a holistic approach with a diplomatic, military, and development side. As Michel said,

> We [...] believe it is unrealistic to wait for the ideal conditions before making a commitment to development co-operation. [...] the ideal conditions for striking a deal will never be achieved unless the international community is prepared to start funding development.[470]

In sum, both postal liberalisation and EU-Africa relations were firmly anchored on the EU agenda. At the same time they closely reflected Belgium's national interests and were therefore prioritised despite numerous obstacles to facilitate agreement on the dossiers.

II. Obstacles: the leadership environment, institutional hurdles, and preference divergence

Postal services

Both economically and politically the Belgian Presidency faced an unfavourable leadership environment to further postal liberalisation. After the September 11 terrorist attacks, business confidence collapsed and partly due to the fierce economic slowdown in the US and German economic weakness, Belgian and EU growth levels fell significantly.[471] Although unemployment levels were declining, the high oil prices caused inflation in the euro zone to rise to its highest level since 1993.[472]

The political situation was similarly challenging. Even though the reform-minded centre-right Flemish liberals VLD had the largest number of seats in parliament, the disparate nature of Verhofstadt's coalition combining liberal, socialist, and green parties made disagreements on liberalisation inevitable.[473] Domestic regional tensions were also increasing following Flemish demands for greater fiscal autonomy and the rise of the right-extremist Vlaams Blok which challenged national unity and threatened cross-party consensus on European issues.

Furthermore, social tensions became apparent after national rail strikes and demonstrations following the collapse of Belgium's national airline Sabena. The incidents did not help the credibility of the government of a country that was still recovering from a series of judicial, administrative, and political scandals.[474] In short, Belgium could not afford to put domestic politics on hold during its presidency.

At EU level, Belgium assumed the presidency in the post-Nice climate marked by unsolved enlargement issues, tensions over the EU's future shape, and rising euroscepticism. After Ireland's rejection of the Nice Treaty in June 2001 and renewed calls to entrust the elaboration of the EU's constitutional texts to a Convention, the Belgian Presidency's key pet project became to address the 'crisis of identity in the EU'[475] and set out a comprehensive agenda for constitutional reform.[476] The rising levels of euroscepticism, in turn, linked to fears of losing the 'European Social model' translated into a lack of commitment towards the Lisbon goals. When the Commission proposed a new stage of postal liberalisation there was strong resistance by the EP, EcoSoc, interest groups, and within the Council.

In its first reading, the EP rejected the postal directive's key provisions. It inserted an across-the-board reserved area weight limit of 150 g which would open only 6% rather than 20% of the market. Moreover, it removed special services and pushed back the directive's expiry date from December 2006 to the end of 2008. Finally, the EP insisted on greater guarantees to preserve a universal service and called for a high level of social protection to be included among the goals of the postal industry. The EP was roughly split along geographic lines. The Dutch, Belgian, and Nordic liberals tended to back the Commission proposal, while French, Greek, and Portuguese MEPs rejected it.

The EP's views were echoed by EcoSoc. Its November 2000 opinion urged for caution over further opening of the postal sector, questioned the full liberalisation of special services and outgoing cross-border mail, and agreed with pushing back the directive's expiry date.[477] While EcoSoc opinions carry little legal weight, politically Belgium could not ignore them. European public postal operators supported them and their voice was much stronger than that of the pro-liberalisation business and consumer organisations which were slow to organise themselves.

The Commission accepted the amendments related to the Community's social tasks, but discarded anything that would water down its initial proposal.[478] This included the EP's changes to the weight limit for monopolies, suggestions to reserve direct and outgoing cross-border mail below 150 g, and the deletion of special services. In addition, it rejected any amendments that allowed the extension of postal monopolies or weakened the detailed timetable laid out.

The directive was not less conflictive in the Council where the Belgian Presidency faced two polarised camps: The Nordic-Germanic camp on the pro-liberalisation side versus the Franco-Mediterranean camp opposing further liberalisation. Austria, Ireland, and the UK did not fall clearly into either grouping. British postal unions predicted up to 50,000 job losses as a result of the Commission proposal. With a general election looming, the government seemed reluctant to side with the liberal camp.

As the Commission and the EP, the Member States differed on the proposed weight limits, outgoing cross-border mail, special services, and the deadline for full liberalisation. France and the UK agreed with the EP on maintaining a monopoly on all letter mail below 150 g. Greece, Luxembourg, and Portugal argued for an even higher weight limit. Sweden, Denmark, Finland, Germany, Austria, Belgium, and the Netherlands, in turn, considered the 150 g limit too high. The pro-liberalisation group defended their position referring to the mandate agreed at Lisbon. The anti-liberalisation camp claimed that the Declaration on Services of General Interest, adopted at the Nice Council, was a mandate for halting liberalisation.[479]

Major differences also existed over the full liberalisation of outgoing cross-border mail. Ireland, Greece, Spain, Luxembourg, and Portugal sought exemptions on the grounds that this category accounted for a bigger part of the national operator's turnover than in other Member States.

As to the provision regarding special services, Spain, France, Greece, and Italy took a similar position to the EP. They argued that exposing all specific services to competition could stifle the universal service's ability to evolve. Instead, they suggested fixing a price, whereby services above that price would be liberalised. The Commission claimed this would cause economic, legal, and technical problems.

The most controversial issue, however, was the deadline for full liberalisation. Austria, Finland, the Netherlands, and Sweden supported Belgian proposals for full liberalisation by 2009, but were prepared to grant exemptions to some Member States as happened with telecommunications liberalisation. Italy preferred a 2012 deadline, while France, Greece, Luxembourg, and Portugal were against a deadline at this stage. Denmark and the UK tried to push for a solution whereby the Commission would assess in 2006 whether fixing a 2009 deadline would adversely affect the universal service. If it did, the Commission would come up with an alternative, but if did not, full liberalisation would happen in 2009.[480]

In the light of these obstacles, observers raised doubts whether Belgium could conclude the dossier during its presidency.[481]

Central Africa

Similarly, Belgium faced significant hurdles to pursue its foreign policy objectives. After September 11 the 'war against terrorism' and military invasion in Afghanistan moved to the top of the Council agenda. Moreover, it damaged Belgium's authority as the EU's external representative. Although European leaders expressed strong solidarity with the US, Bush's handling of the terrorist attacks and his virtual unilateralism led to transatlantic tensions and exacerbated inter-European rivalries on who had most influence over the US. France, Germany, and the UK decided to hold their own private talks on the war without involving the Belgian Presidency.[482]

Belgium's external agenda was complicated further by concerns over enlargement and the ongoing conflicts in the Middle East and Macedonia. Finally, the Belgian Presidency had to prepare the EU for the November WTO meeting and the next round of international climate change negotiations. Both involved dense diplomatic activity given the failure of the 1999 Seattle WTO negotiations and US opposition to the Kyoto Protocol. In the light of this difficult international context, it was by no means obvious that Africa should move up on the EU's external relations agenda.

The developments in the Great Lakes itself were not encouraging either. War had broken out in the DRC in 1998 involving Angola, Chad,

Namibia, and Zimbabwe, whose troops aided the Kinshasa government, and Burundi, Rwanda, and Uganda that supported Congolese rebels. The Lusaka peace deal of July 1999 was never successfully implemented and although the new Head of State Joseph Kabila (son of Congolese President Joseph Kabila assassinated in early 2001) restarted the protracted inter-Congolese dialogue (ICD) during the Belgian Presidency, it was suspended after a week.

A further obstacle to the development of a coherent EU–Africa dialogue was the Belgian Presidency's lack of African counterparts to liaise with. The Organisation of African Unity (OAU) – founded in 1963 to promote development and international cooperation – was ineffective and largely seen as a dictators' club by the EU states.[483] Even though the creation of a successor organisation had been decided in March 2001 to promote democratic institutions and good governance, this new African Union (AU) was not formally launched until July 2002. Similarly, the initiative of a New Partnership for Africa's Development (NEPAD) was in its early stages. Initiated by South Africa, Algeria, and Nigeria, and later joined by Senegal, it was to facilitate economic development and construct a common African platform from which to engage with the international community. However, at the start of the Belgian Presidency it had only just been formally presented.

Political violence in Zimbabwe and the repressive nature of the Mugabe regime also overshadowed Belgium's intentions to advance the EU–Africa dialogue. In October 2001 Zimbabwe rejected the EU's ultimatum to decide whether to allow EU election observers into the country. This led to EU sanctions on the regime a few months later. A senior official judged,

> It is difficult for a presidency to plan anything when it comes to Africa. Something will always happen that takes away your attention of Africa and something will happen in Africa that prevents you from doing anything there.[484]

Apart from the unfavourable external climate, the Belgian Presidency was confronted with institutional hurdles, Member State disinterest, and preference divergence in the Council.

Amongst the institutional hurdles was the fact that so far the Great Lakes had been looked at from a development rather than foreign policy perspective. The EU's development ministers met only three times a year while the foreign ministers met monthly. Hence, despite institutionalised relations with Central Africa ever since the Community's creation, Africa had hardly featured on the Foreign Affairs Council. Michel's immediate challenge was therefore to move Africa from the development into the foreign ministerial domain and bridge the much criticised gap between the EU's development policies and the CFSP. A Belgian official stated,

> Our view was that the EU's relations with Africa have been too development driven. It needed a strong political attitude.[485]

Moreover, there was a lack of interest in Africa. With the end of the Cold War, the continent's geo-strategic importance for Europe declined. The African countries depended much more heavily on Europe for aid, markets, and political support than Europe depended on them. With the exception of the other former colonial powers (mainly France, the UK, and Portugal), the Member States felt unaffected by African events.[486] Instead, Yugoslavia, German reunification, and Eastern Europe dominated the foreign ministers' agenda in the 1990s. Thus, the Belgian Presidency had to 'mobilise interest in the Council'.[487]

However, France and the UK – two of the EU's most powerful Member States and key players in the Great Lakes region – preferred keeping Africa off the EU agenda. Both saw their special relationships with individual African states as part of their national foreign policy prerogatives.[488] A practitioner confirmed,

> The UK and France have for the longest time not been interested in doing anything on Africa on EU level. They were taking their own initiatives, for example the UK initiative of a Commission for Africa. The UK does not want the EU to interfere with what they are doing. The French are the same. The French financed all their projects themselves.[489]

France and the UK were also at odds with themselves on Africa which manifested itself in the EU and UN Security Council. The UK, generally supported by Germany and the Netherlands, seemed inclined to support Eastern Congo's accession to Rwanda who had allegedly sent troops to the region to protect itself from continued attacks by those responsible for the 1994 genocide that had fled to Eastern Congo.[490] France, whose view was shared by Belgium, regarded Rwanda's security concerns as an excuse to gain *Lebensraum* and access to mineral resources in the Eastern Congo. They supported the ICD, preserving the Congo's unity and restoring its sovereignty through the withdrawal of foreign troops and protection of ethnic minorities. Unsurprisingly, the EU's capacity to formulate a common regional policy had been strongly limited in the past.

Furthermore, there was resistance to Belgium's new moral approach. The year 2001 was the international year of mobilisation against racism with a UN world conference being held in September. Belgium saw the event as a unique platform to present its new foreign policy and apologise on behalf of Europe for the sufferings caused by colonialism. Fearing excessive financial implications, the UK and the Netherlands, however, were not ready to issue such an apology.

In the light of these disagreements in the Council, neither Solana nor Patten was keen to prioritise Africa. Solana had assigned an entire unit of the Council's Policy Planning and Early Warning Unit to work on the Western Balkans and only one staff member on Africa:

> Solana was very reluctant. He was afraid that no sufficiently strong common position could be generated to make it worth while for a troika to visit Africa. Instead his key foci were the Balkans and the Middle East. Patten, in turn, used to be development minister for the UK. But Africa was not at all his priority. Also Patten shared the UK view, which we did not share. He needed to be convinced.[491]

How Belgium tried to overcome this long list of obstacles both with regard to postal liberalisation and the EU's Africa policy and with what level of success is examined next.

III. Overcoming the obstacles: the strategic process

Ex-ante presidency preparations

Similar to the Finnish Presidency, to overcome the numerous obstacles, Belgium planned its presidency long before its term. In case of the postal directive, policy preparations involved internal dialogue and assessment of the state of play at EU level. With regard to the EU's Africa policy, Belgium carefully analysed potential deliverables.

Postal liberalisation: assessing the state of affairs

Belgian Presidency preparations began a year to a year and a half before assuming office. To identify the priorities a special presidency cell (SOO) was set up at the PM's office in March 2000 (see below). By June/July 2000 the first brainstorming sessions with the ministers and civil servants were held.[492] From September onwards Belgian officials started producing notes and dossiers on each of the broad priority issues, including postal liberalisation.

Internal dialogue on the domestic impact of further postal liberalisation commenced six months ahead of its presidency. Particularly the trade unions feared rising unemployment. However, Belgium's internal co-ordination system managed to 'get everyone to agree that postal liberalisation was necessary'.[493] It decided not to go for a 'brutal opening of the sector, but something more gradual'.[494] The government also met with the respective Belgian interest groups and attended high-profile lobbying events on postal liberalisation.[495] Finally, in June 2001 the Belgian parliamentary Committee on Infrastructure, Communications, and Public Enterprises organised a hearing on universal services at the Belgian Chamber of Representatives.

To trace the progress of the new postal directive, Belgium started contacting the Council Secretariat and the Commission around September 2000. Most Belgian officials at the Permanent Representation considered the Council Secretariat the best presidency resource during the preparation phase of the IM dossiers and while holding the chair position:

> The role of the Council Secretariat was very much that of an administrative supporter to us. They prepared meetings, sometimes suggested solutions before and after a meeting and helped prepare COREPER.[496]

> The Council Secretariat wrote the memos on the Member State positions and aided the presidency. Its role has been ever more important and growing. I think it can off-set the Commission and any influence that may come from Commission bargaining.[497]

The EU–Africa dialogue: assessing deliverables

Similarly, the decision to focus on the creation of a more coherent EU–Africa dialogue and conflict prevention in the Great Lakes was the result of careful preparations more than one year before taking office. The preparations served to 'anticipate events and assess deliverables, possible outcomes of ministerial meetings and where Belgium [could] take initiative'.[498] The Belgian government initially thought about a common strategy on the Great Lakes rather than 'merely' generating a body of Council conclusions on the region. However, it dismissed this idea after evaluating the poor implementation record of previous common strategies. Council conclusions were considered 'a gentler way to bring about what [Belgium] wanted'.[499]

In addition, during the preparation phase Belgium realised that, to drive forward the EU–Africa dialogue and agree something meaningful, any event on African issues would have to involve African heads of state or ministers:

> We discovered that the Africans were coming in huge numbers to meetings but were unable to negotiate anything. They were not organised enough. By June 2001 we knew that to agree anything meaningful would be difficult – the only level that counts in Africa is the level of head of state or maybe the ministers.[500]

Thus, Belgium decided to pick up under its presidency the ministerial meeting that had been agreed within the Cairo Action Plan.

As the Finnish Presidency, Belgium tried to overcome a number of obstacles *before* its term including the neutrality constraint, the gap between the EU's development cooperation and CFSP policies, and the general disinterest in the region. To ensure its presidency would not be perceived as blatantly pursuing national interests, Belgium started a close dialogue on Africa with the Portuguese Presidency in the first half of 2000 and co-ordinated initiatives regarding conflict prevention with its immediate predecessor, the Swedish Presidency. The Contonou Agreement agreed under the Portuguese Presidency already contained provisions on peace-building and conflict prevention.[501] With a view to operationalising these provisions Portugal, Sweden, and Belgium sponsored six case studies of the EU's political and development response in conflict-affected countries (including the DRC). The studies were to provide the basis for discussions during the Belgian Presidency.

Belgium could also build upon the results of the Gothenburg Summit, which had adopted a programme aimed at improving the EU's capacity for conflict prevention. In addition, it asked the Council to identify priority regions for preventive action, invited recommendations for the further development of the programme and agreed to draw up yearly surveys on potential conflicts in Africa and deepen cooperation with the UN. In close collaboration with Sweden, Belgium achieved the breakthrough at the May GAC which adopted a new Common Position on conflict prevention, management, and resolution in Africa[502] and mandated the Belgian Presidency to develop a conflict prevention concept focused specifically on the Great Lakes:

> The Council [invites] the incoming presidency further to pursue and develop EU policy in the Great Lakes region as a concrete example

of the application of the Common Position and to report back to the Council at an early opportunity.[503]

The Common Position provided the bridge between development and foreign policy interventions that Belgium had sought and legitimised Belgian Presidency attempts further to integrate the political and development dimensions of the EU's Africa policy.

To generate greater interest in the region, in the months ahead of the presidency, Verhofstadt and Michel were very outspoken about the humanitarian crisis in the Great Lakes and the international community's responsibility to prevent and resolve conflict in Africa.[504] Their arguments centred on three elements. First, they made the moral case – hard for any to reject. They stressed Europe's historical responsibility towards former colonies and for their difficulties today. Second, similar to the Finnish case Belgium stressed the positive-sum nature of its initiatives by highlighting the strategic interest to support peace initiatives in regions that are geographically close to it. The Belgian Presidency argued that Europe is the 'natural partner' of Africa just as the US is a natural partner of Latin America and Canada. It introduced the notion of 'continental bilateralism' and insisted that it was implementing and developing already existing initiatives rather than specific Belgian interests. Third, Belgium tried to transmit both to the Great Lakes countries and its EU partners that it did not have a 'hidden agenda'. As Koen Vervaeke, then Belgium's Special Envoy to the Great Lakes region, said,

> Our commitment is an honest one without a hidden agenda. Our only goal is the well-being of the population. Strictly spoken, Belgium no longer has any vital interests to protect in Central Africa, even in the DRC, despite its potential riches. But Belgium is convinced that it has a moral responsibility to demonstrate solidarity with the region in Africa it knows best and where it still has numerous ties.[505]

To give weight to its arguments, Belgium took a number of national initiatives ahead of its presidency. These included a global plan for intervention in the region titled 'The Construction of Peace in the Great Lakes Region: A Belgian Plan of Action', a new 'Peace and Justice programme', an agreement to liberalise state loans frozen since 1990, advocating the establishment of a certification system for diamonds to avoid illegal exportation, and Verhofstadt's visit to the DRC on 30 June to commemorate its 41st independence anniversary. Since 1988 no Belgian leader had been to the country.

Verhofstadt assured the Congolese people that their 'suffering [had] gone on long enough'[506] and of Belgium's commitment to engage its western partners in assisting the peace process:

> What we have come to say in humility is that we will do all we can, with others, with the EU, the US and the whole international community, to create conditions in which the Congo can be reborn.[507]

During the visit bilateral agreements totalling 18 million US dollars were signed. Calling for the demilitarisation of the Eastern provinces of Kisangani and the resumption of the ICD, Verhofstadt also promised to lobby for international debt relief and to consider cancelling the Congolese debt to Belgium.

Belgium's initiatives were echoed at EU level. Prodi signalled Commission willingness to look into the resumption of development aid to the Congo – suspended since the early 1990s. In March 2001 it had already adopted a 28 million aid programme directed at restoring the rule of law and two months later the Commission had released 120 million euros from the EDF for medical care and food supply for a 24-month test period. Patten further pledged 1.9 million Euro to support the Congolese peace process and promised to revisit the so-called National Indicative Programme (NIP) for the DRC which had been designed against the background of the Lusaka peace agreements to provide substantial assistance to the country.

Belgium's efforts also sparked positive reactions in the EP:

> We acknowledge the fact that, precisely because of its historic responsibility for Africa, the Belgian presidency will be making this a particular priority. We support this.[508]

In sum, ahead of its presidency Belgium already started to give impetus to EU Africa policy through its discourse and national initiatives. In addition, it assessed the tools of conflict prevention that were being put into place to then put the Great Lakes region at the fore of the EU's foreign and development policies providing a test-bed for these new structures and processes in conflict prevention. As a Commission official said,

> The process drives the whole thing. The structure for co-ordination had been set up by the Swedish Presidency so that a regular pattern could start.[509]

Thus, by the time Belgium presented its presidency programme with Central Africa ranking ahead of the Western Balkans or the Middle East, the country's heavy emphasis on Africa was respected and took nobody by surprise.

The presidency's agenda-setting powers

Nonetheless, the launch of the Belgian Presidency Programme was widely criticised. To his own team's surprise, Verhofstadt presented it in early May.[510] This offended the Swedish Presidency who still had two months ahead. Belgium also presented an unprecedented long list of 16 priorities. Apart from Belgium's main presidency theme – the future of Europe – each of its 15 ministers had been asked to communicate their key priority to the PM.[511] Unsurprisingly, many judged the Belgian Presidency as 'too ambitious'.[512] Verhofstadt's response was simply to ask for judgement to be reserved for six months and promise the publication of a scoreboard at the end of the Belgian term. How then did Belgium 'score' with regard to the postal liberalisation and the EU's policy towards Central Africa?

Postal liberalisation: progress and setbacks

Upon assuming the presidency Belgium increased diplomatic activity on the postal directive. Indeed, few meetings had dealt with the issue during the previous six months. Belgium ensured that the outstanding technical issues were taken up at working group level and dedicated several COREPER meetings to the directive.[513] Its presidency compromise went considerably further than what the anti-liberalisation camp had in mind, but weakened the Commission proposal slightly. It contained three phases – an idea that had first floated under the 2000 French Presidency. The first phase, to commence in 2003, consisted in reducing the weight threshold for monopolies from 350 g to 100 g. This was lower than the threshold the Southern countries defended and the 150 g that France, the UK, and the EP had advocated. In 2006, the second phase was to start reducing this limit further to 50 g. Thus, the Commission's goal to liberalise 20% of the market by 2003 would only be reached in 2006. Full liberalisation was to be achieved in the third phase in 2009. This was a balanced compromise that pushed for full liberalisation, but gave Member States, including Belgium, time to prepare their national postal operators for competition.

Before its October Telecommunications Council, the Belgian Telecommunications Minister Rik Daems got involved heavily conducting informal bilateral consultations to identify the tricky issues. An official recalled,

> The Council was on a Monday and on the Friday before I had a long meeting with our minister discussing the sticky points. He asked me to get him the mobile numbers of all the ministers who still had concerns. He phoned all of them over the weekend. He held many informal bilateral last minute consultations over the weekend to solve any difficulties. These kind of bilateral consultations are normal for a presidency. This is the reality of politics.[514]

Belgium successfully brokered agreement on the first two phases and the full liberalisation of outgoing cross-border mail in 2003. However, to accommodate the specific characteristics of the postal services of Greece, Spain, Portugal, Ireland, and Luxembourg, Member States in which outgoing cross-border mail accounted for an especially large part of the national postal provider's turnover could get exemptions.

In addition, the Belgian Presidency's common position deleted the paragraph about special services. France argued strongly that exposing such services to full competition would stifle the ability of the public service to evolve.[515] Spain, France, Italy, and Luxembourg considered that additional restrictions may be necessary to guarantee legal clarity and avoid circumvention of universal service. Another group of delegations (Germany, Finland, the Netherlands, Portugal, and Sweden) rejected the definition of special services.

The third phase remained the most difficult and the decision on full liberalisation had to be postponed until 2007. Nonetheless, the Belgian Presidency laid out a process how to reach this decision. It was decided that the Commission should assess the impact of full liberalisation on universal services and present recommendations to the Council and Parliament by 31 December 2006. On the basis of this assessment the Council with the EP was then to decide whether to go ahead with full or further liberalisation. This was a creative solution that made the 2009 deadline favoured by Belgium not impossible, but subject to review and built on similar suggestions by the UK and Denmark:

> We did not achieve to agree on 2009 as the final deadline. However, due to the creativity of the Belgian Presidency, there was an agreement that did not rule out the 2009 deadline. I think we are good at these compromises because we do them a lot internally. Our approach is not to keep hammering on the nail and insist to the

very end, but be creative and suggest solutions without excluding our goal.[516]

The Commission supported the outcome and other governments argued that the decision struck 'the right balance in line with the view of liberalising the market while maintaining the universal service'.[517] The only country that voted against the Belgian Presidency compromise was the Netherlands and Finland abstained. Nonetheless, the nature of the outcome can be considered positive-sum. The agreement made neither the Netherlands nor Finland worse off. Both countries simply would have liked the compromise to go further, but the agreement was preferable to the status quo.

The Great Lakes: greater coherence and more effective conflict prevention?

Belgium used its presidency to sketch out a common policy for the Great Lakes and develop a more pro-active and coherent EU Africa policy. To reconcile Franco-British policy differences towards the region and gain support for increasing aid to assist the peace process, Belgium raised the issue in its tour of the capitals at the start of the presidency and put the Great Lakes on every GAC agenda.[518] At his first GAC Michel briefed the Council about his and Verhofstadt's visit to the Congo, Belgium's national action plan, and their ideas for the region. He argued that unless help was given to the DRC, the window of opportunity that opened with Kabila's son assuming power could be lost. Belgium's presidency conclusions committed the Council to working towards 'an extensive, consistent, coordinated EU role in the Great Lakes region' and specified that 'the desired consistency should be found in particular in [Member States'] political perceptions, [...] diplomatic action and [...] aid and cooperation policies'.[519] The Council agreed to continue monitoring the disarmament, demobilisation, reintegration, and repatriation (DDRR) plan; the withdrawal of foreign troops; and the ICD. In addition, Belgium got the Council's general backing of the gradual resumption of aid should the peace process progress.

To help Kabila meet EU expectations, the Belgian Presidency assumed the role of an external mediator. It engaged the presidents of the Great Lake countries and Zimbabwe in a political dialogue on the main aspects of the Lusaka accord and sent the EU's first ever troika to the region. Under Belgian chairmanship the Council endorsed the troika in support of the peace process[520] and managed to agree the broad aim of the mission: confirm the EU's political and financial commitment to the Great

Lake countries; examine their progress; and inform them about the EU's short-term support measures.[521]

In addition to the DRC, the troika visited Angola, Zimbabwe, Burundi, Rwanda, and Uganda. In Angola, the DRC's most important military ally, the EU delegation affirmed that the Lusaka peace process was the only solution to the conflict. With Zimbabwe's President Robert Mugabe it discussed the withdrawal of troops from the Congo, human rights, and the respect for the rule of law. While visiting Burundi, the troika urged the armed rebels to negotiate a ceasefire and promised to help the government address poverty, rehabilitate its infrastructure, and strengthen democracy. Rwanda, in turn, was encouraged to engage directly with the Congolese authorities to dismiss its security concerns. Crucially, the troika established that the ICD would reopen in early 2002.

By December 2001 the European Council decided to resume aid to the Congo. After considerable debate between Britain, France, and Belgium, it committed itself to release 108 million US dollars in development funds. Given that EDF aid had – unlike emergency funds from the Commission's Humanitarian Aid Office (ECHO) – been frozen since 1990, this was a significant success. Other achievements included the adoption of a common position on Rwanda and a Joint Action on Burundi. The common position on Rwanda established that the EU would pursue a political dialogue with the Rwandan government on its regional foreign and security policy, commitment to the peace processes in the region, and troops present in the DRC.[522] The joint action on Burundi, in turn, released EU funds to support the deployment of a special protection unit for the safe return of exiled politicians. In addition, the mandate of the EU's Special Representative for the Great Lakes region was renewed until December 2002.

Pushing its idea of a more holistic approach that would also include a military and diplomatic dimension, Belgium linked the formulation of a common policy towards the Great Lakes closely to conflict prevention. As provided for by the Gothenburg programme, the Belgian Presidency scheduled an initial discussion on potential conflict situations in July. Following a presentation by Solana, Michel led a debate on the EU's early warning instruments and how they could be used to strengthen conflict prevention. The Council welcomed particularly the Commission's and the Council Secretariat's intention to present to the EU's Political and Security Committee (PSC) more detailed reports on ongoing or emerging conflicts and emphasised the need to increase cooperation with relevant international organisations, NGOs, and civil society.

The role of civil society in conflict prevention and the implementation of the Cotonou Agreement had been the subject of two preceding events held on initiative of the Belgian presidency in cooperation with NGOs and the ACP Secretariat. Their results included recommendations to extend the role of NGOs in creating and implementing development initiatives and the outline of an action plan enhancing political and financial cooperation, dialogue on trade negotiations, decentralised cooperation, civil society, and the implementation of the Cotonou Agreement.

The discussions of the EU's ability to respond to crisis situations continued at a further seminar on the six case studies commissioned with Sweden and Portugal. It recommended a new framework for development assistance consisting of a mix of regional and country-specific strategies and short- and long-term initiatives, the deepening and extending of the political dialogue and mainstreaming conflict prevention across the EU's policy spectrum through addressing it in a greater number of working groups. To strengthen EU capacity, its conclusion argued, the number and quality of EU staff working in conflict-affected regions should be increased and to enable more rapid responses EU delegations be given more decision-making authority over local fund management. Reflecting Belgian arguments for greater flexibility regarding the conditionality principle, the seminar conclusions further suggested donors take risks despite concerns over corruption.

The recommendations and operational conclusions of these seminars were fed into the November Development Council which welcomed the action plan and urged the Commission to submit a communication on the participation of civil society in the EU's development policies and refine its development co-operation tools in fragile and conflict-ridden countries. The Spanish Presidency was invited to further the work done by Belgium, Sweden, and Portugal.[523]

Other concrete achievements in the area of conflict prevention include the Council's Common Position on combating the illicit traffic in conflict diamonds at the GAC on 29–30 October committing the EU members to conduct negotiations to establish an international diamond certification scheme in the context of a binding international agreement.

To develop the EU–Africa dialogue at continental level, the Belgian Presidency took three initiatives: a working meeting with the NEPAD initiators and the OAU; high-level meetings with sub-regional organisations such as the Economic Community of West African States (ECOWAS); and the EU's first Africa–Europe Ministerial Conference.

The working meeting with the NEPAD initiators and the OAU took place on 10 October 2001 to discuss NEPAD's priorities, perspectives, and institutional framework and possible links with existing development and co-operation efforts between the EU and Africa. NEPAD's development strategy and detailed programme of action was hailed as a new phase in the cooperation between Africa and the developed world, in which Africa recognised for the first time that it holds the key to its own development. As the Belgian Presidency programme, the European delegation stressed the importance to develop the EU partnership with the African continent further and expressed strong support for this home-grown effort to resolve African problems.[524] Both sides indicated their resolve to develop a regular dialogue on the New African Initiative and agreed *inter alia*:

- twice-yearly meetings between the initiative's steering committee and the EU;
- a permanent link between the initiative and the European Commission;
- the immediate establishment of a joint reflection group on the relationship between the New African Initiative and the Cotonou Agreement and the Cairo process;
- a pilot project to train civil servants;
- a common group on infrastructure, as a priority area for implementation in the framework of the next European Development Fund Programme; and
- further to consult on the next WTO round to ensure that it addressed the development dimension of trade.

In subsequent Council meetings the Belgian Presidency stressed that NEPAD's success would depend upon developments in the DRC, Burundi, and Zimbabwe. Overall:

> Belgium seized on the NEPAD initiative to organise a meeting with the five presidents. While NEPAD was not Belgium's initiative, they tried to get something out of it.[525]

The high-level meeting with ECOWAS was also held in mid-October. It was the second of its kind to strengthen the cooperation between the two organisations and follow up the Cairo Summit. The meeting reconfirmed the heads of states' desire 'to work towards a new dimension in the global partnership between Africa and Europe'.[526] The EU expressed particular support for ECOWAS' regional integration efforts and welcomed its progress in setting up a mechanism for crisis prevention and settlement in the Mano river countries (Guinea, Liberia, and Sierra Leone). To show the EU's increased support for the peace process in this sub-region, a special EU presidency representative for the Mano River Union (MRU), Hans Dahlgren, had been appointed ahead of the Belgian Presidency. The EU and ECOWAS undertook to maintain regular meetings, while ensuring the continuity of the dialogue through additional meetings with the ECOWAS executive secretary and the EU heads of mission.

As to the first Africa–Europe Ministerial Conference, Belgium fostered agreement on hosting the event as well as a second ministerial conference in 2002. Belgium focused the conference on the eight themes that had been identified at Cairo: regional co-operation, AIDS, food security, conflict prevention, environment, return of cultural objects, debt, and human rights.[527] The meeting reaffirmed the Union's solidarity with the African continent and its attachment to the dialogue initiated in Cairo.[528] Its main outcome was a *communiqué* in which the EU ministers and their African counterparts noted a narrowing of differences and a joint declaration on terrorism. In addition, the African ministers briefed the EU on the transformation of the OAU into the AU and Africa's progress towards political and economic integration.[529] The new NEPAD initiative was formally welcomed as the bases for future cooperation between Europe and Africa. A senior official summarised,

> The ministerial meeting served to present reports – it was an intermediary process to establish initial progress. The Belgian's essentially built on a motion that started at Cairo. They carried it forward and did it well.[530]

Finally, to increase the effectiveness of EU Africa policy, the Belgian Presidency sought to enhance its co-ordination with UN initiatives and international financial institutions. At Belgium's first GAC the Great Lakes region was also among the EU priorities for the forthcoming UN General Assembly. During its presidency, Belgium fostered political agreement on the Member States' commitment to achieve the UN's official public development aid target of 0.7% of GDP and – in conjunction with the Commission – to establish a timetable by when to achieve this target. The October 29 GAC supported an increased coordinating role for the UN Observer Mission in the DRC (MONUC) in the DDRR process, the setting up of an inter-agency consultation mechanism in association with the main donors, and the speeding up of foreign troop withdrawal under UN auspices.

In addition, the joint action on Burundi was a result of co-ordination with the UN. In October 2001, the mediator for Burundi, Nelson Mandela, had requested the EU's financial support for the establishment of an interim multinational security presence in the country and in the context of the peace process UN Security Council Resolution 1375 of 29 October energetically supported the introduction of this multinational presence.

Belgium also participated on behalf of the EU at the Durban UN World Conference against Racism in early September. Despite British and Dutch reservations about any formal apology for colonialism, Michel came up with a text agreeable to everyone. It condemned the suffering caused through slavery and acknowledged that some effects of colonialism persisted into the present. Indeed, his speech on behalf of the EU at the conference itself was not far off an apology:

> Let us remember the many sufferings inflicted by deeds committed at different moments in history. Let us bow respectfully before all the victims. Let us never forget them. Let us pledge to ensure that these misdeeds shall never again be committed.[531]

The EU's conclusions and Michel's statements were echoed in the final conference declaration.[532] Michel also seems to have played a role in saving the conference's face after the US and Israel decided to withdraw from it on the grounds that it contained hateful language against Israel.[533] Rather than staying for three days, as planned, Michel prolonged his stay to a week taking into account that he would be late for the Gymnich informal Council. A senior official judged that Michel's 'personality and commitment made a real difference'.[534]

As to better coordination with international financial organisations to raise funds for the Congo, Belgium convened (with Canada) an informing donor meeting on 3 July followed by a second donor information conference on the DRC on 20 December on World Bank initiative. The first meeting took stock of the recent economic reforms and how to support the nascent recovery process. It agreed to address the country's outstanding debt, develop effective mechanisms for donor coordination and implementation of assistance, and to take a regional approach in some issues. The meeting planned projects amounting to 240 million US dollars for the months ahead. The follow-up meeting subsequently made funds available for the resumption of the ICD and the World Bank, the IMF, and the African Development Bank presented a debt strategy for the DRC.

So far we have seen how Belgium pursued its priorities and that in both postal liberalisation and the EU's Africa policy it achieved many of its goals. But what were the conditions for its success, particularly in the light of the obstacles outlined above?

IV. Conditions for success

The leadership environment, skill, and use of the Council Secretariat

Belgium coped well with the unfavourable domestic and international leadership environment. By publishing its presidency programme so early, it diverted media attention away from its difficult domestic situation (particularly the Sabena bankruptcy) and resolved the coalition's internal wrangling over the presidency priorities.[535] The presidency gave Verhofstadt 'an opportunity to rise above the constraints under which a coalition leader of a smallish, decentralised state must normally labour. [...] For six months [...] Europe gave him a liberty and an authority inside Belgium that he could not hope for when everyday life resumed'.[536] Despite tipping on Swedish toes, the move was strategic. It limited the potential adverse effect of domestic developments on the presidency's agenda-setting power.

To ease regional tensions, the government established an independent commission that agreed – just before the presidency – the Lambermont accord which gave further autonomy and financing to the regions.[537] In addition, the government divided the chairing of the Councils and Belgian country seats in the Council between the federal and the regional governments.[538] Only matters related mainly to federal competence were chaired by federal ministers. Postal liberalisation and the EU's Africa policy fell within these.

Furthermore, Belgium did not allow the rejection of the Nice Treaty to derail its presidency. It treated the incident as 'an internal Irish, not an EU problem'.[539] It continued the accession negotiations as planned and reaffirmed the applicant countries of EU commitment to enlarge.

September 11 had the biggest impact on the presidency's agenda-setting capacity. It took considerable time away off the EU's PSC and 'terrorism, which was barely on the agenda before, moved to the top of the agenda'.[540] It also contributed (together with the Western Balkans) to delay the troika to the Great Lakes. Nonetheless, the troika visit and

Belgium's other Africa presidency initiatives were pursued as planned. One interviewee argued,

> 9/11 led to a lot of additional meetings, but I do not think Africa suffered from this. This shows you that it was a real priority of Belgium.[541]

In fact, the terrorist attacks put the focus on neglected countries and the danger that can stem from them. Indeed, the Council expressed greater commitment to combat poverty, seen as a root cause of terrorism. In this sense it may well have served Africa.

Belgium's quick response to convene extraordinary Foreign and JHA Councils showed that its presidency machinery was able to handle unexpected crises. A senior official recalled,

> 9/11 was completely unexpected. [But ...] it enabled us to show what we were capable of doing. We decided in the night of September 11 that we would convene a special Council. Commissioner Patten and Solana were travelling and it was very difficult to reach them on their planes. So we took the initiative here.[542]

Belgium's reputation of a 'compromise country'[543] was a key asset in dealing with the tensions in the Council in the 9/11 aftermath. Given that successful policy formulation in Belgium depends on the capacity to formulate compromises, package deals and collective bargaining are part of its political culture. Various MEPs argued,

> Belgium is Europe in miniature with all its advantages and disadvantages. This experience is partly the key to the success of the Belgian presidency.[544]

> [Belgium] is traditionally known to be able to reconcile the irreconcilable and, at difficult moments, to have launched visionary proposals that help the European community to progress.[545]

Even though the big Member States talked directly to the US rather than through the Belgian Presidency, Belgium's small size had its advantages, including smooth co-ordination and raising fewer suspicions about its intentions:

> Because of our size limit we worked in small teams and focused very much on our priorities. The advantage of working in small teams is

that you have no problems of co-ordination and the climate is very collaborative.[546]

Small countries often run better presidencies than big countries because the big countries are less trusted than the smalls. People always suspect that big states have hidden interests behind every compromise they put forward, but smaller Member States have fewer national interests to defend, particularly when it comes to the internal market where fewer sectors are economically important to them.[547]

Vital for the successful pursuit of Belgian presidency objectives, particularly with regard to the IM, was the degree of centralisation that was introduced into Belgium's policy co-ordination process. The co-ordination of Belgian EU policy positions is highly 'complicated, time-consuming, and often cumbersome'[548] due to the high number of actors involved and Belgium's complex federal system. It depends not only on co-ordination between ministries, but also on securing agreement between federal and sub-national governments. Apart from the federal government, Belgium has five sub-national governments and parliaments which participate in the development of Belgian EU policy: three community governments and parliaments (Flemish, French, and German) and three regional governments and parliaments (Flanders, Wallonia, and Brussels). The institutions of the Flemish Community and Region have merged.[549] From a constitutional viewpoint there is no hierarchy between the federal government and its sub-national counterparts. Thus, unless each unit's consent is assured on issues that fall within their competencies, Belgium cannot take a position in the Council.[550] How then was such consent achieved during the presidency?

Belgium's system of co-ordination is highly decentralised with different arrangements in each policy sector. Informal technical co-ordination starts with the specialists at the Permanent Representation and so-called 'federal correspondents' feeding Commission initiatives and legislative proposals to their counterparts in the five Belgian governments. The latter are linked through specialised networks and informal contacts which try to establish informal consensus *inter alia* to prevent overload of formal co-ordination mechanisms and the politicisation of issues. The precise structure of these networks differs from sector to sector and tends to be more formalised the greater the intensity of EU activity in a policy area.[551] Belgium's positions in Council working groups are generally established through these specialised networks and informal contacts.

However, once an issue reaches COREPER and ministerial level, formal co-ordination between the federal and the sub-national units as well as the different ministries takes place at the Belgian Ministry of Foreign Affairs (MFA).

The main formal coordinating unit is the MFA's European Integration and Co-ordination Department P11 which brings together the relevant federal and sub-national ministers' personal representatives and the Belgian Permanent Representative in weekly meetings. If they do not reach unanimous agreement on Council positions, the particular matter gets transferred to an Inter-ministerial Conference for Foreign Policy (ICFP), in which the ministers themselves participate. If still no consensus is forthcoming, the so-called Concertation Committee is consulted in which the PM and vice PMs try to foster agreement with the sub-national governments. Should all efforts fail, Belgium is unable to negotiate in the Council and has to abstain if a vote is called. In most cases, however, P11 reaches agreement. Abstaining in the Council is generally worse for Belgian interests than agreeing some package deal between the federal and the sub-national governments.[552] Also, with everybody knowing each other and following the logic of repeated games, the atmosphere in P11 meetings is usually consensual.[553] A senior official confirmed,

> Sometimes it is difficult to reach consensus, but normally this procedure works well. It is the only way consensus can be established[554]

The conclusions reached in P11 are often not rigid, but set the boundaries within which a compromise must fall. Given the large pro-European consensus amongst elites, Belgian civil servants tend to get substantial leeway from their principals.[555] Before COREPER meetings and after Belgium's negotiating position has been agreed through P11, strategic meetings take place how to best defend its position. If these conclude that the mandate given needs adaptation, the issue is referred back to P11.[556] Finally, should difficulties arise during the Council meetings, when competence is shared each Belgian delegation is accompanied by a so-called assessor (either ministers or high-level officials from a sub-national government) allowing for on the spot consultation with regional governments.

The Belgium system of co-ordination for the Council presidency had two key strengths. First, given that representatives from the Permanent Representation (the Belgian ambassador, his deputy, or the Antici and Mertens) participate in the P11 meetings, they could more easily establish their negotiating leverage and bridge the gap between the internal Belgian co-ordination process and the political reality in the Council. In addition, P11 generates personal contact between the people at the Permanent Representation and the ministerial representatives, who could be called informally should problems arise. Compared to other presidencies, Belgian government communication with the Permanent Representation and the EU institutions was also more personal and less costly due to the government's unique advantage of being Brussels based.[557] Belgian Permanent Representative, Frans van Daele, for example, met his most important government interlocutors three or four times a week – common also at lower levels.[558]

Interestingly, the mere fact of holding the Council presidency helped bridge the system's weaknesses including the high number and diversity of P11 participants and its potential of overload. The presidency forced the political leaders to find agreements more speedily:

> In a way things were easier during the presidency, as we could use it to argue that we had a general mandate to find consensus. To be an effective presidency we had to find solutions internally. Thus we used the presidency to find solutions internally. This helped us to work more rapidly.[559]

This was particularly true in case of the postal directive, where internal agreement had been lacking (see above).

The second strength of the Belgian system of co-ordination was the creation, in March 2000, of the SOO at the PM's office introducing a degree of centralisation and a strategic dimension into the co-ordination process. The SOO was headed by a task force presided over by the PM's representative, Peter Moors. It met the day after P11 meetings and was first dedicated to the logistics and the organisation of the presidency and then turned increasingly to content and priorities. It included the chairpersons, Belgium's Permanent Representative, the Director General for EU affairs, and special experts.

The task force followed closely the negotiation progress at the federal, community, and regional levels as well as in the Council and identified problems and strategies how to tackle them:

> The task force was responsible for the day to day co-ordination, to review work in progress, look at the weeks ahead, come up with new initiatives, and to prepare a scoreboard. To assess the progress each week was very important.[560]

This was a significant change. Normally there is little central co-ordination on EU issues. It effectively dealt with the problem that the Belgian ministries enjoy relative autonomy making technical co-ordination problematic.[561] It turned the presidency into a 'strikingly tightly run affair in which a relatively small group of people were involved in most if not all the most important decisions, and one person, the PM, dominated the show'.[562] Finally, the presidency cell strengthened ex-ante co-ordination of positions in the Council:

> The key to our success was – I am absolutely convinced – the consensus we generated on the presidency positions beforehand.[563]

Overall, similar to the Finnish system the set-up was based on political-strategic co-ordination rather than hierarchy. Figure 4 illustrates this complex intra-Belgian intergovernmental and inter-ministerial co-ordination system during the 2001 Council presidency.

Apart from internal co-ordination, the presidency's personal commitment and style, its relations with the other Council members, and the use of the Council Secretariat conditioned its influence.[564]

Personal commitment played a role in both advancing postal liberalisation and developing the EU's Africa policy. Verhofstadt's pro-active 'presidential' leadership style[565] helped to foster agreement on postal liberalisation at domestic level, and Daems' efforts and bilateral ministerial consultations at EU level. One official judged,

> The Belgian Minister was a good chairman. He was good in imagining different compromises and particularly creative about the calendar towards full liberalisation. He worked very hard.[566]

As the only liberal in the Council, Verhofstadt had initially been rather isolated. Nevertheless, Nice had gained him the respect of the other small states whose institutional interests (particularly weighted votes in the Council) he was defending. In addition, since Nice he had successfully cultivated personal relationships with German Chancellor Schroeder and British PM Blair.[567]

Michel's activist style and personal inclination to pursue bold debates which generated tensions on some issue, gained him respect in the area of EU–Africa relations. Given Belgian expertise on

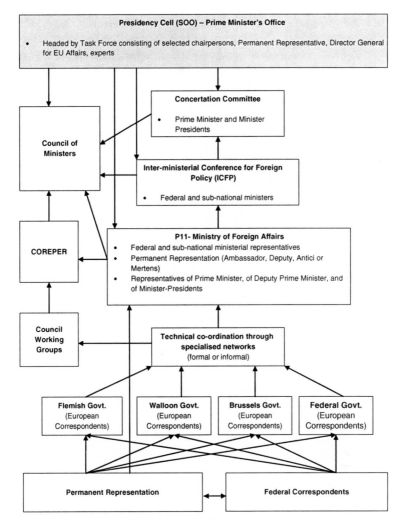

Figure 4 Inter-ministerial Co-ordination During the Belgian 2001 Council Presidency

Central Africa, the presidency felt qualified to lead the EU in this dossier:

> The African diaspora in Belgium, the Belgian networks in Central Africa, and Belgian expertise, make that Belgium can pretend to play the number one in the Central African dossiers and to be the motor of the international Community.[568]

The small group of officials that ran the presidency was also regarded as 'highly competent'.[569] To ensure expertise, Belgium selected the relevant working group chairpersons early and drew upon top-class advisors in Belgium's political and university circles. Training consisted mainly in negotiation simulation and chairing. As Belgium's Permanent Representatives stay in office for much longer than other career diplomats (six years or more), experience, seniority, and negotiation skills at COREPER level were ensured.[570] By the time Belgium assumed the presidency, its Permanent Representative had been in office for five years. Similarly, Belgium's Deputy Permanent Representative had ample Community experience. In areas that where Belgium had less national interests, such as the broad dossier of enlargement, a Dutch and a Luxembourg diplomat were invited into the Belgian Presidency team bridging gaps in staff shortages.[571]

Belgium further enhanced its expertise and information advantage through the extensive use of the Council Secretariat. To determine the negotiation leverage of the individual players a senior official concluded that 'the Council Secretariat is your biggest ally during the presidency':[572]

> The Council Secretariat has a lot of expertise and, even more important, memory. They are a core resource and very useful.[573]

The Council Secretariat's institutional memory was particularly helpful to establish the Member States' negotiation positions on postal liberalisation. As Finland, Belgium tried to look for unanimous, positive-sum agreements rather than bluntly pursuing its own interests.

On occasions Belgium 'had the feeling [it] had to keep the Council Secretariat in check'.[574] Its presidency preparations coincided with the Nice IGC during which the Council Secretariat lobbied hard to establish itself as a player in its own right with a greater political role.[575] However, in the case of the postal liberalisation dossier, Belgium did not let the Council Secretariat dominate the proceedings or formulation of the compromise. One official argued,

> I did not feel that the Council Secretariat took a more political role. We decided which compromise to defend.[576]

In its priority areas Belgium, contrary to some presidencies, wrote all its Council conclusions itself. In this way it kept the Council Secretariat in check.[577] A senior official at the Council Secretariat stated that 'giving policy input rather than technical input only works if a presidency is open to it'.[578] This is much more likely in dossiers that the presidency has not claimed 'its own'.

In case of the development of a more coherent EU–Africa policy, Solana needed to be alerted. Since taking office much of his focus had been on the Western Balkans,

> There was a realisation that we needed to enhance our Africa teams. Michel alerted Solana to this a number of times and Solana [was] listening.[579]

In contrast to the Council Secretariat's IM unit, Solana has taken a political rather than a technocratic role. However, in this case his political role helped Belgium to give Africa a higher status and go beyond lowest common denominator decisions:

> The people at the Council Secretariat were pushing for more than a lowest common denominator outcome. They definitely supported the presidency and took a very pro-active approach.[580]

Heterogeneity, intensity, and distribution of governmental preferences

Both in terms of the heterogeneity and intensity of viewpoints the climate on postal liberalisation in the Council was unfavourable. The Council was split into two blocs. The distribution of governmental preferences, however, was favourable. Germany was particularly supportive of the Belgian compromise. Germany was a crucial ally not only because of its weight in the Council but also because of its close relations with France which needed to be convinced of the Belgian compromise. Furthermore, after Labour had been re-elected in June 2001 the UK's position moved clearly towards the Belgian approach on postal liberalisation. Together with the group of smalls that had already liberalised its postal services and the Commission, this was a powerful coalition.

In case of the EU–Africa relations the heterogeneity of viewpoints was also low centring on the Franco-Belgian versus the UK approach. Portugal and France often gave voice to the presidency's views. Both Portuguese Foreign Minister Jaime Gama and PM Antonio Guterres stressed the need for the EU to play a much more prominent role in development cooperation at various Council meetings and backed Belgium's intention to take initiatives in favour of Africa from the outset.[581] France, in turn, was realising 'that it [did] not have the capacity to deal with different crisis in Africa by itself' and that since the end of the Cold War 'African states [had] become more independent from French influence'.[582] Thus, France became more interested to move things onto the EU level.

Relations between Belgium and France on the Great Lakes had been particularly close since the beginning of 2001. Both countries had invited Mugabe to discuss the possibility of the withdrawal of its 11,000 Zimbabwean troops from the DRC and held bilateral meetings with President Kabila in November 2001. As Belgium, Chirac emphasised the need for the withdrawal of troops from Congo, encouraged Kabila to pursue the ICD, and urged international financial institutions to release aid to the country.

However, through intense activity on the Great Lakes under Belgian chairmanship, the Franco-British differences were easing out. Despite tensions over Zimbabwe and its traditional support for Rwanda, the UK position on the Great Lakes' conflict saw a gradual change during the Belgian Presidency crucial to move towards a common approach and define the troika mission. This change followed a report by Britain's All Party Parliamentary Group on the Great Lakes and Genocide Prevention (APPG) of the House of Commons. After a mission to the DRC, the APPG concluded that although Rwanda's initial intervention in the DRC was justified, its military bases appeared to be more closely linked to the positioning of mineral mines than rebel forces.[583] The group recommended undertaking a study of the threat posed by armed groups operating in the DRC and link British and European aid in the Great Lakes to cessation of illegal exploitation of natural resources and implementation of the Lusaka accords. Furthermore, it urged the UK government to broker a substantially increased aid package for the DRC.

The APPG report also sparked a gathering by fellow national parliamentarians and MEPs who met on 21 November to forge a common policy on resolving the Great Lakes crisis. They concluded that only a regional approach could solve the conflict and that common EU rather than bilateral policies would be needed. They urged the EU governments to prioritise the humanitarian tragedy, especially in eastern Congo. By January 2002 the French and British Foreign Ministers made a joint mission to the Great Lakes to promote peace in the region and foster the impression of a unified EU policy on the area.

Finally, the German and the Dutch national viewpoints were evolving towards the Franco-Belgian approach. Both countries showed more signs of recognising the Kabila government and shifting pressure onto the rebels and the withdrawal of foreign troops. The Netherlands, for example, suspended some of their aid programmes to Rwanda, because of its participation in the Congolese conflict.[584] Hence, the climate in the Council in terms of the heterogeneity, intensity, and distribution of viewpoints became gradually more favourable.

Inter-institutional relations

Inter-institutional relations with the Commission and the EP were similarly important. Belgium has traditionally been a 'very Commission oriented country'[585] and its IM presidency priorities reflected Commission priorities. In its February synthesis report submitted to the Stockholm Council, the Commission had included postal liberalisation as one of its top ten policy priorities for 2001. Hence, from the preparation stages Belgium had discussions with the Commission which became a key ally in dismissing concerns by the more protectionist Member States and socialist MEPs. IM Commissioner Fritz Bolkestein argued that long-term employment in the postal sector could only be safeguarded if it would be able to provide competitive services, responsive to the demand of both business customers and households.[586] Bolkestein also tried to weaken the ideological dimension of the debate by agreeing on the importance of universal services. Nonetheless, the Commission's influence in shaping the final outcome was low (see below) – while backing the Belgian Presidency compromise, it preferred much speedier liberalisation.

With regard to the Great Lakes, Belgium did not have automatic Commission support. Patten had not been to the region before and shared the UK view. Interestingly, under Portuguese Commissioner Joao de Deus Pinheiro responsible for external relations with the ACP states, South Africa, and the Lomé Convention from 1995–1999, the Commission – often in tandem with Belgium – had 'been fighting hard to get more attention for Africa'.[587] However, Belgium managed to get Patten's backing for a Great Lakes troika and its efforts to develop the EU Africa dialogue. An official at the Council Secretariat judged,

> Belgium was crucial to make Patten as well as Solana look at Africa and increase their attention to the region. Now their agenda seems much broader.[588]

As to the EP, in case of the postal directive the PM's unit did not involve the EP much. However, the Permanent Representation was in touch with the Belgian MEPs. Establishing contact with the EP on the directive was important to avoid the directive ending up in the conciliation procedure used in the event of severe disagreement between the Council and the EP.[589] Nonetheless, the EP sided with the anti-liberalisation camp. Compared to the Commission, outcomes in the EP are often more difficult to influence. Much depends on the size of a national delegation within the big party groups – the key structures within the EP. Theoretically, a small state can be relatively influential when it is concentrated, well organised, and ideologically 'median', as the case with the Belgian socialists. These conditions were not, however, met in case of the Belgian liberals. To ensure that the presidency compromise would be acceptable to the EP, Belgium tried to work through its national MEPs and keep regular contact with the presidents of the different committees, in this case the postal committee. These contacts were generated through the Belgian Permanent Representation.[590]

With regard to EU–Africa relations, in contrast, the EP welcomed the Belgian presidency's initiative to give priority status to the DRC and invited the Council to encourage the ICD.[591] In addition, the EP invited Kabila to immediately embark on the process of reconciliation and democratisation, to allow the EU fully to restore its structural aid to Congo. In an emergency session in early July it also adopted a resolution strongly condemning 'the systematic and large-scale pillaging of natural resources and wealth from the DRC'.[592] But was the EP the driving force in the dossier?

V.   Revision of achievements: assessing the counterfactuals

The following section revisits the presidency's achievements and assesses the counterfactuals. Can the outcomes solely be attributed to the Belgian Presidency? What role did the other decision-makers play?

Postal liberalisation

Presidency achievements and the role of other Member States

Postal liberalisation was an area of high political and ideological sensitivity. Although Belgium had to delete the liberalisation of special services and did not reach its goal to fix the 2009 deadline for full liberalisation, the compromise brokered reflected its main interests and took a considerable step forward. Crucially, the timetable agreed did not exclude full liberalisation by 2009. In addition, the Belgian Presidency compromise went much further than the suggestions made by the anti-liberalisation camp. What then was the input by the other Member States? Or had the dossier merely been ready for adoption?

Belgium had not been the only country that tried to conclude the postal dossier. The French 2000 Presidency had also prioritised the directive, but contrary to Belgium, its aim had been to slow liberalisation. Aligning itself with the EP, the French compromise defended the 150 g threshold for monopolies. However, the French Presidency failed to break the deadlock. Even a marathon session of ten hours in Brussels broke down without bridging the gap between the two camps. One official judged, 'The French compromise was simply not enough of a compromise.'[593] In addition, rather than working in tandem, tensions between France and the Commission became increasingly visible and France relied much less upon the Council Secretariat to try to broker its deals.[594]

Given the deep divisions that had been exposed under the French Presidency, the adoption of the dossier was neither inevitable. Since the breakdown of the negotiations in December 2000, the Swedish Presidency – while very much in favour of the directive – hardly touched it. It did not convene the working group on postal liberalisation until very late into its presidency and no further substantive discussions were held at the Telecommunications Councils.[595] The Stockholm European Council of 23–24 March 2001 merely set a deadline of the end of 2001. After informal bilateral consultations, Sweden concluded that 'the positions of delegations have yet to evolve sufficiently to allow for [...] an agreement to be reached'.[596] Thus, even though time pressure was building up to meet the 2001 deadline, the dossier was nowhere closer to a decision when Belgium moved into the chair than under the French presidency.[597]

Although Belgium's three-step compromise built upon ideas that had first floated under the French Presidency and its solution to the deadlock over the time table was aided by suggestions from the UK and Denmark, the detailed balancing of interests and final shape of the compromise was elaborated by Belgium rather than any other Member State. In addition, it was the Belgian administration that did the bridge building behind the scenes both between the opposing camps in the Council and with the EP.

The role of the Commission

Given the sensitivity of the issue and intensity of Member State preferences, supranational Commission leadership was highly limited. While the Commission actively lobbied the Member States and the EP to speed up the adoption of the postal directive, the compromise reached did not originate in the Commission. Indeed, the Commission had to be convinced of its final shape:

> Our allies were the Member States more than anybody else. We had to convince the Commissioner to be flexible and accept the compromise we wanted to go for.[598]

The Commission had initially rejected the suggestions of deleting the notion of special services. Only when both the Council and the EP agreed to exclude special services from the directive, the Commission reigned in. In addition, the Commission proposal had envisaged a less gradual liberalisation process than Belgian's compromise entailed (see above). In short, the final shape of the proposal differed significantly from the Commission's initial proposal and preferences. In accepting the presidency compromise the Commission rendered its agenda influence to intergovernmental leadership. This seems to be the norm rather than the exception:

> All major files generally change quite a bit from the initial proposal. Then the Commission usually backs these changes, in very exceptional cases it turns against a common position reached in the Council. The Commission can think about withdrawing a proposal, but that rarely happens either.[599]

The role of the EP

While the EP got its way on the special services, its overall influence was also low. The majority of EP amendments were outright rejected. Neither the Commission nor the Presidency agreed with the EP provisions to merely liberalise 6% of the postal market or to leave the timetable for further liberalisation open. By March 2002, the EP gave its agreement to open a further 20% of the sector on the condition that the Commission made biannual reports to it and the Council on the application of the directive considering in particular developments concerning economic, social, employment, and technological aspects, as well as the quality of service. In addition, the EP modified some of the directive's final wording. Reference to the 'provision of the universal services', for example, was replaced with 'maintenance of universal services' and reference to 'standard mail services' was replaced by 'items of domestic correspondence'.[600] However, none of the EP amendments changed the Council's political agreement and the directive was adopted without further discussion.

Central Africa

Presidency achievements and the role of other Member States

During the Belgian Presidency the EU reconfirmed its solidarity with Africa and its attachment to the dialogue initiated in Cairo in May 2000. Belgian initiatives contributed to more resources being dedicated to Africa and helped modify the EU framework for providing assistance to crisis-affected countries, in particular the Great Lakes, to one which is more flexible and engages a greater number of actors. In addition, Belgium developed concrete recommendations on how the EU should engage in conflict-affected countries. Officials from the Belgian administration, the Commission, and the Council Secretariat agreed that the Belgian Presidency played an important role in the development of a more pro-active and coherent Africa policy during its term by focussing the mind of the Council and the Commission on conflict resolution and prevention in the Great Lakes:

> The dialogue has become much more active and there is more continuity. The Netherlands had Africa on their agenda and the Irish presidency dealt with it too. So the dialogue is more structured and does not always need the impulse from the presidency.[601]

> The level of attention paid to Africa has changed dramatically. The Belgian presidency was an important building block. It is now on the agenda and even Luxembourg with no tradition of dealing with Africa is now obliged to consider it.[602]

> The Belgian Presidency achieved most progress in the area of conflict prevention when it comes to EU-Africa relations. Conflict prevention had, of course been in the pipeline before. The Commission published a communication on it in April 2001. But Belgium decided to work in depth on this and apply it to Africa. Africa figured much more prominently on the Council agenda than previously. Belgium was trying to push for a fresh look at the situation.[603]

Indeed, although a Belgian diplomat lamented that 'the peace process in the Great Lakes was not sufficiently advanced at the time of the Belgian Presidency to be even more constructive'[604] and it is difficult to assess the precise impact of the presidency, Belgium set the locomotive in motion for long-term EU commitment towards the region.

After the DRC signed peace agreements with Uganda and Rwanda in 2002 both countries withdrew their troops from the Congo and by

•

the spring 2003 the ICD led to an agreement on the formation of a transitional national government formally ending the war. The EU contributed to the stabilisation of the security conditions in the DRC by launching a military operation (Artemis) in 2003 in the Ituri region and its first Police Mission for crisis management in Kinshasa in April 2005. Both were conducted in close co-operation with MONUC. In addition, it decided to establish an assistance mission for security reform in the DRC 'to advice the Congolese authorities in charge of security while ensuring the promotion of policies that are compatible with human rights and international humanitarian law, democratic standards, principles of good public management, transparency and observance of the rule of law'.[605] In 2006, the EU sent 250 election observers to the DRC – the EU's largest mission to that date. The Belgian Presidency can undoubtedly take some credit for generating the political commitment of the EU *vis-à-vis* the DRC:

> The Belgian Presidency wanted to increase EU commitment to the Great Lakes. Look at the Congo now. We are starting to become an actor in the region.[606]

> The Belgian presidency played an as active part as it could. You have to keep in mind that things in this area move very slowly. The EU Africa dialogue was like two elephants that talk.[607]

However, there were also disappointments. For example, there was no systematic follow up of the NEPAD meeting which was judged as 'good in terms of publicity but not strong in terms of long-term results'.[608]

Until the Belgian 2001 Presidency Africa had hardly featured on the GAC agendas, not even Zimbabwe. Similarly, the kind of joint initiatives Belgium started between the Council presidency and the ACP Secretariat General were unprecedented and contributed positively to the EU–Africa dialogue.

None of the other Member States attributed a similar degree of importance to the Great Lakes at this particular point in time. Few countries were interested in Africa and matched Belgian expertise on the Great Lake countries. A Commission official speculated,

> If we would have had a different presidency at the time, for example one with interests in Asia, I think we would have started very differently when it comes to crisis prevention.[609]

Second, those who were interested in the region such as France and the UK were not only reluctant to move their Africa policy onto the EU level, but at odds with each other over their approach. The initiative clearly came from Belgium rather than any of the other Member States.

The role of the Commission

Some have identified the Commission as the key 'entrepreneur' driving forward the EU's Africa policy.[610] In 1996 and 1999 the Commission issued two communications on peace-building and conflict prevention in Africa and co-operation with ACP countries involved in armed conflict.[611] The papers were the EU's first conceptual documents on conflict regulation and the EU's Africa policy.[612] In addition, a joint report on conflict prevention had been prepared by the Commission and the High Representative for the Nice Council in December 2000, and in 2001 the Commission contributed to the European Programme for Conflict Prevention (see below) with another communication that reviewed all recent EU initiatives to promote peace and stability.[613] Its long list of recommendations included setting up a pilot system for the regular exchange of information between the Commission, the Council Policy Unit, and Member State desk officers for the Balkans as well as the Great Lakes. However, in contrast to Belgium, the Commission did not think exclusively about Africa when drawing up its paper on conflict prevention:

> Did the Commission have Africa in mind when it drew up its conflict prevention paper? Yes and no. The paper was not only talking about Africa.[614]

Other contributions by the Commission to develop the EU–Africa dialogue included Commissioner Nielson's visit to the DRC in July 2001 to review the peace process and its impact on EU aid and meeting with Ketumile Masire, the DRC peace facilitator, to cover various aspects of the ICD. His discussions with the signatories to the Lusaka Agreement and Masire paved the way for signing, in January 2002, the DRC's NIP for the Congo worth 32 million euros in humanitarian assistance for health and nutrition/food security as well as relief assistance to the least accessible areas.[615]

However, the Commission had been unable to turn Africa from a passive into an active item on the Council agenda. A Commission official argued,

If you look at the situation before [the Belgian Presidency], Africa was very much off the radar screen even though the Commission had been fighting hard for a while to get more attention for Africa. We were trying to structure the work better and wanted to push Africa up on the list of priorities. But it was Belgium who really helped us to achieve this. In general, vigorous co-ordination by the Commission is refused in the area of foreign policy and there is minimal steering by the Commission.[616]

This suggests that to influence Council priorities in foreign policy matters, forge common views, or change emphasis the Commission depends upon the Council presidency – more so than the other way around. While this relationship is inversed at the implementation stage, the EU dialogue with Africa had not reached this stage yet. In its early beginnings, common approaches had yet to be defined and new emphasis set.

The role of the EP

The EP has limited powers in the development of the EU's foreign policy. Rather than taking initiative, it mostly monitors political and humanitarian developments abroad and issues resolutions. As the Commission, it was unable to elevate the Great Lakes into a policy priority. However, in response to the Belgian programme it took some initiatives in support of conflict prevention in Africa. The EP's Committee on Development and Development Cooperation hosted a conference titled 'Towards a coherent European policy for conflict-prevention in Africa: the challenges of the Belgian Presidency' in Brussels in September. The conference examined the coherence of the Union's policies on the African Continent and the Cotonou Agreement as conflict-prevention instrument.[617] Most important to dismiss EP influence in developing the EU's Africa policy during the Belgian Presidency term, however, is the fact that the EP only became active after Belgium decided to focus the EU on Africa and conflict prevention in the Great Lakes. In sum, while the EP played a constructive role in developing EU–Africa relations, it was not in the driving seat.

Conclusion

Contrary to the neutral broker approach, Belgium used its presidency strategically assuming the leadership both in the postal dossier and in the EU's Africa policy. The liberalisation of postal services had been key to the Belgian liberals despite numerous obstacles at domestic and EU level. The presidency and the institutional changes made for it served as a tool to foster agreement internally and tilt the balance of support towards the pro-liberalisation camp within the Council. Its level of influence can be considered as medium: the final compromise brokered – while not going as far as Belgium had wished – went considerably further than the position of the opposition camp and did not compromise its own preferences. While accommodating its own preferences in the final agreement, it also ensured that all other Member States' concerns were addressed. Despite Dutch and Finnish reservations, the compromise brokered was positive-sum. The presidency's power to set the agenda, lead the discussion, summarise conclusions, and hold informal bilateral discussions were crucial to reach this outcome. The Commission and the Council Secretariat were key allies, but neither assumed the political leadership in this dossier. Belgium firmly kept this role to itself.

Belgian initiatives with regard to the EU's Africa policy are examples of a high level of presidency influence. Despite unexpected international events, Africa and the Great Lakes moved from the backstage into the spotlight. As a former colonial power that sought international recognition and a new image, development assistance and conflict prevention in Africa became the Belgian Presidency's foreign policy theme. Through numerous high-profile events and conferences Belgium nurtured the EU–Africa dialogue and tried to put flesh on the abstract concept of conflict prevention. Belgium used its presidency to be the 'engine for international action in the region'.[618]

In both cases prioritising certain dossiers over others did not automatically lead to results, but required careful preparation, investigation, and coalition-building before and during the presidency:

> The presidency is about having an idea and pushing and pushing over a long period of time. It is not just about the six months you have the presidency. You have to play the game and plan on a grander scheme.[619]

'Playing the game' domestically meant having an effective structure in place to overcome the weaknesses of the Belgian co-ordination system and at EU level constructing a well-functioning relationship with the Commission and Council Secretariat. Equally important in both the postal liberalisation and Africa dossier was to generate allies in the Council. This meant bridging the differences between the Franco-Belgian approach and that of the UK. In Pillar I, the EP and its sceptical stance on the directive was an additional constraint. In Pillar II, Belgium made sure it had the blessing of the Council before the start of its presidency to try to sketch out a common policy for the Great Lakes and seized upon the Swedish Presidency results in the area of conflict prevention.

Despite numerous obstacles and an unfavourable presidency setting, the evidence suggests that a small country can be an effective presidency and broker outcomes that not only satisfy its own preferences but are also beneficial to the EU. Belgium overcame its constraints through early dialogue with all key actors and efficient domestic co-ordination. In both pillars Belgium's efforts were central to reach the desired results. The intensity of Member State preferences and the EP were the biggest constraints in the construction of a compromise on the postal directive, while external events as well as Member State preferences constrained the development of a coherent EU–Africa dialogue and progress in the Great Lakes. Even though Belgium today finds that 'there is still too little attention for African issues at the highest political and international level',[620] under its presidency term it was highly influential in setting the priorities, tone, and pace of the negotiations. A Commission official judged,

> When you have the presidency you can do two things, you can either keep building steadily or try to achieve breakthroughs in certain areas. The case of Belgium and Africa was among the breakthroughs.[621]

To conclude, Verhofstadt's wish with regard to the Laeken declaration 'not to be aloof and neutral' also applied to Belgium's IM and foreign policy priorities.[622]

6
The 2003 Greek Presidency: Internal Market and Foreign Policy Priorities and Achievements

We want to continue the work other EU presidencies began, but we also want to bring forward new ideas, to create new directions.[623]

Introduction

Greece assumed the Council Presidency for the fourth time from 1 January to 30 June 2003. It had joined the Community in 1981, but half-heartedly. EU membership profoundly challenged its political, administrative, and economic structure characterised by endemic statism and clientelism. Significant parts of Greece's state protected business, organised labour, and political class resisted change.[624] The first decade of Greek membership was therefore marked by anti-European sentiment and an intergovernmental approach to integration.[625] Particularly in foreign policy Greece often vetoed common decisions to defend national interests.[626] Unsurprisingly, Greece earned the reputation of an 'unpredictable'[627] presidency with difficulties in 'finding the right combination of language of might, right, and common interests'.[628]

Since the mid-1990s consensus over Greece's role in Europe has grown and reform pressures have taken the upper hand. Today the EU is generally seen as 'a catalyst for political, economic, and social modernisation' and 'a valuable alliance in an unstable neighbourhood'.[629] The Simitis administration was intent to take a more balanced presidency approach than previous governments.

This chapter examines the 2003 Greek Presidency's main IM and foreign policy aims and achievements. On the IM agenda Greece prioritised the Community Patent regulation. The Western Balkans headed its foreign policy agenda. The chapter analyses the presidency's objectives and strategies to pursue them. It closes with a review of Greece's achievements and analysis of the counterfactuals. The chapter shows how the Greek Presidency brokered a common approach on the Community Patent that reflected its national preferences and gave new impetus to Balkan integration.

I. Greek internal market and foreign policy presidency objectives

Enhancing SME competitiveness: the Community Patent

On the Council's IM agenda the Greek Presidency focused on initiatives benefiting small and medium-sized enterprises (SMEs). The latter included the creation of a single system of patent protection through a Community Patent.[630] The regulation formed part of the Lisbon agenda and had been on the Council agenda since July 2000. It aimed at:

- creating a new unitary industrial property right to eliminate barriers to the free movement of goods;
- giving inventors the option of obtaining a single patent valid throughout the EU; and
- reducing the cost of patenting in Europe to encourage innovation and private investment in research and development.

Its key features included equal effect throughout the Community; a centralised Community Patent Court (CPC); a three-language regime (French, English, and German); and a closer link between the European Patent Office (EPO) – which would issue the Community Patent – and the EU. The Community Patent would coexist alongside national and European systems and inventors could choose their preferred protection. These features were to address the perceived shortcomings (legal uncertainty and high costs) of the existing European patent system.

The Greek Presidency programme dedicated a special sub-heading to SMEs stating that it would 'seek to encourage small emerging enterprises, supporting their capacity to innovate'.[631] The adoption of the Community Patent was mentioned under the titles 'The European Knowledge Economy' and 'Bringing a new momentum to research and innovation'.[632] Diplomats and ministers consistently singled it out when presenting Greece's IM priorities.[633]

Greece has traditionally not been a driver behind the IM and is amongst the slowest implementers of IM directives.[634] The EU initiatives regarding SMEs, however, closely reflected its priorities. SMEs play a vital role in the Greek economy. Greece employs 87.5% of its workforce in SMEs.[635] The micro enterprise with less than ten employees is its main business model. SMEs also generate 70% of new jobs in Greece. Unsurprisingly, improving the business environment for SMEs has been a key objective of Greece's Ministry of Development.

Partly due to its high costs, Greek SMEs struggled to access the European Patent system. Thus, Greece fully supported the creation of cheaper protection through the Community Patent.[636] In addition, Simitis 'took a personal interest in intellectual property'.[637] As a former law professor, he had a background in intellectual property and authored a book on patent law. Wrapping up the Community Patent during his presidency was a personal challenge for him.[638] He saw the regulation as an opportunity to show that Greece had matured since its past presidencies and could be an effective broker in sensitive IM issues. One official said,

> Greece wanted to be remembered for its efforts in the Community Patent – a politically very sensitive dossier. It was to some extent a matter of prestige.[639]

However, Greece had qualms about the proposed language regime and the future of its National Patent Office (NPO). Greece defended multilingualism, because many Greek SMEs did not have the linguistic competencies to draft their requests in one of the three EPO languages. As to the future of NPOs, Greece sought to avoid that any enhanced role of the EPO would lead to a major cut in the activities or staff of its NPO.

Strengthening Western Balkan relations

In the foreign policy realm, Greece's key priority was strengthening EU relations with the five Western Balkan countries: Albania, Bosnia-Herzegovina, Croatia, the Former Yugoslav Republic of Macedonia (FYROM), and Serbia-Montenegro.[640] Greece wanted to enhance their 'European prospect' ensuring 'that the EU stands firm in its commitment for eventual full membership of Western Balkan countries'.[641] This was to be achieved by developing the EU's framework for relations with South-Eastern Europe (SEE) – the Stabilisation and Association Process (SAP) – into an 'enlargement-oriented framework',[642] launching a new political forum called the 'Balkan Integration Process' (BIP), and advancing regional co-operation in energy and JHA.

The Western Balkans had been on the EU agenda since the early 1990s. They were recognised as potential EU candidates in June 2000. A special

Summit in Zagreb in October 2000 (Zagreb I) subsequently launched the SAP whose cornerstones are bilateral Stabilisation and Association Agreements (SAAs) to integrate the countries' economies with the EU; strategic financial aid through the Community Assistance for Reconstruction, Development, and Stabilisation Programme (CARDS); and a programme for autonomous trade measures (ATMs) eliminating customs on imports from the Western Balkans. By the time Greece assumed the presidency, SAAs had been concluded with Croatia and FYROM. However, Belgium, Luxembourg, Portugal, Italy, and Greece itself still had to ratify them. The Greek Presidency intended to advance the ratification process, progress towards an SAA with Albania,[643] and launch feasibility studies on the opening of SAA negotiations with Bosnia-Herzegovina and Serbia-Montenegro.

To turn the SAP into an accession process Greece wanted to integrate economic and social cohesion into the EU's policy towards the region and complement the SAP with the BIP. This required substantially more funding. Greece suggested an annual increase of CARDS of 300 million euros during 2004–2006. The funds were to be added to the 4.6 billion euros the EU had allocated to the region for this period and taken from the accession process, from which there were two billion euros left.

The BIP, in turn, was intended to enhance the EU's political dialogue with the region through regular heads of state and ministerial meetings. Greece's plan was to institutionalise annual Western Balkan Summits with the added value of a political scheme for reviewing and achieving SAP objectives. Greece proposed – via the BIP – to discuss issues of common concern, associate the SAP countries to major EU developments, enhance the political visibility of the SAP, deepen the understanding of the association process, and strengthen regional co-operation.[644] A senior Greek official said,

> We want to enrich SAP with aspects learned from the accession process to eventually turn it into an accession process. Our aim is to increase the SAP's visibility and provide political impetus during our presidency. Part of this idea is to create the Balkan Integration Process, a multi-lateral political forum to institutionalise regular meetings.[645]

Greece's focus on the Balkans has geographic, geopolitical, and economic roots. Until the accession of Bulgaria and Romania in 2007 Greece was the only Balkan Member State and shared no land borders with the EU. Enlargement to the Balkans would end its geographic exposure.

Geopolitically, Greece wanted to reduce its external vulnerability. The Balkans have been prone to conflict; the end of the Cold War had revived old nationalist forces and ethnic, political, social, and economic tensions.[646] It brought with it the break up of former Yugoslavia, crises in Kosovo and Macedonia, and difficult political, economic, and social transitions in Albania and Bulgaria. Moreover, illegal immigration, cross-border corruption, and environmental issues became part of Greece's post-cold war security agenda.

Since the mid-1990s, after a sense of threat grew that Balkan instability could inhibit Greek EU integration, Greece had assumed a stabilising role in the region and turned increasingly to multilateral solutions. It initiated biannual ministerial meetings with the Balkans and annual head of state meetings under the South East Europe Co-operation Process (SEECP). The idea of the BIP resembled these initiatives. In addition, Greece became a proponent of a more coherent CFSP with an active defence element.

From an economic point of view, the Balkans – with almost 50 million consumers[647] – are an attractive market. Greece is amongst the largest foreign investors in the region and the only EU country that pursued a comprehensive National Action Plan (2002–2006) for the economic reconstruction and political stability of the Balkans. To co-fund its infrastructure, energy, and institution = building projects, Greece increasingly turned to the EU.

Finally, Greece sought EU engagement to limit economic spill over effects of the crises in the Western Balkans. During the war in former Yugoslavia, Greek EU exports had plummeted given its heavy reliance on road and rail communication through Yugoslavia. Economic crisis in Albania resulted in immigration waves to Greece. Fearing a widening socio-economic gap between Greece and its neighbours and extra pressure on its economy caused by illegal immigration, Greece not only advocated stability in the Balkans, but also a common European frontier policy and border police.[648]

Keen to 'turn a bilateral problem into a European one',[649] the Greek Presidency declared the Western Balkans a 'major priority' and stated that 'capitalising on its knowledge of the region and its tradition of bilateral relations with these countries, [it would] give the necessary impetus to all initiatives [...] aimed at the development of the region'.[650] However, with regard to both its IM and Western Balkan priorities Greece faced a long list of obstacles.

II. Obstacles: the leadership environment, institutional hurdles, and preference divergence

The Community Patent

Both at domestic and, particularly, at EU level Greece was confronted with a tough leadership environment. Economically, the picture was mixed. Although Greek growth rates more than doubled the EU average, the Community entered a period of economic decline with Germany, France, Italy, and Portugal close to or in breach of the SGP. The euro zone was predicted to expand 1% at most and inflation stayed stubbornly above the ECB's 2% target. The outbreak of war in Iraq in March 2003 contributed to the economic uncertainty and the resulting oil price hike overshadowed the outlook for a recovery. Aims to progress with the Lisbon agenda looked therefore bleak. Some even speculated that the Spring Council would be cancelled.[651] European Affairs Minister Tassos Giannitsis feared that the war could 'overthrow [Greece's] work as presidency'.[652]

Politically, the government's fortunes also varied. The ruling Panhellenic Socialist Movement (PASOK) enjoyed a comfortable majority in parliament. Under Simitis it had adopted a resolutely pro-European stance and the conservative opposition had gradually abandoned its traditional automatic dissent of government policy.[653] However, by March 2003 Greece entered the pre-election period and opposition leader Konstantinos Karamanlis began to attack PASOK over its economic policies, failings in infrastructure projects, falling behind in the preparations for the 2004 Olympic Games, and corruption scandals.[654] The election campaign posed an additional burden on the government. It also led to calls for PASOK's reorganisation and leadership rivalry between Simitis and Foreign Minister Giorgos Papandreou.[655]

At EU level, the pending implementation of the Seville Conclusions introducing annual Council work programmes alongside the traditional six-monthly presidency agendas demanded close agenda co-ordination with Greece's successor Italy. Seville also required merging the IM Council with industry, research, and technology. As the agenda of this new Competitiveness Council was wider than the individual sectoral Councils had been, the presidency had to prioritise and allocate time for discussion even more carefully than before.

In addition, Greece assumed the presidency during the highly conflictual Convention endgame and inherited the challenging tasks to facilitate agreement on the EU's new employment strategy, second railway package, energy liberalisation, and occupational pensions, amongst others.

The biggest hurdles as to adopting the Community Patent, however, were disagreements in the Council. Contrary to most IM legislation, it had to be adopted by unanimity (as it involved the creation of a new patent protection system and not mere harmonisation). This proved extremely difficult. Greece was the seventh presidency to inherit the regulation and negotiations seemed increasingly deadlocked. No noteworthy progress had been achieved since the 2002 Barcelona Summit and the Council followed the principle 'nothing is agreed until everything has been agreed'.[656] Thus, Greece had to review all key points of tension: the legal system, the linguistic regime, the division of tasks between the EPO and the NPOs, the latter's quality of work, and the costs and distribution of proceeds from patent processing services.

The main stumbling block with regard to the legal system was fierce German opposition to the centralised CPC. Germany files almost 70% of patent applications in Europe, deals with half of all European patent legal cases, and has courts charged exclusively with patent litigation. It attempted to protect its national tribunals, specialist judges, and expert lawyers.[657] France and the Commission, in contrast, defended the centralised processing of disputes on grounds of judicial coherence and costs.[658]

A further fierce dispute centred on the linguistic regime. The Southern delegations vehemently rejected the Commission's three language approach. Insisting that all official languages were placed on the same footing, they turned the Community Patent into a non-discrimination issue. Germany and Ireland were prepared to accept proposals for a one-language regime. Denmark backed a solution whereby Member States accept that a patent issued in one of the EPO's three official languages has force of law without being translated. Finland suggested publishing every document relating to the patent in one language, but translating their requests and a summary into all official EU languages.

As to the relation between the EPO and the NPOs, Spain, Greece, Portugal, Denmark, Finland, Sweden, France, and the UK recommended a decentralised approach to issuing the EU patent. Contrary to the Commission and reflecting the EP's ideas, they suggested passing much of the EPO's work regarding the processing of Community Patent applications to NPOs. Other delegations, in turn, preferred a centralised management of the system through the EPO. A third group of countries was prepared to accept decentralisation if sufficient guarantees were made on high standards.[659] However, there was disagreement on how to achieve these.

Finally, the cost and distribution of proceeds from patent processing services caused tensions. France and Italy were keen to include rules concerning the allocation of tax revenue in the regulation. The British delegation, however, believed that these rules should be outlined in an agreement between the Community and the EPO. The Spanish, Greek, and Portuguese delegations supported the principle of the allocation of a specific proportion of tax revenue to NPOs in the context of an agreement between the Community and the EPO, but with precise details regarding the allocation of funds set down in the regulation.[660]

The Commission was willing to adjust its initial proposal with regard to the legal system but continued defending the three language regime. Its compromise was to move from an initially fully centralised to a semi-decentralised system, the idea being that litigation would be placed under the exclusive jurisdiction of the CPC until a coherent body of case law had developed. Once this was the case (approximately five years), a number of decentralised chambers – branches of the EC's central jurisdiction rather than national tribunals – would be set up.[661] The Scandinavian countries and the UK supported this compromise. Portugal, Greece, and Italy, in contrast, feared discrimination and selective decentralisation, especially as Germany urged for extremely demanding criteria.[662] The Southern countries wanted to ensure that each country had the option of a regional chamber. However, Germany also opposed any transitional period and – supported by France, Austria, and Italy – argued that decentralised chambers should operate immediately so that the national patent courts would not loose their expertise. In addition, Germany foresaw difficulties connected to the recreation of national patent courts after five years.[663]

As to the EP, its opinion of April 2002 differed considerably from the Commission's. It argued that first instance jurisdiction should be established at national level and national courts should be recognised as 'EU Patent Courts'. Rulings at second instance, in turn, would be adopted by a European Chamber for Intellectual Property. Community Patent applications could be submitted in any EU language. However, for the handling of their application, countries were asked to choose a second 'procedural language' out of a list of five. Applications filed in languages other than these five would subsequently be translated into the chosen procedural language.[664] Finally, the EP supported that NPOs play an important role in the processing of the Community Patent.

The Western Balkans

The Greek Presidency also faced considerable obstacles to pursue its Western Balkan agenda, including the Iraq crisis, the region's slow progress, and scepticism in the Council, Commission, and EP.

The EU's transatlantic relations were severely strained over the legitimacy of the US-led Iraq war. The publication by a number of Member States[665] of letters supporting the US' Iraq policy sparked a political crisis and discredited to an unprecedented degree attempts to develop a common foreign policy. It also threatened to undermine the authority of the Greek Presidency. Rescuing the CFSP, transatlantic relations, as well as the Middle East peace process, and threat of weapons of mass destruction forced themselves on top of the agenda.[666]

The tensions over Iraq spilled over into the enlargement dossier. While Chirac warned the candidate countries backing US policy that they had risked their accession to the EU,[667] Blair congratulated them for their 'courage and leadership in supporting America'.[668] Greek diplomats feared that continued political tensions could derail enlargement and that war with Iraq would 'affect the speed of the decision-making process'.[669]

In addition, the Western Balkans' slow reform progress hindered Greek efforts to advance their accession. Common problems included their weak democratic institutions and rule of law, lack of cooperation with the ICT, and widespread organised crime. The countries were also facing numerous economic problems and restructuring was slow.[670] Another point of tension was the breach of UN sanction by Bosnia-Herzegovina and Serbia-Montenegro by selling arms to Iraq and Liberia.[671] Unsurprisingly, Council members (including the Dutch, British, and Swedish delegations) warned the Greek presidency against moving too quickly in the Balkans.

In addition, the December 2002 Copenhagen Council had only just concluded negotiations with ten candidate countries. Many Member States considered it too early to push Western Balkan integration before mastering this enlargement. Indeed, the Greek Presidency was the first to face the considerable organisational and political challenges after the accession ceremony in April when the ten future members gained observer status in the Council.

The Nice Treaty, which entered into force on 1 February 2003 was supposed to help Greece deal with the problems of increased membership by extending QMV. However, it further expanded co-decision with the EP making careful presidency–EP liaison imperative. The powers of the Commission president were also further enhanced. The Treaty's main institutional changes (composition of the institutions and re-weighting of votes), however, did not affect the Greek Presidency – they did not take effect until November 2004. The constitutional treaty ensuring the future functioning of the Union had not yet been concluded, and the forthcoming IGC promised to be conflictive after the difficult final Convention months. In sum, the immediate and medium-term priority that imposed itself on the EU agenda was fostering agreement on the new treaty followed by a period of consolidation rather than further widening. Sweden emphasised this particularly vehemently.

The Member States further disagreed on the precise approach towards Balkan integration, including whether to follow a policy of conditionality or 'encouragement with fewer strings attached'.[672] While Greece's proposals reflected the latter, the UK and Sweden favoured the former. They developed their own policy approach called 'European Partnerships' which were to serve as a checklist to measure progress. France and Germany were also cautious about Greece's 'unconditional' approach.

Finally, Greece proposed to raise CARDS funding at a time when the EU's key net payers were arguing for a reduced budget. EU support to the region had declined steadily and the Netherlands, the UK, and Sweden thought that the Balkans had already received too much EU money. In addition, they argued that 'after Afghanistan there were other priorities'.[673] In the light of the budget disputes and unfavourable economic climate, Greek demands to increase annual spending on the Balkans by 300 million euros were highly ambitious.

The Commission's response to the BIP was similarly sceptical. It feared a 'duplication of existing processes':[674]

> Every presidency usually wants to invent something new. When Greece approached us with the idea of the Balkan Integration Process we were very sceptical indeed. We did not want any new names to empty shells.[675]

In addition, it was hard to convince Commission technocrats that the region was anywhere close to start accession negotiations. The Commission position was closer to the UK and Sweden than the Greek Presidency, although it proposed slightly more positive 'European *Integration* Partnerships' in a contribution to the Thessaloniki Summit.

'Enlargement fatigue' was also expressed in the EP.[676] In the January plenary on the Greek Presidency priorities MEP Poetterring stressed that Balkan enlargement could only be a long-term project:

> Whilst sharing [the Greek Presidency's] belief that these countries must have the prospect of joining the EU, we must always affirm [...] the long-term nature of that prospect. For the people of the EU will first have to cope with the accession of ten countries [...].[677]

In addition, the EP supported the policy of conditionality and advocated the introduction of yearly benchmarks for measuring each country's reform process. In November 2002 it had recommended suspending a further stage of the SAP and financial assistance if a number of requirements including the respect for democracy, rule of law, and co-operation with the ICT for Yugoslavia were not met.

In the light of the above, official and press circles promised a 'rocky ride' for the EU[678] and wondered if Greece would be 'up to the task'.[679]

III. Overcoming the obstacles: the strategic process

Long-term strategic planning has not been Greece's *forte*. Presidency preparations for pursuing its IM and foreign policy priorities started a year ahead of the Greek term.[680]

Ex-ante presidency preparations

Travaille de Contacte on the Community Patent

Internal brainstorming sessions between the Minister, Deputy Minister, Secretary General, Director General, and the officials at the Greek Permanent Representation commenced in early 2002. During these meetings Council Conclusions were 'de-codified', Commission programmes examined, IM priorities set, and responsibilities divided.[681] It was determined 'where [Greece] wanted to achieve progress, which direction the dossier should go, and what shape an agreement should take'.[682] Once the Community Patent was declared top priority, the Greek Permanent Representation was asked to prepare 'priority papers' and write reports on the dossier.

Contrary to most other Member States, Simitis put the Ministry of Development (General Secretariat for Research and Technology) rather than the Economics Ministry in charge of the regulation. The General Secretariat for Research and Technology took a favourable view of the

Community Patent and Simitis hoped to avoid differences with the Economics Ministry in this way.[683]

At first the geographical distance between Brussels and Athens complicated the presidency preparations. However, this problem was solved by moving staff to the Greek Permanent Representation who – in October 2002 – started to contact the relevant people at the technical and political level in the Council Secretariat, the Commission, and the Member States.[684] One official characterised the preparation phase as *travaille de contacte*.[685]

Reinvigorating the debate on the Western Balkans

The first preparatory sessions on the presidency's foreign policy agenda took place in December 2001.[686] Initially Turkey, Cyprus, and the Balkans topped the agenda. This was gradually narrowed down to the Western Balkans.[687] Papandreou's personal counsellor on the region, Axel-Sotirios Wallden, was subsequently sent to Brussels to prepare the Greek initiative together with Themistokles Dimiris, chair of the Western Balkans working group. A third expert on the Balkans was based at the MFA in Athens.

The presidency preparations revolved around two concerns. First, Greece concentrated on generating political support for a second special Summit between the EU and the Western Balkans (Zagreb II) for June 2003 in Thessaloniki. It was to provide the forum to enhance the SAP and launch the BIP. The Commission was Greece's first contact. A Greek official said,

> The Commission is a necessary ally – it publishes annual reports which are very important. Some Member States have not a precise idea about the issues at stake in the Balkans and they take a lot of inspiration from the Commission. We contacted the Commission in January 2002 immediately after it was clear that the Western Balkans would top our agenda.[688]

Commission support was also crucial because all the instruments Greece proposed as part of the BIP (twinning, technical advice, and exchange programmes) were run by it and its first SAP progress report of April 2002 had suggested

> to establish a new political forum, – the Zagreb process – building on the success of the November 2000 Zagreb Summit, to bring together the political leaders of the region and their EU counterparts

at ministerial level on a regular basis to discuss key issues of common concern.[689]

Seizing upon the Commission recommendations, Greece announced its intention to hold a Zagreb II at the Council's review of the first SAP report on 13 May 2002. To overcome scepticism towards its specific ideas, Greece tried to circumvent Commission technocrats by focusing on the more supportive political level.[690] It held 'as many informal discussions as possible'[691] with Patten and Prodi's Cabinet.

Interestingly, Simitis initially foresaw 'a special troika' to the region rather than a Summit.[692] He was afraid that ministers would not show up at a special Balkan Summit. However, Papandreou judged troika meetings as less effective than ministerial conferences.[693] Thus, during the course of 2002 Greece tried to get the backing of the Member States, the Council Secretariat, and other key actors.

Greece's dialogue with the other Member States commenced immediately after the Commission had published its first annual SAP review and upon announcing its plans to organise a special Summit on the region. Italy, Germany, and France (all big member states) were approached first. By mid-May 2002, a partial success was achieved. The foreign ministers endorsed most of the SAP report's recommendation and welcomed a follow up Zagreb Summit.[694] However, Greece was unable to persuade the Council to turn the Western Balkan Summit into annual events. France, Germany, and the UK refused to commit their heads of state or foreign ministers to yearly meetings.

Once its presidency term neared Greece toured the capitals to discuss the Western Balkans in detail with all Council members.[695] The talks were timed well. They coincided with the launch of three publications on the future of the Western Balkans by a number of respected European think tanks, including the European Stability Initiative (ESI), the Centre for Applied Policy Research in conjunction with the Hellenic Foundation for European and Foreign Policy (ELIAMEP), and the International Crisis Group (ICG).[696] All argued that a new set of policy tools was necessary to guide the Balkans' integration into the EU.

In addition, Greece built upon a number of conferences and ministerial meetings, in particular the London Conference on organised crime in the Western Balkans and the Athens First Ministerial Meeting on a Regional Electricity Market in SEE.[697] Attended by the EU's JHA ministers, the G8 countries, the Balkan states, Solana, representatives from NATO, the OSCE, and other international organisations, the London Conference alarmed policy-makers about organised crime and illegal immigration in the region. The ministerial meeting on electricity in SEE, in turn, set out a strategy to reform the region's electricity sector and integrate it into the EU's internal market (IM). These reports, conferences, and ministerial meetings did not only reinvigorate the debate on the EU's Western Balkan policy,[698] but also legitimised Greece's heavy focus on the region.

The Council Secretariat was contacted last. Relations intensified from October onwards when Papandreou's advisor began fortnightly meetings with Solana and his Western Balkan division. The Council Secretariat agreed that a second Zagreb would be needed and that the Greek Presidency was the 'logical place' to hold it:

> We agreed on the basic notion the Greeks presented to us, namely that we need to enhance SAP and bring it closer to the Balkan States. We thought that Central Europe and their accession path would be a good example for the Western Balkans.[699]

Solana was tasked with sensitising other foreign ministers to the Western Balkans and invited to all key meetings with the region. As his appointment had coincided with the Kosovo reconstruction period, he had been very active in the Balkans. Greece also held special meetings with the other key political actors in the region, such as EU Special Representative for Bosnia-Herzegovina (Lord Paddy Ashdown) and Special Co-ordinator of the Stability Pact (SP) for South-Eastern Europe (Erhard Busek). Both 'pushed hard to help', *inter alia* by writing letters to the Greek Western Balkan team which Greece circulated to the other Council members.[700]

The EP was not involved in the preparations of the Western Balkan dossier. Greece merely kept it informed and Simitis met with the Conference of Presidents of Parliament in December 2002 to explain the presidency priorities.

The second key Greek concern during presidency preparation phase was to draft a working paper on the Western Balkans highlighting six priorities. The first titled 'Peace, Stability, and Democratic Development' was to be ensured by supporting the implementation of international agreements concerning SEE, promoting ethnic and religious tolerance, and combating nationalism. The second was to carry the SAP forward through encouraging the ratification process and establishment of SAAs. Under the third priority of 'Developing the SAP and adapting it to the new environment after enlargement' Greece invited the Council to assess the priorities, effectiveness, and implementation of CARDS and the ATMs and reflect on ways to introduce economic and social cohesion into EU policies.[701] It proposed to enrich the SAP through twinning facilities, increased participation of SAP countries in Community programmes, reviewing mechanisms of the conformity of national with EU legislation, strengthening monitoring mechanisms and assistance in border control management (see above). Fourth, the working document prioritised the launch of the BIP to develop relations between SAP countries and the EU. Fifth, Greece suggested addressing the issues of refugees, protection and rehabilitation of historic and religious monuments, the collection of small arms, investment support, and bilateral free-trade agreements with the Western Balkans. Sixth, it declared the promotion of regional co-operation a prime issue.

On each of these priorities the Greek Presidency prepared detailed policy papers for Council and other sessions which were to generate a special agenda for the integration of the region titled 'Thessaloniki agenda for the Western Balkans: Moving towards European integration' and a joint declaration of the EU and the Western Balkan states. The idea behind adding the Thessaloniki agenda to the joint Summit declaration was to be more concrete than Zagreb I had been. It resembled calls by the CAP and ELIAMEP for an 'Agenda for South-Eastern Enlargement'.[702] A Greek official confirmed,

We wanted an agenda, not simply another declaration.[703]

To overcome Member States' scepticism and the neutrality constraint, Greece cleverly marketed its initiatives by highlighting their positive-sum nature and continuity. The main arguments were that Balkan integration was the safest solution to guarantee regional stability and that its ideas were 'nothing spectacular nor specifically Greek' because it built upon the SAP rather than invented something new and the Commission had already presented a report to this effect.[704] Second, Greece argued that 'after the next enlargement the Balkan States would feel abandoned' if nothing was done.[705] It talked about the importance of avoiding a new dividing line between Europe and the Balkans and maintained that the EU should send a positive message to the region. This would balance the 'feeling of abandonment' and signal to the Western Balkans that EU membership was a distinct possibility. In addition, enhancing their 'European perspective' and thus the prospect of membership, was argued, would provide the necessary incentive for them to pursue their reform path.

The Greek discourse generated high expectations in the region. Ahead of the December Copenhagen Summit, the Western Balkan countries called on the EU to deliver them a 'clear perspective' and recognise them as 'serious candidates'.[706] Croatia's Minister for European Integration stated,

> The Thessaloniki Summit in 2003 planned under the Greek Presidency could be for the Western Balkan countries what the Copenhagen Summit in 1993 was for the current EU candidates from Central and Eastern Europe. It could enrich the SAP and upgrade the status of some Western Balkan countries from potential EU candidates to EU candidates.[707]

The December Copenhagen Summit subsequently underlined 'its determination to support [the Western Balkans'] efforts to move closer to the EU' and like the May Council conclusions welcomed the decision by the incoming Greek Presidency to organise a Summit between the EU Member States and SAP countries.[708]

The presidency's agenda-setting powers

As Finland and Belgium, the Greek Presidency was well aware of its agenda-setting and procedural powers:

> It is your prerogative to set the agenda. Sometimes Member States try to make your life difficult, but in the end you hold the strings.[709]

The joint collaboration with Italy did not hinder Greece to develop SME competitiveness and the Western Balkans into key presidency themes. Indeed, given their geographical proximity, they were 'natural allies' in their political, economic, and strategic engagement in the Balkans.[710]

The Greek Presidency agenda was perceived as 'ambitious but nonetheless realistic'.[711] Prioritising SMEs was regarded as an 'excellent move' in the EP debate[712] and Prodi fully endorsed Greece's programme, especially 'the intense focus on [...] patents [...] and the major obstacles to lasting peace in Europe – the Balkans [...] question'.[713] However, to achieve its presidency goals, the EU's active agendas seemed much more important than Greece's overall programme:

> While the agenda really is the prerogative of the presidency and the presidency's personal work, afterwards [you] hardly look at the document. [...] What is more important is the calendar of meetings and individual agendas which are not just technical, but pure substance.[714]

The Community Patent: towards a common approach?

The Greek Presidency's calendar contained numerous special events on SMEs sending 'positive signals about the Community Patent to all the relevant actors'.[715] Most important were a ministerial conference on SMEs in February in Thessaloniki, a public debate on SME legislation at the March Competitiveness Council, and the Spring Summit. The key conclusions of the events included putting small businesses at the centre of the Lisbon process; integrating the 'Think Small First' principle and SME concerns into every EU and national policy; and proposals for a Commission Action Plan on entrepreneurship before the 2004 Spring Council.

At the same time Greece scheduled numerous intellectual property working group meetings on the Community Regulation. As neither the latest Danish proposals nor the Commission approach enjoyed unanimous support, the Greek Presidency put forward a new compromise. It kept the notion of central jurisdiction granting the ECJ the exclusive right for court action, infringement procedures, or request for damages and of a specialised CPC composed of 15 patent law judges and technical experts attached to the Court of First Instance. The CPC was to be the single court of first instance for the Community Patent, while the EU's Court of First instance was to deal with appeals.

To overcome German opposition to centralised jurisdiction and accommodate southern Member States' – including its own – concerns about selective decentralisation, Greece suggested a transition period towards full centralisation. During the transition, decentralised chambers would operate alongside the ECJ in all Member States interested in hosting national patent courts and paying their operating costs. The decentralised courts would deal with legal action initiated against a resident of the Member State where they are located, while cases concerning residents of several Member States would come under the competence of the ECJ. In short, the national patent courts would continue as decentralised chambers of first instance until the CPC was fully operational. The length of this transitional period was one of the presidency's bargaining chips.

To overcome the language impasse Greece proposed that legal proceedings would be held in the defence party's state of residency language (unless agreed otherwise). Regarding the languages used for registration of patents Greece built upon agreements sketched out during the course of 2002. While a patent should generally be applied for in one of the three official EPO languages, should an inventor file a patent in another Community language the translation costs would be borne by the EU according to a pooling system. If granted, the patentee would only have to translate the claims – rather than the whole document – in all official Community languages. These arrangements were estimated to lower translation costs by more than half.[716]

As to the lesser points of contention, the Greek compromise build upon a common approach defined in May 2001. It continued to attribute an important role to NPOs, *inter alia* advising SMEs and potential applicants for Community Patents, receiving applications and forwarding them to the EPO, and disseminating patent information.[717] While the exact rules relating to fees and how they were to be paid still had to be clarified, Greece suggested that the income from renewal fees would be equally shared between the EPO and the NPOs and that the distribution key of annual fees to NPOs was to be decided by the Council on the basis of unanimity. Finally, to assess the quality and implementation of the regulation Greece proposed five-yearly Commission reviews. These reports were to cover quality and consistency, the deadlines required for decisions, and the costs incurred by inventors.

National diplomats, however, remained unenthusiastic. Greece responded by putting all means at its proposal behind it. Simitis held bilateral consultations and a marathon COREPER session on the Community Patent that took place on 26–27 February. By 3 March, steered by the Greek presidency, the Competitiveness Council unanimously agreed on a common approach. Crucially, Germany softened its stance on the continuation of its national courts on the condition that the transition towards a fully centralised judicial system was extended. While Berlin called for a ten-year transitional period and Greece proposed five, the Council settled on seven years. Although the German press accused its minister of betrayal given the anticipated job losses, the German Secretary of State for Justice seemed satisfied given that the German Courts could put their experience to the service on the ECJ while pursuing their activities until 2010.

In the light of the regulation's difficult history, the Greek common approach was hailed as an 'extraordinary political compromise' and success.[718] The nature of the compromise was a careful balancing of all the Council members' viewpoints without compromising the regulations key objectives of cost effectiveness, greater legal certainty, and high quality. At the same time Greece generated enough allies on key features of the Community Patent system to accommodate its own interests to a great extent. For example, Greece secured the cost reduction to ensure greater SMEs access to and protection by the system. Patent applications could be filed in Greek without the costs being carried by the applicant and all claims *vis-à-vis* Community Patents would be translated into all Community languages. In addition, the important role of NPOs regarding the processing of Community Patent applications was preserved.[719] A Commission official judged,

> in specific details, [Greece's] national positions came through. However, Greece managed to appear rather neutral in this matter as its common approach took all the key concerns of the other Member States into consideration.[720]

This illustrates a more general point: once a presidency compromise gains the 'dominant position,'[721] and thus a presidency discusses its own terms, rallies sufficient support for its solutions, and the compromise has something in stock for everybody, the office holder can afford to be 'neutral', or rather will inevitably appear more neutral.

Even though Germany compromised, it received sufficiently favourable terms to not make it worse off and the outcome was preferable to no agreement. This also applied to the other Member States. The deal brokered did not only accommodate Greek interest, but was positive-sum.

Despite the March success, adopting the final text of the regulation proved difficult. Intellectual property working group meetings resumed in April and by June the presidency had – in line with the common approach – revised the draft regulation three times. The relationship between the EPO and the NPOs re-emerged as an issue with Member States asking for partnership agreements between the two and greater quality assurance. In addition, they did not want to rule out the possibility of extending the role of NPOs. Further clarification on the use of languages, on the appointment procedure of judges, and powers of the CPC was also necessary. Finally, new disagreements emerged on the timing and effect of the translations of the claims of a granted Community Patent. The negotiations were not concluded under the Greek Presidency. The Thessaloniki Council merely acknowledged that intensive work was being conducted on a revised text of regulation, which takes account of the March common political approach. Overall, the common political approach Greece had secured was not detailed enough to allow for the conclusion of the dossier.

From stabilisation to enlargement?

Greece's calendar of events provided the Western Balkans with the highest possible visibility and focused on all relevant policy agendas including external relations, JHA, defence, energy, and the environment. The Thessaloniki Western Balkans Summit was to be the culmination of all the meetings on the region.

From the first day, the Greek Presidency moved the spotlight on the region. The EU's official take over of the UN Police Task Force in Bosnia on 1 January and the programming meeting with the Commission provided it with opportunities to do so. Prodi had developed into an important ally:

> The Hellenic Presidency will help the Union and the Balkan Region to approach each other. This is a really important priority. [...] The door of the Union is open and the Balkans have always been a part of Europe.[722]

It seems hardly coincidental then that Croatia submitted its application for EU membership during the Greek term. To ensure the application would not be overshadowed by Iraq, Greece even told Croatia when best to present it.[723] On initiative of the presidency a special troika followed up the membership bid and by April the Council invited the Commission to present an opinion on granting Croatia candidate status.

Furthermore, Greece capitalised on the Commission's 2003 SAP report and developments in the Western Balkans more generally, to focus Council attention on the region. The assassination of Prime Minister Zoran Djindjic moved Serbia-Montenegro to the centre of the March General Affairs and External Relations Council (GAERC). Greece invited the country's foreign minister to brief the Council on the situation. The Greek Presidency argued that the risk of further instability demanded greater EU involvement and its conclusions declared regional stability a top EU priority.[724] In addition, the Council confirmed its intention to launch a feasibility study on opening SAA negotiations if Serbia-Montenegro created a single economic space.

Most effective to increase the Western Balkans' visibility, however, was – less than two weeks into the presidency – a three-day, high-profile tour of the region by Papandreou with the message that 'Europe [was] ready to help [moving the Western Balkans to candidacy and then membership]'.[725] In Bosnia-Herzegovina, Solana joined Papandreou to launch the EU's first police mission. Solana echoed Papandreou's message declaring that 'Bosnia's future lies in Europe' and the EU '[wants] to help [...] to make this future a reality'.[726] Greece's public relations effort was very well received[727] and the tour rekindled EU interest in the region, while at the same time eliciting commitment from the Western

Balkans to reform. The Greek Presidency also used it as an opportunity to launch its first working paper on the region.[728]

The issues discussed during Papandreou's visit and raised in the working paper were systematically followed up at formal and informal external relations, JHA, defence, energy, and environment Council meetings, conferences, and seminars.[729] At his first GAERC Papandreou briefed the Council on his tour, invited Patten to talk about SAP developments, and scheduled an open debate on the presidency's Western Balkan priorities.[730]

To overcome Member States' scepticism regarding the lack of compliance with the ICT for Yugoslavia by Serbia-Montenegro and conditionality, the Greek Presidency together with Solana insisted that the EU should not be too 'dramatic in the way it presents the issue and that it would be important to offer something positive'.[731] Too much conditionality could be counterproductive. The head of the UN Interim Mission in Kosovo supported them: 'Kosovans must feel that European integration is within their grasp.'[732] Important GAERC outcomes in this respect included the formal backing for boosting EU support for Serbia-Montenegro, the launch of a 'feasibility study' on an SAA with Bosnia-Herzegovina, and a common position putting pressure on indicated war criminals.

The possibility of offering the region more funding was the key question of a presidency non-paper Greece presented at the May GAERC. Papandreou argued that if the EU was 'really serious' about the region, the countries required a 'qualitative step' towards preparing accession.[733] In addition, the Brussels Council had invited the Commission, the EIB, and other international financial institutions 'to examine possible initiatives in support of major infrastructure projects in transport, energy and telecommunications in South-Eastern Europe and in particular in the Western Balkans'.[734] The discussions continued at COREPER. Insisting until the very end, Greece managed to generate consensus to increase funding for the region.[735] However, it had to settle for much less than hoped. The Council was only willing to accept raising CARDS by 71 million euros in 2004 and 70 million euros in 2005 and 2006 – as per a Commission proposal. This did not allow an extension of social and cohesion policy to the region. Nonetheless, the possibility of further funding was not ruled out:

> [...] the Council welcomes the Commission's proposal for an increase in the CARDS budget by more than Euro 200 million over the period 2004–06, as a clear expression of this intent (to offer substantial EU

financial support) and a good basis for the discussions in the ongoing budget procedures. [...] Taking into account the overall balance of the Union's priorities, the possibility of further support, in particularly by mobilising the European Investment Bank, should also be explored.[736]

The Iraq crisis, general tensions over the budget, key Member States' economic situation, and the region's reluctance to co-operate with the ICT all contributed to Member States' reluctance significantly to increase CARDS funding.

More progress was achieved in JHA. In line with its priorities Greece focused the Council debates on fighting drugs and organised crime, police co-operation, and external border protection. Greece exploited Member States' perceived urgency to fight organised crime and created a new horizontal working group on drugs to which it presented, in early February, a draft action plan on drugs between the EU and the Balkans. Building on the London conference, Greece's intention was to create a Balkan version of the EU's Central Asia Action Plan on drugs. The action plan was to co-ordinate the implementation of various EU programmes to strengthen stability and security of the region.[737] It suggested *inter alia*: helping governments draw up national anti-drug plans; a regional anti-drug centre; fighting organised crime; training the judiciary; a network of judicial co-operation; improving co-operation between law enforcement agencies; enhancing cross border security, information exchange, operational co-operation, and the role of Europol in the Balkans; and clamping down money laundering.

To rally consensus on the action plan Greece organised a seminar on Balkan routes of heroin trafficking and an open debate on organised crime in the region at the February JHA Council. Numerous other events were dedicated to this issue.[738] Italy and Austria were Greece's most important allies – both had drugs crime on top of their own policy agendas. Hence the Greek Presidency could voice some of its ideas through them.

Italy announced that it would follow up the issues under its presidency through seminars for EU and Balkan police forces, liaison officers, and witness protection schemes. The French and German European Affairs Ministers also saw organised crime and corruption as key concerns undermining the success of SEE. Although the Scandinavian countries and the UK disagreed with Greece's 'unconditional' approach to the region, they coincided on the need to fight organised crime.[739]

Through the numerous Councils, seminars, national exchanges of views, and the strategic use of its policy papers, the Greek Presidency conveyed a strong message: organised crime threatened stability in the Western Balkans which could affect the EU as a whole. By March, the Council asked Europol to start negotiating agreements with the Western Balkans and in early June 2003 it adopted the Drugs Action Plan.

In the area of immigration and border management Greece concentrated mostly on advancing existing initiatives. After commissioning a comprehensive report on illegal immigration and placing it on top of the June European Council, it finalised the creation of the network of national immigration liaison officers to help control illegal migration through the Western Balkans. However, funding remained a sticking point here as well. The estimated cost for effective border management was 140 million euros. The Commission, however, offered only 80 million euros for 2004–2006 (bringing the budget to 100 million euros). Nonetheless, as the case with the CARDS funding, the Commission was invited to examine further financial possibilities and 'new institutional mechanisms'.[740]

Important outcomes were also achieved in the areas of defence, energy, and the environment. They included adopting the financing mechanism opening the way for the EU's first military mission, Concordia, in FYROM launched on 31 March and commencing discussions on the take over of the Stabilisation Force mission in Bosnia-Herzegovina by presenting a joint report with Solana and a detailed presidency paper. The latter initiative was reviewed at the March Informal Defence Council, received strong French and British backing, and was agreed a year later.[741] The Greek Presidency also concluded the so-called Berlin Plus Agreement, which ensured EU access to NATO resources.

In the area of energy Greece promoted initiatives to extend the regional electricity and gas market in SEE. The May Energy Council conclusions paved the way for developing energy production centres in the Balkans. In line with a Commission Communication, the broader objective was to ensure energy supply and expand the EU energy market. As to the environment an initiative regarding water management in the Balkans was launched after the informal environment Council and a two-day conference had generated consensus on the issue.[742]

The results of the Councils were fed into the EU–Western Balkan Summit Declaration and Thessaloniki Agenda. In addition, the Member States, the Commission, and other interested parties were invited to submit their ideas to strengthen the Union's SAP to the Western Balkans Summit.[743] Contributions were received by the SP, France, the Commission, the Parliamentary Conference, the region's leaders, and the EP.[744] To ensure that the Western Balkan countries were not excluded from formulating their common agenda, Greece invited their Ambassadors to numerous working groups and scheduled meetings with delegations from the Balkans in Zagreb, Rome, and Athens to receive their feedback.[745]

Despite consulting widely, reaching political agreement on the Thessaloniki Agenda was challenging. Greece's first draft received a frosty reception in the Council working group. It was too positive for the 'hardliner group' led by the UK.[746] Greece had to redraft the document trying to strike a better balance between the Western Balkans' EU prospect and their need to reform:

> Here we committed a tactical mistake. We were way too positive. When we presented it to the working group it was a disaster. But then we changed the document's structure, took some of the interests of the other Member States into consideration and the climate changed.[747]

Semantics proved extremely important. While the idea behind the BIP was accepted, the name was too positive as well. What the Commission had referred to as the 'Zagreb Process' and Greece labelled the BIP became the 'EU–Western Balkan Forum' – a more neutral term.

The most fundamental change, however, was the incorporation of the UK's and Sweden's European Partnership idea – supported by France and Patten. Here as well, the Commission's slightly more positive name of European Integration Partnership was dropped. The partnerships made the 'conditionality' concept more explicit than Greece had envisaged. However, the function they fulfilled, namely more effective monitoring of the Balkans' progress, reflected the Greek approach. Moreover, they increased the Commission's role within the SAP – a guarantee that the Western Balkans would not 'slip from the agenda after the 2003 Greek and Italian Presidencies'.[748]

Greece finalised the draft joint declaration and the Thessaloniki agenda at the June GAERC. Both documents confirmed the prospect of EU membership and were endorsed by the Thessaloniki Summit. As per Greece's initial working document new practical initiatives of the Thessaloniki Agenda included twinning arrangements, increased participation of SAP countries in Community programmes, assistance in border control and management, and institutionalised regular ministerial meetings between the EU and the Balkans through the EU–Western

Balkans Forum. Crucially, in the presidency seat Greece reached what it had not achieved at the GAERC in May 2002: increased commitment by the Member States to the Western Balkans through periodical Summits of the heads of state or government of the Western Balkans and their EU counterparts and annual meetings of their foreign and JHA ministers. Other ministers were invited to meet as appropriate. Italy committed itself to organise the first of such ministerial meetings and declared that the Balkans would continue top priority under its presidency.[749]

The Western Balkans accepted the Thessaloniki Agenda as their common agenda and the enhanced SAP as their accession framework at the Western Balkan Summit. They highlighted the EU's commitment to explore supplementary financial aid and, in return, promised to co-operate with the ICT and deal with problems connected to the repatriation of refugees, organised crime, corruption, illegal immigration, and border management. In addition, they expressed their support of the regional co-operation initiatives identified by the agenda in the areas of energy, infrastructure, trade, visas, and reigning in small arms.

The positive signals sent to the region increased their leaders' incentives to progress with reforms – as witnessed by their creation of a common regional approach to combat cross-border organised crime. On the EU side, the ratification procedure of the SAAs with FYROM and Croatia continued with Greece ratifying the SAAs in May. The Commission opened negotiations towards an SAA with Albania in January and pursued Croatia's application by issuing a questionnaire to the country to assess its readiness to start accession negotiations, the feasibility study was launched for an SAA with Bosnia-Herzegovina, and the Thessaloniki Agenda and institutionalisation of the EU–Western Balkans Forum formed a good basis for further progress. Overall, the Greek Presidency's transformed 'the SAP into a more coherent EU integration framework'.[750] As Simitis stated,

> The Greek Presidency had set specific goals for a qualitative change in the relations of the EU with the five West Balkan states. The [...] Thessaloniki Summit and the EU-West Balkans Summit reaffirmed the accession prospects of these countries. A new regular political dialogue process has been adopted between the EU and the West Balkan states, promoting harmonisation of legislation towards the community *acquis* and thereby ensuring a stable financial aid increase in financial aid.[751]

IV.   Conditions for success

The leadership environment, skill, and use of the Council Secretariat

The above results were achieved despite the Iraq crisis. This can partly be explained by Greece's high level of political sensitivity in the management of the crisis and its relations with the other Council members. As Patten put it, Greece was 'a gentleman and politician at the same time'.[752]

Despite the seemingly irreconcilable divisions in the Council, Greece managed to save the EU's face at an emergency summit by enabling the adoption of a joint communiqué which averted an open clash and reasserted the credibility of EU institutions.[753] To do so it carefully juggled PASOK's and the Greek public's fierce opposition to war with the commitment to find a common EU stance and limit the damage to transatlantic relations. Senior PASOK members even criticised Simitis for pursuing European policies at the expense of party priorities.

As Greece appeared relatively objective and clearly separated Iraq from other foreign policy and economic issues, the crisis and tensions in the Council did not prevent it from fostering agreement in its priority dossiers. Greece's small size was undoubtedly an advantage. It is hard to imagine what the Council atmosphere would have been like with France, Germany, the UK, Italy, or Spain in the chair.

The Lisbon Summit went ahead as planned and the Greek Presidency accommodated Iraq on the agenda by postponing a debate on the Convention progress. To avoid overt arguments, Greece – supported by most Member States – stuck mostly to its economic agenda rather than the international situation.[754] Nonetheless, the political tensions between the Franco-German alliance who opposed the war, and the UK, Spain, and Italy supporting US military action, could not be separated entirely from the debates on how to increase the EU's and SME competitiveness.

As to the Western Balkans, Papandreou was determined not to 'allow [...] international crises elsewhere to distract [the presidency] from [its] commitment to bringing this corner of our continent closer to the rest of Europe'.[755] In fact, as the US agreed with the Greek objectives in the Western Balkans and the Berlin Plus Agreement had enhanced EU–US co-operation on Western Balkan issues, it was an area where spill-over effects from the conflict could be prevented.[756] Hence the Iraq war, despite taking much of Greece's time, seemed to have little effect on the region's progress towards the EU.[757]

Despite the leadership tensions between Simitis and Papandreou, together with Giannitsis they proved the strongest team of all past Greek Presidencies. Having overseen his country's most determined restructuring effort to date[758] and a political turnabout since taking office in 1996, Simitis had established himself as an esteemed senior Council member projecting a moderate image abroad. Papandreou was one of Europe's most respected politicians who also enjoyed unrivalled popularity in Greece.[759] Both had good negotiation skills and 'approached the presidency with a vision, had the necessary bureaucratic stamina, and were not scared about drafting papers and solutions'.[760] Indeed Simitis' personal involvement in the Community Patent and Papandreou's in the Western Balkans dossier were crucial for their success.[761]

Greece was also keen to prove that it had learned from the past. Thus, its overall presidency approach was more balanced and its strategy across the policy spectrum 'to not dissatisfy anybody, to not hurt anybody'.[762] As the Finnish and Belgian presidencies, it tried to pursue positive-sum outcomes. Taking neutrality seriously, Greece did not participate in the April mini defence summit by France, Germany, Belgium, and Luxembourg for example. Papandreou repeatedly assured that Greece was 'on a new [...] European track'[763] and its credibility had increased when becoming a euro-zone country. As to external relations, given Greece's change of policy *vis-à-vis* the Balkans since the Kosovo war (at the expense of deepening the rift between Greek public opinion and European priorities) and its intimate knowledge of Balkan history, Member States had slowly come to see it as a legitimate leader in the region.[764]

Although Greece's small size was seen as a constraint in some areas, most interviewees also saw it as a political advantage:

> Even if you are a small country you can translate your small size into power. [...] Being from a small [...] country is a political advantage, because you arouse less suspicion in the chair. Many initiatives are based on interests, but if you are a small country the other Member States more readily accept it.[765]

As important as Simitis' and Papandreou's personal skills and commitment was that Greece addressed deficiencies in its interministerial co-ordination and administration including: competition between the Ministry of National Economy and the MFA; a highly ineffective, hierarchical state apparatus and MFA threatened with overload; a weak bureaucracy owed to the politicisation of recruitment at the expense of merit; and a general underdevelopment of planning mechanisms and lack of clear priorities.

Theoretically, the MFA represents Greek EU policy, mediates between the ministries, and communicates instructions to the Permanent Representation. To prepare the Greek position, the MFA's EU General Directorate holds weekly meetings with representatives from the other ministries, which too have EU General Directorates who co-ordinate the position of their respective ministry.[766] Sometimes it also organises briefings in Brussels or ad-hoc meetings. Since 1993 an Interministerial Committee for the co-ordination of Greece–EU relations brings together all the main technical ministries. It is presided over by the Minister of Foreign Affairs, but meets more often at the Secretary General level.

In practice, the Ministry of National Economy and the MFA compete for the leadership of EU policy co-ordination. In addition, with the increasingly technical nature of EU dossiers, many ministries developed informal direct lines to the Permanent Representation.[767] Thus, to the annoyance of the ministries, co-ordination is sometimes exercised by the Permanent Representation. Unsurprisingly, the Greek administrative system has been characterised as the 'sum of isolated fortresses', and thus highly fragmented with centrifugal political forces resisting formal co-ordination obligations.[768] Part of the presidency preparations was therefore to introduce a clearer division of tasks and greater level of centralisation.

The MFA was put in charge of the overall presidency planning and co-ordination. For the logistics, budget, protocol, and translations the government created – one year ahead of Greece's term – a special 'Office of the Greek Presidency,' which also acted as an intermediary for third parties and the Council Secretariat. The Presidency Office was headed by Giannitsis. Strategy and co-ordination between the ministries, in turn, was assigned to the General Secretary for European Affairs Ilias Plaskovitis. Conflicts between the MFA and other ministries, particularly the Economics Ministry, were settled by him. A senior Greek official confirmed that 'the lead definitely came from the MFA. This was a great success.'[769] To ensure that the competition between the Economics and Foreign Affairs Ministries would not affect the Community Patent and given that co-ordination between the Research and Development and the Foreign Ministries worked well,[770] the Greek Presidency put the latter in charge of the regulation (see above).

Nonetheless, the Greek system kept many ad-hoc features. To address the slow and hierarchical nature of the Greek state apparatus, for example, sole interlocutors with direct lines to the ministers were appointed. Chairpersons could call their interlocutor at any time to ask for instructions or approval of his or her negotiation stance. In this way, bureaucratic structures were sidelined and decisions were taken between officials at the Permanent Representation and their interlocutor (or minister) directly. Interestingly these interlocutors were often outsiders to the Greek administration. As one Greek official described it:

Decision-making in Athens is normally slow and very hierarchical. It is like a pyramid and it is hard to get to the top. We had a novelty that probably other presidencies have not had. Simitis and Papandreou appointed some contact points – often not from the administration. We could call our contacts at any time and usually had an answer in 15 minutes. Thus we skipped the administration in order to be quicker and more effective. Obviously this happened behind the scenes, is not institutionalised, and was only for the presidency. In this way we had access to the highest level. Their answer subsequently was fed back into the administration. This system helped enormously.[771]

This gave the working group and COREPER chairs a much greater margin of manoeuvre:

I would describe our system as a centralised system within a system. We had a sole interlocutor and only ever had to dial one number. If anything was successful, then – in my view – it was this. I feel we sometimes had a *carte blanc* – a much wider margin for manoeuvre than usual.[772]

To address weaknesses in its bureaucracy, Greece recruited experienced people from previous presidencies back into the Greek administration.[773] The government also created a number of advisory committees consisting of university professors or other experts. Some seminars, particularly for working group chairs, were organised by the Minister of European Affairs and the Council Secretariat. However, most of the training consisted in 'learning by doing'.[774] Language problems at the ministries in Athens were the most noticeable consequence of the lack of training.

In addition, as in the Finnish and Belgian cases, to accumulate expertise the chairpersons were – with a few exceptions – selected one year before the Greek Presidency term. Eighty per cent of them were from the Permanent Representation. This ensured familiarity with the EU and the priority dossiers. The key presidency posts, such as the Antici and COREPER chairs, were filled with highly skilled personnel. A senior official from the Council Secretariat confirmed that in the area of the IM individual chairs 'were very often very efficient despite the overall organisation and co-ordination being rather poor'.[775]

Finally, the Greek Presidency managed to develop a 'constructive dialogue' with the Council Secretariat.[776] Given its limited staff, Greece relied heavily on the Secretariat's assessments of Member State positions and leverage. Greek officials considered the Secretariat as the 'best minute taker'.[777] Numerous interviewees mentioned that the nature of the relationship with the Council Secretariat varies depending on whether it has its own 'hidden agenda' and the experience/inexperience of the office holder.[778] The less experienced the office holder, the greater the potential role of the Council Secretariat. With regard to the Community Patent, it did not seem to have a hidden agenda, Greece was a relatively experienced Council presidency and Simitis had the expertise and ambition to assume the political lead in the dossier. Thus, while open to the Secretariat's input, Greece took the overall responsibility and added 'Greek flavour here and there'.[779]

In case of the Western Balkans there was potential of conflict between Solana's office and the presidency and some 'diplomatic struggles' took place on security and defence issues or Turkey's role in NATO.[780] In the Western Balkan dossier, however, there seems to have been a clear separation of functions between Solana's staff and the Greek Presidency. While Solana's office provided operational support and took the lead in the EU's ongoing crisis management operations (where it is much better equipped than a rotating office), the Greek Presidency assumed the political leadership of the Western Balkan dossier:

> The High Representative and the Council Secretariat are more and more in the lead as to management functions, particularly in crisis management. The presidency is nevertheless extremely important in terms of agenda-setting. The whole Thessaloniki Summit was very much led by the presidency. We [the Western Balkan Unit from the Council Secretariat] gave some limited input, but the presidency was clearly in the lead.[781]

While the Council Secretariat provided Greece with a contribution to its Western Balkan working paper, the overall thrust and concept of the document came from the presidency.[782] So did the first draft of the Thessaloniki Agenda. Indeed, had the Council Secretariat had more influence in its development, the first draft agenda may not have caused the initial reactions it did. A senior Council Secretariat official concluded,

> Greece played a very important and useful role. They had very good people and the Council Secretariat would have had great difficulties in doing anything like they did. From Greece came the political push and the initiative. The rotating presidency's advantage is that it provides additional energy for specific policies. If it were not for the Greeks, Thessaloniki would have not been the same thing.[783]

Overall, organisation and logistics did not run as admirably as in the Finnish case. Meetings were frequently cancelled or rearranged and journalists and officials deplored the high number of wrong telephone numbers in the Greek Presidency guide.[784] The FT did not fail to remind its readers that 'chaos is a Greek word'.[785] Regarding the overall leadership and brokerage, however, Greece proved its ability to handle EU affairs and mediation skills in both the difficult case of the Community Patent and foreign affairs. It put structures in place to avoid potential mishaps and provide leadership in its priority areas. The chairpersons' personal qualities, networks, and special contacts partially remedied Greek administrative deficiencies for the presidency term. According to a Commission official there were never any open contradictions and 'even though Greece is amongst the worst IM implementers this did not affect their performance in the chair'.[786] Quite the contrary, Greece was determined to work on its reputation and close as many dossiers as possible. In areas where Greece had no vital interests at stake this often meant taking more flexible positions than previously.[787] In its priority areas, however, this meant offering new dynamism to foster agreement.

Heterogeneity, intensity, and distribution of governmental preferences

In case of the Community Patent, the heterogeneity of viewpoints was high and Greece could move its favoured solutions forward without appearing too biased. Moreover, the distribution of governmental preferences was generally favourable. On all points of contention Greece had at least one big state on its side. France supported the centralised CPC. Spain and Italy shared Greek concerns about the linguistic regime.

Greece's proposals for a decentralised system of issuing the EU patent was backed by France, the UK, and Spain who also supported Greece's ideas about the costs and distribution of proceeds from patent processing services. Germany was relatively isolated on the issue of the CPC and could not mobilise the Franco-German tandem to push for decentralised jurisdiction. Agreement was possible after Germany weakened its position. However, the intensity of preferences prevented Greece to conclude the dossier despite unanimous support for the presidency's common approach.

With regard to the Western Balkans, Greece found itself relatively isolated in its 'unconditional approach' towards the region despite Italian and Austrian support and Greece's well-respected expertise on the Balkans. In addition, the intensity and distribution of preferences was somewhat unfavourable. As seen above, the UK led a coalition resisting major changes to EU Western Balkan policy. Similarly France and Germany were cautious about moving too quickly in the region. While supporting Greek initiatives with regard to the fight against organised crime, on financial issues they (and most other Member States) preferred the more modest proposals by the Commission. Unsurprisingly, Greece had to make some concessions.

Inter-institutional relations

Relations with the Commission were particularly close in the area of SME competitiveness and Anna Diamantopoulou, former Greek Minister for SMEs and then European Commissioner for Employment and Social Affairs, was an important ally. The Commission launched a number of special reports on SMEs during the Greek term and agreement on the Community Patent regulation had been a key Commission priority since 2001. Thus, Greece co-ordinated closely with the Commission, as various officials affirmed,

> Relations with the Commission were fundamental. [...] what we communicated to the Commission was: we do not want surprises; we want a fair game, and a business-like presidency. We also wanted to throw in ideas here and there.[788]

> The Commission was fully associated with our work. To prepare briefings we invited not only the Council Secretariat, but also the Commission. They presented their opinion, but the key role of initiative has the presidency. The dialogue was part of preparing the meetings.[789]

A Commission official confirmed the close relationship between the IM DG and the Greek delegation:

> Our relationship with the Greek Presidency was excellent. There was full transparency and full confidence. In tandem with the Greek Presidency we were devising the 'war game,' how to handle the discussion and sometimes you even decide together who to give the floor to first and when the Commission comes in.[790]

Regarding the Western Balkans, Greece did not rely as heavily on the Commission:

> We produced so many policy papers on the Balkans and had great expertise on the region. So here we did not need the Commission.[791]

Nonetheless, Greece showed the Commission a draft of its priority paper ahead of the presidency and made an effort to accommodate some of its feedback to ensure that the Commission would 'be on board'.[792]

Although both the Greek Presidency and the Commission saw the Western Balkan Summit as an opportunity to enhance the political dialogue with the region, the Commission favoured – through the European Integration Partnerships – more stringent conditionality than Greece. In its contribution to the Western Balkan Summit, it stressed that the Western Balkans need further to develop concrete political and economic cooperation among themselves particularly in areas of refugee return, migration, fight against organised crime, trade, energy, and transport. Patten tried to strike a balance between the highly positive Greek discourse and the Commission approach:

> The destiny of the people of southeast Europe is membership with the EU. [. . .] Of course, they have to make changes on their part and should continue the economic and political reform on which they embarked. But we wish to be more hands-on in helping them with that process; and we proposed that we should turn the annual assessments on the progress they make on economic and political reform into partnerships.[793]

Relations with the EP were non-systematic and sporadic with regard to both the IM and foreign policy. In fact, because of the Greek Presidency's general lack of consultation with the EP, a major inter-institutional row broke out over the amount of subsidies paid to the accession countries.

As the EP has the right to approve budget-related decisions and was not given enough time to draft its opinion on the accession treaties, it threatened to delay its approval of the treaties. The conflict was solved through informal meetings with the President of the Committee on Constitutional Affairs, the Secretary Generals of the parties, and various politicians.[794] Most Greek interviewees saw the EP as the 'troublemaker' within the EU's decision-making triangle.

V.   Revision of achievements: assessing the counterfactuals

The Community Patent

Presidency achievements and the role of other Member States

Given the economic importance of SMEs, there was no critical opposition towards initiatives benefiting them. Most of the preceding 14 Council presidencies had mentioned SMEs in their presidency programmes. However, Member States seemed to have lost their faith in the Community Patent and lacked political commitment to agree on a common approach. This had become clear under the Swedish and Belgian 2001 Presidencies. Although the Feira Summit had established the end of 2001 as the deadline for the regulation's adoption, both countries struggled to achieve agreement. After a six-hour discussion in the March IM Council under the Swedish Presidency, and 12 working group and four COREPER meetings on the regulation, the Stockholm Summit merely urged the Council and the Commission to speed up the work on the regulation.

The succeeding Belgian Presidency devoted an entire Council meeting to the dossier and although the Member States managed to outline general policy guidelines for the Community Patent, they rejected the presidency compromise.[795] Partly due to Belgium's lack of involvement at the highest level, the file was not taken up at European Council level.[796] Similarly, Denmark failed to generate agreement on the dossier. Unlike Greece and in the light of Member State opposition, it did not dare to tackle certain aspects of the regulation:

> There was a clear difference between the Danish Presidency and the Greek Presidency and how they approached this dossier. Quite frankly, Denmark was really discouraged by the difficult history of the dossier. A presidency can definitely make a difference.[797]

France may have played a role in pressuring Germany to compromise on the issue of the patent's judicial regime. However, it was the

Greek Presidency's level of initiative and Simitis' personal expertise and commitment that helped greatly to find an acceptable compromise. While – in retrospect – not facilitating the breakthrough it hoped for, Greece's main achievement was to generate agreement on the difficult issue of the Community Patent's future jurisdiction and formulate a common approach for future presidencies to build upon which replaced the 'nothing is agreed until everything is agreed' approach from before.

The role of the Commission

The Commission reports played an important role in reinvigorating the debate on initiatives benefiting SMEs. However, the Commission could not move SMEs (and with it the Community Patent) into the spotlight by itself. A Commission official argued,

> The presidency gives the direction to the process. It tells us what their views are and what they would like to focus on ahead of time, so that we can incorporate their input and adjust our schedule accordingly. They also tell us their no-go areas. When the presidency has no will in a certain area, they will not put it on the agenda, so we will not waste our time.[798]

Indeed, in the Community Patent dossier, the Commission receded its agenda-setting powers to the Greek Presidency. It supported Greece's compromise for the sake of an agreement and given it was 'defendable', not because it was its preferred choice.[799] In fact, the Commission's attempts to present a workable compromise on the Community Patent's future jurisdiction failed. The Commission argued for a centralised judicial system that would – once a coherent body of case law had been generated at Community level – gradually introduce decentralisation (see above). However, the Greek Presidency and three of the EU big Member States did not support this compromise. Germany (supported by France, Austria, and Italy) argued that decentralised chambers should operate immediately so that the national patent courts would not loose their expertise. In addition, the Commission's language regime proposals were more pragmatic than Member States would accept. Both national and Commission officials agreed that the influence of the Commission is often exaggerated as their proposals usually change – sometimes drastically – in the Council negotiations and if the alternative is no agreement at all, it usually accepts the Council's compromises:

Even if the Commission has a different view, it then generally changes its view, because it wants the agreement between Council and Commission. The Commission has a consultative role, but it is not the broker of deals. I certainly have not seen the Commission in this role and I doubt that it could be done, because it is in the interest of the Commission not to stop the matter. They want a proposal to be adopted and want to avoid delays.[800]

A Commission official confirmed,

The aim is to reach agreement. To do so the proposals always change. Once the presidency has a compromise, the Commission usually accepts it.[801]

This suggests that the presidency has a 'degree of discretion and autonomy' when it comes to shaping final outcomes[802] and may even broker deals the Commission profoundly dislikes.[803]

One may argue that the Commission's contribution to the compromise was to generate pressure to agree before the EU Spring Summit by threatening to withdraw the regulation. But for two reasons it is doubtful that this threat had much influence on the Council. First, it had already been voiced under the Spanish and Danish 2002 Presidencies, never materialised, and has rarely been used in the history of the EU. Second, the Commission's weapon of withdrawing a proposal is only credible when the Council decides by QMV, not by unanimity as in the Community Patent case.

The role of the EP

The EP has also supported SME initiatives. As early as 1983 it called for a 'Year of SMEs and the Craft Industry' and since then has issued a number of resolutions related to SMEs.[804] In the specific case of the Community Patent, the EP urged the Council repeatedly to overcome its differences. It considered the regulation 'of fundamental importance for promoting the creativity of European enterprises and improving their competitiveness on the international scene'.[805] However, the EP did not manage to move its April 2002 opinion into the dominant position. Although the Greek Presidency coincided with the EP on the role of NPOs, the final compromise differed significantly from the EP opinion on the judicial and linguistic system. The EP suggested decentralised jurisdiction at first instance, but Greece brokered agreement on a transition towards fully centralised jurisdiction. While the EP wanted inventors to apply for a Community Patent in any language and subsequently create five 'procedural languages', the Council's common approach expected inventors to file their application in one of the EPO's three official languages. Only if this was impossible, the translation costs into one of these three would be borne by the EU.

Indeed, the Greek Presidency did not involve the EP in the Council negotiations as evidenced by the EP's repeated questions to both the Council and the Commission to explain the sticky points and what steps the Council was planning to take with a view to reaching an agreement. Only those EP suggestions that enjoyed the backing of the Greek Presidency and a critical mass of Member States were incoproated. In sum, the EP had little overall influence in shaping the Community Patent.

The Western Balkans

Presidency achievements and the role of other Member States

Before Greece took over the presidency, the Western Balkans were considered 'a topic that [was] not a live issue'[806] and that was '[sliding] down the list of hot issues for EU Foreign Ministers'.[807] By the end of the 2002 Danish Presidency, 'many people in the Western Balkans concluded [...] that the EU had little time for them'.[808] Portugal, Ireland, Belgium, and the Scandinavian countries were particularly uninterested. The Greek Presidency, however, revived the Western Balkans on the EU agenda:

> Greece of course wanted much stronger EU objectives in the Balkans. This was not important for Portugal, Ireland, or the Scandinavian countries. Greece wanted it more than the rest and I think they got quite a lot.[809]

> Depending on who is in the chair, the tone of the debate changes very clearly. The Danes were an excellent presidency, but on the Balkans extremely neutral and did not take any new initiatives. Instead they very much focused on enlargement and let the Commission run the show. The Greeks in turn have real ambitions to push the agenda on the Western Balkans forward.[810]

The Western Balkan Summit (and the run up to it) sent a clear message to the region that it belongs in the EU and created a special dynamic reinvigorating policy debates related to the region '[increasing] the likelihood that the Western Balkans will be in rather than out'.[811] The formulation that the Balkans have a 'real European perspective' was significantly more than Zagreb I promises. In addition, the declaration adopted at the EU–Western Balkans Summit, together with the Thessaloniki Agenda, provided a more coherent basis for directing future reform efforts in the region and connecting reform efforts to enhanced EU support. Putting the Balkans on every single GAERC meeting and all relevant Councils was Greece's work rather than the leadership of other Member States. In addition, the networking behind the scenes to forge agreement on the Thessaloniki Agenda and on the measures to enrich the SAP was done by the Greeks. Busek described the work of the Greek Presidency as an 'impressive process of consultations between the EU, the countries of the region, and all the players involved in supporting the region in its efforts'.[812] In addition, it was Greece's initiative to create a special horizontal working group on drugs in the Western Balkans as part of fostering greater regional co-operation in JHA.

Austria and Italy were Greece's closest allies. Given their geographic proximity to the region they have – together with Greece – been instrumental in moving the Balkans onto the EU agenda. Austria fully supported Greek objectives and regarded the prospect of increasing integration the most effective incentive for the countries to speed up their national reform processes.[813] Italy, in turn, told Greece that if the Greek Presidency did not do anything special on the Balkans it definitely would.[814] Indeed, Italy kept the Balkans and the implementation of the Thessaloniki Agenda on top of the EU's foreign policy agenda.

However, Greek achievements fell short of the high expectations in the Western Balkan states. Even though their funding was increased, the Western Balkan Summit did not extent the EU's cohesion policy to them, grant them candidate status or a timetable for accession. Instead the EU stuck to the 'potential candidates' terminology that had been introduced at the Feira Summit and stressed that much relied on the region's own reform efforts. This shows that despite its increased agenda-setting powers, the presidency works within the constraints of other EU institutions and actors whose interests have to be accommodated. Hence, the final Thessaloniki agenda was not entirely 'made in Greece'. A senior official judged that '85 per cent of what was obtained came from Greece', while 15% came from other decision-makers. The UK and Sweden who enjoyed French support, for example, insisted on a greater degree of conditionality than Greek proposals entailed and put forward the European Partnerships. Although the Partnerships did not go against Greece's thinking, they moderated the highly positive and ambitious Greek discourse. The main thrust of the EU's Western Balkan policy did therefore not change dramatically. Overall, even if 15% was input from other actors, achieving 85% of its original Western Balkan agenda is still a lot, particularly in the light of the Iraq crisis.

The role of the Commission

The Commission had limited influence on the Greek Western Balkans priority document. A Greek official argued,

> We took some changes from the Commission, but nothing fundamental that would have changed our view or approach.[815]

However, the Commission made a number of key contributions to the development of the EU's relations with the Western Balkans, most crucially its 2002 and 2003 SAP progress reports and May 2003 communication on energy policy. In its first SAP progress report, the Commission had proposed to bring together the political leaders of the region and their EU counterparts at ministerial level on a regular basis. Greece seized upon the Commission's policy recommendations and pushed the idea of a second Zagreb meeting. In addition, as Greece had suggested in its priority document, the Commission's March 2003 recommendations included extending twinning, further developing a review of the countries' conformity with EU legislation, gradually extending Community programmes to the Western Balkans (particularly visa regime and migration policy), developing a regular joint political dialogue, and sending a strong message to the Western Balkans about the EU's commitment to the region. Similarly, the Commission's energy communication coincided with Greece's broader objective to expand the EU energy market into the Western Balkans.

Although the Commission tried to balance the UK and Swedish approach with Greece' ambitions, it had to reign in to the dominance of the Member States in EU foreign policy. Its concept of European Integration Partnership was dropped. The Commission nonetheless achieved an important victory in the sense that the British and Swedish European Partnerships increased its role within the SAP guaranteeing it potentially greater agenda influence in the future.

On determining the precise levels of funding, the Commission was more influential. As per its proposal the Council accepted raising CARDS by 71 million euros in 2004 and 70 million euros in 2005 and 2006. Similarly, the Commission's proposals regarding the budget for sharing border management costs were approved. Particularly in the first case, Greece's ambitious proposals had to be scaled down. Nonetheless,

had Greece not taken the initiative to increase Western Balkan funding, it is unlikely that any increase would have happened. The political
push for initiative of the dossier came from the presidency, while the
Commission followed suit:

> The Commission was positive, but the driver was the presidency. The
> Commission was reluctant at the beginning and then they came with
> us. But in some critical issues they left us alone.[816]

The role of the EP

The EP's role in shaping EU Western Balkan policy during the Greek Presidency was insubstantial. Although the EP took an interest in the region,
regularly sent parliamentary election observers to the Western Balkans,
and supported initiatives to reinforce the SAP, it was not proactive in
developing the EU's Western Balkan policy during the Greek term. In
fact, the EP's June contribution to the Western Balkan Summit expressed
serious concerns about the economic and social situation in the region
and warned that integration of the Western Balkans would take considerable time.[817] The EP was reluctant to push for further integration
before the success of the EU's first Eastern enlargement was secured. Its
key foci in the first half of 2003 were the Middle East and Iraq.

Regarding the additional CARDS funding for the region MEPs were
informed, but they gave no relevant input. Indeed, as seen above, the EP
had supported freezing funding in November 2002. It insisted on strict
conditionality and the evaluation of the integration of the SP countries
on the basis of the Copenhagen economic and political criteria. While
the conditionality approach was reflected in the European Partnerships,
the initiative for such Partnerships did not come from the EP, but the
Member States and the Commission.

In addition, the EP was an observer rather than active participant at
the Western Balkan Summit. The opening statements of the Summit
declaration read that the participating Heads of State or Government
agreed the Thessaloniki agenda for the Western Balkans 'in the presence'
of the EP rather than 'together' with it.

Finally, and perhaps most important to dismiss the EP as a causal factor for the progress received with regard to the EU's Western Balkan
policy under the Greek Presidency, the main demands by the June EP
resolution were already contained in the Greek January working document. They included calls for the Western Balkans' full co-operation
with the International Criminal Tribunal for Former Yugoslavia (ICTY),
the implementation of UN Security Council Resolution 1244 on Kosovo,

the return of refugees, increased participation of SAP countries in Community programmes, the importance of regional cooperation, strengthening monitoring mechanisms on the implementation of commitments by SAP countries, the lifting of visa requirements for the EU, and parliamentary cooperation between the Member States and the SEE countries.[818]

In sum, the ideas put forward in the area of the Western Balkans and initiatives to develop them under the Greek Presidency did not come from the EP. While supporting improved implementation of existing programmes, it was sceptical about the Balkans' progress and enhanced Balkan integration. Thus, the EP left the leadership in this dossier to other actors. To conclude,

> It was crucial that Greece had the chair. The results would have been very different if any other Council member would have had it. Other countries may also not have been willing to organise a Summit. While the Commission contributed with a communication before the Thessaloniki Summit, the Greek Presidency added the major political elements. Even after the Greek presidency, the atmosphere changed – it would have been difficult to achieve what the Greeks achieved.[819]

Conclusion

This Chapter has shown that – numerous constraints not withstanding – the presidency agenda exhibited uniquely Greek contours. Greece pursued its objectives through extensive networking and strategic use of the presidency's formal and informal powers. Its preferred presidency tools were open debates and presenting policy papers.

Rather than developing new IM initiatives, Greece focused on existing projects and sought to shape the Community Patent regulation in a way that it would not compromise its own preferences. Greece had a particular interest in making the Community Patent accessible to SMEs because its economic sector consists largely of SMEs. In addition, it was Simitis' personal ambition to close the Community Patent negotiations and prove that Greece can handle difficult IM dossiers effectively.

Greece's alliance with the Commission was crucial to foster agreement on the Community Patent. It also relied heavily on its PM's expertise, engagement, and political weight. Greece's level of influence was medium to low. It managed to accommodate its own interest in the common approach brokered and no provision went against its interests.

However, some parts of the common approach were left vague and the subsequent failure by numerous presidencies to finalise the Community Patent regulation shows (a) that the political commitment generated by Simitis was not as robust as initially thought; and (b) that in case of a high intensity of preferences, a mutually acceptable outcome on the *Pareto* frontier may not be detected even if presidency initiative behind a certain dossier is sustained.

The overall strategy in the Community Patent debate was not to dissatisfy anybody and hence generate positive-sum outcomes. Given the unanimity rule, the presidency's influence consisted in guiding the Council towards agreement on its preferred choice without disregarding other Member States, in particular German interests. This was successfully done by the Greek Presidency whose compromise was more acceptable to Germany than previous proposals and the suggestions by the Commission.

In the foreign policy realm, the Greek Presidency reinvigorated the debate on the Western Balkans and developed an agenda for the further integration of the region based on the SAAs. For reasons of geopolitical proximity and historical connections, the Balkans are more vital to Greek interests than to any other EU Member State.[820] The prospect of a second Western Balkan Summit at the end of the Greek term generated a positive dynamic and growing understanding of the need to discuss issues of common concern in the areas of JHA, energy, defence, and the environment. Here too, Greece had to synthesise its own ideas with those developed by the Commission and other Council members most of which were more hesitant in their financial and political support of the region.[821] Hence, Greek presidency influence can be considered as medium. We observe a medium correlation between presidency preferences and outcomes brokered.

Politically most relevant, Greece – in the role of the presidency – managed to institutionalise regular Western Balkan meetings at both heads of state and ministerial level. While this idea was not new and had also been proposed by the Commission, as a 'regular' Council member it did not manage to generate sufficient support behind the Summits. Under its presidency, however, seizing upon its own expertise and policy papers as well as contributions by other relevant regional actors and think tanks, Greece succeeded to move the spotlight on the region and foster agreement on institutionalising high-level dialogue between the EU and the Western Balkans. In addition, the horizontal approach taken ensured that the Western Balkans were discussed in all relevant Council formations with important successes reached in the area of JHA.

The Thessaloniki Western Balkan Summit was no second Copenhagen – the five Western Balkan states were not granted candidate status or accession dates. However, the SAP was enriched with practical elements from the enlargement process that anchor Balkan integration on the EU agenda and make enlargement to the Western Balkans more feasible than previously the case. The Greek Presidency acted as the catalyst of this policy development. For the Western Balkans the steps taken may have been small, but for the EU in the light of the constraints it was facing – particularly the demanding international situation and the Iraq crisis – the Greek Presidency took a big qualitative step forward.

Policy entrepreneurship 'requires consistency and political courage'.[822] In the area of the Community Patent and the EU's Western Balkan policy Greece showed both. Although the Greek Presidency could not reinvent the EU's wheels, it set distinct accents and advanced its priority dossiers by generating outcomes that – while in line with its own interests – everybody could accept. A senior official concluded,

> The rotating Presidency is very useful for small countries. Usually, we – as small countries – follow the key decisions, but do not elaborate them. They are elaborated by the big countries and then presented to us. But during our presidency you do elaborate them yourself.[823]

7
Conclusion

In the light of the fierce reform debates of the Council presidency over the past few years and the divide it triggered between the big and small Member States – reflected most recently in the arguments by Irish voters for rejecting the Lisbon treaty in the June 2008 referendum – this book set out to investigate two interlinked questions: (a) why the rotating presidency was the single most contentious issue in the institutional reform discussions over the past years?; and (b) why especially small states have been such adamant supporters of the status quo and hence rotation? To answer these questions, it presented a systematic and comparative study of the presidency's role and influence within the EU's system of governance and challenged a number of common assumptions both in the presidency literature and in the reform debate.

I. The presidency, national interests, and levels of influence

The first is that the presidency is a mere administrative task and 'neutral broker'[824] whose ability to 'promote initiatives or [...] deliver to domestic expectations is heavily constrained.'[825] An assessment of the presidency's evolution and agenda-setting power, as well as in-depth case studies of the recent Finnish, Belgian, and Greek presidencies, showed that the presidency's institutional role grew over time and that its combination of formal and informal powers gives the office holder important leadership tools to broker compromises and shape EU policies in line with national interests.

Unsurprisingly, the office has been particularly important to small states whose decision-making power is more limited than that of the EU's big Member States. As a Greek official put it:

> The most positive aspect of the rotating presidency is that it gives us a chance to hold an influential role and that you manage to get totally different people to look at the same issue which you move into the spotlight.[826]

The book constructed a precise link between the domestic politics of the countries in the chair and how they influenced presidency priorities and strategies. In the area of the IM the selected presidencies all emphasised issues in which they had key economic interests. Importantly, they did so even if the obstacles to achieve agreement in these dossiers were considerable. Finland, the EU's pioneer in information technologies, prioritised the e-commerce and copyright directives despite their technical difficulties and contentious nature. The liberal-led Belgian government, keen to advance with domestic postal liberalisation, put the EU's postal service directive on top of its IM agenda even though there was a fierce split between a pro- and anti-liberalisation camp in the Council. Greece, concerned about its large sector of SMEs, tried to create better conditions for them by prioritising the Community Patent – a highly sensitive dossier that had been on the EU agenda for numerous presidencies without progressing. As none of these dossiers was new, they can be seen as examples of 'agenda structuring' by the presidency.[827]

Similarly, in the foreign policy realm there were clear links between domestic and presidency priorities. The three presidencies tried to introduce new initiatives or dimensions that reflected their geographical and geo-strategic interests as well as historical ties. Again, the three selected small state presidencies were not intimidated by unfavourable leadership environments or opposition. Seeking to strengthen EU foreign policy in the North, especially towards the neighbouring Russia, the Finnish Presidency managed to develop the ND into a central theme in the EU's external relations[828] despite the Chechnya crisis, scepticism from the Member States, Community institutions, as well as the partner countries. Belgium, with its African colonial ties, pushed for greater attention being paid to the region and a more holistic policy that would include a diplomatic, development, and military (conflict prevention) dimension when Member States were focused on the 'war against terrorism' and military invasion in Afghanistan and despite the disagreements between France and the UK on the Great Lakes. In an attempt to end its geographic exposure and economic and security reasons, the Greek Presidency pushed the Western Balkan countries ahead on their road to the EU at a time when 'enlargement fatigue' seemed to gain the upper hand and despite the crisis over Iraq. In contrast to IM initiatives, in the foreign policy realm presidencies sought policy innovation rather than merely going with the flow of the existing agenda.

Crucially, in both policy areas the respective (small state) presidencies did not simply pick undisputed dossiers that were 'easy' to conclude. They did not 'merely' concentrate on efficiency optimisation as some have argued, but prioritised those dossiers which they wanted to get to the *Pareto* frontier *and* influence in their favour (see Chapter 3). These tend to be issues in which the presidencies also have a high level of expertise. Expertise, in turn, is crucial for shifting an outcome into one's preferred direction and avoiding deadlock which can arise when pushing domestic interests.

While this emphasis on both efficiency (facilitating agreement) and distribution (shifting the agreement towards the chair's preferred outcome) hold in a presidency's priority area, in other ongoing agenda issues where the presidency may not have particular interests at stake or weak preferences it may focus more on efficiency than on distribution or indeed leave the leadership to others. This may be particularly true in the case of small state presidencies whose scope of interests tends to be narrower. While it may be worth investigating this more systematically, what mattered in our analysis is whether small states manage to impact distribution when they *have* strong preferences. This was shown to be the case. All outcomes accommodated presidency interests to a great extent and no compromises brokered were against the presidencies' preferences.

Finnish influence with regard to the e-commerce dossier was high. The directives most important aspects, such as the legal liability of intermediaries, were solved in line with Finnish interests despite disagreements in the Council. Finnish influence over the copyright dossier, however, was low. While the directive progressed considerably during the Finnish term and – as in case of e-commerce – the presidency solved the legal liability issue, Finland did not reach overall agreement on copyright. The succeeding Portuguese Presidency compromise differed from Finland's preferred solutions on the issues of exemptions and exhaustion of copyrights.

The Belgian Presidency's level of influence in case of postal liberalisation was medium. Its compromise on the directive reflected its own interests, but Belgium made concessions on special services and the timetable for full liberalisation which weakened its initially preferred policy choice.

Greece's presidency influence with regard to the Community Patent was medium to low. Although the political agreement on the Community Patent was in line with the interests Greece had been fiercely defended (the EU's multiple language regime, centralisation of patent jurisdiction, while safeguarding an important role for NPOs), the dossier is still pending. In other words, a mutually acceptable outcome has so far not been discernible. Indeed, by 2008 governments started to propose other legal agreements outside the EU's legal framework to reduce, for example, translation costs.

In the foreign policy dossiers, both the Finnish and the Belgian Presidencies exerted a high level of influence despite the unanimity requirement, and Greece's presidency influence can be considered as medium despite the numerous obstacles outlined above. All in all, in the three cases examined we detect more variance in IM than in foreign policy initiatives. This counters Whitman's (1998) analysis who found that particularly in foreign affairs, the presidency may not be the best vehicle to advance national policy objectives. Table 10 summarises these results.

Table 10 The Level of Presidency Influence in Selected IM and Foreign Policy Dossiers

Presidency	Policy Area	Priority	Level of Influence	Compromise reached by
Finland 1999	IM	• E-commerce directive	High	Unanimity
		• Copy-right directive	Low	No agreement
Belgium 2001		• Postal directive	Medium	Qualified majority
Greece 2003		• Community Patent	Medium to low	Unanimity
Finland 1999	Foreign Policy	• Northern Dimension	High	Unanimity
Belgium 2001		• Africa (Great Lakes)	High	Unanimity
Greece 2003		• Western Balkans	Medium	Unanimity

The case studies suggest that our hypothesis that the rotating presidency has evolved into an influential institution providing states with a window of opportunity to shape policy outcomes in line with the office holder's interests, holds. This finding agrees with Tallberg's (2006) investigation into the influence wielded by the chair of multilateral negotiations. However, the cases have also shown that the Council presidency cannot impose its will and that the level of presidential influence varies from dossier to dossier.

The presidency operates within a delicate resource-constraint structure which explains this variance. This leads us to the second empirical claim that has been challenged. It concerns the resources and constraints of the presidency and particularly the effects of the size of the office holder.

II.   A question of size? On the presidency's resources and constraints

This book has shown that small states are not overburdened with the presidency tasks. They generate similar levels of legislative output during their presidencies to big state presidencies (see Appendix) and the (small) size of a country, and hence limited material resources, does not hinder the office holder to shape the EU agenda and facilitate policy outcomes that reflect domestic preferences and priorities. Regardless of their size governments have greater influence over decision outcomes in the presidency seat than when not in the presidency seat. This has become particularly clear in the foreign policy realm where the agenda is less predetermined.

As an ordinary Council member Finland anchored the ND on the EU's systemic agenda, but only in the presidency seat could it put flesh on the initiative by convening numerous events on it and moving it onto the Council's active agendas. Similarly, it was the position of the chair that helped Belgium to develop a more pro-active and coherent EU Africa policy. The region had hardly featured on GAC agendas before. While holding the presidency, Greece reached what it had not achieved as an ordinary Council member at the GAERC in May 2002: sending a clear message to the Western Balkan countries that they belong into the EU; giving new impetus to Balkan integration by complementing the EU's Western Balkan policy with elements of the enlargement process; institutionalising regular meetings at head of state and ministerial level; and increasing financial support to the region.

The same holds for IM dossiers. As an ordinary Council member, Belgium did not manage to shift its preferred compromise into the center of debate given French resistance to liberalisation efforts. Similarly, the 2000 Portuguese Presidency compromise on the copyright dossier opposed the previous Finnish Presidency's preferred choices on a number of key aspects. No longer in the chair, the Finnish Presidency positions were no longer in the centre of debate.

This may have broader theoretical implications. Intergovernmentalism seems to underestimate the influence of small member states in the EU and tends to argue that bargaining reflects the interests and priorities of the big member states. This book has shown that small member states can have significant impact when they hold the presidency. Rather than their bargaining power, it is the small states' entrepreneurial behaviour within the resources/constraint structure that explains this outcome.

Rather than size as a condition for presidential success, four sets of resources and constraints were put forward: (a) the leadership environment (internal and external political and economic developments), (b) the heterogeneity, intensity, and distribution of governmental preferences in the Council, (c) inter-institutional relations with the Commission and the Parliament, and (d) the presidency's skill and effective use of the Council Secretariat. These, in turn, can be grouped into three broader categories of context-specific factors, the institutional environment, and country characteristics. This is illustrated in Figure 5.

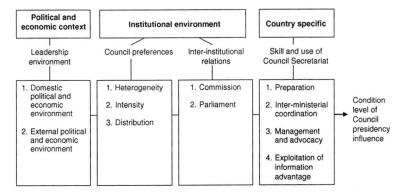

Figure 5 The Council Presidency's Resource/Constraint Structure

The case studies in this book suggest that presidency influence is likely to be highest when:

- its domestic and external political and economic environment is favourable;
- the heterogeneity of views in the Council is high and the intensity of preferences is low allowing the presidency to construct winning coalitions around its favoured points of view;
- it has no big state coalition against its proposals;
- it works in tandem with the Commission and generates Commission backing for its compromise;
- it mobilises support in the EP; and
- it prepares its priorities well and legitimises them at EU level through effective management and advocacy tactics, ensures efficient domestic co-ordination, and skilfully exploits its information advantage by using the Council Secretariat.

While the country in the chair cannot influence its leadership environment, it can manipulate the other factors by investing its resources and technical expertise to mobilise support for its preferred solution.[829] All three states (despite their differences in terms of interests and identity (North/South), the degree of commitment to European integration, and level of experience) concentrated on these strategies particularly as they could not rely on their political weight or voting power in the Union.

Further research is needed if we want to establish the weight of each of the factors that condition a presidency's success. The cases of the copyright dossier and the aftermath of the Community Patent agreement suggest, however, that the intensity and distribution of Member State preferences are the biggest constraints to a country's presidency influence. Much of what the presidency can or cannot do will depend on how and how deeply the Council is divided and on the quality of the compromise, that is what it offers to whom. This gives weight to the arguments put forward by intergovernmentalism.

While more work needs to be done accurately to rank the importance of the conditions for success, differences were detected given the different institutional environment in Pillars I and II. Building alliances with the Commission and the EP was generally more important for the presidency in IM legislation than in foreign policy issues. However, both institutions' influence in shaping the final policy outcome of a presidency's priority dossier was found to be exaggerated.

In the e-commerce case, the Finnish Presidency deleted the articles in which the Commission tried to sketch out additional powers for itself and rejected any EP amendments which questioned its approach. The Belgian Presidency compromise on postal liberalisation weakened the initial Commission proposal and the notion of special services was dropped even though the Commission had fiercely defended it. The EP's potential supranational leadership was also limited. Trying to slow the liberalisation pace, the Belgian Presidency compromise rejected most of its amendments. The Community Patent is an example where the Commission clearly relinquished its agenda-setting power entirely to the Council presidency. The final shape of the Greek Presidency compromise, particularly concerning the patent's judicial regime, was directly opposed to the compromise the Commission had put forward. Similarly, the EP had little overall influence in shaping the Community Patent. Only those EP suggestions that enjoyed the backing of the Greek Presidency (and a critical mass of Member States) were considered.

This poses difficult questions for neofunctionalism and for accounts that analyse supranational leadership without investigating the strategies and policy entrepreneurship of the presidency.[830] Commission proposals change – often significantly – in Council negotiations and the co-decision procedure and, as noted by one interviewee, only 'in very exceptional cases [the Commission] turns against a common position reached in the Council'.[831]

In Pillar II issues the case studies showed that the Commission through its permanence, policy papers, and alliances with key Member States can ensure a degree of policy continuity. To advance the ND and Western Balkans, both the Finnish and the Greek Presidencies had to lobby the Commission and make some concessions to it, especially on the budgetary front. However, neither in the ND, the EU's Africa nor in Western Balkan's policy, the Commission or EP were the driving forces. This is contrary to Krause's (2003) finding that the Commission was the key player in the development of the EU's Africa policy. Only when the Belgian Presidency took it on board, was progress made.

Merely focusing on supranational players – according to neofunctionalism the most important actors shaping European integration – would present difficulties in explaining both negotiation outcomes in Pillar I and the origins and development of foreign policy initiatives. Moreover, the empirical findings of this book suggest that the neofunctionalist logic of spill-over effects whereby integration between states in one area will create strong incentives to integrate another is overly optimistic, particularly in Pillar II. This analysis has shown that to have issues, such as the ND, the Great Lakes or the Western Balkans, considered on EU level or move them forward, the interested actors have to put in a lot of time, effort, and resources. There is no automaticity about this process or indeed its success.

III. The presidency as a policy entrepreneur

The institutionalist concept of a policy entrepreneur describes the nature and influence of the rotating Council presidency well. It captures its inherent bias and subtle informal powers. As Schattschneider once argued, 'The outcomes of the game of politics depends on which of a multitude of possible conflicts gains the dominant position.'[832] This book showed that the government who holds the Council presidency has a unique comparative advantage to move certain issues and solutions into the dominant position by increasing an issues' visibility, the intensity with which it is debated, and by exploiting its procedural powers and information advantages.[833] Indeed, the latter can be seen as the most important informal power of the presidency. It ensures that it is very difficult for the Council to agree anything against a presidency country's wish.

Once the presidency manages to focus the Council on a certain set of solutions or generates broad agreement on a general approach, it can afford to be more 'neutral' – or rather will inevitably appear more neutral: the set of solutions being discussed is already in the presidency's interest and has a critical mass on its side. The strategy to achieve such broad agreement, particularly in CFSP issues where the neutrality constraint is most obvious, involved convincing Member States of the European value added of an initiative and explaining why it is the right time to look at a particular dossier. In all cases, Council conclusions on a presidency initiative were generated before taking office. This legitimised presidential initiatives and gave the respective Council presidencies a mandate to pursue them during their term.

In one important aspect, however, this analysis differed from Kingdon's policy entrepreneurship and agenda-setting model. This difference stems from the Council Presidency's hybrid nature as a supranational office and intergovernmental policy entrepreneur at the same time. As argued repeatedly, the institution of the presidency itself can be seen as a (predictable) window of opportunity for individual governments to shape the EU agenda and policy outcomes. However, in so far as the government in office has to manipulate its resource/constraint environment before and during its term to ensure the successful pursuit of its priorities, individual presidencies do not resemble a 'surfer who waits for the big wave', but policy actors that actively seek and even create windows of opportunity once they move into the chair. In other words, windows of opportunity for the chair do not necessarily open automatically, but the presidency country has to increase the likelihood for them to open and thus create the conditions for maximising presidential influence. While sometimes a presidency may be able to seize on opportunities and tap into the perception of urgency of a certain matter by other Council members, more often it seeks to create these windows of opportunity.

The findings support rational choice institutionalism in that it sees the presidency as a set of rules and incentives and the office holder as a self-interested utility maximiser. Outcomes are determined by strategic rationality and manipulation of the presidency's resource/constraint structure. However, the office holder also 'plays its games' within a social and institutional culture of consensus. While utility maximising will remain the primary motivation of the presidency and appears to be exogenous, the country in the chair realises that its goals can be achieved most effectively by keeping consensual relations with the other decision-makers, particularly the Council members. Hence some preferences may be endogenous to the presidency. The culture of compromise in the Council is an important informal norm that is often underestimated by non-institutionalist versions of rational choice theory. To defend its national interests successfully, a presidency does not only exploit its procedural powers, but has to show solidarity for its Council partners, understand their domestic constraints, and adjust its preferences and policy style before and during its period in office. Consensus outweighs the formal decision-making rule of QMV. In other words, presidencies – while shaping compromises in their favour – often seek unanimous agreement even if formally a qualified majority suffices to adopt a dossier. Ungerer has termed this way of operating a 'refined form of defending national interests'.[834] In sum, the country in the chair finds that its behaviour is shaped by the presidency as an institution and it rationally chooses to be constrained by it to some extent.[835] The normative implications of this argument are explored in greater detail below.

These findings make it difficult to come to a clear-cut conclusion on whether the Council presidency is an intervening or causal variable when explaining policy outcomes. In one sense, it can be seen as an intervening variable – an opportunity for national governments to exploit the formal and informal powers which come with the office. On the other hand, the Council Presidency also has independent effects on policy outcomes. In making the Member State in the chair absorb the institutional culture of consensus, rethink preferences and shape strategies, the Council presidency as an institution plays a leading part. Indeed, the adaptation to the institutional environment and other actors' preferences is a condition for success in advancing a national government's priority or goal.

In focusing on the presidency's research-constraint structure and relying on institutionalism and Kingdon's agenda-setting theory, the book has tried to move away from the stale debate between intergovernmentalism and neofunctionalism. Instead it has stressed the interdependence of actors and institutions. The investigation has shown that it is too simplistic to assume that any one actor or governments alone are fully in control of the integration process. As the EU is highly polycentric, leadership dispersed, and dominance by one actor not tolerated, establishing coalitions, channelling ideas through other actors, and utilising other actors' resources are crucial. In their coalition-building efforts, however, any actor, whether Member State or supranational institution, will need to work closely with the presidency and vice versa.

IV.   The value of the rotating Council presidency

The results of this study have a number of normative implications. Given that the rotating Council presidency can shape policy in line with the holder's preferences, is this development contrary to the spirit of the European integration project? The findings of this analysis suggest quite the contrary. First, Chapter 2 has shown that the rotating presidency has been an important symbol of the European construct. As any system with federal traits, the EU's effective functioning relies upon the notion of equality amongst its ever more diverse Member States, particularly the big and small. To guard equality and avoid the creation of a strong permanent centre, the EU's founding members agreed multiple mechanisms to tame pure power politics in the EU and share out leadership. Out of these mechanisms (the combination of supranational and intergovernmental elements, weighted votes in the Council, and balanced appointment procedures to the EU institutions), the rotating Council presidency has been the only one that guards the equality principle in its pure form.[836] As such, it fulfils a crucial political objective characteristic of federalism. As Alexander Hamilton once argued in the course of the US Constitutional Convention:

> [...] if the smaller states renounce their equality, they renounce at the same time their liberty.[837]

The importance of this symbolism should not be underestimated in a Community that is becoming ever more diverse. Indeed, it merits much closer and more systematic investigation after the 2004 and 2007 enlargements.

Second, the case studies demonstrated that the presidency has an important educational effect. Training takes place, interministerial co-ordination systems are enhanced, and by exposing officials to managing highly technical dossiers and Community processes, the presidency contributes to skill development.[838] As Menon argues,

> Holding the presidency represents by far the most effective way of ensuring the effective Europeanisation of national administrations. This is not a question of making them pro-European but rather of ensuring that they are adequately prepared for the onerous task of ensuring smooth administrative interaction between the EU and national levels. Holding the presidency represents a kind of "Shock Therapy" which forces national administrations to devise ways of working effectively with Brussels.[839]

Third, the short six-month presidency term seems to work as a continuous motor for policy innovation. The case studies showed that each six-month presidency brings new ambitions and solutions to the job and thereby injects renewed dynamism into EU – decision-making. Former Commission President Jacques Santer pointed out:

> My personal experience confirms the fact that every six months, impetus and new dynamism are given to the work of the EU, while a longer term presidency would no doubt curtail "permanent motivation".[840]

This is particularly important since the running of the Union can easily 'fall prey to bureaucratic routine'.[841]

Finally, this book has shown that the bias of the presidency is not contrary to the spirit of European integration, because the Council presidency operates within a consensus-driven, positive-sum culture (see above). In the two cases which fell under QMV (e-commerce under the Finnish chair and postal liberalisation under the Belgian Presidency), the compromises catered for more than the required qualified majority. Our empirical evidence suggests that the general philosophy of the presidency is 'not to dissatisfy anybody' and treat the other Council members as the office holder would expect them to treat it when no longer in the chair. Hence, presidencies look for balanced outcomes that are acceptable to all even if formally only a qualified majority may be required. Prioritising IM dossiers that are closest to national interest thus happens neither at the expense of the majority interest nor to the detriment of the minority. Lane and Mattila (1998) estimate that 75–81% of decisions in the Council are based on unanimity rather than the required QMV and even after enlargement decision outcomes continue to 'be sensitive to the positions taken by all actors'.[842]

As one analyst argues, EU bargaining and the institution of the presidency is characterised by 'a collective rationality based on the dual responsibility to deliver the goods at home and collectively at the EU level'.[843] Uniquely placed at the interface of the national and Community level, the Council presidency tries to reconcile self-interest with solidarity. Alternatively, this behaviour may be driven by short-term versus long-term rationality. The country in the chair may be willing to accommodate other states' interests as much as possible, because in repeated games it pays off to be accommodating in the long run. For each time a country has the presidency, it is 26 times an ordinary Council member. Hence, what may happen when a country is no longer holding the presidency surely weighs heavily on its calculations.

Similarly, in the area of foreign policy the successful presidency was pushing on its own regional priorities stressing the value added for all and without downgrading other foreign policy initiatives. Contrary to the compromises presented in IM dossiers, there were no radical changes from presidency to presidency. Instead we observed shifts of emphasis and path dependency. Despite Greece's enthusiasm for speedy Balkan integration, the conditionality principle was not dropped or EU accession criteria weakened. Rather than seeking a radical overhaul of the EU's Africa policy, Belgium's initiatives in the Great Lakes built upon the existing Cotonou Agreements and conflict-prevention measures. The political need to minimise confrontation (as well as the unanimity requirement in foreign policy) prevents the presidency office for being exploited for pure self-interest at the expense of others. This may explain in part why the presidency has remained unreformed for so long.

These insights into the way the presidency operates suggest that the logic of repeated games is strong in the EU and that the principle of diffused or deferred reciprocity underlies Council negotiations. The latter was clearly visible in the case of the ND. Finland started hosting events related to the Mediterranean Partnership years before its presidency in order to generate the Southern countries' support of its own regional initiative and convince them that the ND was not designed to compete with the Barcelona Process. Subsequently, the 2000 Portuguese Presidency committed itself to adopt the first action plan on the initiative.

Moreover, even if the Council presidency may be able to shape policy outcomes in line with its own interests, this may be considered as legitimate. The three presidencies examined here prioritised not only those IM and foreign policy dossiers that were of national interest to them, but also on which they had a greater level of expertise than other Council members, the Commission, and the EP. This greater level of expertise arguably turns them into legitimate leaders who try to 'customise the EU' and hence '[emphasise] some feature over others so that the Union would resemble the country itself'.[844] The presidency can therefore be seen as a unique tool to ensure that the EU serves its 'customers'. The rotation principle and brief period of office guarantee that no customers are systematically preferred over others.

V. Are the alternatives better?

Whether these key values of the Council presidency, including the Council's consensus culture, spirit of shared leadership in the EU, and incentive for policy innovation, will be upheld under the new Lisbon Treaty remains to be seen. If ratified in the end, the EU will get a new differentiated presidency of the Council. This differentiated presidency disconnects the European Council presidency from the presidency of the Council of Ministers and takes away external representation from rotation. A permanent presidency is introduced at the European Council level (elected for a two and a half year term, renewable once) along with a permanent double-hatted High Representative for foreign policy who is also Vice-President of the Commission.

Rotation is preserved at the Council of Minister level and its substructures. Here, the presidency (with the exception of foreign affairs) is to be held by pre-established groups of three Member States (made up on a basis of equal rotation taking into account Member States diversity and geographical balance) for a period of 18 months. This new 'troika presidency' is to work together on the basis of a common programme. Each of the three states can take the lead for six months as is the case today – or the countries in the team can decide alternative arrangements among themselves.

These are the most far-reaching presidency reforms to date and they present both opportunities and risks. A permanent European Council President could develop experience and political capital to ensure better implementation records especially of projects that were a particular country's hobby horse. In addition, separating the European Council clearly from legislative affairs in the Council of Ministers would allow for a greater focus on political leadership, strategic debate, and longer-term agenda setting. This could include a more permanent and structured relationship with the supranational decision-makers, which together with the new mechanisms of dismissal could enhance the new institution's accountability.[845]

At the same time, the introduction of a permanent European Council president as head of the EU's most powerful decision-making institution could introduce an additional source of conflict between the EU institutions, the different Council layers, and the Member States. This was a key concern in the Convention debates; particularly should the elected European Council President be from a big Member State.[846] In addition, the challenge of coordination between the new permanent President and the rotating presidency is largely unchartered by the Treaty and their precise division of tasks not yet clear. The new arrangement raises the question, to what extent was such effectiveness predicated on the joint chairing of both the European Council and the Council of Ministers? Finally, it is doubtful, that the permanent European Council President will provide the EU a long sought face, given the continued existence of the High Representative, the rotating presidency of the Council of Ministers, and of course the presidents of the Commission and the European Parliament. A straight answer to Henry Kissinger's agonising question as to whose phone to call when dealing with the EU remains more elusive than ever.

At Council of Minister level, troika presidencies present opportunities to enhance agenda coordination between the Member States. The 2007–2008 trio partners, Germany, Portugal, and Slovenia, for example, already agreed to work more closely together during their 18 months to improve the implementation of the issues that all three presidencies treat as priorities and to enhance their political cooperation (through joint cultural projects, joint training programmes, and personnel exchanges). This way, potential administrative shortcomings of single Member States could be bridged. Nonetheless, so far Member States continue to draw up their own 'national' presidency programme along side the joint programmes and the troika presidency set-up does not prevent the tendency of some big states from treating the small as junior partners.

To conclude, the main arguments presented against rotation, namely that the EU needs a powerful figurehead and that small states are over-burdened with the task rest on shaky empirical ground. Even inexperienced small states, such as Finland in 1999 or more recently the 2008 Slovenian Presidency, have highly encouraging records. Ultimately, the EU's institutional set-up should be designed in a way that primarily serves its Member States. This book has shown that the rotating presidency does so by alternating agenda-shaping power between them and by making a difference in terms of both the bargaining outcomes it generates and the functioning of the EU as a whole.

Appendix

I. The Council's legislative activity from 1999–2007

Year	Presidency	Directive	Regulation	Decision	Recommendation	Common Strategy/Joint Action	Other	Total
1999	Germany Finland	22 16	117 80	162 135	2 2	5 11	16 38	324 282
1999 Total		38	197	297	4	16	54	606
2000	Portugal France	19 32	80 115	130 133	4 1	5 8	13 16	251 305
2000 Total		51	195	263	5	13	29	556
2001	Sweden Belgium	19 24	77 85	152 122	8 2	12	16 15	272 260
2001 Total		43	162	274	10	12	31	532
2002	Spain Denmark	36 26	80 80	153 128	7 1	8 8	29 18	313 261
2002 Total		62	160	281	8	16	47	574
2003	Greece Italy	29 34	77 115	131 156	7 5	12 10	14 10	270 330
2003 Total		63	192	287	12	22	24	600
2004	Ireland Netherlands	47 11	129 97	120 168	1 1	5 17	16 10	318 304
2004 Total		58	226	288	2	22	26	622

(Continued)

Year	Presidency	Directive	Regulation	Decision	Recommendation	Common Strategy/Joint Action	Other	Total
2005	Luxembourg United Kingdom	10 27	58 84	143 152	5 8	12 26	16 9	244 306
2005 Total		37	142	295	13	38	25	550
2006	Austria Finland	22 43	71 139	109 194	6 3	20 12	18 10	246 401
2006 Total		65	210	303	9	32	28	647
2007	Germany Portugal	5 16	63 82	103 163	1 1	21 22	15 16	208 300
2007 Total		21	145	266	2	43	31	508
1999–2007 Total		438	1629	2554	65	214	295	5195
(A) Average per 6 month term (1999–2003)		25.7	90.6	140.2	3.9	7.9	18.5	286.8
(B) Average per 6 month term (2004–2007)		23.6	91.6	141.3	3.6	16.1	13.4	289.6
(C) = (B) − (A)		−2.13	0.97	1.09	−0.33	8.24	−5.07	2.77
(D) Average/Smalls (1999–2003)		22.17	79.83	133.00	4.00	8.00	19.00	266.00
(E) Average/Smalls (2004–2007)		26.60	98.80	146.80	3.20	13.20	14.00	302.60

(F) = (E) − (D)	4.43	18.97	13.80	−0.80	5.20	−5.00	36.60
(G) Average/Bigs (1999–2003)	31	106.75	151.00	3.75	7.75	17.75	318.00
(H) Average/Bigs (2004–2007)	16	73.50	127.50	4.50	23.50	12.00	257.00
(I) = (H) − (G)	−15.00	−33.25	−23.50	0.75	15.75	−5.75	−61.00
(A) − (D)	3.53	−26.92	−18.00	0.25	0.25	1.25	−52.00
(B) − (E)	−3.03	25.30	19.30	−1.30	−10.30	2.00	45.60
(A) − (G)	−5.30	−16.15	−10.80	0.15	0.15	0.75	−31.20
(B) − (H)	7.57	18.07	13.79	−0.93	−7.36	1.43	32.57
(D) − (G)	−8.83	−26.92	−18.00	0.25	0.25	1.25	−52.00
(E) − (H)	10.60	25.30	19.30	−1.30	−10.30	2.00	45.60

Note: The category entitled 'Other' includes: Addendums, Budget decisions, Common Positions, Final Acts, Joint Positions, Joint Statements and Council Statements, Memorandums, Staff Regulations, Rules of Procedure, Implementing Rules, Declarations, Agreed Minutes. The total number of EU Legislation published in the Official Journal of the European Communities from 1999 to 2007 and revised to elaborate this table is 34,638. König et al. (2006)'s dataset using CELEX and EUR-Lex supports the overall results. However, the precise numbers of adopted acts they record are much lower. Such discrepancies can be explained by various factors: (a) differences in the search queries; (b) as König et al. (2006) find, the Celex data were integrated into the EUR-Lex framework in January 2005. Accordingly, these two sources may not be viewed as entirely independent; (c) the above numbers include binding and non-binding legislation that may or may not be in force any longer; and (d) binding legislation may occasionally involve both multiple Commission initiatives and/or multiple final adopted acts.

Source: Self-Elaboration based on Official Journal of the European Communities (**http://eur-lex.europa.eu/JOIndex.do?ihmlang=en**).

Notes

1. Flash Eurobarometer No. 245, 18 June 2008.
2. Magnette and Nicolaïdis (2003).
3. Westlake (1995), p. 37.
4. Dewost (1984), p. 31; Wallace (1985), in O'Nuallain (1985), p. 10.
5. Schout (1998).
6. O'Nuallain (1985); De Bassompiere (1988); Kirchner (1992); Elgström (2003); Tallberg (2006).
7. Bulmer and Wessels (1987); Troy Johnston (1994); Dinan (1994, 1999); Hayes-Renshaw and Wallace (1997); Westlake (1995); Nugent (1995); Hix (1999); Peterson and Bomberg (1999); Sherrington (2000).
8. Kirchner and Tsagkari (1993); Garel-Jones (1993); Höll (1998); Ludlow (1998); Henderson (1998a, 1998b); Duke (1998); Anderson (1999); Luther (1999); Maurer (2000); Stubb (2000a); Tiilikainen (2000); Bjurulf (2001); Edwards and Wiessala (2001); Lequesne (2001); Vos and Bailleul (2002); Martinez Sierra (2002); Van Keulen (2004); Bunse (2004); Whitman and Thomas (2005); Quaglia and Moxon-Browne (2006); Quaglia, Hough, and Mayhew (2007).
9. See also Elgström (2003).
10. Other comparative works include Kirchner (1992, 1993); Elgström (ed.) (2003).
11. Wallace, in O'Nuallain (1985), p. 271.
12. Hayes-Renshaw and Wallace (1995), p. 146.
13. Westlake (1995), p. 45; Dewost (1984); Wallace (1985a).
14. Nugent (1995), p. 128; Hix (1999), pp. 28–30, 63–66; Bulmer and Wessels (1987).
15. De Bassompiere (1988); Verbeke and Van de Voorde (1994); Nugent (1995).
16. Verbeke and Van de Voorde (1994), p. 35.
17. Tallberg (2002a), p. 3.
18. Ibid.
19. See also Mazzucelli (2003).
20. See also Schmidt (2001).
21. Underdahl (1994), in Metcalfe (1998), p. 426. *Blackwell Encyclopaedia of Political Science* (1991), p. 321.
22. Beach (2005), p. 18.
23. Bachrach and Baratz (1962); Schattschneider (1960).
24. Peters (1998).
25. Jones (1984); Peters (1994b). For functionalist theories see Almond and Coleman (1960); Almond and Powell (1966).
26. King, Keohane, and Verba (1994).
27. Thelen and Steinmo (1992), p. 9; Wessels et al. (2003); Bulmer (1994).

28. Pollack (1996), pp. 431–442.
29. Thelen and Steinmo (1992), p. 2.
30. Peters (1996b), p. 206.
31. Other types include sociological and historical institutionalism. See Hall and Taylor (1996); Immergut (1998); Peters (2005).
32. North (1990); Peters (2005), p. 49.
33. Weingast (1996), p. 168.
34. See Garret and Weingast (1993); Tsebelis (1994, 1995); Garrett and Tsebelis (1996); Pollack (1996, 2003) for rational choice approaches to the EU and Bulmer and Armstrong (1998) or Pierson (1998) for historical institutionalism.
35. Haas (1958, 1964, 1975); Lindberg (1963); Lindberg and Scheingold (1970, 1971); Sandholtz and Zysman (1989); Transholm-Mikkelsen (1991).
36. Hoffmann (1966); Keohane and Hoffmann (1991); Garrett (1992); Moravcsik (1993, 1998).
37. Pollack (1996), p. 430.
38. Moe (1990), p. 213; Puchala (1999), p. 318.
39. Moravcsik (1997).
40. Wozniak Boyle (2006), p. 23.
41. King, Keohane, and Verba (1994) call these systematic and non-systematic differences.
42. Bachrach and Baratz (1963); Beach (2005).
43. For quantitative research on the presidency, see Thomson (2008).
44. Kelstrup (1993).
45. For other definitions, see Rothstein (1968); Keohane (1969); Thorhallson (2000).
46. Dinan (1999), p. 231. See also Bengtsson (2003), p. 56.
47. Mill (1846); Przeworski and Teune (1970); Lijphart (1971); Meckstroth (1975); King et al. (1994); Peters (1998).
48. Elgström (ed.) (2003).
49. Stubb (2000a), p. 52. The EU's three pillar design was introduced in 1992 by the Maastricht Treaty.
50. Enhancing the EU's relations with the Western Balkans under the Greek Presidency included putting them on enlargement track. Enlargement, in turn, is a more comprehensive template than merely foreign policy. It combines elements of the EU's external and internal policies.
51. Whitehead (2002), pp. 186–212.
52. Other challenges include the numerous definitions of institutions, leadership, and influence. Peters (1996b).
53. In December 2005 the Council decided to publish initial discussions and final votes on EU legislation that falls under the co-decision procedure. But the discussions in between, when compromises are being brokered, will remain secret. EU Observer 22 December 2005.
54. See also Bunse (2000); Tallberg (2003).
55. Wallace and Wallace (2000), p. 38.
56. See Laffan (1997b); Hix (1994), p. 1; Sbragia (1992), p. 257; Risse-Kappen (1996), p. 56.

57. Wallace and Wallace (2000), p. 3 and 5.
58. Elazar (2001), p. 49.
59. Majone (1994).
60. Hix (1999); Schuppert (1994).
61. Nicolaïdis and Howse (2001). See also Sandholtz and Stone Sweet (1998), p. 1; Olsen (2002), p. 584.
62. Magnette and Nicolaïdis (2003).
63. Strictly speaking the EC remains a separate entity (Pillar I) within the EU. Magnette and Nicolaïdis (2003); Kohnstamm and Durand (2003).
64. Treaty of Paris Art. 9; Treaty of Rome Art. 157.
65. Simmenthal v. Commission (Case 92/78). Stein (1981); Burley and Mattli (1993).
66. George (1991), p. 3.
67. Nugent (1995), p. 112.
68. Kohnstamm and Durand (2003), p. 4.
69. For a study of Commission-small state relations, see Bunse, Magnette, and Nicolaïdis (2005b).
70. Kohnstamm and Durand (2003), p. 3.
71. QMV was rarely used until the latter half of the 1980s.
72. For detailed discussions, see Moravcsik and Nicolaïdis (1999); Peterson and Bomberg (1999); Magnette and Nicolaïdis (2003).
73. Nice Treaty, Protocol on EU enlargement, Article 3(i) and (ii).
74. Baldwin and Widgrén (2003); Baldwin, Berglof, Giavazzi, and Widgrén (2001); Raunio and Wiberg (1998).
75. If after 12 months no agreement is forthcoming, the countries supporting the proposal may move ahead by themselves.
76. See also Baldwin and Widgrén (2004).
77. Ahern, in Brown (2004).
78. Art 157, EC.
79. EU Observer, 13.1.2004.
80. EU Observer, 9.7.2004.
81. Magnette and Nicolaïdis (2003), p. 6.
82. Geurts (1998), p. 56.
83. Nice Treaty, Protocol on enlargement, Art. 4, Provisions concerning the Commission.
84. Interview, Finnish PermRep, 2.3.2005.
85. Bunse, Magnette, and Nicolaïdis (2005b).
86. Magnette and Nicolaïdis (2003), p. 7.
87. Wallace (1985b), p. 2; Westlake (1995), p. 37.
88. *Financial Times (FT)*, 4.12.2000.
89. Raili Seppnen, in *Sunday Business*, 27.6.1999.
90. Tiilikainen, *Convention*, 21.1.2003.
91. Dick Roche, *Convention*, 21.1.2003.
92. Gijs de Vries, *Convention*, 21.1.2003.
93. See Balazs and Maij-Weggen, *Convention*, 20–21.1.2003; Rupel and Kelam, *Convention*, 15.5.2003; Interview, Commission, 7.3.2003.
94. Coussens and Crum (2003); Kollman (2003); Tallberg (2003).
95. Coussens and Crum (2003), p. 21.

96. Ferrero-Waldner, *BBC News*, 16.1.2003.
97. Costa Neves, *BBC News*, 16.1.2003.
98. Aznar, in Martinez Sierra (2002), p. 15.
99. Magnette and Nicolaïdis (2004).
100. James Madison, Federal Convention, 9.6.1787. See also debate on 11.6.1787 (http://www.constitution.org/dfc/dfc-1787.txt).
101. Nicolaïdis and Howse (2001), p. 4.
102. ECSC, Art. 27.
103. EEC, Art. 146, Euratom, Art. 116. The 1965 Merger Treaty adopted the six-month period for all three Communities.
104. Wallace and Edwards (1976), p. 536.
105. Edwards and Wallace (1977), p. 1.
106. Wallace, in O'Nuallain (1985), p. 3.
107. Maastricht Treaty, Art. 4.
108. Ludlow (2002a), p. 5–15.
109. Interview, Commission, 7.3.2003.
110. Kirchner (1992), p. 73.
111. The European Council was not formally institutionalised until 1986 and the presidency was not officially charged to chair it until 1992.
112. Kirchner (1992), p. 72. See also Bulmer and Wessels (1987), pp. 103–109; Dinan (1994), pp. 231–239; Westlake (1995), pp. 37–49; Hayes-Renshaw and Wallace (1997), pp. 134–157.
113. If the Conciliation Committee fails to deliver a result acceptable to both EP and Council, the proposal falls.
114. See also Westlake (1995), p. 37; Ludlow (1994), p. 146.
115. Title III, Art. 40 10. (b).
116. Title III, Art. 40 10. (g).
117. Hayes-Renshaw and Wallace (1997), p. 175.
118. Beyers and Dierickx (1998), p. 290; Sloot and Verschuren (1990), pp. 64–65.
119. Annex I and II, Council of the European Communities (2002c).
120. Kirchner (1992), p. 71.
121. Westlake (1995), p. 37.
122. Council (2002b).
123. Kirchner (1992); Westlake (1995); Hayes-Renshaw and Wallace (1997); Sherrington (2000).
124. Esbøll, in O'Nuallain (1985), p. ix.
125. See also Kirchner (1992); Westlake (1995); Wurzel (1996a, b); Hayes-Renshaw and Wallace (1997); Sherrington (2000).
126. Lautso (1997), p. 4.
127. Schout (1998), p. 1.
128. Wallace (1985b), p. 16.
129. Moravcsik (1999a), p. 271. Puchala (1999).
130. Kingdon (1995), p. 179.
131. Moravcsik (1999a), p. 272.
132. Young (1991), in Young (1999), p. 806.
133. Beach (2005), pp. 18–19.
134. Kingdon (1984, 1995).

135. Peters (1994a).
136. Kingdon (1995), p. 3.
137. Ibid. (1995).
138. Peters (1996a), p. 62.
139. Peters (1994a), p. 11.
140. Sandholtz and Zysman (1989); Cram (1997); Pollack (1998); Jones and Clark (1998); Wendon (1998); Jabko (1999); Krause (2003); Wozniak (2006).
141. Schmidt (2001) is an exception.
142. Moravcsik (1999a), p. 270.
143. Ibid., p. 273.
144. Wallace and Edwards (1976), p. 536.
145. Council (1996a).
146. Bainbridge and Teasdale (1997), p. 372.
147. Metcalfe (1998), p. 419.
148. McCubbins and Schwartz (1984); McCubbins and Page (1987); McCubbins, Noll, and Weingast (1987, 1989); Moe (1987); Pollack (1997, 1998).
149. Whitman (1998), p. 15, in Tallberg (2003), p. 4.
150. Bengtsson, Elgström, and Tallberg (2004), p. 315. See also Amstrup (1976); Lindell and Persson (1986); Handel (1990).
151. The Lisbon Treaty changes this. See Chapter 7.
152. Schmidt (2001), p. 126.
153. Interview, Greek PermRep, 4.5.2004.
154. Ungerer (1988), p. 101.
155. Whitman (2006), p. 3.
156. Voss and Bailleul (2002), p. 6.
157. Bulmer and Wessels (1987), p. 138.
158. Vos and Bailleul (2002), p. 7.
159. Verbeke and Van de Voorde (1994), p. 35.
160. Interviews, Finnish Ministry of Finance, 27.8.2003; Finnish EU Presidency Secretariat, 21.6.1999.
161. *EU Observer*, 12.1.2004. Irish Independent 12.1.2004.
162. Wallace and Edwards (1976), p. 538.
163. Wallace (1985a), pp. 272–273.
164. Olsen (2002), p. 597. See also Pollack (1997, 1998).
165. Hayes-Renshaw and Wallace (1997), p. 145; Bunse (2000), p. 29.
166. Wallace (1985a), p. 272.
167. See European Information Service (EIS), 29.1.2003.
168. Kerr, EP Plenary, 18.2.1998.
169. While visiting Israel's Premier Ariel Sharon, for example, he did not meet the then leader of the Palestinian Authority, Yasser Arafat. *EU Observer*, 30.12.2003.
170. Mazzucelli (2003).
171. *European Voice (EV)*, 14–20.12.2000.
172. Gray and Stubb (2001), p. 11.
173. Luif (1999).
174. Wallace (1986), p. 586.
175. Interview, Finnish PM's Office, 22.6.1999.
176. Bunse (2000). Tallberg (2003) labels these three forms of agenda influence 'agenda-exclusion', 'agenda-structuring', and 'agenda-setting'.

177. Peters (1994a), p. 9.
178. Schattschneider (1960), p. 69.
179. Hix (1999), p. 66.
180. Wallace and Edwards (1976), p. 536.
181. *EU Observer*, 20.10.2005 and 3.12.2005.
182. Interview, UK PermRep, 5.3.2003.
183. Bachrach and Baratz (1962, 1963).
184. Examples include the 1982 Belgian Presidency who set the annual farm prizes by vote and the 1985 Italian Presidency who 'forced through' the convening of an IGC by vote. Bulmer and Armstrong (1998), p. 14.
185. Interview, UK PermRep, 5.3.2003.
186. Interview, Finnish Ministry of Foreign Affairs (MFA), 29.8.2003. In the latter case, German Chancellor Gerhard Schröder ordered the chairman of the environment Council, Jürgen Trittin, to delay decision-making and change the directive to protect the interests of the German car industry. *The Guardian*, 5.7.1999, *EV*, 24.-30.6.1999.
187. *Deutsche Welle*, 30.12.2003.
188. Interview, UK PermRep, 5.3.2003.
189. Interview, Finnish PM's Office, 29.8.2003.
190. Kollman (2003), pp. 56–57.
191. Hix (1999), p. 66.
192. Wurzel (1996a), p. 281.
193. Westlake (1995), p. 116.
194. Ibid.
195. Given the Seville Council decision to reduce the number of sectoral Councils to nine, this strategy is unlikely to be pursued in the future. However, the broader focus of the new Councils may make it easier to include new issues than the former narrow sectoral Councils.
196. See ministerial meetings under the 1988 Greek Presidency, the 1992 Portuguese Presidency, or the Italian Presidencies in 1990 and 1996.
197. Hayes-Renshaw and Wallace (1997), p. 141.
198. Tallberg (2003).
199. Senior official, UACES Presidency Conference, 21.3.2003.
200. Tallberg (2003).
201. Greek Foreign Minister Papoulias on the Programme of the Greek Presidency 5.7.1988.
202. Interview, then Finnish PermRep, 7.3.2003.
203. Review of Council's Work (1989, 1995, 2002).
204. The Barcelona Process, launched in 1995, is a framework of political, economic and social relations between the EU and ten Mediterranean states.
205. Non-papers are frequently presented ahead of informal Councils.
206. This conclusion was reached after consulting presidency websites, the public register of Commission and Council documents and interviews at the Commission, Permanent Representations, and Council Secretariat. Westlake (1995) supports this finding. A comprehensive list of all papers and non-papers does not exist.
207. Crenson (1971), p. 30.
208. Interview, UK PermRep, 5.3.2003.

209. Interview, Greek Embassy, Washington DC, 13.2.2003.
210. Interview, Finnish PM's Office, 29.8.2003.
211. Interview, Greek PermRep, 27.4.2004.
212. Interview, Greek PermRep, 4.5.2004.
213. Westlake (1995), p. 115.
214. Gray and Stubb (2001), p. 13.
215. Schout (1998), p. 4.
216. Hayes-Renshaw and Wallace (1997), p. 145.
217. Endo (1999), p. 84.
218. Interview, then Belgian PM's Office, 25.2.2005.
219. *Irish Times* 12.12.1996, in Lautso (1997), p. 31.
220. Sarkozy (2008), EP plenary, 21 October 2008.
221. Bengtsson (2003), p. 60.
222. Interview, Greek PermRep, 26.4.2004.
223. See also König and Bräuniger (2004); Hosli (1999). For an assessment of the impact of enlargement on EU legislative decision-making, see Thomson (2007).
224. Interview, Finnish Ministry of Trade, 27.8.2003.
225. The initiatives of the direct election of the EP, the EMS, and the IM are examples.
226. Simonian (1985).
227. Werts (1992), pp. 91–95.
228. France and Germany also submitted numerous joint contributions to the Convention. See Dehousse, Maurer, Nestor, Quermonne, and Schild (2003); Bunse, Magnette, and Nicolaïdis (2007).
229. *Le Figaro*, 14.1.2004; *FT*, 15.1.2004 and 21.1.2004; *EU Observer*, 15.1.2004 and 21.1.2004; *Economist*, 31.1.2004–6.2.2004.
230. See, for example, the trilateral Summit held on 18.2.2004 in Berlin.
231. Interview, Commission, 11.5.2004.
232. Interview, then Finnish PermRep, 27.8.2003.
233. Interview, Finnish PermRep, 9.3.2005.
234. Interview, Finnish PermRep, 16.3.2005.
235. Bunse, Magnette, and Nicolaïdis (2005b).
236. Pollack (1997), p. 102. Schmidt (2001), pp. 126–127.
237. Kirchner (1992), p. 5.
238. *Agence Europe (AE)*, 2.7.1996 and 15.1.1997. See also Gillespie (1996), in the *Irish Times*, 12.12.1996.
239. Edwards and Lund (1993), p. 65.
240. *EU Observer*, 22.12.2003.
241. Duke (1998), p. 1.
242. Bretherton and Vogler (1999), in Bengtsson (2003), p. 61.
243. Cameron (2002).
244. Tsebelis (1994), p. 128.
245. See also Lautso (1997), p. 20.
246. Bonvicini and Regelsberger (1987), p. 161.
247. Interview, Finnish PM's Office, 21.6.1999.
248. Kirchner (1992), p. 110; Menon (2003), p. 6; Vos and Bailleul (2002).
249. Interview, Greek Embassy, Washington DC, 13.2.2003.
250. *AE*, 15–16.12.1997.

251. See, for example, *Le Monde*, 12.12.2000; *EV*, 14–20.12.2000; Gray and Stubb (2001).
252. Interview, Finnish PM's Office, 22.6.2003.
253. *AE*, 7.1.1998.
254. For a detailed analysis, see Kassim, Peters, and Wright (2000).
255. *EV*, 24–30.6.1999.
256. Whitman and Thomas (2005).
257. Westlake (1995), p. 293.
258. Westlake (1995).
259. Interview, Finnish PM's Office, 29.8.2003. Schout (1998), p. 5; Wallace and Edwards (1976), p. 23.
260. Bulmer and Wessels (1987), p. 54.
261. Endo (1999), p. 87.
262. Neustadt (1990), p. 40.
263. *EU Observer*, 27.11.2003.
264. Watson, EP Plenary, 16.12.2003.
265. Interview, Commission, 7.3.2003.
266. Wallace (1986), p. 584.
267. Blair, 5.12.1997.
268. Interview, Finnish Ministry of Trade, 26.8.2003.
269. Interview, then Danish PermRep, 21.3.2003.
270. Interview, Finnish Ministry of Trade, 27.8.2003.
271. Puchala (1999), p. 318.
272. Interview 1, then Finnish PermRep, 29.8.2003.
273. Interview 2, then Finnish PermRep, 29.8.2003.
274. For a detailed discussion on Council coalition building, see Spence (1995).
275. Westlake (1995), p. 326.
276. Sherrington (2000), pp. 49–52.
277. Esbøll (1992), in Westlake (1995), p. 322.
278. Interview, Finnish MFA, 29.8.2003.
279. Wise Men Report (1979).
280. General Secretariat's Staff Regulations (1993).
281. Esbøll (1992), in Westlake (1995), p. 327.
282. Edwards and Wallace (1977), p. 25.
283. Wise Men Report (1979).
284. Interview, Commission, 7.3.2003.
285. Interview, EP, then Finnish PM's Office, 3.3.2003.
286. See Tallberg (2002a).
287. Kirchner (1992), p. 91.
288. Interview, Finnish Ministry of Finance, 27.8.2003.
289. George (1991) p. 230. See also Rosenthal (1975).
290. Paavo Lipponen, in *FT*, 1.7.1999.
291. 'Mainstream' is defined here as a country with no policy opt-outs.
292. Halonen (1998b).
293. Tiilikainen (2003), p. 104.
294. Linden, in Billboard Bulletin 3.7.1999.
295. Finnish MFA (1999a).
296. Commission of the European Communities (1998a).
297. Commission (2000c).

298. Evans (2003).
299. Interview, Finnish MFA, 29.8.2003.
300. Corley (2002).
301. Verrue 20.1.1999.
302. *EIS*, 24.7.1999.
303. Interview, Finnish PM's Office, 21.6.1999.
304. Catellani (2001), p. 65.
305. Commission (1998b), in Ojanen (1999). See also Council (2000e).
306. Council (1999h).
307. Wellman (1998), p. 9.
308. Lipponen (1997).
309. Catellani (2001), p. 64.
310. Finnish MFA (1999a).
311. Heininen (2001), p. 23.
312. Besides the Social Democrats (SDP), the Rainbow Coalition comprised the conservative National Coalition Party (KOK), the ex-Communist Left Wing Alliance (VAS), the Green Party and the Swedish People's Party (SFP).
313. *EV*, 6.–11.5.1999.
314. *EIS*, 8.12.1999.
315. *FT*, 6.12.1999.
316. *AE*, 3.12.1999 and 1.12.1999.
317. *EIS*, 4.12.1999.
318. *EIS*, 19.6.1999.
319. Commission (1999d).
320. *EIS*, 26.4.2000.
321. *EIS*, 26.4.2000.
322. *FT*, 1.7.1999.
323. Catellani (2001), p. 71; Arter (2000).
324. Haukkala (2001), p. 107.
325. Commission (1998b).
326. Arter (2000), p. 687; Novak (2001).
327. Slava Hodko, in VF 6.4.1999.
328. Arter (2000), p. 693.
329. Interview, Finnish PM's Office, 22.6.1999.
330. Ibid.
331. Interview, Finnish Ministry of Trade and Industry, 29.8.2003.
332. Ibid., 27.8.2003.
333. Kingdon (1995), p. 165.
334. Interview, Finnish PM's Office, 22.6.1999.
335. Interview, Finnish MFA, 3.3.2000.
336. Commission (1998b).
337. Ibid.
338. Heininen (2001), p. 30.
339. Interview, Finnish PM's Office, 9.10.2002.
340. See seminars/lectures at the Academy for Social and National Development of Uzbekistan (8.1.1999), the Finnish Embassy in Washington DC (13.1.1999) and the Baltic Sea Institute (Tampere, 22.2.1999). ND Workshops took place in London (5.2.1999), Manchester (26.2.1999) and the London School of Economics (4.5.1999). Conferences and international

fora on the ND included the Conference on Baltic Sea Security and Co-operation (Stockholm, 19.11.1998), the meeting of the Council of the Baltic Sea States (22.–23.1.1999), the joint meeting of the Nordic Council and the Assembly of the Baltic States (Helsinki, 8.–9.2.1999), the EU-Russia Summit (Moscow, 18.2.1999) and the second Co-operation Council between the EU and Russia (Brussels, 17.5.1999).

341. Interviews, Finnish MFA, 3.3.2000 and Finnish PM's Office, 9.10.2002. Ahtisaari raised the ND in his October 1998 visit to Moscow, Finnish Ambassador Stenlund discussed it with German officials in December 1998, and Lipponen in his talks with then Russian PM Primakov in St Petersburg in February 1999.

342. Baldersheim and Stålberg (1999).

343. Halonen, Ahtisaari, and Lipponen met Aznar on various occasions in February and March 1999.

344. *Helsingin Sanomat* 1.11 and 4.11.1997.

345. See *FT*, 4.3.1999.

346. Ilves, in *FT*, 19.5.2000.

347. Haukkala (2001), pp. 111–112.

348. See Ojanen (1999), p. 17.

349. Ojanen (1999), p. 17.

350. Interviews Finnish MFA, 29.8.2003; Finnish PM's Office, 10.10.2002.

351. Interview, Finnish MFA, 3.3.2000.

352. Ibid.

353. Council (1999b).

354. Arter (2000), p. 685.

355. Interview, Finnish PM's Office, 21.6.1999.

356. Harle (2000), p. 11.

357. Tuomioja (1999); Finnish MFA (1999d); *AE*, 5.7.1999.

358. COREPER on 20.10.1999.

359. See, Working Group on Economic Questions (information society services), 4.10.1999; 7.10.1999; 29.10.1999; 4.11.1999; 11.–12.11.1999; and 23.11.1999.

360. COREPER I on 17.11.1999; 19.11.1999; and 1.12.1999.

361. Interview, Finnish MFA, 29.8.2003.

362. Interview, Finnish Ministry of Trade and Industry, 27.8.2003.

363. *AE*, 3.12.1999.

364. *EIS*, 8.12.1999.

365. Council (1999i).

366. Belgium remained concerned about the inclusion of financial services in the directive.

367. Interview, Finnish MFA, 29.8.2003.

368. The directive was adopted after the EP's second reading on 4.5.2000.

369. See Working Party on Intellectual Property (copyright) on 14.7.1999; 2.–3.9.1999; 13.9.1999; 27.9.1999; 5.10.1999; 20.–21.10.1999; 3.–4.11.1999; and 1.12.1999.

370. Interview, Finnish Ministry of Trade, 27.8.2003.

371. *Hufvudstadsbladet* 6, in VF, 9.2.1999.

372. Finnish MFA (1999e).

373. The expert seminar on Northern Europe's Forest Sector was held in Petroza-vodsk, Russia on 12–13.10.1999, while the working group on gas of the CBSS met in Berlin on 9–10.9.1999. The conferences on the ND included the Barents conference (15.7.1999), the conference of the Chairmen of the Foreign Affairs Committees of the Parliaments of the EU Member States, the applicant countries and the EP in Helsinki (20.–21.7.1999) and the Ripon Educational Fund's 1999 transatlantic conference in Stockholm (19.8.1999). Euro-Arctic co-operation within the framework of the ND in the youth fields was discussed at a conference organised by the Finnish Education Min-istry in conjunction with the Commission and the Centre for International Mobility in Rovaniemi on 10–12.9.1999.
374. Van Ham and Trenin (2000).
375. Ibid., p. 58.
376. Commission (1999f).
377. Patten (1999).
378. Council (2000e).
379. Patten (1999).
380. Ivanov 12.11.1999, in Leshukov (2001), pp. 137–138.
381. Council (1999f).
382. Interview, Finnish PM's Office, 9.10.2002.
383. *FT*, 13.11.1999; *EIS*, 17.11.1999.
384. Former Danish Foreign Minister, 8.3.2000.
385. Stubb (2000a), p. 52.
386. See, for example, Lipponen, in *FT*, 13.11.1999. See also *EIS*, 1.12.1999.
387. *EIS*, 22.12.1999.
388. *EIS*, 20.11.1999.
389. Katiforis, EP plenary, 21.7.1999.
390. Interview, Finnish PM's Office, 10.10.2002.
391. Nordic Business Report, 22.2.1999. *Sunday Business*, 27.6.1999.
392. Interview, Finnish PM's Office, 29.8.2003.
393. *Irish Times*, 11.12.1999. Interview, former Danish Foreign Minister, 8.3.2000. Schröder, in *AE*, 13.12.1999.
394. Rehn (2003), p. 17. See also Kassim, Peters, and Wright (2000).
395. Interview, Finnish PM's Office, 10.10.2002.
396. Ibid., 22.6.1999.
397. Interview, then Finnish PM's Office, 3.3.2003.
398. Interview, EU Secretariat for the Finnish Presidency, 21.6.1999.
399. Interview, Finnish Ministry of Trade and Industry, 27.8.2003.
400. Interview, Finnish Ministry of Defence, 10.10.2002.
401. Rehn (2003). See also EV 29.7–4.8.1999.
402. Interview, Finnish PM's Office, 10.10.2002.
403. Kassim (2000); Wright (1996).
404. Palacio Vallersundi, EP plenary, 21.7.1999. *Die Welt* 8.2.1999. See also *FT*, 13.12.1999.
405. Interview, Finnish MFA, 29.8.2003.
406. *Frankfurter Allgemeine Zeitung* (FAZ), 13.8.1999.
407. Industry (2–3.7), Culture (18–19.7), Education (14–15.9), and Housing (17–18.9).
408. Lipponen, in *Helsingin Sanomat*, VF, 16.8.1999.

409. Interview, Finnish PM's Office, 10.10.2002.
410. Interview, Council Secretariat, 6.4.2004.
411. Interview, Finnish PM's Office, 9.10.2002.
412. Interview, Finnish Ministry of Trade and Industry, 26.8.2003.
413. Interview, Council Secretariat, 3.5.2004.
414. Interview, Finnish Ministry of Trade and Industry, 27.8.2003.
415. Interview, Council Secretariat, 3.5.2004.
416. See, for example, Thors and Swoboda, EP plenary, 21.7.1999.
417. Halonen on 27.8.1999, 31.8.1999, 15.9.1999, 24.11.1999, and 1.12.1999; Lipponen on 27.10.1999 and 14.12.1999; Niinistö on 3.11.1999 and 7.12.1999; Sasi on 6.10.1999 and 17.11.1999; Hassi on 21–22.9.1999 and 6.10.1999; Perho on 14.10.1999; Heinonen on 23.9.1999 and 12.10.1999; Tuomioja on 21.9.1999; Biaudet on 21.9.1999; and Häkämies and Koskinen on 2.9.1999.
418. Arter (2000), p. 687.
419. Harbour, EP plenary, 21.7.1999.
420. Matikainen-Kallström; Myller; Hautala; Väyrynen, EP plenary, 21.7.1999.
421. Halonen, EP plenary, 31.8.1999.
422. Posselt, EP plenary, 14.12.1999.
423. See, for example, Halonen (1998b).
424. Rehn (2003), p. 12.
425. Commission (2000d).
426. See Patten (1999).
427. Interview, Finnish Ministry of Trade and Industry, 27.8.2003.
428. Interview, Commission, 6.5.2004.
429. Interview, Finnish PermRep, 2.3.2005.
430. Bunse, Magnette, and Nicolaïdis (2005b).
431. Council (1999c).
432. Interview, Commission, 6.5.2004.
433. Ibid.,
434. Interview, Finnish MFA, 29.8.2003.
435. Commission (1999b).
436. After the Finnish Presidency term, Finland complained that the Commission's commitment in the energy sector dropped leading to disappointing implementation records.
437. Interview, Finnish PM's Office, 10.10.2002.
438. Interview, Finnish MFA, 11.10.2002.
439. Ojanen (2001), p. 14. See also Kononenko (2000).
440. Haukkala (2001), p. 107.
441. Interview, Finnish MFA, 11.10.2002.
442. Patten (1999).
443. European Parliament (1999a, 1999b).
444. MEP Wallis (2003).
445. Ibid. (2003).
446. Interview, Finnish MFA, 9.10.2002.
447. Haukkala (2001), p. 113.
448. Leshukov (2001), p. 131.
449. Interview, then Finnish PM's Office, 3.3.2003.
450. Charles Picqué (2001).

451. De Winter and Türsan (2001), p. 11.
452. Commission (1997b).
453. Geradin and Humpe (2002).
454. Belgian Ministry of Foreign Affairs, Foreign Trade, and International Cooperation (2001a).
455. Verhofstadt, EP plenary, 4.7.2001.
456. Interview, Belgian PermRep, 28.2.2005.
457. Ludlow (2002a), p. 49.
458. Interview, then Belgian PM's Office, 25.2.2005.
459. Interview, then Belgian MFA, 24.2.2005.
460. Van Bellinghen (2001).
461. Holland (2002).
462. Ibid., pp. 208–209.
463. Interview, Council Secretariat, 1.3.2005.
464. Africa–Europe Summit (2000a).
465. Michel (2003a).
466. Interview, then Belgian MFA, 24.2.2005.
467. Belgian MFA (2001a).
468. Ibid.
469. Verhofstadt, EP plenary, 4.7.2001. See also AE 2.7.2001 and 4.7.2001. Van Daele, in AE 22.6.2001.
470. Michel (2003a).
471. Commission (2002e).
472. *Eurostat*, 18.6.2001.
473. His 'blue-red-green' coalition consisted of the VLD, the francophone liberals *Parti Reformateur Liberal* (PRL), *Front Democratique des Francophones* (FDF) and the *Mouvement des Citoyens pour le Changement* (MCC), and the Flemish and Francophone Socialist and Green parties including the *Socialistische Partij, Parti Socialiste* (PS), *Anders Gaan Leven* (Agalev), and Ecolo.
474. These included the Dutroux paedophile case and a crisis over dioxin-contaminated food.
475. Verhofstadt, EP plenary, 4.7.2001. See also *AE*, 5.7.2001 and *The Independent*, 29.6.2001.
476. See Vos and Bailleul (2002); Ludlow (2002a).
477. *EIS*, 7.12.2000.
478. Of the 47 EP amendments the Commission rejected 36.
479. *EIS*, 3.1.2001.
480. *EIS*, 5.10.2001.
481. Weber Shandwick (2001).
482. *The Guardian*, 7.11.2001.
483. *BBC News*, 8.7.2002. Interview, Council Secretariat, 1.3.2005.
484. Interview, Council Secretariat, 1.3.2005.
485. Interview, then Belgian MFA, 24.2.2005.
486. Fiedler (2004).
487. Interview, then Belgian MFA, 21.3.2005.
488. Lister (1997).
489. Interview, Council Secretariat, 1.3.2005.
490. Krause (2002).
491. Interview, then Belgian MFA, 24.2.2005.

492. Interview, then Belgian PM's Office, 25.2.2005.

493. Interview, then Belgian PermRep, 8.9.2005.

494. Ibid.

495. See, for example, the Conference on Postal Services on 19.6.2001 bringing together government and Commission officials, representatives of the Universal Postal Union (UPU), MEPs, etc.

496. Interview, Belgian MFA, 24.2.2005.

497. Interview, Belgian PermRep, 17.2.2005.

498. Interview, then Belgian MFA, 24.2.2005.

499. Ibid.

500. Ibid.

501. Commission of the European Communities (2001d).

502. Council (2001q). See also Council (1997b).

503. Council (2001h).

504. Interview, Commission, 22.3.2005.

505. Vervaeke (2003).

506. Verhofstadt, in UN Office for the Co-ordination of Humanitarian Affairs (IRIN-CEA), 30.6.2001–6.7.2001.

507. Verhofstadt, in Info Congo-Kinshasa, April–June 2001, Issue 168–169.

508. Poettering, EP plenary, 4.7.2001. See also Baron Crespo and Ducarme.

509. Interview, Commission, 22.3.2005.

510. Interview, Belgian MFA, 24.2.2005.

511. De Winter and Türsan (2001), p. 4.

512. See Earl of Stockton and Wurtz, EP plenary, 4.7.2001.

513. See working group meetings on 20.6.2001, 10.9.2001 and COREPERs on 19.9.2001, 3.10.2001, 10.10.2001.

514. Interview, then PermRep, 8.9.2005.

515. Council (2001t).

516. Interview, then Belgian PermRep, 8.9.2005.

517. Douglas Alexander, British Minister of Trade and Industry, in *The Independent*, 16.10.2001.

518. See GACs on 16.7.2001; 8–9.10.2001; 29–30.10.2001; 9–10.11.2001; 10.12.2001.

519. See Council (2001k).

520. See GAC 8–9.10.2001.

521. Council (2001l).

522. Council (2001o).

523. Presidency Press Release, 19.12.2001.

524. Presidency Press Release, 10.10.2001.

525. Interview, Council Secretariat, 1.3.2005.

526. Second EU–ECOWAS ministerial meeting: final press release, 12.10.2001.

527. Presidency Press Release, 9.9.2001.

528. Council (2001r).

529. Africa–Europe Ministerial Conference (2001).

530. Interview, Council Secretariat, 1.3.2005.

531. Michel, 1.9.2001.

532. UN (2001).

533. Others argued that the US walked out over the issue of reparations for slavery and colonialism. International Action Centre (2001).

534. Interview, Council Secretariat, 21.3.2001.
535. Kerremans and Drieskens (2003), p. 158.
536. Ludlow (2002a), p. 38.
537. *The Economist*, 7.7.2001.
538. As per the 1994 Co-operation Agreement.
539. Interview, Belgian MFA, 24.2.2005.
540. Interview, Council Secretariat, 1.3.2005.
541. Interview, then Belgian MFA, 21.3.2005.
542. Interview, Belgian MFA, 24.2.2005.
543. Interview, former senior Belgian official, 2.3.2005.
544. Grosch, EP plenary, 4.7. 2001.
545. Thyssen, EP plenary, 4.7.2001.
546. Interview, Belgian MFA, 24.2.2005.
547. Interview, former senior Belgian official, 2.3.2005.
548. Kerremans (2000), p. 183.
549. Kerremans and Beyers (2001), p. 202.
550. Only General Affairs, Defence, Economy and Finance, the Budget, JHA, Telecommunications, Consumer Protection, Development co-operation, Civil protection, and Fisheries are under exclusive federal competence. Culture, Education, Tourism, Youth, Housing, Industry, and Research are either entirely or mainly within the jurisdiction of the Communities and the Regions. Agriculture, IM, health, energy, environmental policy, social affairs, and transport fall mainly within federal jurisdiction but with some implications for Regions or Communities competencies. Coolsaet and Voet (2002), p. 67 and Belgian MFA (2001b).
551. Kerremans (2000).
552. Interview, Belgian MFA, 24.2.2005.
553. Kerremans (2000), p. 191.
554. Interview, Belgian MFA, 24.2.2005.
555. De Winter and Türsan (2001), p. 14.
556. Kerremans and Beyers (2001), p. 200.
557. Interview, former senior Belgian official, 2.3.2005.
558. Ludlow (2002a), p. 37.
559. Interview, Belgian MFA, 24.2.2005.
560. Interview, then Belgian PM's Office, 25.2.2005.
561. Kerremans (2000), p. 185.
562. Ludlow (2002a), p. 36.
563. Interview, Belgian MFA, 24.2.2005.
564. Kassim (2000); Wright (1996).
565. Ludlow (2002a).
566. Interview, the Belgian PermRep, 8.9.2005.
567. Ludlow (2002a), p. 39.
568. Vervaeke (2003).
569. Ludlow (2002a), p. 37.
570. Kerremans and Beyers (2001), p. 195.
571. Interview, Belgian MFA, 24.2.2005.
572. Interview, Belgian PermRep, 28.2.2005.
573. Interview, Belgian MFA, 24.2.2005.
574. Interview, then Belgian PM's Office, 25.2.2005.

575. Ibid.
576. Interview, Belgian MFA, 24.2.2005.
577. Interview, then Belgian PM's Office, 25.2.2005.
578. Interview, Council Secretariat, 21.3.2005.
579. Ibid.
580. Interview, Commission, 22.3.2005.
581. See, Laeken Council, 14–15.12.2001. Gama, in AE 16.7.2001.
582. Interview, Council Secretariat, 21.3.2005.
583. APPG (2001).
584. See *Congo-Kinshasa News*, November 2001.
585. Interview, then Belgian PM's Office, 25.2.2005.
586. *The Independent*, 23.12.2000.
587. Interview, Commission, 22.3.2005.
588. Interview, Council Secretariat, 21.3.2005.
589. Interview, Belgian PermRep, 18.2.2005.
590. Interview, Belgian MFA, 24.2.2005.
591. *AE*, 6.7.2001.
592. EP (2001a).
593. Interview, then Belgian PermRep, 8.9.2005.
594. *EIS*, 19.1.2001.
595. Council (2001v).
596. Council (2001u).
597. This supports Thomson's (2008) analysis which shows that a legislative proposal is not more likely to be adopted the larger the political distance between the current and preceding president's positions. Instead, whether or not an agreement is achieved depends on other factors, including the level of polarisation.
598. Interview, then Belgian PermRep, 8.9.2005.
599. Commission official, Brussels, 14.3.2005.
600. See texts adopted by the EP on 13.3.2002.
601. Interview, then Belgian MFA, 21.3.2005.
602. Interview, Council Secretariat, 21.3.2005.
603. Interview, Commission, 22.3.2005.
604. Interview, then Belgian MFA, 21.3.2005.
605. Council Secretariat (2005a).
606. Interview, Council Secretariat, 21.3.2005.
607. Interview, Commission, 22.3.2005.
608. Interview, then Belgian MFA, 21.3.2005.
609. Interview, Commission, 22.3.2005.
610. Krause (2003).
611. Commission (1996b, 1999e)
612. Krause (2003), p. 225.
613. Commission (2001e).
614. Interview, Commission, 22.3.2005.
615. *AE*, 12.7.2001.
616. Interview, Commission, 22.3.2005.
617. *AE*, 18.9.2001.
618. Michel (2003a).
619. Interview, Council Secretariat, 1.3.2005.

620. Vervaeke (2003).
621. Interview, Commission, 22.3.2005.
622. Verhofstadt, in *The Guardian*, 3.5.2001.
623. Costas Simitis (http://www.greece.gr/POLITICS/EuropeanUnion/Greece-saims.stm).
624. Tsoukalis (2003).
625. Mavris (2004).
626. The 1983 Greek Presidency blocked the EU from condemning the USSR's shooting down of a South-Korean airliner and in 1994 the Greek Presidency unilaterally imposed an embargo on Macedonia.
627. Dokos (2003), p. 64.
628. Tsoukalis (2003), p. 328.
629. Ibid., pp. 324–325; Mavris (2004), pp. 133–134.
630. Commission (2000b).
631. Hellenic MFA (2002).
632. Ibid.
633. See Agathocles or Christodoulakis, in *AE*, 16–17.12.2002 and 14.1.2003 respectively.
634. The 1988 Greek Presidency had opposed key aspects of the 1992 IM project. Similarly, in 1994 it was hesitant to push the EU's liberalisation agenda. Dimitrakopoulos and Passas (2004).
635. Hellenic Organisation of SMEs (www.eommex.gr). The EU average is 70%. This figure predates enlargement and includes Norway, Iceland, Lichtenstein, and Switzerland. European Observatory for SMEs (2003).
636. The target was a 40% cost reduction.
637. Interviews, Commission, 11.5.2004, Council Secretariat, 3.5.2004.
638. Simitis (2003), EP plenary, 14.1.2003.
639. Interview, Council Secretariat, 3.5.2004.
640. Serbia-Montenegro is the same legal entity as the Federal Republic of Yugoslavia (FRY) and includes Kosovo.
641. Hellenic MFA (2003d). Papandreou (2003a).
642. Bechev (2003).
643. The GAERC of 21.10.2002 had invited the Commission to begin SAA talks with Albania.
644. Hellenic MFA (2003d).
645. Interview, Greek PermRep, 28.2.2003.
646. Tziampiris (2003), p. 137; Tsoukalis (2003), p. 326.
647. Including Romania and Bulgaria.
648. Simitis, in *EV*, 19.12.2003–8.1.2004.
649. Interview, EP, 26.4.2004.
650. Hellenic MFA (2002).
651. *AE*, 20.3.2003.
652. *EV*, 19.12.–8.1.2003.
653. Couloumbis (2003), p. 39.
654. *Athens News Agency* (ANA) 1.3.2003 and 6.4.2003.
655. *The Economist*, 4.1.2003.
656. Council (2002e).
657. *EIS*, 4.3.2003.
658. *AE*, 5.9.2002 and 13.11.2002.

659. *EIS*, 2.11.2001.
660. Ibid., 15.5.2001.
661. *AE*, 7.11.2002
662. Ibid., 15.11.2002.
663. Lenoir, in *AE*, 14.11.2002.
664. Euractiv, 16.04.2002.
665. UK, Italy, Spain, Denmark, and the Netherlands.
666. EP plenary, 14.1.2003.
667. Poland, Hungary, the Czech Republic (CR), Estonia, Latvia, Slovakia, Bulgaria, and Romania.
668. *EV*, 20–26.2.2003.
669. Giannitsis, in Kathimerini 5.1.2003. *EV*, 19.12.2002–8.1.2003. *Süddeutsche Zeitung (SZ)* 18.2.2003.
670. Commission (2003f, 2003g, 2003h).
671. Council (2002g, 2002h).
672. Interview, UK PermRep, 11.3.2003. Hellenic MFA (2003e).
673. Interview, Greek PermRep, 4.5.2004.
674. Interview, UK PermRep, 11.3.2003.
675. Interview, Commission, 7.5.2004.
676. *FT*, 26.5.2003; *EIS*, 14.1.2003.
677. Poettering, EP plenary, 14.1.2003.
678. *The Independent*, 12.1.2003.
679. *New York Times*, 11.1.2003.
680. The Greek MFA mentions two-year presidency preparations. All interviewees coincided that preparations started one year before.
681. Interview, Greek PermRep, 30.4.2004.
682. Interview, Greek PermRep, 4.5.2004.
683. Interview, Commission, 11.5.2004.
684. Interview, Greek PermRep, 4.5.2004.
685. Interview, Greek PermRep, 30.4.2004. Guggenbühl (forthcoming) calls this process 'intelligence management.'
686. Interview, Greek PermRep, 28.2.2003.
687. Interview, Greek PermRep, 4.5.2004.
688. Interview, Greek PermRep, 28.2.2003.
689. Commission (2002d), p. 13.
690. Interview, Greek PermRep, 4.5.2004.
691. Interview, Greek PermRep, 28.2.2003.
692. Interview, Greek PermRep, 4.5.2004.
693. Interview, Commission, 7.5.2004.
694. Council (2002i).
695. Interview, Greek PermRep, 4.5.2004.
696. European Stability Initiative (ESI) (2002); Van Meurs and Yannis (2002); International Crisis Groups (ICG) (2002).
697. See also, Brussels Conference on investment in SEE, 7.11.2002; SEE Poverty Reduction Strategies Forum, 29.10.2002–1.11.2002; Ljubljana Social Cohesion Conference, 4–5.11.2002.
698. Centre for European Policy Studies (2002).
699. Interview, Council Secretariat, 6.4.2004.
700. Interview, Greek PermRep, 4.5.2004.

701. The ESI made this proposal (2002).
702. Van Meurs and Yannis (2002).
703. Interview, Greek PermRep, 4.5.2004.
704. Ibid., 28.2.2003.
705. Ibid., 4.5.2004.
706. Boris Traijekovski, President of FYROM, 3.12.2002. *EIS*, 3.12.2003.
707. Mimica (2002).
708. Council (2002d).
709. Interview, Greek PermRep, 30.4.2004.
710. Ibid.
711. Karamanou, EP plenary, 14.1.2003.
712. Folias, EP plenary, 14.1.2003.
713. Prodi, EP plenary, 14.1.2003.
714. Interview, Greek PermRep, 30.4.2004.
715. Interview, Commission, 7.5.2004.
716. Commission (2003i).
717. Hellenic MFA (2003a).
718. See *Legal Week Global* 12.8.2003; Council (2003c); Interview, Commission, 11.5.2004.
719. Hellenic Ministry for Development (2003b).
720. Interview, Commission, 11.5.2004.
721. Schattschneider (1988), p. 60.
722. Prodi (2003).
723. *AE*, 18.2.2003.
724. Council (2003a).
725. Papandreou, in *EIS*, 14.1.2003.
726. Solana, in *EIS*, 17.1.2003.
727. *EIS*, 17.1.2003.
728. Hellenic MFA (2003c).
729. See GAERCs on 24.2.2003, 18.3.2003, 14.4.2003, 19.5.2003, 16.6.2003. JHA on 27.2.2003, 28.–29.3.2003, 8.5.2003, 5–6.6.2003; Environment 4.3.2003, 13.6.2003; Energy 27–28.3, 14.5.2003, 5.6.2003; Informal Councils on JHA 28–29.3.2003, Defence on 14–15.3.2003. Spring summit on 20–21.3.2003. Seminars on Balkan routes of Heroin Trafficking 10–12.2.2003, on organised crime in the Balkans in April, on conflict prevention and the lessons learned from the Balkans, 4–7.5.2003; Ministerial Conference for the promotion of co-operation in Research and Technological Development between the EU and the Balkan countries, 26–27.6.2003; Conference for the promotion of the 6th Framework Program to candidate and third countries, 17–19.2.2003; Preparatory Meeting for the promotion of the Scientific and Technological Development co-operation between the EU and the Balkans, 20–22.2.2003.
730. Hellenic MFA (2003b).
731. *EIS*, 15.2.2003.
732. Michael Steiner, in *EIS*, 11.6.2003.
733. Papandreou, Hellenic MFA (2003f).
734. Council (2003c).
735. Interview, Greek PermRep, 4.5.2004.
736. Council (2003e).
737. Council (2003d).

738. See the ministerial meeting with the Western Balkans on 3.3.2003 and the special troika on 22.4.2003.
739. See JHA Council open debate, 27.2.2003.
740. Council (2003g).
741. It was adopted on 12 July 2004.
742. The latter was organised jointly with the World Bank.
743. Council (2003c).
744. The recommendations of the Athens WEF which focused on SEE's European prospect were also fed into the Summit.
745. Interview, Greek PermRep, 4.5.2004.
746. Ibid., 28.3.2003.
747. Ibid., 4.5.2004.
748. Bechev (2003).
749. See JHA ministerial meeting 28.11.2003 and foreign ministers' meeting 9.12.2003.
750. Bechev (2003).
751. Simits, EP plenary, 1.7.2003.
752. Patten, in *Athens News Agency*, 17.6.2003.
753. For a detailed discussion, see Ludlow (2003a).
754. Ludlow (2003b); *AE*, 23.3.2003.
755. Papandreou (2003a).
756. Interview, Greek PermRep, 28.2.2003.
757. See also Bechev (2003).
758. Tsoukalis (2003), p. 322.
759. *Le Monde*, 5.3.2004.
760. Interview, Greek PermRep, 30.4.2004.; *EV*, 19.12.2002–8.1.2003 and 16–22.1.2003.
761. Interview, Commission, 11.5.2004.
762. Interview, EP, 26.4.2004.
763. Papandreou, in *NYT*, 11.1.2003. Giannitsis, in *E!Sharp* January 2003, p. 32.
764. EKEME (2002), pp. 203–212.
765. Interview, EP, 6.4.2004.
766. The EU General Directorate of the MFA has four directorates (External Affairs; European Integration and Economic and Monetary Policy; IM, Agriculture, and New Community Policies; and JHA) and an EP Bureau.
767. Galatsinou (1996); Minakaki (1992); Spanou (2000).
768. Spanou (2000), p. 165; Dimitrakopoulos and Passas (2004), p. 4; Passas and Stephanou (1997).
769. Interview, Greek PermRep, 30.4.2004.
770. Spanou (2000).
771. Interview, Greek PermRep, 27.4.2004.
772. Interview, Greek PermRep, 30.4.2004.
773. Ibid., 4.5.2004.
774. Ibid., 30.4.2004.
775. Interview, Council Secretariat, 3.4.2004.
776. Ibid., 3.5.2004.
777. Interview, Greek PermRep, 30.4.2004.
778. Ibid., 4.5.2004; Greek Embassy (Brussels), 3.5.2004; Commission, 6.5.2004.
779. Interview, Council Secretariat, 3.5.2004.

780. Interview, Greek PermRep, 27.4.2004.
781. Interview, Council Secretariat, 6.5.2004.
782. Ibid.
783. Ibid., 6.5.2003.
784. *EV*, 13.–19.2.2003.
785. *FT*, 1.1.2003.
786. Interview, Commission, 11.5.2004.
787. Interview, Greek PermRep, 30.4.2004.
788. Ibid., 4.5.2004.
789. Interview, Greek Embassy in Brussels, 3.5.2004. See also Interview, Greek PermRep, 4.5.2004.
790. Interview, Commission, 11.5.2004.
791. Interview, Greek PermRep, 30.4.2004.
792. Ibid., 4.5.2004.
793. Patten, Press Conference, 20.6.2003 (http://www.eu2003.gr/en/articles/2003/6/20/3118/).
794. Interview, *EP*, 26.4.2003.
795. Council (2001b).
796. Interview, Commission, 11.5.2004.
797. Ibid.
798. Interview, Commission, 6.5.2004.
799. Ibid., 11.5.2004.
800. Interview, Greek PermRep, 27.4.2004.
801. Interviews, Commission, 18.3.2005 and 14.3.2005.
802. Ibid., 11.5.2004.
803. A prominent example is the take-over directive which sought to establish common principles for cross-border take-over bids, create a level playing field for shareholders, and establish disclosure obligations throughout the EU. Articles 9 (ensuring shareholders can vote on defensive measures after a bid has been publicised) and 11 (neutralising measures that could be interpreted as pre-bid defences) were particularly contentious. Despite strong Commission opposition, the 2003 Italian Presidency compromise made articles 9 and 11 optional.
804. EP (1997a, 1997b, 2002a, 2002c).
805. Ibid., 2002d.
806. Swoboda, EP plenary, 14.1.2003.
807. *EIS*, 12.3.2002.
808. RFE/RL Newsline, Vol. 7, No. 13, Part II, 22.1.2003.
809. Interview, Council Secretariat, 6.5.2004.
810. Interview, UK PermRep, 11.3.2003.
811. Interview, EP, 6.4.2004.
812. Busek (2003).
813. Interview, UK PermRep, 11.3.2003.
814. Ibid., 4.5.2004.
815. Ibid.
816. Ibid.
817. EP (2003a).
818. Hellenic MFA (2003c); EP (2003a).
819. Interview, Finnish PermRep, 2.3.2005.

820. Dokos (2003), p. 52.
821. Patten (2003).
822. Spanou (2000), p. 179.
823. Interview, Greek PermRep, 27.4.2004.
824. Schout (1998).
825. Hayes-Renshaw and Wallance (1997), p. 147. See also De Bassompiere (1988); Ludlow (1993); Kirchner and Tsagkari (1993); Coombes (1998); Corbett (1998).
826. Interview, EP, 26.4.2004.
827. Tallberg (2003).
828. Haukkala (2001), pp. 111–112.
829. Moravcsik (1999a), p. 272.
830. For example, Wozniak Boyle (2006).
831. Interview, Commission, 14.3.2005. See also, Interview, Commission, 18.3.2005.
832. Schattschneider (1960, 1988 edition), p. 60.
833. See also Bunse (2000) and Tallberg (2006).
834. Ungerer (1993), p. 82.
835. Peters (2005).
836. Magnette and Nicolaïdis (2003).
837. See debates in the Constitutional Convention, as cited by Hamilton, 19 June, 1787 (http://www.san.beck.org/WASH8-Constitution.html).
838. O'Nuallain (1985).
839. Menon (2003), p. 6.
840. Jacques Santer, in *AE*, 10.1.1998.
841. Magnette and Nicoalïdis (2003), p. 32.
842. Thomson (2007), p. 18.
843. Lewis (1998), p. 484.
844. Ojanen (1999), p. 13.
845. Crum (2007).
846. See Balazs and Maij-Weggen, Convention Plenary 20–21.1.2003; Rupel and Kelam, Convention Plenary 15.5.2003; Interview, Commission, 7.3.2003.

Bibliography

Aho, E. (1994) *Speech delivered at the University of Tartu, 15 March 1994*.

Ahtisaari, M. (1995) 'Finlande: du sang neuf pour l'Union européenne'. *Politique Internationale* (Summer) No. 68, pp. 143–156.

Ahtisaari, M. (1997) 'Towards a Global International System in the 21st Century'. *Speech delivered at Harvard University, 15 October 1997* (http://www.vn.fi/tpk/puheet-1996/P971005.harwen.html).

Ahtisaari, M. (1999a) Interview with *Die Welt*, 15 July 1999.

Ahtisaari, M. (1999b) *Speech delivered during the dinner in connection with the Ministerial Conference on the Northern Dimension, Helsinki, 11 November 1999* (http://www.vn.fi/tpk/puheet-1999/P991111.pohjen.html).

Ahtisaari, M. (1999c) *Speech delivered at Chatham House, London, 24 November 1999*.

Almond, G. and Coleman, J. Eds. (1960) *The Politics of Developing Areas* (Princeton: Princeton University Press).

Almond, G. and Genco, S.J. (1977) 'Clouds, Clocks, and the Study of Politics'. *World Politics*, Vol. 29, No. 4 (July 1977), pp. 489–522.

Almond, G.A. and Powell, G.B. (1966) *Comparative Politics: A Developmental Approach* (Boston: Little, Brown).

Amstrup, N. (1976) 'The Perennial Problem of Small States: A Survey of Research Efforts'. *Cooperation and Conflict*, Vol. 11, No. 3, pp. 163–182.

Anderson, P.J. (1999) 'The British Presidency of 1998'. *Journal of Common Market Studies/The European Union: Annual Review 1998/1999*, Vol. 37, pp. 63–64.

Antola, E. (1991a) 'EFTA and its Limits'. In: Wallace, H. (ed.) *The Wider Western Europe, Reshaping the EC/EFTA Relationship* (London: Pinter Publishers), pp. 233–245.

Antola, E. (1991b) 'Finland'. In: Wallace, H. (ed.) *The Wider Western Europe, Reshaping the EC/EFTA Relationship* (London: Pinter Publishers), pp. 146–158.

Antola, E. (1991c) 'From the European Rim to the Core: The European Policy of Finland in the 1990s'. In: Wallace, H. (ed.) *Northern Dimensions, Yearbook 1999* (Helsinki: Finnish Institute of International Affairs), pp. 5–12.

APPG. (2001) *Report DRC Visit 2001*. (http://www.appggreatlakes.org/content/pdf/report_visit_2001.pdf).

Armstrong, K.A. and Bulmer, S. (1998) *The Governance of the Single European Market* (Manchester: Manchester University Press).

Arter, D. (1995) 'The EU Referendum in Finland on 16 October 1994: A Vote for the West, not for Maastricht'. *Journal of Common Market Studies*, Vol. 33, No. 3, pp. 361–387.

Arter, D. (2000) 'Small State Influence Within the EU'. *Journal of Common Market Studies*, Vol. 38, No. 5, pp. 677–697.

Aspinwall, M. (2000) 'Structuring Europe: Power Sharing Institutions and British Preferences on European Integration'. *Political Studies*, Vol. 48, pp. 415–442.

Aspinwall, M. and Schneider, G. Ed. (2001) *The Rules of Integration, Institutionalist Approaches to the Study of Europe* (Manchester: Manchester University Press).

Bachrach, P. and Baratz, M.S. (1962) 'Two Faces of Power'. *American Political Science Review*, Vol. 56, No. 4, pp. 947–952.

Bachrach, P. and Baratz, M.S. (1963) 'Decisions and Non-Decisions: An Analytical Framework'. *American Political Science Review*, Vol. 57, No. 3, pp. 632–642.

Bainbridge, T. (2002) *The Penguin Companion to European Union* (London: Penguin Books).

Bainbridge, T. and Teasdale A. (1997) *The Penguin Companion to European Union* (London: Penguin Books).

Baldersheim, H. and Stålberg, K. (1999) *Nordic Region-Building in a European Perspective* (Aldershot: Ashgate).

Baldwin, R., Berglof, E., Giavazzi, F., and Widgren, M. (2001) 'Nice Try: Should the Treaty of Nice be Ratified?' *Monitoring European Integration*, No. 11, April 2001 (London: CEPR).

Baldwin, R. and Widgrén, M. (2003) 'The Draft Constitutional Treaty's Voting Reform Dilemma'. *CEPS Policy Brief*, No. 44, November 2003 (Brussels: Centre for European Policy Studies).

Balwin, R. and Widgrén, M. (2004) 'Council Voting in the Constitutional Treaty: Devil in the Details'. *CEPS Policy Brief*, No. 53, July 2004 (Brussels: Centre for European Policy Studies).

Banchoff, T. (2002) 'Institutions, Inertia and European Union Research Policy'. *Journal of Common Market Studies*, Vol. 40, No. 1, pp. 1–21.

Barbarinde, O. and Faber, G. (2004) 'From Lomé to Cotonou: Business as Usual?' *European Foreign Affairs Review*, Vol. 9, pp. 27–47.

Beach, D. (2005) *The Dynamics of European Integration* (London: Palgrave/Macmillan).

Bechev, D. (2003) 'Balancing Disappointment and Enthusiasm: Developments in EU-Balkan Relations During 2003'. *SEESP Opinion Piece* (Oxford: European Studies Centre, University of Oxford).

Bellou, F. (2003) 'The Political Scene: Consolidating Democracy'. In: Couloumbis, T.A., Kariotis, T., and Bellou, F. (eds.) *Greece in the Twentieth Century* (London: Frank Cass).

Bengtsson, R. (2003) 'The Council Presidency and External Representation'. In: Elgström, O. (ed.) *European Union Council Presidencies – A Comparative Perspective* (London: Routledge).

Bengtsson, R., Elgström, O., and Tallberg, J. (2004) 'Silencer or Amplifier? The European Union Presidency and the Nordic Countries'. *Scandinavian Political Studies*, Vol. 27, No. 3, pp. 311–334.

Beyers, J. and Dierickx, G. (1998) 'The Working Groups of the Council of the European Union: Supranational or Intergovernmental Negotiations?' *Journal of Common Market Studies*, Vol. 36, No. 3, pp. 289–317.

Bjurulf, B. (2001) 'How did Sweden Manage the European Union'. *ZEI Discussion Paper* C 96 2001 (Bonn: Zentrum für Europäische Integrationsforschung).

Blackwell Encyclopaedia of Political Science. (1991) (Oxford: Blackwell).

Blair, T. (1997) *Speech held on 5 December 1997*.

Blair, T. (2002) 'A Clear Course for Europe'. *Speech delivered at Cardiff, 28 November 2001*.

Bourque, A. and Sampson, P. (2001) 'The European Union's Political and Development Response to the Democratic Republic of the Congo'. *European Centre for Development and Policy Management (ECDPM) Discussion Paper 28* (Maastricht: ECDPM).

Börzel, T. (2003) 'What Can Federalism Teach us about the European Union? The German experience'. *Paper prepared for the Conference Governing together in the New Europe; Robinson College, Cambridge, 12–13 April 2003* (London: Royal Institute for International Affairs).

Bonvicini, G. and Regelsberger, E. (1987) 'The Decision-Making Process in the EC's European Council'. *International Spectator*, Vol. 22, No. 3, pp. 152–175.

Branch, A.P. and Ohrgaard, J.C. (1999) 'Trapped in the Supranational-Intergovernmental Dichotomy: A Response to Stone Sweet and Sandholtz'. *Journal of European Public Policy*, Vol. 6, No. 1, pp. 123–143.

Brassine, J. (1990) *Investigation into the Murder of Patrice Lumumba*, Doctoral Thesis (Brussels: Free University of Brussels).

Bretherton, C. and Vogler, J. (1999) *The European Union as a Global Actor* (London: Routledge).

Broman, M. (2005a) 'Small State Influence in the European Union: Small State Smart State?' *Paper presented at the 46th Annual ISA Conference, 1–5 March 2005*, Honolulu, Hawai.

Broman, M. (2005b) 'Small States and the Art of Influence in the EU – Swedish and Irish Experiences'. *Paper presented at the 14th NOPSA Conference, August 2005*.

Brömmelhörster, J. and Paes, W. (2003) *The Military as an Economic Actor – Soldiers in Business* (Basingstoke: Palgrave/Macmillan).

Brown, T. (1995) *Finland in the European Union* (Dublin: Institute of European Affairs).

Brown, T. (2004) 'Achieving Balance: Institutions and Member States'. *Federal Trust Online Paper 1/04* (London: Federal Trust).

Bulmer, S. (1994) *Economic and Political Integration in Europe: Internal Dynamics and Global Context* (Oxford: Blackwell Publishers).

Bulmer, S. (1995) 'Four Faces of EU Governance: A New Institutional Research Guide'. *Manchester Papers in Politics, EPRU Paper No. 2/1995*.

Bulmer, S. (1998) 'New Institutionalism and the Governance of the Single European Market'. *Journal of European Public Policy*, Vol. 5, No. 3, pp. 365–386.

Bulmer, S. and Armstrong, K. (1998) *The Governance of the Single European Market* (Manchester: Manchester University Press).

Bulmer, S. and Wessels, W. (1987) *The European Council, Decision-making in European Politics* (Basingstoke: Macmillan Press).

Bunse, S. (2000) *The Presidency of the Council of Ministers as a Policy Entrepreneur?* MPhil Thesis (Oxford: Oxford University).

Bunse, S. (2004) 'The 2003 Greek Council Presidency'. *Mediterranean Politics*, Vol. 9, No. 2, pp. 248–257.

Bunse, S., Magnette, P., and Nicolaïdis, K. (2005a) 'Shared Leadership in the EU: Theory and Reality'. In: Curtin, D., Kellermann, A.E., and Blockmans, S. (eds.) *The EU Constitution: The Best Way Forward?* (The Hague: T.M.C. Asser Press).

Bunse, S., Magnette, P., and Nicolaïdis, K. (2005b) 'Is the Commission the Small Member States' Best Friend?' *Swedish Institute for European Policy Studies, September 2005* (Stockholm: SIEPS).

Bunse, S., Magnette, P., and Nicolaïdis, K. (2007) 'Big Versus Small: Power Politics in the Convention'. In: Mazzucelli, C. and Beach, D. (eds.) *Leadership in the Big Bangs of European Integration* (London: Palgrave/Macmillan).

Burley, A. and Mattli, W. (1993) 'Europe Before the Court: A Political Theory of Legal Integration'. *International Organization*, Vol. 47 (Winter), pp. 41–76.

Busek, E. (2003) 'South Eastern Europe Beyond Thessaloniki: The Stability Pact and Regional Cooperation'. *EU-Western Balkans Summit, Thessaloniki, 21 June 2003*.

Cameron, D.R. (1992) 'The 1992 Initiative: Causes and Consequences'. In: Sbragia, A. (ed.) *Euro-Politics: Institutions and Policy-Making in the New European Community* (Washington DC: Brookings Institute).

Cameron, F. (2002) 'The European Union on the International Scene'. *EPC Working Papers, 8 October 2002*.

Carey, G.W. and McClellan, J. Ed. (2001) *The Federalist* (Indianapolis: Liberty Fund).

Catellani, N. (2001) 'The Multilevel Implementation of the Northern Dimension'. In: Ojanen, H. (ed.) *The Northern Dimension: Fuel for the EU?* (Helsinki: Finnish Institute of International Affairs).

CEPS. (2002) *Europa South-East Monitor*, Issue 40, November 2002.

CEPS. (2003a) *Europa South-East Monitor*, Issue 42, January 2003.

CEPS. (2003b) *Europa South-East Monitor*, Issue 43, February 2003.

CEPS. (2003c) *Europa South-East Monitor*, Issue 44, March 2003.

CEPS. (2003d) *Europa South-East Monitor*, Issue 45, April 2003.

CEPS. (2003e) *Europa South-East Monitor*, Issue 46, May 2003.

CEPS. (2003f) *Europa South-East Monitor*, Issue 47, June/July 2003.

Chirac, J. (2002) *Speech held in Strasbourg, 6 March 2002*.

Christoph, J.B. (1993) 'The Effects of Britons in Brussels: The European Community and the Culture of Whitehall'. *Governance*, Vol. 6, pp. 518–537.

Church, C.H. and Phinnemore, D. (1994) *European Union and European Community – A Handbook and Commentary on the 1992 Maatricht Treaties* (Harvester Wheatsheaf: Prentice Hall).

Coolsaet, R. and Voet, A.-S. (2002) 'Belgium'. In: Hocking, B. and Spence, D. (eds.) *Foreign Ministries in the EU* (Basingstoke: Palgrave/Macmillan).

Coombes, D. (1998) 'The Commission's Relationship with the Presidency'. *Paper presented at the Conference of the Presidency of the European Union, Dublin, 15–16 October 1998*.

Corbett, R. (1987) 'The 1985 Intergovernmental Conference and the Single European Act'. In: Pryce, R. (ed.) *The Dynamics of European Union* (London: Croomhelm), pp. 238–272.

Corbett, R. (1998) 'The Council Presidency as seen from the European Parliament'. *Paper presented at Conference of 'The Presidency of the European Union', Belfast, 15–16 October 1998*.

Corley, W. (2002) 'Finland, Northern Lights on American Exports'. *Export America*, November 2002.

Coufoudakis, V. (2003) 'The Cyprus Question: International Politics and the Failure of Peacemaking'. In: Couloumbis, T.A., Kariotis, T., and Bellou, F. (eds.) *Greece in the Twentieth Century* (London: Frank Cass).

Couloumbis, T. (2003) 'Greek Foreign Policy: Debates and Priotities'. In: Couloumbis, T.A., Kariotis, T., and Bellou, F. (eds.) *Greece in the Twentieth Century* (London: Frank Cass).

Couloumbis, T.A. and Dalis, S. (2004) 'Greek Foreign Policy Since 1974 – From Dissent to Consensus'. In: Dimitrakopoulos, D.G. and Passas, A.G. (eds.) *Greece in the EU* (London: Routledge).

Couloumbis, T.A., Kariotis, T., and Bellou, F. (2003) *Greece in the Twentieth Century* (London: Frank Cass).

Coussens, W. and Crum, B. (2003) 'Towards Effective and Accountable Leadership of the Union'. *EPIN Working Paper, No. 3, January 2003* (http://ceps.be).

Cram, L. (1997) *Policy-Making in the EU* (London: Routledge).

Cram, L. (2001) 'Governance "to go": Domestic Actors, Institutions, and the Boundaries of the Possible'. *Journal of Common Market Studies*, Vol. 39, No. 4, pp. 595–618.

Crenson, M.A. (1971) *The Un-Politics of Air Pollution: A Study of Non-Decision-Making in the Cities* (Baltimore: Johns Hopkins Press).

Crum, B. (2005) 'Getting the Constitution into Shape'. *Paper presented at the ECPR Joint Sessions, Granada, 14–19 April 2003.*

Crum, B. (2007) 'Accountability and Personalisation of the European Council Presidency'. *Paper prepared for the Symposium 'Wither the EU's Shared Leadership? (Re)assessing the Value of the European Union Council Presidency in the Context of the 2007 IGC', University of Oxford, 10–11 October 2007.*

Dankert, P. (1992) 'Challenges and Priorities'. In: Pijpers, A. (ed.) *The European Community at the Cross-Roads; Major Issues and Priorities for the EC Presidency* (Dordrecht: Martinus Nijhoff).

De Bassompiere, G. (1988) *Changing the Guard in Brussels: An Insider's View of the EC Presidency* (New York: Praeger).

De Schoutheete, P. and Wallace, H. (2002) 'The European Council'. *Notre Europe Research and European Issues*, No. 19, September 2002 (http://www.notre-europe.asso.fr/Fichiers/Etud19-fr).

De Winter, L. and Türsan, H. (2001) 'The Belgian Presidency 2001'. *Notre Europe Research and Policy Paper, No. 13, June 2001.*

De Witte, L. (Engl. Translation) (2001) *The Assassination of Lumumba* (London: Verso).

Dehousse, R., Maurer, A., Nestor, J., Quermonne, J.-L., and Schild, J. (2003) 'The Institutional Architecture of the European Union: A Third Franco-German way? Notre Europe'. *Research and European Issues*, No. 23, April 2003 (http://www.notre-europe.eu/uploads/tx_publication/Etud23-en.pdf).

Delors, J. (2003) In: Magnette, P. and Nicolaïdis, K. (2003) 'Large and Small Member States in the European Union: Reinventing the Balance'. *Research and European Issues*, No. 25, Notre Europe, June 2003.

Dewost, J.-L. (1984) 'La Présidence dans le cadre institutionnel des Communautés Européennes'. *Revue du Marché Commun*, No. 273, pp. 31–34.

Dimitrakopoulos, D.G. and Passas, A.G. (2004) *Greece in the EU* (London: Routledge).

Dinan, D. (1994) *Ever Closer Union?* (London: Macmillan).

Dinan, D. (1999) *Ever Closer Union?* (London: Macmillan).

Dinan, D. (2002) 'Institutions and Governance 2001–2002: Debating the EU's Future'. *Journal of Common Market Studies*, Vol. 40, Annual Review, pp. 29–43.

Dixit, A. and Skeath, S. (1999) *Games of Strategy* (New York: Norton).

Dokos, T.P. (2003) 'Greece in a Changing Strategic Setting'. In: Couloumbis, T.A., Kariotis, T., and Bellou, F. (eds.) *Greece in the Twentieth Century* (London: Frank Cass).

Dominguez, L. (1995) 'Greece in the European Union: Awkward and Backward'. (http://www.psa.ac.uk/cps/1995/domi.pdf), pp. 816–823.

Dooge, J. and Keating, P. Eds. (2001) *What the Treaty of Nice Means* (Dublin: Institute of European Affairs).

Duke, S. (1998) 'Assessing the UK Presidency: A Second Pillar Perspective'. *EIPA Working Paper 98/W/04* (http://unpan1.un.org/intradoc/groups/public/documents/NISPAcee/UNPAN007417.pdf).

Eckstein, H. (1971) *The Evaluation of Political Performance: Problems and Dimensions* (Beverly Hills: Sage Publications).

Edwards, G. and Lund, C. (1993) 'Der Ministerrat'. In: Weidenfeld, W. and Wessels, W. (eds.) *Jahrbuch der Europäischen Integration 1992–1993* (Bonn: Europa Union Verlag), pp. 63–71.

Edwards, G. and Wallace, H. (1977) *The Council of Ministers of the European Community and the President in Office* (London: The Federal Trust for Education and Research).

Edwards, G. and Wiessala, G. (2001) 'Conscious Resolve: The Portuguese Presidency of 2000'. *Journal of Common Market Studies/The European Union: Annual Review of the EU 2000/2001*, Vol. 39, pp. 43–46.

Edwards, G.C., Kessel, J.H., and Rockman, B.A. (1993) *Researching the Presidency* (Pittsburgh: University of Pittsburgh Press).

EKEME. (2002) *Greece in the European Union* (Athens: EKEME).

Elazar, D. (2001) 'The United States and the European Union: Models for their Epochs'. In: Nicolaïdis, K. and Howse, R. (eds.) *The Federal Vision* (Oxford: Oxford University Press).

Elgstöm, O., Bjurulf, B., Johansson, J., and Sannerstedt, A. (2001) 'Coalitions in European Union Negotiations'. *Scandinavian Political Studies*, Vol. 24, No. 2, pp. 111–128.

Elgström, O. Ed. (2003) *European Union Council Presidencies – A Comparative Perspective* (London: Routledge).

Endo, K. (1999) *The Presidency of the European Commission under Jacques Delors* (Basingstoke: Macmillan).

European Observatory for SMEs. (2003) 'SMEs in Europe', July 2003.

European Peacebuilding Liaison Office (EPLO). (2001) 'Towards a Coherent EU Conflict Prevention Policy in Africa: Challenges for the Belgian Presidency'. *Conference Report and Policy Recommendations*, Brussels, 7 September 2001.

European Policy Centre. (2002) *Convention on the Future of Europe – End of Term Report*, Brussels, 9 September 2002 (http://www.lf.svekom.se/demos/sjalvstyrelse_i_sverige_och_eu/sjalvstyrelse_och_eu/End_of_term_report.pdf).

European Stability Initiative (ESI). (2002) *Western Balkans 2004: Assistance, Cohesion and the New Boundaries of Europe*, 3 November 2002 (Berlin: ESI).

Evans, A. (2003) 'Private Copying in the EU: The Technological Protection and the "three-step test".' *Copyright Reporter*, Vol. 21, No. 2 (July 2003), pp. 36–55.

Evert, S. (2003) 'Time to Abolish the EU's Rotating Presidency'. *CER Bulletin*, No. 21 (http://www.cer.org.uk/articles/n_21_everts.html).

Fearon, J.D. (1991) 'Counterfactuals and Hypothesis Testing in Political Science'. *World Politics*, Vol. 43, No. 2 (January 1991), pp. 169–195.

Featherstone, K. (1994) 'Jean Monnet and the "Democratic Deficit" in the European Union', *Journal of Common Market Studies*, Vol. 32, No. 2, pp. 149–180.

Feldman, M. (1993) 'Organisation Theory and the Presidency'. In: Edwards, G.C., Kessel, J.H., and Rockman, B.A. (eds.) *Researching the Presidency* (Pittsburgh: University of Pittsburgh Press), pp. 267–288.

Fiedler, A. (2004) 'The Great Lakes Region: Testing Ground for a European Union Foreign Policy'. In: Mahncke, D., Ambos, A., and Reynolds, C. (eds.) *European Foreign Policy from Rhetoric to Reality? College of Europe Studies No. 1* (Brussels: P.I.E.-Peter Lang).

Finnish Institute of International Affairs. (2002) 'Chronology of Finnish Foreign Policy (1999)', as of 28 August 2002 (http://www.upi-fiia.fi/english/navigation/publications_frameset.htm).

Fisher, R. and Brown, S. (1988) 'A note on Tit for Tat'. *Getting Together: Building Relationships as We Negotiate* (London: Penguin Books), pp. 197–302.

Fitzmaurice, J. (1996) 'National Parliamentary Control of EU Policy in the Three New Member States'. *West European Politics*, Vol. 19, No. 1, pp. 88–96.

Fitzmaurice, J. (2000) 'The Belgian Elections of 13 June 1999: Near Melt Down or Soft Landing? *West European Politics*, Vol. 1, No. 1, pp. 175–179.

Fletcher, Y. (2002) ' "History will One Day have its Say": New Perspectives on Colonial and Postcolonial Congo'. *Radical History Review*, No. 84, Fall 2002, pp. 195–207.

Franck, C., Leclercq, H., and Vandevievere, C. (2003) 'Belgium: Europeanisation and Belgium Federalism'. In: Wessels, W., Maurer, A., and Mittag, J. (eds.) *Fifteen into one? The European Union and its Member States* (Manchester: Manchester University Press).

Frangakis, N. and Papayannides, A.D. (2003) 'Greece: A Never-Ending Story of Mutual Attraction and Estrangement'. In: Wessels, W., Maurer, A., and Mittag, J. (eds.) *Fifteen into One? The European Union and its Member States* (Manchester: Manchester University Press).

Franklin, M. (1990) 'Britain's Future in Europe'. *Chatham House Papers* (London: Royal Institute of International Affairs).

Gabriel, R.H. (1954) *Hamilton, Madison and Jay on the Constitution, Selections from the Federalist Papers* (New York: The Liberal Arts Press).

Galatsinou, M. (1996) *Organisational and Operational Adjustments of Greek Administration for the Co-ordination of Agricultural Policy in the EU*, Master's thesis (Athens: University of Athens).

Garel-Jones, T. (1993) 'The UK Presidency: An Inside View'. *Journal of Common Market Studies*, Vol. 31, No. 2, pp. 261–267.

Garrett, G. (1992) 'International Cooperation and Institutional Choice: The European Community's Internal Market'. *International Organization*, Vol. 46, No. 2, pp. 533–560.

Garrett, G. (1995) 'From the Luxembourg Compromise to Codecision: Decision Making in the European Union'. *Electoral Studies*, Vol. 14, No. 3, pp. 289–308.

Garrett, G. and Tsebelis, G. (1996) 'An Institutional Critique of Intergovernmentalism'. *International Organization*, Vol. 50, No. 2, pp. 269–299.

Garrett, G. and Weingast, B. (1993) 'Ideas, Interests, and Institutions: Constructing the European Community's Internal Market'. In: Goldstein, J. and Keohande, R. (eds.) *Ideas and Foreign Policy* (Ithaca: Cornell University Press).

Gaventa, J. (1982) *Power and Powerlessness* (Urbana and Chicago: University of Illinois Press).

George, S. (1990) *An Awkward Partner – Britain in the European Community* (Oxford: Oxford University Press).

George, S. (1991) *Politics and Policy in the European Community* (Oxford: Oxford University Press).

Geradin, D. and Humpe, C. (2002) 'The Liberalisation of Postal Services in the European Community: An Analysis of Directive 97/67'. In: Geradin, D. (ed.) *The Liberalisation of Postal Services in the European Union* (The Hague/London/New York: Kluwer Law International), pp. 91–119.

Geurts, C.-M. (1998) 'The European Commission: A Natural Ally of Small States in the EU Institutional Framework?' In: Goetschel, L. (ed.) *Small States Inside and Outside the European Union – Interests and Policies* (Dordrecht: Kluwer Academic Publisher), pp. 49–64.

Gillespie, P. (1996) International Report with the Irish Times, 12 December 1996.

Goetschel, L. (1998) *Small States Inside and Outside the European Union – Interests and Policies* (Dordrecht: Kluwer Academic Publisher).

Golub, J. (1999) 'In the Shadow of the Vote? Decision-Making in the European Community'. *International Organization*, Vol. 53, No. 4, pp. 733–764.

Gomez, R. (1998) 'The EU's Mediterranean Policy: A Common Foreign Policy by the Back Door?' In: Peterson, J. and Sjursen, H. (eds.) *A Common Foreign Policy for Europe?* (London: Routledge).

Goodin, E. and Klingemann, H.-D. (1996) *A New Handbook of Political Science* (Oxford: Oxford University Press).

Granell, F. (1995) 'The European Union's Enlargement Negotiations with Austria, Finland, Norway and Sweden'. *Journal of Common Market Studies*, Vol. 33, No. 1, pp. 117–142.

Grant, C. (1994) *Delors: Inside the House that Jacques Built* (London: Routledge).

Gray, M. and Stubb, A. (2001) 'Keynote Article: The Treaty of Nice – Negotiating a Poisoned Chalice?' *Journal of Common Market Studies*, Vol. 39, Annual Review, September 2001, pp. 5–23.

Grimwade, N. (2002) 'Developments in the Economies of the European Union'. *Journal of Common Market Studies*, Vol. 40, Annual Review, pp. 157–172.

Grønbech-Jensen, C. (1998) 'The Scandinavian Tradition of Open Government and the EU: Problems of Compatibility'. *Journal of European Public Policy*, Vol. 5, No. 1, pp. 185–199.

Guggenbühl, A. (2004) 'Cookbook of the Presidency of the European Union'. In: Meerts, P. and Cede, F. (eds.) *Negotiating European Union* (London: Palgrave/Macmillan), pp. 171–198.

Guiliani, M. (1998) 'Sul concetto di Imprenditore di Policy'. *Rivista Italiana di Scienza Politica*, Vol. XXXVIII, No. 2, pp. 357–377.

Haas, E. (1958) *The Uniting of Europe: Political, Social and Economic Forces, 1950–1957* (Stanford: Stanford University Press).

Haas, E. (1964) *Beyond the Nation State: Functionalism and International Organisation* (Stanford: Stanford University Press).

Haas, E. (1968) *The Uniting of Europe* (Stanford: Stanford University Press).

Haas, E. (1975) *The Obsolescence of Regional Integration Theory* (Berkeley: Institute of International Studies, University of California).

Hall, B. (2000) 'Europe's Revolving Door'. *CER Bulletin*, No. 11, April/May Bulletin (http://www.cer.org.uk/articles/n_11_2.html).

Hall, P.A. and Taylor, R.C.R. (1996) 'Political Science and the Three Institutionalisms'. *Political Studies*, Vol. 44, No. 4, pp. 936–957.

Hall, P.A. and Taylor, R.C.R. (1998) 'The Potential of Historical Institutionalism: A Response to Hay and Wincott'. *Political Studies*, Vols. 46, 5, pp. 958–962.

Halonen, T. (1998a) 'We Have a Lot of Potential'. *International Affairs* (Moscow), Vol. 44, No. 2, pp. 126–167.

Halonen, T. (1998b) *Finland in the EU – Perspective of a Small Member State, Speech held in Nicosia*, Nicosia, 12 October 1998.

Handel, M. (1990) *Weak States in the International System* (London: Frank Cass).

Hanf, K. and Soetendorp, B. (1998) *Adapting to European Integration. Small States and the EU* (London-New York: Longman).

Harle, V. (2000) 'Martti Ahtisaari, a Global Rationalist'. *Northern Dimensions 2000* (Helsinki: Finnish Institute of International Affairs).

Haukkala, H. (2001) 'Comment: National Interests Versus Solidarity – Towards Common Policies'. In: Ojanen, H. (ed.), *The Northern Dimension: Fuel for the EU?* (Helsinki: Finnish Institute of International Affairs).

Haukkala, H. (2003) 'The Role of the Northern Dimension in Tackling the Challenges of a Growing EU Presence in Northern Europe'. *FIIA Occasional Paper Series, No. 36* (Helsinki: Finnish Institute of International Affairs).

Hay, C. and Wincott, D. (1998) 'Structure, Agency and Historical Institutionalism'. *Political Studies*, Vol. 46, No. 5, pp. 951–957.

Hayes-Renshaw, F. (1997) 'The Presidency'. In: Hayes-Renshaw, F. and Wallace, H. (eds.) *The Council of Ministers* (London: Macmillan Press), pp. 134–157.

Hayes-Renshaw, F. (2001) 'The Council and Enlargement: A Challenge or an Opportunity?' *Journal of International Relations and Development*, Vol. 4, No. 1, pp. 9–12.

Hayes-Renshaw, F. (2002) 'The Council of Ministers'. In: Peterson, J. and Shackleton, M. (eds.) *The Institutions of the European Union* (Oxford: Oxford University Press).

Hayes-Renshaw, F. and Wallace, H. (1995) 'Executive Power in the European Union: The Functions and Limits of the Council of Ministers'. *Journal of European Public Policy*, Vol. 2, No. 4, pp. 559–582.

Hayes-Renshaw, F. and Wallace, H. (1997) *The Council of Ministers* (London: Macmillan).

Hayes-Renshaw, F., Lequesne, C., and Mayor-Lopez, P. (1989) 'The Permanent Representation of the Member States of the European Communities'. *Journal of Common Market Studies*, Vol. 28, No. 2, pp. 119–136.

Heininen, L. (1998). 'Integral Role of the European North'. *OSCE Review*, Vol. 6, No. 2.

Heininen, L. (2001) 'Ideas and Outcomes: Finding a Concrete Form for the Northern Dimension Initiative'. In: Ojanen, H. (ed.) *The Northern Dimension: Fuel for the EU?* (Helsinki: Finnish Institute of International Affairs).

Henderson, D. (1998a) 'The UK Presidency: An Insider's View'. *Journal of Common Market Studies*, Vol. 36, No. 4, pp. 563–572.

Henderson, D. (1998b) 'The British Presidency of the EU and British European policy'. *ZEI Discussion Paper C7* (Bonn: Zentrum für Europäische Integrationsforschung).

Hine, D. (1995) 'Italy and Europe; the Italian Presidency and the Domestic Management of the EC'. In: Leonardi, R. and Anderlini, F. (eds.) *Italian Politics; A Review* (London: Pinter).

Hix, S. (1994) 'The Study of the European Community: The Challenge to Comparative Politics'. *West European Politics*, Vol. 17, No. 1, pp. 1–30.

Hix, S. (1998) 'The Study of the European Union II: The "New Governance" Agenda and its Rival'. *Journal of European Public Policy*, Vol. 5, No. 1, pp. 38–65.

Hix, S. (1999) *The Political System of the EU* (Basingstoke: Macmillan).

Hochschild, A. (1999) *King Leopold's Ghost: A Story of Greed, Terror and Heroism in Colonial Africa* (Boston: Houghton Mifflin Co.).

Hocking, B. and Spence, D. (2002) *Foreign Ministries in the EU* (Basingstoke: Palgrave/Macmillan).

Hoffmann, S. (1966) 'Obstinate or Obsolete? The Fate of Nation State and the Case of Western Europe'. *Daedalus*, Vol. 95, pp. 862–915.

Hoffmann, S. (1982) 'Reflections on the Nation State'. *Journal of Common Market Studies*, Vol. 21, No. 1, pp. 21–38.

Höll, O. Ed. (1998) *The Austrian Presidency of the European Union* (Laxenburg: Austrian Institute for International Affairs).

Holland, M. (2002) *The European Union and the Third World* (London: Palgrave/Macmillan).

Hosli, M.O. (1999). 'Power, Connected Coalitions, and Efficiency: Challenges to the Council of the European Union'. *International Political Science Review*, Vol. 20, No. 4, pp. 371–397.

Humphreys, J. (1997) *Negotiating in the European Union: How to Make the Brussels Machine Work for You* (London: Century).

Hurrell, A. and Menon, A. (1996) 'Politics like Any Other? Comparative Politics, International Relations and the Study of the EU'. *West European Politics*, Vol. 19, No. 2, pp. 386–402.

Ilves, T.H. (1999) 'Promoting Stability Through Economic Integration'. *Statement at the Conference on the Northern Dimension, 12 November 1999* (http://64.233.187.104/search?q=cache:BdaSTVFX73EJ:www.vm.ee/eng/kat_140/1214.html+Toomas+Hendrik+Ilves+Helsinki+12+November+1999&hl=es).

Immergut, E.M. (1992) 'The Rules of the Game: The Logic of Health Policy-Making in France, Switzerland and Sweden'. In: Steinmo, S., Thelen, K., and Longstreth, F. (eds.) *Structuring Politics – Historical Institutionalism in Comparative Analysis* (Cambridge: Cambridge University Press).

Immergut, E.M. (1998) 'The Theoretical Core of the New Institutionalism'. *Politics and Society*, Vol. 26, No. 1, pp. 5–34.

Info Congo-Kinshasa. (2001) Issue 168–169, April–June 2001 (http://www.web.net/~ iccaf/humanrights/congoinfo/aprjuncongo01.htm#suffering).

Ingebritsen, C. and Larson, S. (1997) 'Interest and Identity: Finland, Norway and the EU'. *Co-operation and Conflict*, Vol. 32, No. 2, pp. 207–222.

Inotai, A. (2002) 'Regional Cooperation and European Integration – the Case of the Western Balkan'. *Bertelsmann Stiftung, Zentrum für Angewandte Politikforschung, Planungsstab des Auswärtigen Amtes* (http://www.cap.uni-muenchen.de/download/2002_Balkans_Gutachten_Inotai.pdf).

International Action Centre. (2001) 'As US, Israel Walk Out: World Conference condemns racism' (http://www.iacenter.org/durban_israel.htm).

International Crisis Groups (ICG). (2001) 'The Inter-Congolese Dialogue: Political Negotiation or Game of Bluff?' *Africa Report*, No. 37, 16 November 2001 (http://www.unhcr.org/refworld/docid/3de6206f4.html).

International Crisis Group (ICG). (2002) 'Moving Macedonia Toward Self-Sufficiency: A New Security Approach for NATO and the EU'. *Europe Report*, No. 135, 15 November 2002.

Jabko, N. (1999) 'In the Name of the Market: How the European Commission Paved the Way for Monetary Union'. *Journal of European Public Policy*, Vol. 6, No. 3, pp. 475–495.

Jackson, R. (2001) 'Conflict Resolution in Africa: Intervention, Indifference and Indigenous Solutions'. *African Affairs*, Vol. 100, No. 399, pp. 321–328.

Jacobs, F.B. (1997) *Legislative Codecision: A Real Step Forward?* Paper for ECSA. Conference in Seattle.

Jakobson, M. (1998) *Finland in the New Europe*, The Washington Papers CSIS (London: Praeger).

Jepperson, R.L. (1991) 'Institutions, Institutional Effects, and Institutionalism'. In: Di Maggio, P.J. (ed.) *The New Institutionalism in Organisational Analysis* (Chicago: University of Chicago Press).

Jones, A. and Clark, J.R.A. (1998) 'The Agri-Environment Regulation EU 2078/92: The Role of the European Commission in Policy Shaping and Setting'. *Government and Policy*, Vol. 16, pp. 51–68.

Jones, A. and Clark, J.R.A. (1999) 'The European Parliament: Agenda Territories and Agri-Environment Policy-Making'. *Government and Policy*, Vol. 17, pp. 127–144.

Jones, C.O. (1984) *An Introduction to the Study of Public Policy*, 2nd ed. (Monterey, CA: Brooks/Cole).

Kariotis, T.C. (2003) 'The Economy: Growth Without Equity'. In: Couloumbis, T. A., Kariotis, T., and Bellou, F. (eds.) *Greece in the Twentieth Century* (London: Frank Cass).

Kassim, H. (2000) 'The National Coordination of EU Policy: Confronting the Challenge'. In: Kassim, H., Peters, G., and Wright, V. (eds.) *The National Coordination of EU Policy: The Domestic Level* (Oxford: Oxford University Press).

Kassim, H., Menon, A., Peters, G., and Wright, V. (2001) *The National Co-ordination of EU Policy: The European Level* (Oxford: Oxford University Press).

Kassim, H., Peters, G., and Wright, V. (2000) *The National Co-ordination of EU Policy: The Domestic Level* (Oxford: Oxford University Press).

Kazakos, P. and Iokimidis, P.C. Eds. (1994) *Greece and EC Membership Evaluated* (London: Pinter Publishers).

Kelstrup, M. (1993) 'Small States and European Political Integration: Reflections of Theory and Strategy'. In: Tiilikainen, T. and Petersen, I.D. (eds.) *The Nordic Countries and the EC* (Copenhagen: Copenhagen Political Studies Press), pp. 136–162.

Keohane, R. (1969) 'Lilliputians Dilemmas: Small States in International Politics'. *International Organisation*, Vol. 23, No. 2, pp. 291–310.

Keohane, R. Ed. (1989) 'Neoliberal Institutionalism: A Perspective on World Politics'. *International Institutions and State Power* (Boulder: Westview), pp. 1–20.

Keohane, R. and Hoffman, S. (1991) *The New European Community: Decision-making and Institutional Change* (Boulder: Westview).

Kerremans, B. (1996) 'Do Institutions Make a Difference? Non-Institutionalism, Neo-Institutionalism, and the Logic of Common Decision-Making in the European Union'. *Governance*, Vol. 9, No. 2, pp. 217–240.

Kerremans, B. (2000) 'Belgium'. In: Kassim, H., Peters, G., and Wright, V. (eds.) *The National Co-ordination of EU Policy: The Domestic Level* (Oxford: Oxford University Press).

Kerremans, B. and Beyers, J. (2001) 'The Belgian Permanent Representation to the European Union: Mailbox, Messenger, or Representative?' In: Kassim, H., Menon, A., Peters, G., and Wright, V. (eds.) *The National Co-ordination of EU Policy: The European Level* (Oxford: Oxford University Press).

Kerremans, B. and Drieskens, E. (2003) 'The Belgian Presidency of 2001'. In: Elgström, O. (ed.) *European Union Council Presidencies – A Comparative Perspective* (London: Routledge).

King, A. (1993) 'Foundations of Power'. In: Edwards, G.C., Kessel, J.H., and Rockman, B.A. (eds.) *Researching the Presidency* (Pittsburgh: University of Pittsburgh Press), pp. 415–452.

King, G. (1993) 'The Methodology of Presidential Research'. In: Edwards, G.C., Kessel, J.H., and Rockman, B.A. (eds.) *Researching the Presidency* (Pittsburgh: University of Pittsburgh Press), pp. 387–414.

King, G., Keohane, R.O., and Verba, S. (1994) *Designing Social Inquiry* (Princeton: Princeton University Press).

Kingdon, J.W. (1984) *Agendas, Alternatives and Public Policies* (Boston: Little, Brown).

Kingdon, J.W. (1995) *Agendas, Alternatives and Public Choices* (New York: Harper Collins College Publishers).

Kirchner, E.J. (1992) *Decision-Making in the European Community – The Council Presidency and European Integration* (Manchester: Manchester University Press).

Kirchner, E.J. (1993) *The EC Council Presidency: The Dutch and Luxembourg Presidencies, UACES Proceedings 9* (University Association for Contemporary European Studies).

Kirchner, E.J. and Tsagkari, A. (1993) *The EC Council Presidency: The Dutch and Luxembourg Presidencies, UACES Proceedings 9* (University Association for Contemporary European Studies).

Kohnstamm, M. and Durand, G. (2003) 'Common Nonsense – Defusing the Escalating "Big Versus Small" Row'. *EPC Commentary, 12 May 2003* (Brussels: EPC).

Kollman, K. (2003) 'The Rotating Presidency of the European Council as a Search for Good Policies'. *European Union Politics*, Vol. 4, No. 1, pp. 51–74.

Kononenko, V. (2000) 'Swedish Foreign Policy Towards Russia and the Northern Dimension'. *Paper presented at the Research Seminar on the Northern Dimension, Finnish Institute of International Affairs, Helsinki, 24–26 August 2000*.

König, T. and Bräuninger, T. (2004) 'Analysis of Eastern Enlargement and the constitutional Reform Accession and Reform of the European Union: A Game-Theoretical Analysis of Eastern Enlargement and the Constitutional Reform'. *European Union Politics*, Vol. 5, No. 4, pp. 419–439.

König, T., Luetgert, B., and Dannwolf, T. (2006) 'Quantifying European Legislative Research: Using CELEX and PreLex in EU Legislative Studies'. *European Union Politics*, Vol. 7, No. 4, pp. 553–574.

Krause, A. (2002) 'Die EU als internationaler Akteur in Afrika', *Aus Politik und Zeitgeschichte*, No. 13–14, 29 März 2002 (http://www.bpb.de/publikationen/6YAPM0,1,0,Die_EU_als_internationaler_Akteur_in_Afrika.html#art1).

Krause, A. (2003) 'The European Union's Africa Policy: The Commission as Policy Entrepreneur in the CFSP'. *European Foreign Affairs Review*, Vol. 8, No. 2, pp. 221–237.

Laffan, B. (1997a) 'From Policy Entrepreneur to Policy Manager: The Challenge Facing the European Commission'. *Journal of European Public Policy*, Vol. 4, No. 3, pp. 422–438.

Laffan, B. (1997b) 'The European Union: A Distinctive Model of Internationalisation?' *European Integration Online Papers, No. 18* (http://www.eiop.or.at/eiop/texte/1997-018a.htm).

Laffan, B. (2001) 'Amsterdam to Nice'. In: Dooge, J. and Keating, P. (eds.) *What the Treaty of Nice Means?* (Dublin: Institute of European Affairs).

Lane, J.-E. and Mattila, M. (1998) 'Der Abstimmungsprozeß im Ministerrat'. In: König, T., Rieger, E., and Schmitt, H. (eds.) *Europa der Bürger? Voraussetzungen, Alternativen, Konsequenzen* (Frankfurt: Campus Verlag).

Lautso, M. (1997) *The Council Presidency and Domestic Politics*, Master Thesis (Brugge: College of Europe).

Lavdas, K.A. (1997) *The Europeanization of Greece* (London: Macmillan).

Lemola, T. (2001) 'National Specificities Versus Pressure Towards Convergence in Finnish Science and Technology Policy'. *Nelson and Winter Conference Paper Draft (24 May 2001) Aalborg, Denmark, 12–15 June 2001.*

Lequesne, C. (2001) 'The French Presidency: The Half Success of Nice', *Journal of Common Market Studies/The European Union: Annual Review of the EU 2000/2001*, Vol. 39, pp. 47–50.

Leshukov, I. (2001) 'Can the Northern Dimension Break the Vicious Circle of Russia-EU Relations?' In: Ojanen, H. (ed.) *The Northern Dimension: Fuel for the EU?* (Helsinki: Finnish Institute of International Affairs).

Lewis, J. (1998) 'Is the "Hard Bargaining Image" of the Council Misleading? The Committee of Permanent Representatives and the Local Elections Directive'. *Journal of Common Market Studies*, Vol. 38, No. 4, pp. 479–504.

Lijphart, A. (1971) 'Comparative Politics and the Comparative Method'. *American Political Science Review*, Vol. 65, No. 3, pp. 682–693.

Lijphart, A. (1992) *Parliamentary Versus Presidential Government* (Oxford: Oxford University Press).

Lindberg, L. (1963) *The Political Dynamics of European Economic Integration* (Stanford: Stanford University Press).

Lindberg, L. and Scheingold, S.A. (1970) *Europe's Would-be Polity: Patterns of Change in the European Community* (Englewood Cliffs: Prentice Hall).

Lindberg, L. and Scheingold, S.A. (1971) *Regional Integration: Theory and Research* (Cambridge: Harvard University Press).

Lindell, U. and Persson, S. (1986) 'The Paradox of Weak State Power: A Research and Literature Overview'. *Cooperation and Conflict*, Vol. 21, No. 2, pp. 79–98.

Linz, J.J. (1994) 'Presidential or Parliamentary Democracy: Does it Make a Difference?' In: Linz, J.J. and Valenzuela, A. (eds.) *The Failure of Presidential Democracy – Comparative Perspectives Vol. 1* (Baltimore and London: Johns Hopkins University Press).

Lipponen, P. (1997) 'The European Union Needs a Policy for the Northern Dimension'. *Speech delivered at the Conference on the Barents Region Today, Rovaniemi, 15 September 1997*.

Lipponen, P. (1999a) 'The Northern Dimension of the EU'. *Speech delivered at the Joint Meeting of the Nordic Council and the Baltic Assembly, Helsinki, 8–9 February 1999*.

Lipponen, P. (1999b) *Opening Speech delivered at the Foreign Ministers' Conference on the Northern Dimension, Helsinki, 12 November 1999* (http://www.vn.fi/vn/english/speech/991112e.htm).

Lipponen, P. (2000a) 'Baltic Sea Region and the Northern Dimension'. *Speech delivered at Tartu University, 9 May 2000* (http://www.vn.fi/vn/english/speech/20000905e.htm).

Lipponen, P. (2000b) 'The European Union Policy for the Northern Dimension from an Arctic Angle'. *Speech delivered at the Fourth Conference of Parliamentarians of the Arctic Region, Rovaniemi, 28 August 2000*.

Lipponen, P. (2000c) Statement on the Presidency Experience (http://presidency.finland.fi/).

Lister, M. (1997) *The EU and the South* (London: Routledge).

Ludlow, P. (1993) 'The UK Presidency: A view from Brussels'. *Journal of Common Market Studies*, Vol. 31, No. 2, pp. 246–259.

Ludlow, P. (1994) 'The Presidency of the Council, A New Power in the European Union?' In: Various Authors (eds.) *L'équilibre européen; Etudes rassemblées et publiées en hommage á Niels Esboll, Secrétaire général du Conseil de l'Union européenne (1980–1994)* (Brussels: Council General Secretariat), pp. 145–162.

Ludlow, P. (1998) 'The 1998 UK Presidency: A View from Brussels'. *Journal of Common Market Studies*, Vol. 36, No. 4, pp. 573–583.

Ludlow, P. (2002a) *The Laeken Council* (Brussels: EuroComment).

Ludlow, P. (2002b) 'The Greek Presidency'. *EuroComment Briefing Note, No. 1.9, 6 December 2002* (Brussels: EuroComment).

Ludlow, P. (2003a) 'The European Council and Iraq: Beyond the Conclusions'. *EuroComment Briefing Note, No. 1.13, 21 February 2003* (Brussels: EuroComment).

Ludlow, P. (2003b) 'The Spring European Council'. *EuroComment Briefing Note, No. 1.14, 31 March 2003* (Brussels: EuroComment).

Ludlow, P. (2003c) 'The Thessaloniki European Council'. *EuroComment Briefing Note, No. 2.3, 3 July 2003* (Brussels: EuroComment).

Luif, P. (1999) *The Austrian EU Presidency Analysis and Comment*, Unpublished Conference Paper.

Luther, K.R. (1999) 'Small and New, but Nonetheless Competent: Austria and the EU Presidency'. *Journal of Common Market Studies/The European Union: Annual Review 1998/1999*, Vol. 37, pp. 63–64.

Lyra, M. (1998) 'Finnish-Russian Relations'. *International Affairs – Russian Journal of World Politics, Diplomacy and International Relations*, Vol. 44, No. 2, pp. 128–132.

Majone, G. (1994) 'The Rise of the Regulatory State in Europe'. *West European Politics*, Vol. 17, No. 3, pp. 77–101.

Magnette, P. and Nicolaïdis, K. (2003) 'Large and Small Member States in the European Union: Reinventing the Balance'. *Research and European Issues, No. 25, Notre Europe, June 2003*.

Magnette, P. and Nicolaïdis, K. (2004) 'What Lessons to Learn from Europe's Crises? Is There Really a Crisis of European Leadership?' *Challenge Europe, EPC Issue 11, 19.4.2004*.

Mahncke, D., Ambos, A., and Reynolds, C. Eds. (2004) *European Foreign Policy from Rhetoric to Reality? College of Europe Studies No. 1* (Brussels: P.I.E.-Peter Lang).

Majone, G. (1994) 'The Rise of the Regulatory State'. *West European Politics*, Vol. 17, No. 3, pp. 77–101.

Malnes, R. (1995) 'Leader and Entrepreneur in International Negotiations: A Conceptual Analysis'. *European Journal of International Relations*, Vol. 1, No. 1, pp. 87–112.

March, J.G. and Olsen, J.P. (1989) *Rediscovering Institutions: The Organisational Basis of Politics* (New York: Oxford: Free Press; Maxwell Macmillan International).

Marks, G. (1993) 'Structural Policy and Multilevel Governance in the EC'. In: Cafruny, A. and Rosenthal, G. (eds.) *The State of the European Community II: The Maastricht Debates and Beyond* (Boulder: Lynne Rienner).

Marks, G. (1996) 'European Integration from the 1980s: State-Centric v. Multi-Level Governance'. *Journal of Common Market Studies*, Vol. 34, No. 3, pp. 341–378.

Martinez Sierra, J.M. (2002) 'The Spanish Presidency – Buying More than it Can Choose'. *ZEI Discussion Paper 112* (Bonn: Zentrum für Europäische Integrationsforschung).

Maurer, A. (2000) 'The German Presidency of the Council: Continuity or Change in Germany's European Policy?' *Journal of Common Market Studies*, Vol. 38, No. 4, Annual Review, pp. 43–47.

Mavris, Y.E. (2004) 'From Accession to the Euro – The Evolution of Greek Attitudes Toward European Integration 1981–2001'. In: Dimitrakopoulos, D.G. and Passas, A.G. (eds.) *Greece in the EU* (London: Routledge).

Mazzucelli, C. (2003) 'Understanding the Dutch Presidency's Influence at Amsterdam: A Constructivist Analysis.' *Paper presented at EUSA's 8th Biennial International Conference, Nashville, TN, 27–29 March 2003*.

McCubbins, M. (1989) 'Structure and Process, Policy and Politics: Administrative Arrangements and the Political Control of Agencies'. *Virginia Law Review*, Vol. 75, pp. 431–482.

McCubbins, M., Noll, R., and Weingast, B. (1987) 'Administrative Procedures as Instruments of Political Control'. *Journal of Law, Economics and Organisation*, Vol. 3, No. 2, pp. 243–277.

McCubbins, M., Noll, R., and Weingast, B. (1989) 'Structure and Process, Policy and Politics: Administrative Arrangements and the Political Control of Agencies'. *Virginia Law Review*, Vol. 75, pp. 431–482.

McCubbins, M. and Page, T. (1987) 'A Theory of Congressional Delegation'. In: McCubbins, M. and Sullivan T. (eds.) *Congress: Structure and Policy* (New York: Cambridge University Press).

McCubbins, M.D. and Schwartz, T. (1984) 'Congressional Oversight Overlooked: Police Patrols versus Fire Alarms'. *American Journal of Political Science*, Vol. 28, No. 1, pp. 165–179.

Meckstroth, T. (1975) 'Most Different Systems and Most Similar Systems: A Study in the Logic of Comparative Inquiry'. *Comparative Political Studies*, Vol. 8, No. 2 (July 1975), pp. 132–157.

Medvedev, S. (1999) 'Russia as the Subconscious of Finland'. *Security Dialogue*, Vol. 30, No. 1, pp. 95–107.

Menon, A. (2003) *Towards an Effective CFSP: Institutional Proposals, Notre Europe* (http://www.notre-europe.asso.fr/fichiers/AMenon.pdf).

Menon, A. and Wright, V. (1998) 'The Paradoxes of "Failure": British EU Policy Making in Comparative Perspective'. *Public Policy and Administration*, Vol. 13, No. 4, pp. 46–66.

Metcalfe, D. (1998) 'Leadership in European Union Negotiations: The Presidency of the Council'. *International Negotiation*, Vol. 3, No. 3, pp. 414–434.

Metcalfe, L. (1987) 'Measures of Effectiveness in EC Bargaining'. *EIPA Working Paper* (Maastricht: European Institute of Public Administration).

Michel, L. (2003a) 'Central Africa: Belgium Calls for a Concerted Effort'. *Humanitarian Affairs Review*, Spring 2003 (http://www.humanitarian-review.org/upload/pdf/LouisMichelsarticle.pdf).

Michel, L. (2003b) 'How Belgium Put Africa Back on the EU Agenda'. *Humanitarian Affairs Review*, Spring 2003 (http://www.humanitarian-review.org/upload/pdf/LouisMichelInterview.pdf).

Miles, L. (1993) *Scandinavia and EC Enlargement: Prospects and Problems for Sweden, Finland and Norway* (Hull: European Community Research Unit).

Miles, L. (1996) *The European Union and the Nordic Countries* (London: Routledge).

Mill, J.S. (1846) *A System of Logic, Ratiocinative and Inductive* (New York: Harper).

Milward, A.S. (1992) *The European Rescue of the Nation State* (Berkeley: University of California Press).

Mimica, N. (2002) 'Steps Ahead'. *Speech delivered at Centre for European Policy Studies (CEPS) 11 December 2002.*

Minakaki, T. (1992) 'The Communication of Central Administration with the EC and the Role of the European Affairs Units of the Ministries in Greece'. *Administrative Reform*, Vol. 51, No. 2, pp. 33–56.

Moe, T. (1987) 'An Assessment of the Positive Theory of Congressional Dominance'. *Legislative Studies Quarterly*, Vol. 12 (November 1987), pp. 475–520.

Moe, T. M. (1990) 'Political Institutions: The Neglected Side of the Story'. *Journal of Law, Economics, and Organization*, Vol. 6, Special Issue, pp. 213–253.

Moe, T.M. (1993) 'Presidents, Institutions and Theory'. In: Edwards, G.C., Kessel, J.H., and Rockman, B.A. (eds.) *Researching the Presidency* (Pittsburgh: University of Pittsburgh Press), pp. 337–386.

Moravcsik, A. (1991) 'Negotiating the Single European Act: National Interests and Conventional Statecraft in the European Community'. *International Organization*, Vol. 45, No. 1, pp. 651–688.

Moravcsik, A. (1993) 'Preferences and Power in the European Community: A Liberal Intergovernmentalist Approach'. *Journal of Common Market Studies*, Vol. 31, No. 4, pp. 473–524.

Moravcsik, A. (1995) 'Liberal Intergovernmentalism and Integration: A Rejoinder'. *Journal of Common Market Studies*, Vol. 33, No. 4, pp. 611–628.

Moravcsik, A. (1997) 'Taking Preferences Seriously: A Liberal Theory of International Politics'. *International Organisation*, Vol. 51, No. 4, pp. 513–553.

Moravcsik, A. (1998) *The Choice for Europe* (London: UCL Press).

Moravcsik, A. (1999a) 'A New Statecraft? Supranational Entrepreneurs and International Co-operation'. *International Organisation*, Vol. 53, No. 2, pp. 267–306.

Moravcsik, A. (1999b) 'Theory and Method in the Study of International Negotiation: A Rejoinder to Oran Young'. *International Organisation*, Vol. 45, No. 4, pp. 811–814.

Moravcsik, A. and Nicolaïdis, K. (1999) 'Explaining the Treaty of Amsterdam: Interests, Influence, Institutions'. *Journal of Common Market Studies*, Vol. 37, No. 1, pp. 59–85.

Moses, J.W. (1997) 'Trojan Horses: Putnam, ECU Linkage and the EU Ambitions of Nordic Elites'. *Review of International Political Economy*, Vol. 4, No. 2, pp. 382–415.

Mouritzen, H. (1993) 'The Two Musterknaben and the Naughty Boy: Sweden, Finland and Denmark in the Process of European Integration'. *Co-operation and Conflict*, Vol. 28, No. 4, pp. 373–402.

Nentwich, M. and Falkner, G. (1997) *'Towards a New Institutional Balance' European Online Papers* (EIoP), Vol. 1, No. 15 (http://eiop.or.at/eiop/texte/1997-015.htm).

Neustadt, R.E. (1990) *Presidential Power and the Modern Presidents: The Politics of Leadership from Roosevelt to Reagan* (New York: Free Press).

Nicolaïdis, K. and Howse, R. (2001) *The Federal Vision* (Oxford: Oxford University Press).

North, D.C. (1990) *Institutions, Institutional Change and Economic Performance* (Cambridge: Cambridge University Press).

Noutcheva, G. (2003) *In CEPS Europa South-East Monitor, January 2003*, Issue 42 (http://www.ceps.be/files/ESF/Monitor42.pdf).

Novak, J. (2001) 'The Northern Dimension in Sweden's EU policies: From Baltic Supremacy to European Union?' In: Ojanen, H. (ed.) *The Northern Dimension: Fuel for the EU?* (Helsinki: Finnish Institute of International Affairs).

Nugent, N. (1994) *The Government and Politics of the European Union* (London: Macmillan).

Nugent, N. (1995) *The Government and Politics of the European Union* (London: Macmillan).

Nugent, N. (2000) 'Enlargement and the Cyprus Problem'. *Journal of Common Market Studies*, Vol. 38, No. 1, pp. 131–150.

O'Nuallain, C. Ed. (1985) *The Presidency of the European Council of Ministers, Impacts and Implications for National Governments* (London: Croom Helm in association with the European Institute of Public Administration).

Ojanen, H. (1998a) 'Fresh Foreign and Security Policy Impact'. *OSCE Review*, Vol. 6, No. 2.

Ojanen, H. (1998b) 'The Comfort of Ambiguity, or the Advantages of the CFSP for Finland'. *Upi Working Papers, No. 11* (Helsinki: Finnish Institute of International Affairs).

Ojanen, H. (1999) 'How to Customize Your Union: Finland and the Northern Dimension of the EU', *Northern Dimensions Yearbook 1999* (Helsinki: Finnish Institute for International Affairs), pp. 13–26.

Ojanen, H. (2001) *The Northern Dimension: Fuel for the EU?* (Helsinki: Finnish Institute of International Affairs).

Olsen, J.P. (2002) 'Reforming European Institutions of Governance'. *Journal of Common Market Studies*, Vol. 40, No. 4, pp. 581–602.

Olsen, J.P. and March, J.G. (1989) *Rediscovering Institutions* (New York: Free Press).

Paes, W. and Shaw, T. (2003) 'Praetorians or Profiteers? The Role of Entrepreneurial Armed Forces in Congo-Kinshasa'. In: Brömmelhörster, J. and Paes, W. (eds.) *The Military as an Economic Actor – Soldiers in Business* (Basingstoke: Palgrave/Macmillan).

Pagoulatos, G. (2002) 'Greece, the European Union and the 2003 Presidency'. *Research and European Issues, No. 21, Notre Europe, December 2002*, pp. 1–38 (http://www.notre-europe.eu/uploads/tx_publication/Etud21-en_04.pdf).

Papandreou, G. (2002) *Message of Foreign Minister G. A. Papandreou Marking Greece's Taking on of the Presidency of the European Union, 31 December 2002* (www.eu2003.gr/en/articles/2002/12/31/1416/).

Papandreou, G. (2003a) *Speech Given at St Antony's College, University of Oxford, 6 May 2003*.

Papandreou, G. (2003b) *Press Release: EU Council of Ministers – External Relations session 19 May 2003*. (http://64.233.187.104/search?q=cache:1qnmqobHL6AJ: europa-eu-un.org/articles/en/article_2363_en.htm+Council+of+Ministers+ External+Relations+session+19+May+2003&hl=es).

Parenti, M. (1970) 'Power and Pluralism: A View from the Bottom'. *Journal of Politics*, Vol. 32, pp. 501–530.

Passas, A. and Stephanou, C. (1997) 'Grèce'. In: Rideau, J. (ed.) *Les États Membres de l'Union Européenne. Adaptations – Mutations – Résistances* (Paris: LGDJ), pp. 237–258.

Patten, C. (1999) A Northern Dimension for the Policies of the Union: Current and Future Activities. *Foreign Ministers' Conference on the Northern Dimension, Helsinki, 12 November 1999*.

Patten, C. (2003) *Interview after the Publication of the Second Stabilisation and Association Reports, 26 March 2003* (http://64.233.187.104/ search?q=cache:n3liyJ8Bts0J:europa.eu.int/comm/external_relations/news/ patten/sap260303.htm+It+is+for+the+countries+in+the+region+to+take+ their+own+political+decisions+and+the+speed+with+which+they+take+ those+decisions+is+going+to+affect+the+speed+with+which+they+move+ towards+Europe&hl=es).

Peters, G. (1994a) 'Agenda-Setting in the European Community'. *Journal of European Public Policy*, Vol. 1, No. 1, pp. 9–26.

Peters, G. (1994b) *American Public Policy*, 4th ed. (Chatham, NJ: Chatham House).

Peters, G. (1996a) 'Agenda-Setting in the European Union'. In: Richardson, J.J. (ed.) *European Union Power and Policy-Making* (London: Routledge), pp. 61–76.

Peters, G. (1996b) 'Political Institutions, Old and New'. In: Goodin, R. E. and Klingemann, H.-D. (eds.) *A New Handbook of Political Science* (Oxford: Oxford University Press), pp. 205–222.

Peters, G. (1998) *Comparative Politics – Theory and Methods* (London: Macmillan).

Peters, G. (2005) *Institutional Theory in Political Science – The New Institutionalism* (London: Continuum).

Peterson, J. (1995) 'Decision-making in the European Union: Towards a Framework for Analysis'. *Journal of European Public Policy*, Vol. 2, No. 1, pp. 69–89.

Peterson, J. (1997) 'Britain, Europe and the World'. In: Dunleavy, P., Gamble, A., Holliday, I., and Peele, G. (eds.) *Developments in British Politics 5* (New York: St Martin's Press).

Peterson, J. (1999) 'The Santer Era: The European Commission in Normative, Historical and Theoretical Perspective'. *Journal of European Public Policy*, Vol. 6, No. 1, pp. 46–65.

Peterson, J. (2001) 'The Choice for EU Theorists: Establishing a Common Framework for Analysis'. *European Journal of Political Research*, Vol. 39, No. 3, pp. 289–318.

Peterson, J. and Bomberg, E. (1999) *Decision-making in the European Union* (London: Macmillan).

Peterson, J. and Shackleton, M. (2002) *The Institutions of the European Union* (Oxford: Oxford University Press).

Peterson, J. and Sjursen H. (1998) *A Common Foreign Policy for Europe?* (London: Routledge).

Picqué, C. (2001) *Speech on the Economic Priorities of the Belgian Presidency* (http://64.233.187.104/search?q=cache:4mzzL254Z4kJ:attac.org/cec/doc/ecofin02en.htm+Belgian+priorities+economy+minister+consumer+protection&hl=en).

Pierson, P. (1998) 'The Path to European Integration: A Historical-Institutionalist Analysis'. In: Sandholtz, W. and Stone Sweet, A. (eds.) *European Integration and Supranational Governance* (Oxford: Oxford University Press).

Pijpers, A. (1992) *The European Community at the Cross-roads; Major Issues and Priorities for the EC Presidency* (Dordrecht: Martinus Nijhoff).

Plano, J. C. (1982) *Dictionary of Political Analysis* (Santa Barbara, CA: ABC-CLIO).

Pollack, M. (1996) 'The New Institutionalism and EC Governance: The Promise and Limits of Institutional Analysis'. *Governance*, Vol. 9, No. 4, pp. 429–458.

Pollack, M. (1997) 'Delegation, Agency, and Agenda Setting in the European Community'. *International Organization*, Vol. 51, No. 1, pp. 99–134.

Pollack, M. (1998) 'The Engines of Integration? Supranational Autonomy and Influence in the European Union'. In: Sandholtz, W. and Stone Sweet, A. (eds.) *European Integration and Supranational Governance* (Oxford: Oxford University Press), pp. 217–249.

Pollack, M. (2003) *The Engines of European Integration* (Oxford: Oxford University Press).

Preston, C. (1995) 'Obstacles to EU Enlargement: The Classical Community Method and the Prospects for a Wider Europe'. *Journal of Common Market Studies*, Vol. 33, No. 3 (September 1995), pp. 451–463.

Preston, C. (1997) *Enlargement and Integration in the European Union* (London: Routledge).

Prodi, R. (2003) *Press-Conference by the Greek Prime Minister C. Simitis and the President of the European Commission, Mr. Romano Prodi, 10 January 2003* (http://www.greekembassy.org/Embassy/content/en/Article.aspx?office=1&folder=167&article=130).

Przeworski, A. and Teune, H. (1970) *The Logic of Comparative Social Inquiry* (New York: Wiley-Interscience).

Puchala, D. (1999) 'Institutionalism, Intergovernmentalism and European Integration: A Review Article'. *Journal of Common Market Studies*, Vol. 37, No. 2, pp. 317–331.

Putnam, R. (1988) 'Diplomacy and Domestic Politics: The Logic of Two Level Games'. *International Organisation*, Vol. 42, No. 3, pp. 427–460.

Quaglia, L. and Moxon-Browne, E. (2006) 'What Makes a Good EU Presidency? Italy and Ireland Compared'. *Journal of Common Market Studies*, Vol. 44, No. 2, pp. 377–395.

Quaglia, L., Hough, D., and Mayhew, A. (2007) 'You Can't Always Get What You Want, But Do You Sometimes Get What You Need? The German Presidency of the EU in 2007'. *Working Paper of the Sussex European Institute, N 98*.

Raunio, T. (1999) 'Facing the European Challenge: Finnish Parties Adjust to the Integration Process'. *West European Politics*, Vol. 22, No. 1, pp. 138–159.

Raunio, T. and Tiilikainen, T. (2003) *Finland in the European Union* (London: Frank Cass).

Raunio, T. and Wiberg, M. (1998) 'Winners and Losers in the Council: Voting Power Consequences of EU Enlargements'. *Journal of Common Market Studies*, Vol. 36, No. 4, pp. 549–562.

Rehn, O. (2003) 'Can a Neutralist Nordic Become a Core European? – Historical Trajectory and Political Culture in the Making of Finland's EU Policy'. *Revised Version of a Paper presented at the ECPR Joint Session of Workshops, March–April 2003 (Edinburgh) Workshop #2: National Political Cultures and European Integration, 10 September 2003.*

Richardson, J.J. (1996) *European Union Power and Policy-making* (London: Routledge).

Risse-Kappen, T. (1996) 'Exploring the Nature of the Beast: International Relations Theory and Comparative Policy Analysis Meet the European Union'. *Journal of Common Market Studies*, Vol. 34, No. 1, pp. 53–80.

Rometsch, D. and Wessels, W. (1994) 'The Commission and the Council of Ministers'. In: Geoffrey, E. and David, S. (eds.) *The European Commission* (London: Longmans), pp. 202–224.

Rose, R. (1991) 'Comparing Forms of Comparative Politics'. *Political Studies*, Vol. 39, No. 4, pp. 446–462.

Rose, R. (1993) 'Evaluating Presidents'. In: Edwards, G.C., Kessel, J.H., and Rockman, B.A. (eds.) *Researching the Presidency* (Pittsburgh: University of Pittsburgh Press), pp. 453–484.

Rosenthal, G. (1975) *The Men Behind the Decisions: Cases in European Policy-Making* (Lexington, Mass.: D.C. Heath).

Rothstein, B. (1996) 'Political Institutions: An Overview'. In: Goodin, R. E. and Klingemann, H.-D. (eds.) *A New Handbook of Political Science* (Oxford: Oxford University Press), pp. 133–166.

Rothstein, R. (1968) *Alliances and Small Powers* (New York, London: Columbia University Press).

Sandholtz, W. (1996) 'Membership Matters: Limits of the Functional Approach to European Institutions'. *Journal of Common Market Studies*, Vol. 34, No. 3, pp. 403–427.

Sandholtz, W. and Stone Sweet, A. (1998) *European Integration and Supranational Governance* (Oxford: Oxford University Press).

Sandholtz, W. and Zysman, J. (1989) '1992: Recasting the European Bargain'. *World Politics*, Vol. 42, No. 1, pp. 95–128.

Santer, J. (1991) 'Luxembourg's Prime Minister discusses his country's Presidency of the EC Council of Ministers'. *Europe*, January/February 1991, pp. 33–36.

Sarkozy, N. (2008) *Speech Held at the EP plenary*, 21 October 2008.

Sbragia, A. Ed. (1992) *Euro-Politics: Institutions and Policy-making in the New European Community* (Washington DC: Brookings Institute).

Scharpf, F. (1988) 'The Joint-Decision Trap: Lessons from German Federalism and European Integration'. *Public Administration*, Vol. 66, No. 4, pp. 239–278.

Scharpf, F. (1994) 'Community and Autonomy; Multi-Level Policy-Making in the EU'. *Journal of European Public Policy*, Vol. 1, No. 2, pp. 219–242.

Scharpf, F. (1997) *Games Real Actors Play* (Boulder: Westview Press).

Schattschneider, E.E. (1960) *The Semisovereign People* (Orlando: Harcourt Brace Jovanovich College Publishers).

Schattschneider, E.E. (edition 1988) *The Semisovereign People* (Orlando: Harcourt Brace Jovanovich College Publishers).

Schmidt, S.K. (2001) 'A constrained Commission: Informal Practices of Agenda-Setting in the Council'. In: Aspinwall, M. and Schneider, G. (eds.) *The Rules of Integration, Institutionalist Approaches to the Study of Europe* (Manchester: Manchester University Press).

Schmitter, P.C. (1992) 'Interests, Powers and Functions'. *April Working Paper* (Stanford: Centre for Advanced Study in the Behavioural Science).

Schout, A. (1998) 'The Presidency as Juggler: Managing Conflicting Expectations'. *Eipascope*, No. 2, pp. 2–10.

Schuppert, G.F. (1994) 'Zur Staatswerdung Europas: Überlegungen zu Bedingungsfaktoren und Perspektiven der europäischen Verfassungsentwicklung'. *Staatswissenschaften und Staatspraxis*, Vol. 5, pp. 35–76.

Selznick, P. (1957) *Leadership in Administration: A Sociological Interpretation* (Evanston, Illinois: Row, Peterson and Company).

Sherrington, P. (2000) *The Council of Ministers – Political Authority in the European Union* (London: Pinter).

Sie Dian Ho, M. and Keulen, M.v. (2004) 'The Dutch at the Helm: Navigating on a Rough Sea'. *Research and European Issues, No. 34, June 2004* (Paris: Notre Europe).

Simonian, H. (1985) *The Privileged Partnership: Franco-German Relations in the EC, 1969–1984* (Oxford: Oxford University Press).

Sinclair, B. (1993) 'Studying Presidential Leadership'. In: Edwards, G.C., Kessel, J.H., and Rockman, B.A. (eds.) *Researching the Presidency* (Pittsburgh: University of Pittsburgh Press), pp. 203–232.

Singleton, F. (1998) *A Short History of Finland* (Cambridge: Cambridge University Press).

Sloot, Th. and Verschuren, P. (1990) 'Decision-Making Speed in the European Community'. *Journal of Common Market Studies*, Vol. 28, No. 1, pp. 75–85.

Simitis, D. (2003) as cited by http://www.greece.gr/POLITICS/EuropeanUnion/Greecesaims.stm.

Solana, J. (2002) *Speech delivered at Lancaster House Ministerial Conference on 'Defeating Organised Crime in South Eastern Europe', London, 25 November 2002.*

Spanou, C. (2000) 'A Truncated Pyramid?' In: Kassim, H., Peters, G., and Wright, V. (eds.) *The National Co-ordination of EU Policy: The Domestic Level* (Oxford: Oxford University Press).

Spence, D. (1995) 'Negotiations in the Council of Ministers'. In: Westlake, M. (ed.) *The Council of the European Union* (London: Cartermill).

Stein, A. (1990) *Why Nations Cooperate: Circumstance and Choice in International Relations* (Ithaca: Cornell University Press).

Stein, E. (1981) 'Lawyers, Judges, and the Making of a Transnational Constitution'. *American Journal of International Law*, Vol. 75, pp. 1–27.

Steinmo, S., Thelen, K., and Longstreth, F. (1992) *Structuring Politics – Historical Institutionalism in Comparative Analysis* (Cambridge: Cambridge University Press).

Stenback, P. (1995) 'Nordic Co-operation and EU Membership of Finland and Sweden'. *Yearbook of Finnish Foreign Policy*, Vol. 22, pp. 23–28.

Stenlund, P. (1999a) 'Policies for the Northern Dimension'. *Speech delivered at the Meeting of the DG X Directors, Rovaniemi, 18 June 1999.*

Stenlund, P. (1999b) 'The EU's Northern Dimension: Future Perspectives'. *Speech delivered at the European Finance Convention Foundation, Helsinki, 22 November 1999.*

Stenlund, P. (2000). *Speech delivered at UACES Conference on the Finnish Presidency, Manchester, 3 March 2000.*

Stenlund, P. and Nissinen, M. (2001) *A Northern Dimension for the Policies of the European Union, Virtual Finland, 13 November 2001.*

Stepan, A. and Scatch, C. (1994) 'Presidentialism and Parliamentarism in Comparative Perspective', In: Linz, J.J. and Valenzuela, A. (eds.) *The Failure of Presidential Democracy – Comparative Perspectives Vol. 1* (Baltimore and London: Johns Hopkins University Press).

Stubb, A. (2000a) 'The Finnish Presidency'. *Journal of Common Market Studies*, Vol. 38, Annual Review (September 2000), pp. 49–53.

Stubb, A. (2000b) 'Negotiating Flexibility in the Amsterdam Treaty'. In: Neunreither, K. and Wiener, A. (eds.) *Amsterdam and Beyond* (Oxford: Oxford University Press).

Stubb, A. (2000c) 'Dealing with Flexibility in the IGC'. In: Best, E., Gray, M., and Stubb, A. (eds.) *Rethinking the European Union: IGC 2000 and Beyond* (Maastricht: EIPA).

Svensson, A.-C. (2000) *In the Service of the European Union. The Role of the Presidency in Negotiating the Amsterdam Treaty 1995–1997*, Ph.D. dissertation (Uppsala: Uppsala University).

Svetlicic, M. and Trtnik A. (1999) 'European Union Enlargement: Is Enthusiasm Waning'. *Eastern European Economics*, Vol. 37, No. 4, pp. 70–96.

Tallberg, J. (2000) 'The Anatomy of Autonomy: An Institutional Account of Variation in Supranational Influence'. *Journal of Common Market Studies*, Vol. 38, No. 5, pp. 843–864.

Tallberg, J. (2002a) 'The Power of the Chair in International Bargaining'. *Paper presented at the 2002 ISA Annual Convention, New Orleans, 24–27 March 2002.*

Tallberg, J. (2002b) 'Delegation to Supranational Institutions: Why, How, and with What Consequences?' *West European Politics*, Vol. 25, No. 1, pp. 23–46.

Tallberg, J. (2003) 'The Agenda-Shaping Powers of the EU Council Presidency'. *Journal of European Public Policy*, Vol. 10, No. 1, pp. 1–19.

Tallberg, J. (2004) 'The Power of the Presidency'. *Journal of Common Market Studies*, Vol. 42, No. 5, pp. 999–1022.

Tallberg, J. (2006) *Leadership and Negotiation in the European Union* (Cambridge: Cambridge University Press).

Taylor, P. (1983) *The Limits of European Integration* (London: Croom Helm).

Taylor, P. (1996) *The European Union in the 1990s* (Oxford: Oxford University Press).

Thelen, K. (1999) 'Historical Institutionalism in Comparative Politics'. *Annual Review of Political Science*, Vol. 2, pp. 369–404.

Thelen, K. and Steinmo, S. (1992) 'Historical Institutionalism in Comparative Politics'. In: Steinmo, S., Thelen, K., and Longstreth, F. (eds.) *Structuring Politics – Historical Institutionalism in Comparative Analysis* (Cambridge: Cambridge University Press).

Theodoropoulus, B. (2003) 'Greek-Turkish Relations: A New Era?' In: Couloumbis, T.A., Kariotis, T., and Bellou, F. (eds.) *Greece in the Twentieth Century* (London: Frank Cass).

Thomson, R. (2007) 'The Impact of Enlargement on Legislative Decision Making in the European Union'. *Prepared delivered at the 2007 Annual Meeting of the American Political Science Association, 30 August–2 September 2007*.

Thomson, R. (June 2008) 'The Council Presidency in the EU: Responsibility with Power'. *Journal of Common Market Studies*, Vol. 46, No. 3, pp. 593–617.

Thomson, R., Stokman, F.N., Achen, C.H., and Koenig, T. (2006) *The European Union Decides* (Cambridge: Cambridge University Press).

Thorhallson, B. (2000) *The Role of Small States in the European Union* (Ashgate: Aldershot).

Tiilikainen, T. (1994) 'The Finns as Constructors of a United Europe – Reflections Upon the European Political Heritage of Finland'. *Yearbook of Finnish Foreign Policy 1994*, No. 21, pp. 20–28.

Tiilikainen, T. (1998) *Europe and Finland: Defining the Political Identity of Finland in Western Europe* (Aldershot: Ashgate).

Tiilikainen, T. (2000) 'Finland Guided the EU into the New Millennium'. *Northern Dimensions 2000* (Helsinki: Finnish Institute of International Affairs).

Tiilikainen, T. (2001) 'Finland in the EU'. In: Huldt, B., Tiilikainen, T., Vaahtoranta, T., and Helkama-Rågård, A. (eds.) *Finnish and Swedish Security – Comparing National Policies, Swedish National Defence College and the Programme on the Northern Dimension of the CFSP* (Helsinki: Finnish Institute of International Affairs and Institute d'Etude Politiques).

Tiilikainen, T. (2003) 'Finland: Smooth Adaptation to European Values and Institutions'. In: Wessels, W., Maurer, A., and Mittag, J. (eds.) *Fifteen into One? The European Union and its Member States* (Manchester: Manchester University Press).

Timmers, P. and Van der Veer, J. (1999) 'Electronic commerce: A challenge for Europe'. *European Commission – Information Society Directorate-General, 12 July 1999*.

Tornudd, K. (1996) 'Ties that Bind to the Recent Past: Debating Security Policy in Finland Within the Context of Membership of the European Union'. *Cooperation and Conflict*, Vol. 31, No. 1, pp. 37–68.

Transholm-Mikkelsen, J. (1991) 'Neo-Functionalism: Obstinate or Obsolete? A Reappraisal in the Light of the New Dynamism of the EC'. *Millennium*, Vol. 20, No. 1, pp. 1–22.

Troy Johnston, M. (1994) *The European Council: Gatekeeper of the European Community* (Boulder: Westview).

Tsebelis, G. (1994) 'The Power of the European Parliament as a Conditional Agenda Setter'. *American Political Science Review*, Vol. 88, No. 1, pp. 128–139.

Tsebelis, G. (1995) 'Conditional Agenda-Setting and Decision-Making Inside the European Parliament'. *Journal of Legislative Studies*, Vol. 1, No. 1, pp. 65–93.

Tsebelis, G. and Garrett, G. (1996) 'Agenda Setting Power, Power Indices, and Decision Making in the EU'. *International Review of Law and Economics*, Vol. 16, No. 3, pp. 345–361.

Tsebelis, G. and Garrett, G. (2001) 'The Institutional Foundations of Intergovernmentalism and Supranationalism in the European Union'. *International Organisation*, Vol. 55, No. 2, pp. 357–390.

Tsoukalis, L. (2003) 'The Future of Greece in the European Union'. In: Couloumbis, T.A., Kariotis, T., and Bellou, F. (eds.) *Greece in the Twentieth Century* (London: Frank Cass).

Tuomioja, E. (1999) *Opening Remarks of Mr Erkki Tuomioja, Minister of Trade and Industry, at the Press Conference, Oulu, 3 July 1999* (http://presidency.finland.fi/netcomm/news/showarticle420_258.html).

Tziampiris, A. (2003) 'Greece and the Balkans in the Twentieth Century'. In: Couloumbis, T.A., Kariotis, T., and Bellou, F. (eds.) *Greece in the Twentieth Century* (London: Frank Cass).

Underdahl, A. (1994) 'Leadership Theory: Rediscovering the Arts of Management'. In: Zartman, I.W. (ed.) *International Multilateral Negotiation. Approaches to the Management of Complexity* (San Francisco: Jossey-Bass).

Ungerer, W. (1988) 'EC progress under the German Presidency'. *Aussenpolitik*, Vol. XXXIX, p. 4.

Ungerer, W. (1993) 'Institutional Consequences of Broadening and Deepening: The Consequences for the Decision-Making Process'. *Common Market Law Review*, Vol. 30, No. 1, pp. 71–83.

Vahl, R. (1997) *Leadership in Disguise* (Aldershot: Ashgate).

Valtasaari, J. (1999) 'Finland and the EU Presidency – An Agenda for the New Millennium'. *Speech delivered in London, 4 May 1999*.

Van Bellinghen, M. (2001) 'La Coopération avec l'Afrique: Perspectives européennes'. *Seminar Organised by the Institute of European Studies, University of Montreal and McGill, Montreal, 12 November 2001*.

Van Ham, P. and Trenin, D. (2000) 'Russia and the United States in Northern European Security'. *Programme on the Northern Dimension of the CFSP, Vol. 5* (Finnish Institute of International Affairs and Institut für Europäische Politik).

Van Keulen, M. (2004) *The Netherlands 2004 EU Council Presidency: Dutch EU Policy-Making in the Spotlights* (Stockholm: Swedish Institute for European Policy Studies SIEPS).

Van Meurs, W. (2003) 'The Next Europe: South-Eastern Europe After Thessaloniki'. *South-East Europe Review*, No. 3, pp. 9–16 (http://www.boeckler.de/pdf/South_East_Europe_Review_2003_03_meurs.pdf).

Van Meurs, W. and Weiss, S. (2003) *The Next Europe: Southeastern Europe after Thessaloniki* (Gütersloh and München: Bertelsman CAP, July 2003).

Van Meurs, W. and Yannis, A. (2002) *The European Union and the Balkans – From Stabilisation Process to Southeastern Enlargement*, Hellenic Foundation for European and Foreign Policy, Bertelsmann Stiftung and Centre for Applied Policy Research, September 2002.

Van Schendelen, M.P.C.M. (1996) 'The Council Decides – Does It?' *Journal of Common Market Studies*, Vol. 34, No. 4, pp. 531–548.

Vayrinen, R. (1993) 'Finland and the European Community – changing Elite Bargains'. *Cooperation and Conflict*, Vol. 28, No. 1, pp. 31–46.

Verbeke, J. and Van de Voorde, W. (1994) 'The Presidency of the EU, Some Reflections on Current Practice and Recent Evolutions'. *Studia Diplomatica*, Vol. 47, No. 3, pp. 29–40.

Verheugen, G. (1999) 'Germany and the EU Council Presidency, Expectations and Reality'. *ZEI Discussion Paper, C 35, 1999*, pp. 3–14.

Verhofstadt, G. (2000) 'A Vision for Europe'. *Speech to the European Policy Centre, 21 September 2000*.

Verney, D.V. (1992) 'Parliamentary Government and Presidential Government'. In: Lijphart, A. (ed.) *Parliamentary Versus Presidential Government* (Oxford: Oxford University Press).

Verrue, R. (1999) 'Electronic Commerce in Europe: The Present Situation'. *Speech delivered at the Seminar on Electronic Commerce, Kangaroo Group, European Parliament, Brussels, 20 January 1999* (http://europa.eu.int/comm/information_society/speeches/verrue/ecommerce_en.htm).

Vervaeke, K. (2003) 'Peace, Mediation and Reconciliation: The Belgian Experience'. *Presentation by the Special Envoy for the Great Lakes Region, FPS Foreign Affairs, Belgian-Norwegian Seminar on Peace, Mediation and Reconciliation, Brussels, 21 May 2003*.

Von Bogdandy, A. (1999) 'Die Europäische Union als supranationale Föderation'. *Integration*, Vol. 22, No. 2, pp. 95–112.

Von Kyaw, D. (1999) 'Prioritäten der deutschen EU-Präsidentschaft unter Berücksichtigung des Europäischen Rates in Wien'. *ZEI Discussion Paper C33*, pp.1–16 (http://www.zei.de/download/zei_dp/dp_c33_kyaw.pdf).

Voss, H. and Bailleul, E. (2002) 'The Belgian Presidency and the Post-Nice Process after Laeken'. *ZEI Discussion Paper C102*, pp. 1–32 (http://aei.pitt.edu/182/01/dp_c102_voss-baillieul.pdf).

Wahlbäck, K. (2000) *Svenska rollskiften 1156–2001, Uppsats presenterad vid SEB's råd för samhällsekonomiska frågor, 14 November 2000*.

Wallace, H. (1985a) 'EC Membership and the Presidency; A Comparative Perspective'. In: O'Nuallain, C. and Hoscheidt, J.-M. (eds.) *The Presidency of the European Council of Ministers; Impacts and Implications for National Governments* (London: Croom Helm in association with the European Institute of Public Administration), pp. 261–278.

Wallace, H. (1985b) 'The Presidency: Tasks and Evolution'. In: O'Nuallain, C. and Hoscheidt, J.-M. (eds.) *The Presidency of the European Council of Ministers; Impacts and Implications for National Governments* (London: Croom Helm in association with the European Institute of Public Administration), pp. 1–21.

Wallace, H. (1986) 'The British Presidency of the European Community's Council of Ministers: The Opportunity to Persuade'. *International Affairs*, Vol. 62 (Autumn 1986), pp. 583–599.

Wallace, H. (1989) 'Widening and Deepening: The European Community and the New European Agenda'. *RIIA Discussion Paper, No. 23* (London: Royal Institute of International Affairs).

Wallace, H. (1997) 'At Odds with Europe'. *Political Studies*, Vol. 45, No. 4, pp. 677–688.

Wallace, H. and Edwards, G. (1976) 'The Evolving Role of the Presidency of the Council'. *International Affairs*, Vol. 52, No. 4, pp. 535–550.

Wallace, H. and Edwards, G. (1977) 'The Council of Ministers of the EC and the President in office'. *A Federal Trust Paper* (London: Federal Trust).

Wallace, H. and Hayes-Renshaw, F. (1997) *The Council of Ministers* (London: Macmillan Press).

Wallace, H. and Hayes-Renshaw, F. (2003) *Reforming the Council – A Work in Progress* (Stockholm: SIEPS).

Wallace, H. and Wallace, W. (2000) *Policy-Making in the European Union* (Oxford: Oxford University Press).

Wallace, H., Wallace, W. and Webb, C. Eds. (1983) *Policy-Making in the European Community* (New York: Wiley).

Wallace, W. (1982) 'Europe as a Confederation: The Community and the Nation State'. *Journal of Common Market Studies*, Vol. 21, pp. 57–68.

Wallace, W. (1983) 'Less than a Federation, More than a Regime: The Community as a Political System'. In: Wallace, H., Wallace, W., and Webb, C. (eds.) *Policy-making in the European Community* (New York: Wiley).

Wallis, D. (2003) *Speech by Diana Wallis MEP delivered to the Seminar: 'The High North, the EU-Northern Dimension and the Arctic Window – Challenges and Policy Options'* 29 April 2003 (http://www.dianawallismep.org.uk/speeches/3.html).

Weaver, O. (1992) 'Nordic Nostalgia: Northern Europe after the end of the Cold War'. *International Affairs*, Vol. 68, No. 1, pp. 77–102.

Weaver, R.K. and Rockman, B.A. (1993) *Do Institutions Matter, Government Capabilities in the United States and Abroad* (Washington DC: Brookings Institution).

Weber, S. (2001) *Guide to the Belgian Presidency of the European Union July 1 to December 31, 2001* (Brussels: Weber Shandwick).

Weber, S. (2003) *Inside the Greek Presidency* (Brussels: Weber Shandwick).

Wehr, P. and Lederach, J.P. (1996) 'Mediating Conflict in Central America'. In: Bercovitch, J. (ed.) *Resolving International Conflicts – The Theory and Practice of Mediation* (London: Lynne Rienner).

Weiler, J. (1982) 'The Community System: The Dual Character of Supranationalism'. *Yale Law Review*, Vol. 1, pp. 257–306.

Weiler, J. (1997) 'The Reformation of European Constitutionalism'. *Journal of Common Market Studies*, Vol. 35, No. 1, pp. 97–131.

Weiler, J. (2000) Federalism and Constitutionalism: Europe's *Sonderweg*. *Harvard Jean Monnet Working Paper 10/00* (Cambridge, MA: Harvard Law School, 2000).

Weiler, J. and Haltern, U.R. (1996) 'The Autonomy of the Community Legal Order – Through the Looking Glass'. *Harvard International Law Journal*, Vol. 37, No. 2, pp. 411–419.

Weingast, B.R. (1996) 'Political Institutions: Rational Choice'. In: Goodin, R. E. and Klingemann, H.-D. (eds.) *A New Handbook of Political Science* (Oxford: Oxford University Press), pp. 167–190.

Wellman, C. (1998) 'A Complement to EU Enlargement', *OSCE Review*, Vol. 6, No. 2.

Wendon, B. (1998) 'The Commission as Image-Venue Entrepreneur in EU Social Policy'. *Journal of European Public Policy*, Vol. 5, No. 2, pp. 339–353.

Werts, J. (1992) *The European Council* (The Hague: T.M.C. Asser Institute).

Wessels, W. (1998) *National vs. EU-Foreign Policy Interests. Mapping 'Important' National Interests*, Final report of a Collective Project by TEPSA and Member Institutes, Summer 1998.

Wessels, W., Maurer, A., and Mittag, J. (2003) *Fifteen into One? The European Union and its Member States* (Manchester: Manchester University Press).

Westlake, M. (1995) *The Council of the European Union* (London: Cartermill).

Wheare, K.C. (1963) *Federal Government*, 4th ed. (Oxford: Oxford University Press).

Whitehead, L. (1996) 'Comparative Politics: Democratisation Studies'. In: Goodin, E., Klingemann, H.-D. (eds.) *A New Handbook of Political Science* (Oxford: Oxford University Press).

Whitehead, L. (2002) *Democratisation: Theory and Experience* (Oxford: Oxford University Press).

Whitman, R. (1998) 'The Role of the Presidency in Promoting a CFSP'. *Paper presented at the Conference 'The Presidency of the European Union', Belfast, 15–16 October 1998.*

Whitman, R. (2006) 'The UK's Six Months at the EU Helm: A Triumph of Substance Over Style?' *In European Newsletter, January 2006* (London: Federal Trust).

Whitman, R. and Thomas, G. (2005) 'Two Cheers for the UK's EU Presidency'. *RIIA Briefing Paper, December 2005* (London: Chatham House).

Wozniak Boyle, J. (2006) *Conditional Leadership* (Lanham, MD: Lexington Books).

Wright, V. (1996) 'The National Co-ordination of European Policy-Making: Negotiating the Quagmire'. In: Richardson, J.J. (ed.) *European Union Power and Policy-making* (London: Routledge), pp. 148–169.

Wurzel, R.K.W. (1996a) 'The Role of the EU Presidency in the Environmental Field: Does It Make a Difference Which Member State Runs the Presidency?' *Journal of European Public Policy*, Vol. 3, No. 2, pp. 272–291.

Wurzel, R.K.W. (1996b). 'What Role Can the Presidency Play in Co-ordinating European Union Environmental Policy Making? An Anglo-German Comparison'. *European Environmental Law Review*, Vol. 14, No. 3, March 1996, pp. 74–79.

Wurzel, R.K.W. (2000) 'Flying into Unexpected Turbulence: The German EU Presidency in the Environmental Field'. *German Politics*, Vol. 9, No. 3, pp. 23–44.

Wurzel, R.K.W. (2001) 'The EU Presidency and the Integration Principle: An Aglo-German Comparison'. *European Environmental Law Review*, Vol. 19, No. 1 (January 2001), pp. 5–15.

Ylä-Anttila, P., Ali-Yrkkö, J., Paija, L., and Reilly, C. (2000) 'Nokia: A Big Company in a Small Country'. *The Research Institute of the Finnish Economy (ETLA) Series* B 162 Taloustieto Oy Helsinki (http://www.finnfacts.com/english/country/story/worldeconomy/nokia.html).

Young, R.O. (1991) 'Political Leadership and Regime Formation: On the Development of Institutions in International Society'. *International Organisation*, Vol. 45, No. 3, pp. 281–308.

Young, R.O. (1999) 'Comment on Andrew Moravcsik, A New Statecraft? Supranational Entrepreneurs and International Co-operation'. *International Organisation*, Vol. 52, No. 4, pp. 805–809.

Youngs, R. (2004) 'A New Approach in the Great Lakes? Europe's Evolving Conflict-Resolution Strategies'. *Journal of Contemporary Africa Studies*, Vol. 22, No. 3, pp. 305–323.

II. Official EU and Member State documents

Africa-Europe Ministerial Conference (2001) Communiqué, 11 October 2001 (http://europa.eu.int/comm/development/body/eu_africa/docs/communique_en.pdf#zoom=100).

Africa-Europe Summit (2000a) 'Cairo Plan of Action,' 3–4 April 2000 (SN 106/4/00 REV 4).

Africa-Europe Summit (2000b) 'Cairo Declaration,' April 2000.

Auswärtiges Amt (1998) 'Ziele und Schwerpunkte der deutschen Präsidentschaft im Rat der Europäischen Union,' 2 December 1998.

Belgian Ministry of Foreign Affairs, Foreign Trade and International Cooperation (2001a) The Belgian Presidency of the European Union, 1 July–31 December 2001, Work Programme (http://www.eu2001.be/Main/Frameset.asp?reference=01%2D01&lang=en&sess=869625146&).

Belgian Ministry of Foreign Affairs, Foreign Trade and International Cooperation (2001b) 'Distribution of the Belgian Presidency and the Belgian Seat Between the Federal Government, the Regions and the Communities, within the European Council of Ministers,' 15 March 2001.

Commission of the European Communities (1988) Green Paper on Copyright and the Challenge of Technology – Copyright Issues Requiring Immediate Action (COM(88) 172, June 1988).

Commission of the European Communities (1991) Green Paper on the Development of the Single Market for Postal Services (communication from the Commission) (COM(91) 476, June 1991).

Commission of the European Communities (1993) Guidelines for the Development of Community Postal Services – Communication from the Commission to the Council and the European Parliament (COM (93) 247, 2 June 1993).

Commission of the European Communities (1995) Green Paper on Copyright and Related Rights in the Information Society, 27 July 1995 (COM/95/0382 final).

Commission of the European Communities (1996a) Communication from the Commission – Follow-up to the Green Paper on Copyright and Related Rights in the Information Society, Brussels, 20 November 1996 (COM(96) 586 final).

Commission of the European Communities (1996b) The European Union and the Issue of Conflicts in Africa: Peace-Building, Conflict Prevention and Beyond, Communication from the Commission to the Council, Brussels (SEC 96(3)).

Commission of the European Communities (1997a) 'A European Initiative in Electronic Commerce,' Communication to the European Parliament, the Council, the Economic and Social Committee and the Committee of the Region (COM (97) 157, 15 April 1997) (http://www.cordis.lu/esprit/src/ecomcom.htm).

Commission of the European Communities (1997b) Directive 97/67/EC of 15 December 1997 on Common Rules for the Development of the Internal Market of Community Postal Services and the Improvement of the Quality of Service.

Commission of the European Communities (1998a) 'Proposal for a European Parliament and Council Directive on Certain Legal Aspects of Electronic Commerce in the Internal Market,' 18 November 1998 (COM (1998) 586 final 98/0325 (COD)).

Commission of the European Communities (1998b) A Northern Dimension for the Policies of the Union (COM/98/0589/fin.1998/11/25)(http://www.europa.eu.int/comm/external_relations/north_dim/doc/com1998_0589en.pdf).

Commission of the European Communities (1998c) Single Market Scoreboard, No. 2, May 1998 (http://europa.eu.int/comm/internal_market/score/docs/score02/score2_en.pdf).

Commission of the European Communities (1999a) A Northern Dimension for the Policies of the EU: An Inventory of Current Activities, 11 November 1999,

Working Document of the Commission Services (http://www.europa.eu.int/comm/external_relations/north_dim/doc/inventory.pdf).

Commission of the European Communities (1999b) Amended Proposal for a European Parliament and Council Directive on Certain Legal Aspects of Electronic Commerce in the Internal Market (COM (1999) 427 final 98/0325 (COD)) (http://europa.eu.int/comm/internal_market/en/ecommerce/com427en.pdf).

Commission of the European Communities (1999c) Green Paper on the Community Patent and the Patent System in Europe (COM (1999) 42 final, 5 February 1999).

Commission of the European Communities (1999d) Amended Proposal for a European Parliament and Council Directive on the Harmonisation of Certain Aspects of Copyright and Related Rights in the Information Society (COM/99/0250 final – COD 97/0359) (Official Journal C 180, 25/06/1999 P. 0006) (http://europa.eu.int/eur-lex/lex/LexUriServ/LexUriServ.do?uri=CELEX: 51999PC0250:EN:HTML).

Commission of the European Communities (1999e) Co-operation with ACP Countries Involved in Armed Conflict, Communication of the Commission to the Council and the European Parliament, Brussels (COM (1999) 240 final, 19 May 1999).

Commission of the European Communities (1999f) Communication of 8 November 1999, 'Strengthening the Northern Dimension of European Energy Policy' (COM(99)548).

Commission of the European Communities (2000a) 'Growth and Employment Initiative – Measures on Financial Assistance for Innovative and Job Creating Small and Medium Sized Enterprises (SMEs),' Report from the Commission to the European Parliament and the Council, 31 December 1999 (COM(2000) 266 final – Not published in the Official Journal).

Commission of the European Communities (2000b) Proposal for a Council Regulation on the Community patent (COM/2000/0412 final) (Official Journal C 337 E, 28.11.2000) (http://europa.eu.int/smartapi/cgi/sga_doc? smartapi!celexplus!prod!CELEXnumdoc&lg=SL&numdoc=52000PC0412).

Commission of the European Communities (2000c) Directive 2000/31/EC of the European Parliament and of the Council of 8 June 2000 on Certain Legal Aspects of Information Society Services, in Particular Electronic Commerce, in the Internal Market (Official Journal of the European Communities L 178/1, 17.7.2000).

Commission of the European Communities (2000d) E-policy News – Monthly Overview of E-Commerce Related Developments in European Politics and Legislation January 2000 (http://europa.eu.int/ISPO/ecommerce/epolicy/2000-01.html).

Commission of the European Communities (2000e) Proposal for a European Parliament and Council Directive Amending Directive 97/67/EC with Regard to the Further Opening to Competition of Community Postal Services, Brussels, 30 May 2000 (COM/2000/0319 final – COD 2000/0139) (Official Journal C 337 E, 28/11/2000 pp. 0220–0224).

Commission of the European Communities (2000f) Amended Proposal for a European Parliament and Council Directive Amending Directive 97/67/EC with Regard to the Further Opening to Competition of Community Postal

Services, Brussels, 26 June 2001 (COM/2001/0109 final – COD 2000/0139) (Official Journal 180 E, 26/6/2001 pp. 0291–0300).

Commission of the European Communities (2001a) Commission Opinion Pursuant to Article 251 (2) (c) of the EC Treaty, on the European Parliament's Amendments to the Council's Common Position Regarding the Proposal for a Directive of the European Parliament and of the Council on the Harmonisation of Certain Aspects of Copyright and Related Rights in the Information Society Amending the Proposal of the Commission Pursuant to Article 250 (2) of the EC Treaty (COM/2001/0170 final – CPD 97/0359).

Commission of the European Communities (2001b) 'Growth and Employment – Initiative Measures on Financial Assistance for Innovative and Job Creating Small- and Medium Sized Enterprises (SMEs),' Report from the Commission to the European Parliament and the Council (COM(2001) 399 Final – Not published in the Official Journal).

Commission of the European Communities (2001c) Directive 2001/29/EC of the European Parliament and of the Council of 22 May 2001 on the Harmonisation of Certain Aspects of Copyright and Related Rights in the Information Society (Official Journal of the European Communities L167/10, 22 June 2001).

Commission of the European Communities (2001d) The Cotonou Agreement (http://europa.eu.int/comm/development/body/cotonou/agreement_en.htm).

Commission of the European Communities (2001e) Communication from the Commission on Conflict Prevention, Brussels, 11 April 2001 (COM(2001) 211 final).

Commission of the European Communities (2001f) Amended Proposal for a European Parliament and Council Directive Amending Directive 97/67/EC with Regard to the Further Opening to Competition of Community Postal Services, Brussels, 21 March 2001 (COM(2001) 109 final, 2000/0139 (COD)).

Commission of the European Communities (2002a) 'Growth and Employment Initiative – Measures on Financial Assistance for Innovative and Job Creating Small and Medium-Sized Enterprises (SMEs),' Report from the Commission to the European Parliament and the Council, 31 December 2001 (COM(2002) 345 final – Not Published in the Official Journal).

Commission of the European Communities (2002b) 'Growth and Employment Initiative: Measures on Financial Assistance for Innovative and Job-Creating Small and Medium-Sized Enterprises (SMEs),' Report from the Commission to the European Parliament and the Council, 29 May 2002 (COM(2003) 758 Final – Not Published in the Official Journal).

Commission of the European Communities (2002c) 'For the European Union, Peace, Freedom, Solidarity,' Communication of the Commission on the Institutional Architecture, Brussels, 4 December 2002 (COM (2002) 728 final) (http://europa.eu.int/futurum/documents/offtext/com051202_en.pdf).

Commission of the European Communities (2002d) 'The Stabilisation and Association process for South East Europe – First Annual Report,' (COM (2002) 163 final).

Commission of the European Communities (2002e) 'Economic Forecasts Spring 2002,' European Economy, No. 2/2002.

Commission of the European Communities (2002f) Directive 2002/39/EC of the European Parliament and of the Council of 10 June 2002 Amending Directive 97/67/EC with Regard to the Further Opening to Competition of Community

Postal Services, 5 July 2002 (Official Journal of the European Communities L 176/21).

Commission of the European Communities (2002g) Report 'Growth and Employment Initiative,' Brussels, 10 December 2002.

Commission of the European Communities (2003a) 'Measures on Financial Assistance for Innovative and Job Creating Small and Medium-Sized Enterprises (1998 Growth and Employment Initiative),' Report from the Commission to the European Parliament and the Council, 31 December 2002 (COM(2003)480 Final – Not Published in the Official Journal).

Commission of the European Communities (2003b) 'Creating An Entrepreneurial Europe – The Activities of the European Union for Small and Medium-Sized Enterprises (SMEs),' Staff Working Paper, Brussels, 21 January 2003 SEC(2003) 58 (http://europa.eu.int/comm/enterprise/entrepreneurship/promoting_entrepreneurship/doc/2003sec58_en.pdf).

Commission of the European Communities (2003c) 'The SME Envoy: An Active Interface Between the Commission and the SME Community,' Staff Working Paper, Brussels, 21 January 2003 SEC(2003) 60.

Commission of the European Communities (2003d) Communication on 'Thinking Small in An Enlarged Europe,' Brussels, 21 January 2003 (COM(2003) 26 final).

Commission of the European Communities (2003e) Report from the Commission to the Council and the EP on the Implementation of the European Charter for Small Enterprises, Brussels, 13 February 2003 (COM (2003) 21 final/2).

Commission of the European Communities (2003f) 'Albania – Stabilisation & Association Report,' Staff Working Paper, Brussels, 26 March 2003 – SEC (2003) – 339.

Commission of the European Communities (2003g) 'Bosnia & Herzegovina Association Report,' Staff Working Paper, Brussels, 26 March 2003 – SEC (2003) – 340.

Commission of the European Communities (2003h) 'Croatia – Stabilisation & Association Report,' Staff Working Paper, Brussels, 26 March 2003 – SEC (2003) – 341.

Commission of the European Communities (2003i) Translation Cost Estimation (http://europa.eu.int/comm/internal_market/en/indprop/patent/docs/2003-03-patent-costs_en.pdf).

Commission of the European Communities (2003j) Report from the Commission to the Council and the European Parliament on the Implementation of the European Charter for Small Enterprises Brussels, 13 February 2003 (COM(2003) 21 final/2) (http://europa.eu.int/eur-lex/en/com/rpt/2003/com2003_0021en02.pdf).

Commission of the European Communities (2003k) Communication from the Commission to the Council and the EP on the Development of Energy Policy for the Enlarged European Union, Its Neighbours and Partner Countries, Brussels, 26 May 2003 (COM(2003) 262 final/2).

Commission of the European Communities (2008) Flash Eurobarometer No. 245, Post Referendum Survey in Ireland – Preliminary Results, June 18, 2008 (http://ec.europa.eu/public_opinion/flash/fl_245_en.pdf).

Council of the European Communities (1992) Directive: 92/100/EEC on Rental Right and Lending Right and on Certain Rights Related to Copyright in the

Field of Intellectual Property (Official Journal L 346, 27 November 1992, pp. 0061–0066).

Council of the European Communities (1993a) Directive 93/83/EEC on the Co-ordination of Certain Rules Concerning Copyright and Rights Related to Copyright Applicable to Satellite Broadcasting and Cable Transmission (Official journal NO. L 248, 6 October 1993, pp. 0015–0021).

Council of the European Communities (1993b) Directive 93/98/EEC Harmonising the Term of Protection of Copyright and Certain Related Rights (Official Journal L 290, 24 November1993).

Council of the European Communities (1994a) Council Resolution of 7 February 1994 on the Development of Community Postal Services (Official Journal C 048, 16 February 1992, pp. 0003–0004).

Council of the European Communities (1995) Barcelona Declaration 28 November 1995 (http://europa.eu.int/comm/external_relations/euromed/bd.htm).

Council of the European Communities (1996a) Council Guide, Presidency Handbook, EC/2 1996 (1) General Secretariat – Council of the European Union.

Council of the European Communities (1996b) Directive 96/9/EC on the Legal Protection of Databases (Official Journal L 77, 27 March 1996).

Council of the European Communities (1997a) Conclusions of the Presidency, Luxembourg, 12–13 December 1997.

Council of the European Communities (1997b) Common Position Concerning Conflict Prevention and Resolution in Africa, Brussels, 2 June 1997.

Council of the European Communities (1998a) Decision 98/347/EC of 19 May 1998 on Measures of Financial Assistance for Innovative SMEs Creating Employment (Growth and Employment Initiative) (Official Journal L 155, 29 May 1998).

Council of the European Communities (1998b) Conclusions of the Presidency, Cardiff, 15–16 June 1998.

Council of the European Communities (1998c) Conclusions of the Presidency, Vienna, 11–12 December 1998.

Council of the European Communities (1999a) Conclusions of the Presidency, Berlin, 24–25 March 1999.

Council of the European Communities (1999b) 2186th Council Meeting, General Affairs, Brussels, 31 May 1999.

Council of the European Communities (1999c) Conclusions of the Presidency, Cologne, 3–4 June 1999.

Council of the European Communities (1999d) Conclusions of the Presidency, Tampere, 15–16 October 1999.

Council of the European Communities (1999e) 2219th Council Meeting, Health, Brussels, 18 November 1999.

Council of the European Communities (1999f) Conclusions of the Presidency, Helsinki, 10–11 December 1999.

Council of the European Communities (1999g) 2230th Council Meeting, Energy, Brussels, 2 December 1999.

Council of the European Communities (1999h) Common Strategy of the EU of 4 June 1999 on Russia (1999/414/CFSP) (Official Journal of the European Communities L 157/1 24 June 1999).

Council of the European Communities (1999i) Internal Market Council, 7 December 1999 – Press Release: 393 – Nr: 13690/99.

Council of the European Communities (2000a) Conclusions of the Presidency, Lisbon, 23–24 March 2000.

Council of the European Communities (2000b) 'Action Plan for the Northern Dimension with external and cross-border policies of the European Union 2000-3,' 14 June 2000 (http://europa.eu.int/comm/external_relations/north_dim/ndap/06_00_en.pdf).

Council of the European Communities (2000c) Common Position on the e-commerce directive (14253/1/99/REV 1).

Council of the European Communities (2000d) Decision 2000/819/EC on a Multi-Annual Programme for Enterprise and Entrepreneurship, and in Particular for Small and Medium-Sized Enterprises (SMEs) (2001–2005) (Official Journal L 333, 29 December 2000).

Council of the European Communities (2000e) Action Plan for the Northern Dimension with External and Cross-Border Policies of the European Union 2000–2003, Brussels, 14 June 2000 (9401/00 LIMITE NIS 76).

Council of the European Communities (2000f) Common Council Position, 28 February 2000 (14263/1/99 REV 1).

Council of the European Communities (2001a) Laeken Declaration, 15 December 2001 (http://europa.eu.int/futurum/documents/offtext/doc151201_en.htm).

Council of the European Communities (2001b) Results of Internal Market Council, Brussels, 20 December 2001.

Council of the European Communities (2001c) Conclusions of the Presidency, Gothenburg, 15–16 June 2001.

Council of the European Communities (2001d) 2327th Council Meeting, General Affairs, 22 January 2001 (Press:19 Nr: 5279/01).

Council of the European Communities (2001e) 2331st Council Meeting, General Affairs, 26 February 2001 (Press:61 Nr: 6506/01).

Council of the European Communities (2001f) 2338th Council Meeting, General Affairs, 19 March 2001 (Press:110 Nr: 6933/01).

Council of the European Communities (2001g) 2342nd Council Meeting, General Affairs, 9 April 2001 (Press: 141 Nr: 7833/01).

Council of the European Communities (2001h) 2346th Council Meeting, General Affairs, 14–15 May 2001 (Press: 169 Nr: 8441/01).

Council of the European Communities (2001i) 2356th Council meeting, General Affairs, 11–12 June 2001 (Press:226 Nr: 9398/01).

Council of the European Communities (2001j) 2362nd Council Meeting, General Affairs, 25 June 2001 (Press:250 Nr: 10228/01).

Council of the European Communities (2001k) 2367th Council meeting, General Affairs, 16 July 2001 (Press: 282 Nr: 10609/01).

Council of the European Communities (2001l) 2372nd Council Meeting, General Affairs, Brussels, 8–9 October 2001 (Press:337 Nr: 12330/01).

Council of the European Communities (2001m) 2379th Council Meeting, General Affairs, Luxembourg, 29–30 October 2001 (Press: 390 Nr: 13291/01).

Council of the European Communities (2001n) 2383rd Council Meeting, Development, Brussels, 8 November 2001 (Press: 403 Nr: 13573/01).

Council of the European Communities (2001o) 2386th Council Meeting, General Affairs, Brussels, 19–20 November 2001 (Press:414 Nr: 13802/01).

Council of the European Communities (2001p) 2397th Council Meeting, General Affairs, Brussels, 10 December 2001 (Press: 460 Nr: 15078/01).

Council of the European Communities (2001q) Common Position Concerning Conflict Prevention, Management, and Resolution in Africa, 14 May 2001.

Council of the European Communities (2001r) Conclusions of the Presidency, Laeken, 14–15 December 2001.

Council of the European Communities (2001s) 2374th Council Meeting, Transport and Telecommunications, 12609/01 (Presse 353), Luxembourg, 15–16 October 2001.

Council of the European Communities (2001t) Report from Group of Attachés responsible for Postal Services to COREPER, 9 October 2001 (12569/1/01 REV 1 ECO 269 CODEC 981).

Council of the European Communities (2001u) Note from the Presidency to COREPER/Council, Brussels, 31 May 2001 (9303/01 LIMITE ECO 144 CODEC 483).

Council of the European Communities (2001v) Report from COREPER to the Council, Brussels, 10 October 2001 (12642/01 ECO 273 CODEC 999).

Council of the European Communities (2002a) 2425th Council meeting, General Affairs, 8649/02 (Presse 124) Brussels, 13 May 2002 (http://ue.eu.int/ueDocs/cms_Data/docs/pressData/en/gena/70459.pdf).

Council of the European Communities (2002b) 'Measures to Prepare the Council for enlargement,' Report by the Presidency to the European Council, Brussels, 13 June 2002 (9939/02 POLGEN25) (http://ue.eu.int/pressdata/EN/reports/71245.pdf).

Council of the European Communities (2002c) Conclusions of the Presidency, Seville, 21–22 June 2002.

Council of the European Communities (2002d) Conclusions of the Presidency, Copenhagen, 12–13 December 2002 (http://ue.eu.int/ueDocs/cms_Data/docs/pressData/en/gena/75004.pdf).

Council of the European Communities (2002e) Results of the Internal Market, Consumer Affairs and Tourism Council, Brussels, 21 May 2002.

Council of the European Communities (2002f) 2475th Council Meeting, General Affairs, 15184/02 (Presse 383), Brussels, 10 December 2002 (http://ue.eu.int/ueDocs/cms_Data/docs/pressData/en/gena/73608.pdf).

Council of the European Communities (2002g) 2464th Council Meeting, External Relations, 14184/02 (Presse 351), Brussels, 19 November 2002 (http://ue.eu.int/ueDocs/cms_Data/docs/pressData/en/gena/73286.pdf).

Council of the European Communities (2002h) 2463rd Council Meeting, General Affairs, 14183/02 (Presse 350), Brussels, 18 November 2002 (http://ue.eu.int/ueDocs/cms_Data/docs/pressData/en/gena/73248.pdf).

Council of the European Communities (2002i) 2425th Council Meeting, General Affairs, 8649/02 (Presse 124), Brussels, 13 May 2002 (http://ue.eu.int/ueDocs/cms_Data/docs/pressData/en/gena/70459.pdf).

Council of the European Communities (2003a) 2495th Council Meeting, External Relations 6941/03 (Presse 63), Brussels, 18 March 2003.

Council of the European Communities (2003b) 2496th Council Meeting, General Affairs, 6942/03 (Presse 64), Brussels, 19 March 2003 (http://ue.eu.int/ueDocs/cms_Data/docs/pressData/en/gena/75012.pdf).

Council of the European Communities (2003c) Conclusions of the Presidency, Brussels, 20–21 March 2003.

Council of the European Communities (2003d) Draft Action Plan on Drugs Between the EU and Countries of Western Balkans and Candidate Countries Brussels, 3 June 2003 5062/2/03 REV 2 COR 1 CORDROGUE 3 COWEB 76 (http://europa.eu.int/comm/external_relations/drugs/docs/wb.pdf).

Council of the European Communities (2003e) 2519th Council Meeting, General Affairs, 10370/03 (Presse 167) Luxembourg, 16 June 2003 (http://ue.eu.int/ueDocs/cms_Data/docs/pressData/en/gena/76202.pdf).

Council of the European Communities (2003f) 2518th Council Meeting, External Relations, 10369/03 (Presse 166) Luxembourg, 16 June 2003 (http://ue.eu.int/ueDocs/cms_Data/docs/pressData/en/gena/76201.pdf).

Council of the European Communities (2003g) Conclusions of the Presidency, Thessaloniki, 19–20 June 2003.

Council Secretariat (2005a) 'The European Union's Engagement Towards Stability and Security in the Democratic Republic of Congo (DRC),' RDC/00 (initial) 23 May 2005.

Danish Ministry of Foreign Affairs (2002) 'One Europe,' Presidency Work Programme (http://www.eu2002.dk/programme/default.asp?MenuElementID= 30004).

European Convention, The Secretariat (2002) 'Preliminary Draft Constitutional Treaty,' (CONV 369/02) Brussels, 28 October 2002.

European Parliament (1993a) Resolution Concerning the Commission Green Paper on the Development of the Single Market for Postal Services, 22 January 1993.

European Parliament (1993b) Resolution on the Single Market for Postal Services, 25 June 1993.

European Parliament (1993c) Resolution on Postal Services, 29 October 1993.

European Parliament (1997a) Resolution on the Internationalisation of Small Businesses, 18 September 1997.

European Parliament (1997b) Resolution Calling for the Banking and Credit Industries to Grant Facilities to Small Businesses, 24 April 1997.

European Parliament (1999a) Resolution on the Communication from the Commission – A Northern Dimension for the Policies of the Union ((COM(98)0589 – C4-0067/99) A4-0209/99 final).

European Parliament (1999b) Report on the Communication of the Commission – A Northern Dimension for the Policies of the Union (PE 230.181/fin).

European Parliament (2000a) Report on the Proposal for a European Parliament and Council Directive Amending Directive 97/67/EC with Regard to the Further Opening to Competition of Community Postal Services (COM(2000) 319 - C5-0375/2000 - 2000/0139(COD)) (http://www2. europarl.eu.int/omk/sipade2?PUBREF=-//EP//NONSGML+REPORT+A5-2000-0361+0+DOC+WORD+V0//EN&L=EN&LEVEL=5&NAV=S&LSTDOC=Y).

European Parliament (2000b) Resolution on the Proposal for a European Parliament and Council Directive Amending Directive 97/67/EC with Regard to the Further Opening to Competition of Community Postal Services (COM(2000) 319 – C5-0375/2000 – 2000/0139(COD)).

European Parliament (2001) Resolution on the Illegal Exploitation of Natural Resources in the Democratic Republic of Congo, 5 July 2001 (http://www2.europarl.eu.int/omk/sipade2?PUBREF=-//EP//TEXT+TA+P5-TA-2001-0409+0+DOC+XML+V0//EN&LEVEL=3&NAV=X).

European Parliament (2002a) Resolution on the Commission Communication 'Sustaining the Commitments, Increasing the Pace,' 13 June 2002.

European Parliament (2002b) Report on the Community Patent Regulation, 26 February 2002, (A5-0059/2002 final) (OJ 29 May 2003 C127E/519–526).

European Parliament (2002c) Resolution on the Commission Report 'Growth and Employment Initiative,' 10 October 2002.

European Parliament (2002d) Oral question H-0585/02 to the Council, for Question Time at the Part-Session in September I 2002 Pursuant to Rule 43 of the Rules of Procedure by Concepció Ferrer to the Council, Tabled: 17 July 2002 (http://www.europarl.eu.int/registre/questions/heure_questions/2002/0585/P5_QH(2002)0585_EN.doc).

European Parliament (2003) Daily Notebook: 'Western Balkans and the Stability Pact,' EP03-024EN (http://www.europarl.eu.int/omk/sipade3?SAME_LEVEL=1&LEVEL=3&NAV=X&PUBREF=-//EP//TEXT+PRESS+DN-20030605-1+0+DOC+XML+V0//EN).

Finnish Ministry of Foreign Affairs (1999a) 'A Strong and Open Europe into the New Millennium,' Programme of the Finnish Presidency of the European Union, July–December 1999 (SN 2940/2/99 REV 2).

Finnish Ministry of Foreign Affairs (1999b) Conclusions of the Foreign Ministers' Conference on the Northern Dimension, 12 November 1999.

Finnish Ministry of Foreign Affairs (1999c) 'Copyright in the Digital Age' (http://presidency.finland.fi) 29 October 1999.

Finnish Ministry of Foreign Affairs (1999d) Presidency Summary, Informal Meeting of the Ministers of Industry, 3 July 1999 (http://presidency.finland.fi/netcomm/news/showarticle421.html).

Finnish Ministry of Foreign Affairs (1999e) 'Illegal Migration in Russia and EU Member States is to a Large Extent Organised by Organised Criminal Groups,' Presidency Press Release, 6 July 1999 (http://presidency.finland.fi).

Finnish Ministry of Foreign Affairs (1999f) Handout, EUE/RK/AST, 10.6.1999.

Finnish Ministry of Foreign Affairs (1999g) 'The Handling of EU Matters in Finland,' (http://presidency.finland.fi/doc/eu/fin_2hand.htm).

Finnish Ministry of Foreign Affairs, Secretariat for EU Affairs (2000) The Finnish Presidency of the European Union – A Preliminary Summary of Achievements, 11 January 2000.

Hellenic Ministry for Development (2003a) Thessaloniki's Ministerial Conference on Small Business and Entrepreneurship, Conclusions of the Presidency, Thessaloniki, 14 February 2003 (http://www.ypan.gr/eu2003/pdf/smes-presidencyconclusions-eng.pdf).

Hellenic Ministry for Development (2003b) Information Notice – Community Patent (http://www.ypan.gr/eu2003/pdf/patent05032003eng.pdf).

Hellenic Ministry of Foreign Affairs (2002) 'Our Europe – Sharing the Future in a Community of Values,' Programme of the Greek Presidency of the European Union, January–June 2003 (December 2002) (http://www.eu2003.gr/en/cat/68/).

Hellenic Ministry of Foreign Affairs (2003a) Proposal for a Council Regulation on the Community Patent – Revised Text, Council, Brussels, 16 April 2003.

Hellenic Ministry of Foreign Affairs (2003b) Draft Background Notes, General Affairs and External Relations Council, 27–28 January 2003 (http://www.eu2003.gr).

Hellenic Ministry of Foreign Affairs (2003c) Working Document: Greek Presidency Priorities for the Western Balkans, 13 January 2003.

Hellenic Ministry of Foreign Affairs (2003d) Thessaloniki's Ministerial Conference on Small Business and Entrepreneurship: Conclusions of the Presidency, 14 February 2003.

Hellenic Ministry of Foreign Affairs (2003e) Presidency Press Release: Session of the General Affairs and External Relations Council, 27 January 2003 (http://www.eu2003.gr/en/articles/2003/1/27/1706/).

Hellenic Ministry of Foreign Affairs (2003f) Press Release : EU Council of Ministers – External Relations session, 19 May 2003 (http://www.eu2003.gr/en/articles/2003/5/21/2868/).

Irish Ministry of Foreign Affairs (2003) 'Europeans-Working Together,' Programme of the Irish Presidency of the European Union, January–June 2004 (PRN 1487).

Italian Ministry of Foreign Affairs (2003) 'Europe: Citizens of a Shared Dream,' Programme of the Italian Presidency of the European Union, 1 July–31 December 2003.

Office for Official Publications of the European Communities (1997) European Union Consolidated Treaties, Luxembourg.

Official Journal of the European Communities (1999) Debates of the European Parliament, English Edition.

Secretary-General of the Council of the European Union (1999) 'Operation of the Council with an Enlarged Union,' SN 2139/99, 10 March 1999 (Trumpf-Piris Report).

UN (2001) Declaration, Durban World Conference Against Racism, Racial Discrimination, Xenophobia and Related Intolerance, 31 August–8 September 2001 (http://www.un.org/WCAR/durban.pdf).

Wise Men Report (1979) Report on European Institutions, Presented by the Committee of the Three to the European Council (Luxembourg: Office for Official Publications of the European Communities 1979).

III. News Sources and Websites

Agence Europe (http://www.agenceurope.com/).

Agence France (http://www.afp.com/).

Athens News Agency (http://www.ana.gr/anaweb/).

BBC News (http://news.bbc.co.uk/).

Belgian Presidency Website (http://www.eu2001.be/).

Billboard Bulletin (http://www.billboard.com/bb/biz/newsroom/topnews/index.jsp).

Business Week (http://www.businessweek.com/).

Congo Chronicle (http://www.congoned.dds.nl/coengli.html).

Convention (http://european-convention.eu.int).

Council Conclusions (http://europa.eu.int/council/off/conclu/index.htm).

Deutsche Welle (http://www.dw-world.de/).

Die Welt (http://www.welt.de/).
E!Sharp (http://www.peoplepowerprocess.com/).
Eblida Hot News (http://www.eblida.org/hot_news/).
Economist Intelligence Unit (EIU) (http://www.eiu.com/).
E-Policy News (http://europa.eu.int/ISPO/ecommerce/epolicy/Welcome.html).
EU Business (http://eubusiness.com).
EU Observer (http://www.euobserver.com).
Euractiv (http://www.euractiv.com/).
Europa (http://europa.eu.int/).
European Employment Observatory (http://www.eu-employment-observatory. net).
European Information Service (www.eis.com).
European Observatory for SMEs (http://www.eim.nl/english/index.cfm) and (http://europa.eu.int/comm/enterprise/enterprise_policy/analysis/ observatory_en.htm).
European Parliament Plenary Debates (http://www.europarl.eu.int/plenary/ default_en.htm).
European Voice (http://www.european-voice.com/).
Eurostat (http://epp.eurostat.cec.eu.int/portal/page?_pageid=1090,1&_dad= portal&_schema=PORTAL).
Financial Times (http://news.ft.com/home/uk/).
Finnish Ministry of Foreign Affairs (http://presidency.finland.fi/frame.asp).
Frankfurter Allgemeine Zeitung (http://www.faz.net/).
Futurum public debate website (http://europa.eu.int/futurum/index_en.htm).
GreeceNow (http://www.greece.gr).
Greek Presidency Website (http://www.eu2003.gr/).
Guardian (http://www.guardian.co.uk/).
Hellenic Organisation of Small Medium Sized Enterprises & Handicrafts S.A. (www.eommex.gr).
Helsingin Sanomat International Edition (www.helsinki-hs.net).
Hufvudstadsbladet (http://www.hbl.fi/).
Iltalehti (http://www.iltalehti.fi/).
Irish Times (http://www.ireland.com/).
Kathimerini (http://www.ekathimerini.com/).
Le Monde (http://www.lemonde.fr/).
Legal Week Global (http://www.legalweekglobal.net).
New York Times (http://www.nytimes.com/).
Nordic Business Report (NBR).
Notre Europe (http://www.notre-europe.asso.fr/).
OECD (http://www.oecd.org/).
Oxford Analytica (http://www.oxan.com/).
Reuters EU Briefing (http://www.factiva.com/eurounion/).
RFE/RL Newsline (http://www.rferl.org/newsline).
Süddeutsche Zeitung (http://www.sueddeutsche.de/).
Sunday Business (http://static.highbeam.com/s/sundaybusinesslondonengland/).
The Economist (http://www.economist.com/).
The Independent (http://www.independent.co.uk/).
Virtual Finland (http://virtual.finland.fi/).
World Bank (http://www.worldbank.org/).

Index

The letter 'n' denotes note numbers.

accession
  and negotiations, 86, 139, 168, 183
  and state, 5, 23
ACP, 35, 117, 118, 135, 149, 154
Afghanistan, 63, 123, 168, 203
African, Caribbean and Pacific (ACP)
  states, 35, 117, 155
agenda
  and presidency, 3, 4, 16, 45, 57, 58,
    64, 87–94, 131–3, 139, 174–83
  -setting, 3, 5, 6, 16, 33, 39–73,
    87–94, 131–3, 139, 174–83, 188,
    193, 196, 202, 209, 210, 212
Ahern, Bertie, 24
Ahtisaari, Martti, 82
Albania, 161, 162, 163, 183
Algeria, 124
ally/alliance, 20, 59, 61, 60, 71, 75, 84,
  85, 95, 103, 114, 116, 134, 146,
  147, 149, 159, 170, 178, 184, 190,
  199
amendments, 36, 61, 80, 89, 106, 107,
  122, 152, 209
Amsterdam Treaty, 33, 79
Angola, 123, 134
Antici, 65, 142, 145, 188
Austria, 11, 21, 28, 30, 80, 81, 85, 100,
  122, 123, 166, 180, 193, 196, 220
Austrian Presidency
  in 1998, 48, 52
Aznar, José Maria, 31

Balkan Integration, 160, 161, 162,
  167, 168, 173, 199, 201, 206, 214
Balkans, 12, 13, 53, 120, 126, 131,
  139, 147, 155, 159, 161–3,
  167–74, 177–85, 188, 189, 191,
  195–9, 200, 201, 205, 209
Baltic Sea, 77–8, 83, 85, 92, 111
Baltic States, 77, 92

Barcelona Process, 52, 82, 86, 86, 92,
  215
bargaining power, 63, 207
Barroso, José Manuel, 49
Belgian Presidency
  in 1993, 29
  in 2001, 53, 58, 114–58, 192, 204,
    209, 213
Belgium, 11, 13, 21, 29, 30, 52, 57, 63,
  80, 81, 82, 90, 101, 114–58, 162,
  174, 185, 192, 195, 203–7, 214,
  219
Berlin Plus Agreement, 181, 184
Berlusconi, Silvio, 47, 66
bias, 16, 40, 46, 47–8, 213
  see also partiality
big states, 1, 11, 15, 16, 19, 20, 21, 24,
  26, 28, 30, 31, 59, 63, 69, 71, 101,
  103, 104, 105, 141, 189, 206, 208,
  216
bilateral, 46, 54, 59, 65, 84, 85, 91,
  106, 108, 129, 130, 132, 144, 148,
  151, 157, 162, 163, 173, 176
Blair, Tony, 31, 47, 63, 66, 144, 167
blocking minority (BM), 21, 22, 23
Bolkestein, Fritz, 105, 149
border
  and crime, 77
  and mail, 122, 132
  and management, 78, 181, 183, 197
Bosnia, 58, 161, 162, 167, 172, 178,
  179, 181, 183
Budget, 49, 58, 60, 78, 86, 109, 168,
  179, 180, 181, 186, 192, 197
Bulgaria, 11, 162, 163
Burundi, 117, 124, 134, 136, 138

Cairo Action Plan, 118, 128
Canada, 46, 91, 92, 111, 129, 138
CBSS, 83, 87, 91, 92, 93

Central and Eastern European
  Countries (CEECs), 86
CFSP, 12, 13, 20, 35, 61, 62, 125, 128,
  163, 167, 210
Chad, 123
Chechnya, 47, 82, 94, 95, 102, 110,
  203
checks and balances, 19
  see also institutional balance
Chirac, Jacques, 31, 47, 148, 167
co-decision, *see* European Parliament
Cold War, 95, 118, 125, 163
co-legislator, *see* European Parliament
Committee of Permanent
  Representation (COREPER), 35,
  41, 45, 51, 65, 87–91, 104, 127,
  131, 142, 145, 146, 176, 179, 187,
  188, 192
Common Agricultural Policy (CAP),
  33, 53, 173
common market, *see* internal market
common position, 37, 54, 62, 90, 104,
  107, 117, 126, 128, 129, 132, 134,
  135, 152, 179, 209, 221
Common Strategy on Russia, 77, 91,
  92, 113
Community Assistance for
  Reconstruction, Development,
  and Stabilisation Programme
  (CARDS), 162, 168, 172, 179, 180,
  181, 197, 198
community exhaustion, 76, 81, 104
Community Patent, 12, 159, 160–1,
  164–7, 169–70, 175–7, 189,
  192–5, 200, 209
  and Court (CPC), 160, 165, 166,
  175, 177, 189, 190
competition, 76, 97, 115, 123, 131,
  132, 185, 186
compromise, 1, 8, 14, 18, 37, 39, 44,
  47, 49, 50, 54, 56, 57, 59, 61,
  66–70, 89, 90, 95, 101, 102,
  104–6, 112, 131–3, 140, 142, 144,
  146, 147, 149–52, 157, 158, 166,
  175–7, 192–4, 199, 200, 202, 204,
  204, 207–9, 211, 213, 214
Concordia, 181

conditionality, 117, 118, 120, 135,
  168, 169, 179, 182, 191, 196, 198,
  214
confessionals, 15, 54, 65
conflict prevention, 115, 117–20, 127,
  128, 130, 133–9, 153, 155, 156,
  157, 158, 203, 214
Congo (DRC), 117, 118, 119, 123, 125,
  128, 129, 130, 133, 134, 136, 137,
  138, 139, 148, 150, 153, 154, 155
Consensual, consensus, 14, 19, 38, 39,
  40, 47, 48, 59, 66, 67, 68, 69, 71,
  72, 84, 99, 100, 116, 121, 141,
  142, 144, 159, 179, 180, 181, 211,
  213, 215
Constitutional Treaty, 57, 168
constraint, institutional, 46, 53
consumer protection, 51, 104
Convention
  and Constitutional, 121, 168, 212
co-operation, 3, 6, 18, 19, 31, 33, 34,
  43, 44, 46, 75, 77, 82, 85, 91, 92,
  93, 99, 102, 107, 119, 110, 117,
  120, 135, 136, 137, 154, 155, 161,
  162, 163, 173, 180, 183, 184, 196,
  198
Copenhagen, 51, 167, 173, 174, 198,
  201
Cotonou, 118, 120, 135, 136, 156, 214
Council conclusions, 41, 105, 115,
  127, 169, 181
Cologne, 87, 105
Council of Ministers
  Competitiveness, 15, 88, 107, 160,
    164, 174, 175, 176, 184
  Energy, 92
  Environment, 3, 51, 56, 71, 88, 108,
    139, 181, 184, 212
  Foreign Affairs, 63, 125, 215
  General Affairs and External
    Relations (GAERC), 133, 178,
    179, 182, 183, 196, 206
  General Affairs (GAC), 86, 87, 95,
    128, 135
  Health, 92
  Industry, 88, 100, 164
  Internal Market, 5, 172

Council of Ministers – *continued*
  Justice and Home Affairs (JHA), 20,
      34, 47, 89, 140, 161, 171, 178,
      179, 180, 183, 196, 200
  Telecommunications, 88, 117, 131,
      151
Council negotiations, 4, 60, 61, 105,
      193, 195, 209, 214
Council Rules of Procedure, 36
Council Secretariat, 5, 10, 17, 34, 40,
      45, 56, 62, 64, 68–72, 83, 89, 94,
      99, 100, 101, 104, 112, 114, 127,
      134, 139, 144, 146, 147, 149, 151,
      153, 157, 170, 171, 172, 184, 186,
      187, 188, 189, 190, 207, 208
Croatia, 161, 162, 174, 178, 183
Cyprus, 11, 21, 23, 170
Czech Republic, 11, 21, 30

Daems, Rik, 131, 144
Danish Presidency
  in 2002, 55, 195
De Bassompiere, 34
degressive proportionalism, 26
Denmark, 11, 21, 29, 30, 52, 80, 81,
      82, 93, 108, 110, 122, 123, 132,
      151, 165, 192, 219
digital market, 75
directive
  copyright, 12, 74, 75, 76, 80, 81, 88,
      91, 101, 104, 111, 112, 203
  e-commerce, 12, 13, 74, 75, 76, 80,
      81, 83, 84, 87–91, 95, 99, 101–7,
      111–13, 203, 204, 205, 209, 213
  postal services, 114, 115
distribution of preferences, 5, 16, 59,
      101, 104, 190
domestic, 43, 46, 57, 63, 64, 69, 70,
      71, 74, 79, 99, 121, 127, 139, 144,
      152, 157, 158, 164, 202, 203, 204,
      206, 207, 208, 211
Dutch Presidency
  in 1991, 47
  in 2004, 50, 51

East, 47, 85, 120, 123, 126, 131, 163,
      167, 198
Economic and Social Committee
  (EcoSoc), 93, 121, 122

election
  Belgian (2007), 132
  German (2005), 57
  observers, 124, 154, 198
electronic signatures, 80, 88, 103
emergency summit, 184
empty chair crisis, 32, 58
enlargement, 11, 21, 23, 24, 26, 33,
      37, 44, 45, 50, 60, 67, 82, 86, 108,
      113, 121, 123, 146, 161, 169, 172,
      173, 177, 195, 198, 201, 204, 206,
      213, 214
Estonia, 11, 21, 77, 85
EU-Africa dialogue, 117, 124, 127,
      128, 135, 154, 155, 157, 158
Euro, 33, 52, 57, 60, 79, 85, 87, 92,
      109, 121, 130, 164, 179, 185
European Central Bank (ECB), 23, 50,
      164
European Coal and Steel Community
  (ECSC), 19, 20, 31
European Commission, 136, 190
  and composition, 19, 21, 24, 168
  DGs, 82
  interim report, 84
  interservice group, 82, 108
  and proposal, 190
  and resignation, 58
European Commissioner, 190
European Council, 23, 28, 30, 32, 33,
      38, 51, 57, 84, 86, 94, 97, 113,
      134, 151, 181, 215–16
European Court of Justice (ECJ), 20,
      24, 175, 176
European Development Fund (EDF),
      117, 130, 134, 136
European Integration Partnerships,
      168, 182, 191, 197
European Parliament, 26–31, 216
  and co-decision, 33, 34, 89, 168
  and co-legislator, 20, 33, 79
  and composition, 19, 21, 24, 25, 27
  and elections, 79, 124, 198
  members of (MEPs), 26–8, 34, 37,
      79, 96, 102, 121, 140, 148, 149,
      150, 198
European Patent Office (EPO), 160,
      161, 165, 166, 175, 176, 177

European Political Cooperation (EPC), 34
Euroscepticism, 121
EU Western-Balkans Forum, 183
exemptions
  and Belgian 2001 Council Presidency, 145
  and Finnish 1999 Council Presidency, 58
  expertise, 2, 4, 40, 53, 61, 64, 66, 67, 68, 72, 75, 76, 83, 95, 99, 100, 101, 104, 105, 109, 112, 144, 145, 146, 154, 166, 188, 190, 191, 193, 200, 204, 208, 215

federal
  correspondents, 141, 145
federalist, 11, 13, 47, 52, 74, 114
Feira Action Plan, 108
Ferrero-Walder, Benita, 30
Finland, 1, 2, 11, 13, 28, 30, 45, 74–113, 122, 123, 132, 133, 146, 165, 174, 203, 204, 205, 206, 214, 217, 219
Finnish Presidency
  in 1999, 11, 74–113, 126, 203, 207
  and ministerial conference, 87, 91, 92, 103, 107, 111
  priorities, 12, 74–113
foreign policy, 5, 10, 12, 34, 47, 53, 61, 62, 74–113, 114, 115, 119, 123–6, 129, 142, 145, 156, 157, 159–201, 203–6, 208, 214, 215
France, 1, 11, 21, 24, 29, 30, 57, 59, 61, 81, 82, 102, 105, 116, 122, 123, 125, 131, 132, 134, 147, 148, 151, 155, 164–6, 168, 171, 181, 182, 184, 185, 189–93, 203, 219
Franco-German axis/alliance/tandem, 32, 56, 59, 60, 75, 103, 105, 116, 149, 151, 159, 184, 190, 191, 199, 208, 209
  dominance, 20, 61, 197, 212
French Presidency
  in 1965, 49
  in 1989, 57
  in 1995, 57
  in 2000, 48, 53, 63, 64, 131
  in 2008, 52, 58

General Affairs Council (GAC), *see* Council of Ministers
German Presidency
  in 1983, 51
  in 1988, 50
  in 1999, 58, 64, 65, 110
Germany, 11, 21, 24, 26, 29, 30, 57, 59, 60, 80, 81, 85, 100, 102, 105, 122, 123, 125, 132, 147, 164, 165, 166, 168, 171, 176, 177, 184, 185, 190, 192, 193, 216, 219, 220
Giannitsis, Tassos, 164, 185, 186
Gibraltar, 81
Giscard d'Estaing, Valéry, 32, 59
Great Lakes, 12, 13, 114, 115, 117–20, 123, 124, 125, 127–30, 133, 134, 137, 139, 148, 149, 153–8, 203, 205, 209, 214
Greece, 11, 13, 29, 47, 50, 52, 53, 81, 122, 123, 132, 159–206, 214, 219
Greek Presidency
  in 1983, 50, 51
  in 2003, 45, 50, 53, 58, 109, 159–201, 204, 209

Hamilton, Alexander, 212
harmonisation, 51, 75, 76, 165, 183
hegemon, 16, 19, 30, 38, 114
Helsinki Summit, 35, 91, 94
heterogeneity of preferences, 5, 16, 40, 56, 58, 59, 69, 71, 101, 147, 189, 208
High Representative, 23, 61, 62, 155, 188, 215, 216
Historical Institutionalism, 6, 7, 211, 212
Hungary, 11, 21
hybrid, 2, 4, 39, 70, 72, 210

Iceland, 77, 85
IMF, 139
immigration, 47, 78, 102, 163, 172, 181, 183
impartial, 24, 39, 43, 45, 47, 55, 67, 69
influence
  level of, 8, 9, 40, 56, 111, 157, 199, 204, 205

informal Council/Summit
  on Cultural and Audio-visual, on
    Industry, 88
  on Defence, 51, 181
  on Environment, 51
information advantage, 5, 10, 16, 40,
    46, 54, 55, 56, 66, 68, 70, 71, 72,
    146, 207, 208, 210
institution
  and presidency, 2, 5, 6, 7, 8, 12, 28,
    39, 56, 59, 206, 210, 211, 212,
    214
  institutional balance, 2, 5, 16,
    18–38, 39
intellectual property, 88, 103, 161,
    166, 175, 177
intensity of preferences, 9, 69, 71, 75,
    190, 200, 208
inter-Congolese dialogue (ICD), 124,
    125, 130, 133, 134, 138, 148, 150,
    154, 155
intergovernmental
  and entrepreneurship, 42, 72, 210
intermediaries' liability, 80, 101
inter-ministerial coordination, 98,
    207
internal market (IM), 13, 75–9,
    115–20, 160–3
  see also Council of Ministers
International Criminal Court (ICT),
    167, 169, 179, 180, 183
international exhaustion, 76, 81, 104,
    106
Interreg, 108, 109
Iraq, 45, 47, 58, 63, 164, 167, 178,
    180, 184, 197, 198, 204
Ireland, 1, 11, 21, 24, 29, 30, 61, 63,
    68, 81, 121, 122, 132, 165, 195,
    219
Irish Presidency
  in 1996, 57
  in 2004, 63
Italian Presidency
  in 2003, 61
Italy, 11, 21, 28, 29, 30, 66, 79–82,
    101, 102, 122, 123, 162, 164, 166,
    171, 174, 180, 183, 184, 189, 193,
    196, 219

Kabila, Joseph, 124, 133, 148, 150
Kaliningrad, 77, 93, 107, 108
Kirchner, Emil, 2, 3, 33
Kosovo, 58, 82, 163, 179, 185, 198
Kyoto, 123

language, 86, 96, 100, 138, 159, 161,
    165–7, 175–7, 187, 193, 195, 205
Latvia, 11, 21, 77, 85
leadership, 5, 12, 16, 18, 32, 40,
    56–58, 79–81
  context, 4, 5, 16, 40, 56, 79
  shared, 18, 31, 215
legal liability, 80, 104, 107, 112, 204
legitimacy, 4, 19, 30, 31, 38, 62, 79,
    167
liberalisation
  postal, 12, 13, 116, 120, 121, 126,
    127, 131, 139, 144, 146, 147,
    149, 150, 151, 157, 204, 209,
    213
Lipponen, Paavo, 77, 79, 84
Lisbon Treaty, 1, 18, 22, 23, 25, 26, 38,
    57, 202, 215
Lithuania, 11, 21, 77, 85
lobby, 84, 102, 103, 105, 127, 130, 209
Lomé Conventions, 117, 149
Ludlow, Peter, 116
Lumumba, Patrice, 119
Lusaka peace, 124, 130, 134
Luxembourg, 11, 21, 29, 30, 47, 50,
    57, 63, 68, 81, 84, 85, 110, 122,
    123, 132, 146, 153, 162, 185, 219
Luxembourg Presidency
  in 1997, 50, 63
  in 2005, 57

Maastricht Treaty, 35, 57
Macedonia, 123, 161, 163
Magnette, Paul, 224 n.63, 224 n.69,
    228 n.228
Malta, 11, 21, 23, 26
mediator/mediation, 1, 33, 36, 66, 75,
    97, 133, 138, 189
Mertens, 65, 142, 145
Michel, Louis, 119, 120, 125, 129, 133,
    134, 138, 144, 147
Middle East, 47, 120, 123, 126, 131,
    167, 198

ministerial conference/meeting
and Belgium 2001 Council
Presidency, 13, 205
and Finnish 1999 Council
Presidency, 58
MONUC, 137, 154
Mugabe, Robert, 124, 134, 148
multilateralism, 18
multilingualism, 161

Namibia, 124
national, 2, 3, 5, 6–7, 12, 14, 23, 24,
32, 43–4, 76, 78, 121, 186,
202–6
and preferences, 8, 39, 46, 72, 74,
114, 160
nation state, 18
NATO, 50, 58, 171, 181, 188
negotiation
and bilateral, 85
and IGC, 4, 54, 58
and multilateral, 43, 206
and positions, 36, 54, 61, 65, 92,
142
and set-up, 99
and style, 81, 99
neighbourhood policy, 108
NEPAD, 124, 135, 136, 137, 154
Netherlands, 11, 21, 29, 30, 57, 80,
81, 122, 123, 125, 126, 132, 133,
148, 153, 168, 219
neutral broker, 2, 39, 42, 43, 44, 45,
46, 47, 48, 50, 51, 53, 55, 156,
202
neutrality
and constraint, 16, 43–4, 48, 128,
173, 210
New Institutionalism (NI), 6, 7, 8, 14,
15, 38
New Institutionalists, 7, 32, 46
Nice Treaty, 11, 22, 23, 25, 121, 139,
167
Nicolaïdis, Kalypso, 224 n.61,
224 n.69, 228 n.228
Nigeria, 124
non-decisions, 49, 50
Nordic
and Council of Ministers, 78, 93
and Investment Bank, 78

normative implications, 211, 212
North, 24, 77, 86, 92, 203, 223
and Northern Dimension Action
Plan, 87, 93, 107, 108, 110, 111
and Northern Summit, 111
Norway, 77, 85, 110
nuclear safety, 77, 78, 86, 102

organisation, 1, 2, 3, 18, 35, 37, 38,
43, 45, 46, 48, 56, 64, 65, 77, 82,
83, 85, 92, 93, 95, 96, 98, 99, 110,
111, 115, 121, 122, 124, 134, 135,
136, 138, 143, 164, 167, 171, 188,
189
Organisation of African Unity (OAU),
124, 135, 136, 137
organised crime, 61, 167, 171, 180,
181, 183, 190, 191
OSCE, 171

P11, 142, 143, 145
package deal, 3, 45, 140, 142
Panhellenic Socialist Movement
(PASOK), 164, 184
Papandreou, Giorgos, 164, 170, 171,
172, 178, 179, 184, 185, 187
pareto frontier, 40, 41, 200, 204
Paris Treaty, 31
partiality, 24, 39
see also bias
Patten, Christopher, 93, 95, 110, 126,
130, 140, 149, 171, 179, 182, 184,
191
Permanent Representation, 64, 65, 83,
96, 97, 98, 99, 112, 127, 141, 143,
145, 149, 150, 169, 170, 186, 187,
188
Phare, 108, 109
Pillar
I, 12, 20, 44, 60, 62, 158, 209
II, 12, 53, 158, 209
III, 20, 44
Poland, 11, 21, 77, 85
policy entrepreneur, 7, 16, 39–73, 201,
209, 210
political conditionality, 117
Political and Security Committee
(PSC), 134, 139

Portugal, 1, 11, 21, 28, 29, 30, 81, 104,
    122, 123, 125, 128, 132, 135, 147,
    162, 164, 165, 166, 195, 216, 219,
    220
Portuguese Presidency
    in 2000, 118, 128, 204, 207, 215
positive sum, 14, 17, 40, 67, 75, 86,
    90, 99, 113, 129, 133, 146, 157,
    177, 185, 200, 213
power
    to persuade, 53, 64, 65, 66
    politics, 16, 19, 20, 212
preference divergence, 79, 120, 124,
    164
presidency
    compromise, 14, 70, 89, 104, 105,
        112, 131, 133, 149, 150, 152,
        177, 192, 204, 207, 209
    programme, 52, 78, 110, 116, 119,
        131, 136, 139, 160, 192, 216
principal-agent theory, 7
principle
    of conditionality, 117, 118, 135, 214
    of country of origin, 75
    of equality, 19, 24, 25, 212
procedural control, 51, 89
Prodi, Romano, 130, 171, 174, 178
property right, 88, 103, 160
Putin, Vladimir, 47

qualified majority (QM), 12, 21, 22,
    100, 205, 211, 213, 214

Rational Choice Institutionalism, 7,
    211
reciprocity, reciprocal, 67, 85, 94, 102,
    113, 118, 214
referendum
    French, 50
    Irish, 38
reform, 1, 6, 109, 172, 183, 191, 196,
    202, 215
    and Council presidency, 1
regional, 52, 53, 77, 82, 83, 85, 87, 93,
    108, 109, 110, 111, 113, 115, 117,
    118, 120, 121, 126, 129, 134, 135,
    137, 138, 139, 141, 142, 143, 148,
    161, 162, 166, 171, 172, 173, 178,
    180, 181, 183, 196, 199, 200, 214

representation
    under-, 21
    over-, 21
resource, 1, 3, 4, 6, 8, 11, 12, 13, 40,
    45, 48, 50, 56, 58, 60, 63, 67, 68,
    69, 70, 71, 75, 77, 78, 80, 83, 86,
    93, 94, 98, 100, 103, 112, 118,
    127, 146, 148, 150, 153, 181, 206,
    207, 208, 210, 211, 212
Rome Treaty, 117
rotation principle, 28, 53, 215
Russia, 45, 46, 47, 58, 77, 78, 82, 83,
    85, 86, 91, 92, 94, 95, 102, 107,
    108, 109, 111, 113, 203
Rwanda, 117, 119, 124, 125, 134, 148,
    149, 153

St Petersburg, 107
Santer, Jacques, 84, 213
Satuli, Antti, 79, 117
security, security threats, security
    structure, 12, 23, 48, 51, 62, 74,
    77, 86, 103, 111, 116, 118, 125,
    134, 137, 138, 154, 155, 163, 180,
    188, 198, 204
Senegal, 124
September 11/terrorist attacks, 45, 58,
    120, 123, 139, 140
Serbia-Montenegro, 161, 162, 167,
    178, 179
Simitis, Costas, 159, 161, 164, 169,
    170, 171, 172, 176, 183, 184, 185,
    187, 188, 193, 199, 200
simple majority, 23, 24
Single European Act (SEA), 3, 34, 35
single market, *see* internal market (IM)
size, 5, 11, 14, 17, 20, 21, 23, 26, 28,
    37, 40, 63, 64, 67, 71, 75, 95, 140,
    150, 160, 184, 185, 206, 207
Slovakia, 11, 21
Slovenia, 11, 21, 30, 216, 217
small and medium sized enterprise
    (SME), 160, 174, 175, 184, 190,
    194
small states, 1, 2, 4, 5, 6, 8, 10, 11, 12,
    14, 15, 16, 17, 19, 20, 21, 23, 26,
    28, 30, 31, 37, 38, 43, 61, 63, 66,
    68, 70, 96, 100, 102, 105, 144,
    202, 203, 204, 206, 207, 217

Sociological Institutionalism, 6, 211, 212
Solana, Javier, 126, 134, 140, 147, 149, 171, 172, 178, 179, 181, 188
solidarity, 33, 85, 119, 123, 129, 146, 153, 211, 214
South, 11, 107, 109, 124, 149, 161, 163, 172, 173, 179, 208
South Africa, 124, 149
South-Eastern Europe (SEE), 161, 172, 179, 180, 181, 199
South East Europe Co-operation Process (SEECP), 163
sovereign/ty, 18, 31, 52, 125
Spain, 1, 11, 21, 28, 29, 30, 47, 50, 52, 80, 81, 82, 102, 122, 132, 165, 184, 189, 190, 219
Spanish Presidency
  in 1989, 29, 52
  in 1995, 29, 52
  in 2002, 47, 52, 63
spill over effects, 163, 184, 209
Stabilisation and Association Agreements (SAAs), 162, 172, 183, 200
Stabilisation and Association Process (SAP), 161, 162, 169–74, 178, 179, 182, 183, 196, 197, 198, 199, 201
Summit
  Barcelona (2002), 165
  Copenhagen (1993), 174
  Copenhagen (2002), 167
  Corfu (1994), 75
  EU-Africa/Cairo, 117, 118, 120, 124, 127, 128, 135, 144, 147, 150, 153, 154–8
  Feira (2000), 108
  Gothenburg (2001), 128
  Hanover (1988), 50
  Lisbon (2000), 51
  Lisbon (2003), 184
  Luxembourg (1997), 29
  Nice (2000), 155
  Stockholm (2001), 49
  Thessaloniki (2003), 170
  Vienna (1998), 84
  Western Balkan, 162, 171, 181, 183, 191, 195, 196, 198, 200, 201
  Zagreb (2000), 162

Supranational
  and entrepreneurship, 42
Sweden, 11, 21, 28, 30, 49, 80, 81, 82, 89, 93, 110, 122, 123, 128, 132, 135, 151, 165, 168, 182, 196, 219
Swedish Presidency
  in 2001, 192

Tacis, 102, 108, 109
Tallberg, Jonas, 4, 49, 52, 206, 226 n. 176
Thessaloniki Agenda, 173, 181, 182, 183, 189, 196, 198
tour des capitals, 44, 54
transatlantic relations, 33, 167, 184
troika, 115, 125, 126, 133, 134, 139, 148, 149, 171, 178, 215, 216

Uganda, 117, 124, 134, 153
UK, 1, 11, 21, 33, 47, 49, 52, 57, 60, 65, 66, 68, 81, 82, 85, 102, 105, 117, 122, 123, 125, 126, 131, 132, 147, 148, 149, 151, 155, 158, 165, 166, 168, 171, 180, 182, 184, 190, 196, 197, 203
UK Presidency
  in 1977, 66
  in 1981, 66
  in 1992, 57
  in 1998, 47, 85
  in 2005, 49, 65
unanimity, 12, 20, 44, 53, 59, 61, 99, 165, 176, 194, 200, 205, 214
universal postal service, 115
UN Security Council, 125, 138, 198
USA, North America, American, 31, 47, 92, 93

Verhofstadt, Guy, 116, 117, 118, 120, 121, 129, 130, 131, 133, 139, 144, 158
Vervaeke, Koen, 129
veto, 32, 49, 101, 116, 159
Voss and Bailleul, 44, 45

Wallace, Helen, 32, 55, 66
weighted votes, 19, 21–4, 37, 144, 212

West, 21, 74, 107, 135, 183
Westlake, Martin, 227 n.206
working group, 34, 35, 41, 45, 53, 64,
    83, 87, 88, 89, 90, 91, 96, 112,
    131, 133, 141, 145, 146, 151, 170,
    175, 177, 180, 182, 187, 192, 196
WTO, 82, 123, 136
Wurzel, Rüdiger, 3

Yaoundé Conventions, 117
Yugoslavia, 52, 125, 163, 169, 179, 198

Zagreb, 162, 170, 171, 172, 173, 182,
    196, 197
    see also Summit
Zimbabwe, 124, 133, 134, 136, 148,
    154

LaVergne, TN USA
26 May 2010
184073LV00001B/21/P